Negative Intelligence

The Army and the American Left, 1917–1941

Twentieth-Century America Series
Dewey W. Grantham, General Editor

Negative Intelligence
The Army and the American Left, 1917–1941

Roy Talbert, Jr.

UNIVERSITY PRESS OF MISSISSIPPI
Jackson & London

Library of Congress Cataloging-in-Publication Data

Talbert, Roy.
  Negative intelligence : the army and the American Left, 1917–1941
/ Roy Talbert, Jr.
  p.   cm. — (Twentieth-century America series)
  Includes bibliographical references and index.
  ISBN 0-87805-495-2
  1. United States.   Dept. of the Army.   General Staff.   Military
  intelligenceDivision.   I. Title.   II. Series.
  UB251.U5T35   1991
  355.3'432'0973—dc20   90-23047
                                                                   CIP

British Library Cataloging-in-Publication data available

UB
251
.U5
T35
1991

All photographs courtesy of National Archives.

For my wife,
Jane Boyd Holbert Talbert

Contents

Acknowledgments

I am grateful to Coastal Carolina College and to the University of South Carolina for the generous support that made this project possible. In the dean's office, Shirell Mishoe and Marie Lovero were indispensable in photocopying and in keeping me and the paperwork in order. A major contribution toward the purchase of essential microfilm came from the university's Research and Productive Scholarship program, and my travel was considerably enhanced by free access to the university's air service to Washington. A grant from my college's Faculty Development Committee, endowed by the Horry County Higher Education Commission, made additional travel possible, as did an allocation from the college's Honors Program. Precious time for research came through a grant from the university's Faculty Exchange and Development program, and the writing was accomplished during a sabbatical provided by my college.

The editor of this series, Dewey W. Grantham, has guided me for many years, and one of the most important lessons he taught me about historical writing is the necessity of placing even a narrowly defined topic into the broader context of the times. In that endeavor I am grateful for the work of a large community of scholars who have added immensely to my knowledge of the American left, and the right, in the twentieth century. It would have been impossible, however, for me to examine so many of these studies without the aid of the reference and interlibrary loan staff at my own Kimbel Library. Mary Bull, Margaret Fain, Sallie Clarkson, Linda Brumfield, and Marchita Phifer not only wrought miracles in acquiring books so new or so scarce that few libraries had them, but they also took an active and encouraging interest in the project. I was supported too by the interlibrary loan office of the university system.

I owe an especially large debt to those who read early drafts of this work and who offered numerous suggestions for its improvement. Dewey Grantham's meticulus scrutiny is legendary among the many writers who have benefited from his editing. Richard Polenberg, of x · *Acknowledgments*

Cornell University, and Athan Theoharis, of Marquette University, both major contributors to the general study of domestic intelligence, blended encouragement and criticism so skillfully that the process of revision was never an unpleasant chore. At professional meetings, my discussions with Joan M. Jensen and Theodore Kornweibel, Jr., aided my work immensely.

My friend Gary W. Reichard, of Florida Atlantic University, was especially helpful in introducing me to the National Archives. Once there, I was aided immeasurably by archivist John E. Taylor and his colleagues, as well as by the staff at the branch at Suitland, Maryland, where I was allowed into the underground labyrinth to pick and choose from its vast holdings. I am particularly grateful for the convenient shuttle that connects the main archives building with Suitland. Working at the Franklin D. Roosevelt Library in Hyde Park, New York, was, as always, a pleasure, and the staff was long-suffering in handling problems for me over the telephone. My stay in Albany at the New York State Archives was also pleasant. Similarly, the librarians at the Western Reserve Historical Society in Cleveland, Ohio, aided my research, using the mails, the telephone, and the copier. The Library of Congress generously loaned me the microfilmed papers of Newton D. Baker. In Atlanta, Emory University and Georgia State University gave me kind assistance, as did East Carolina University in Greenville, North Carolina. Were the intelligence agencies themselves as helpful and forthcoming as libraries and archival centers, this would be a better book and the world a better place. Yet with all the aid provided by so many, this work, whatever its merits or flaws, is my own.

The timely production of a book demands a certain amount of single-mindedness and, sometimes, outright compulsive behavior. My gratitude to my wife for abiding with me during this process is inadequately reflected in the dedication. Our children, Matt, Drew, Becky, and Beth, were also enormously patient with a father who too frequently locked himself away, although the youngest, spying me organizing the bibliography, did express some skepticism that a book would ever emerge from "those scraps of paper." To my partner and friend, James R. Holbert, Jr., I am grateful for the temporary release from my share of labor in the vineyard.

Introduction

My interest in the army's surveillance of radicals began just over twenty years ago when, with a commission in the Military Intelligence branch, I was assigned to the Counterintelligence Division of the Office of the Assistant Chief of Staff for Intelligence, Department of the Army, in the Pentagon. At that time, I was largely unaware of the immense program of negative intelligence in the period 1917–41; I thought that the greatest level of domestic spying on the left had occurred in the late 1960s. When I prepared the initial outline for this book, I assumed that I could handle the pre-1967 years in one or two chapters and then concentrate on the army's recent spying. For sources, I anticipated that the confidential archival material I had collected for the Pentagon would be available after so many years, and I planned to use other documents released during a revealing investigation by Senator Samuel J. Ervin, Jr. The North Carolina civil libertarian had scrutinized Military Intelligence in an inquiry that began in 1971 and in some fascinating ways seemed to have served as a prelude to his Watergate role.

Although the papers Ervin had insisted be declassified were available, I had only partial success in finding the material I had collected, and much of that was still classified and thus denied me. I knew I was in trouble when I asked to see the army's dossier on Margaret Mead, the famous anthropologist. My delight in having the fat file delivered to my desk evaporated when every page turned out to be a notice that the document had been withdrawn for reasons of national security.

If the recent period was less open than I had hoped, the years from 1917 to 1941 had developed into a bonanza. Starting in the late 1970s, a veritable mountain of material had been declassified which wonderfully illuminated the era before World War II. Hundreds of thousands of documents are now available in the National Archives, many of them made even more accessible by having been released on microfilm or in print by the archives and private publishing firms. I have described these treasures, along with a historiographical overview, in the bibliographical essay, and I expect they will be of immense aid to historians in a variety of fields. For the purposes of my work, I was so impressed with the coverage they afforded that I chose to postpone an examination of the recent past and treat only the earlier years in this study. I could have continued the story, using my own experience and records released through Ervin's investigation, but to have done so would have meant largely skipping the years from World War II to the 1960s, a period that remains hidden in records still classified. It seemed proper for me to tell here that part of the story which could be told best and to wait for further material to become available. I hope that in a few years I will be able to resume this chronicle with as much detail as I think I have provided in this narrative.

Beyond the availability of sources, the period from 1917 to 1941 has a definite significance in the context of the development of domestic intelligence. Earlier efforts notwithstanding, the founding of this country's intelligence program dates from the United States's involvement in World War I, and so my story begins in 1917. I conclude by defining the army's place in the modern domestic intelligence community, a process that did not begin to take shape until World War II. Marking the beginning of a new era in which domestic intelligence was ruled by the Federal Bureau of Investigation, and the roles of the army and navy were more or less carefully delimited, 1941 is an appropriate place to end. The reemergence of a domestically active Military Intelligence after World War II and the restrictions on intelligence agencies developed in the mid-1970s deserve separate study.

The years from 1917 to 1941 do not, however, represent a period of continuous and uniform expansion of the army's negative intelligence apparatus. In fact, the energy and the resources for spying on radicals dissipated to a considerable extent after 1920. Because nearly all of the significant activity occurred in the World War I and Red Scare eras, my coverage of these frantic times accounts for the majority of the book. Despite the relative lack of domestic spying in the 1920s and 1930s, those decades contain a number of fascinating episodes which I have recounted. I found the army's relationship with private spy groups especially interesting, and I hope that my story of the army's connection with professional patriots and ultraconservatives will assist in clarifying our view of the right in the 1920s and 1930s.

Although my purpose has not been to write the history of either the right or the left, I have been naturally drawn into each because one represented the major target of Military Intelligence and the other a significant source for it. Both are magnetic topics, to be sure, and both have demanded attention, but my focus is on Military Intelligence as a reactionary agency responding to what it regarded as domestic threats to the American way of life. Nor is this a story of international espionage or an account of the larger intelligence community of which Military Intelligence was only a part. I have tried to place the army within the spy world, and I have examined its relations with other agencies, especially the Departments of Justice and Navy, but, again, my concentration has been on army domestic intelligence. I have not dealt with combat intelligence at all, and I have mentioned foreign intelligence only when it relates to Americans abroad.

In placing the army firmly in the national fight against radicalism, I have not attempted any sophisticated analysis of the motives of the people who took Military Intelligence down that path. Their reasons seem plain enough, and I have generally let the spies speak for themselves. I have also accepted the army's definition of American radicalism, and the result is a very broad movement indeed. With the hindsight of knowing that Pearl Harbor was coming in 1941, it is easy to make the judgment that the military should have eliminated negative intelligence and accentuated the positive. Most studies, except those that un-critically defend the army, leave it at that: the military foolishly chased radical ghosts at home and failed in the far more important arena of foreign espionage. That analysis, though basically correct, does not admit the awful domestic circumstances which, when viewed by the contemporary intelligence agencies, seemed to warrant the emphasis on the negative. I think that in looking at the early years of this century we have had a tendency, ever so slight, to romanticize the radicals and to downplay the violence from the extreme left. It seems to me that we have underestimated, just a bit, the level of social tension in this country, especially during World War I, the Red Scare, and the Great Depression. I have asked the reader from time to time to look at American history from the standpoint of a negative intelligence officer, and I have purposely highlighted the threats and the possible conspiracies which such a perspective always generates.

The army was so alarmed after 1917 that an immersion in its files puts the researcher at risk of accepting its view of the world and of seeing the times solely in terms of mad bombers and lunatic vigilantes. I do not believe the situation was ever as bad as the analysts of the Negative Branch of the Military Intelligence Division feared. I think Robert K. Murray was essentially correct when he said in his seminal *Red Scare* that fear of the left was "more peripheral than basic" to the American experience. Surely most Americans were not overwhelmed by paranoia of a radical revolution. Yet there were moments when the country did seem, as Theodore Roosevelt said in 1912, to "stand at Armageddon." I know that Military Intelligence and thousands of Americans saw a domestic war that required the sternest of measures, with no time for the niceties of law and due process.

It is a dark and bizarre story, and there were days when I came up from the microfilm reader or walked out of the archives depressed over the misdeeds of my countrymen. All investigative agencies at one time or another abused civil liberties, but that the army should do so in involving itself in political affairs has been especially dismaying to nearly every student who has considered the topic. For that reason, I have given particular attention to efforts to restrict the army from such activities. Following the conclusion of World War I, policies were repeatedly promulgated expressly forbidding the military from engaging in domestic espionage, only to be rescinded or violated when the next social crisis arose. Most Americans, I dare say, have had a pristine vision of a country unencumbered by a meddling army. Like so much else in our history, that belief turns out to be largely mythical.

Negative Intelligence
The Army and the American Left, 1917–1941

CHAPTER 1

Origins of Military Intelligence

The use of spies and informers is as old as warfare itself, yet it was not until the early twentieth century that the United States military developed modern agencies responsible for the collection of what by then had come to be called "intelligence." On paper, however, Military Intelligence in the army and its sister service, the Office of Naval Intelligence, trace their beginnings to the Gilded Age. The navy established its intelligence office first, in 1882, and it maintained a clear superiority at least until the middle of 1917. The navy's edge, however, was hardly measurable because its intelligence center remained small, poorly staffed, and meagerly funded. It was not until 1897, with support from Assistant Secretary of the Navy Theodore Roosevelt, that the naval function blossomed, especially when congressional funding increased two years later.[1]

The year 1885 is the accepted date for the creation of a clearly identifiable army office with the specific responsibility of handling intelligence. At that time the Division of Military Information, with several civilian clerks, was established within the War Department's Miscellaneous Branch, a location suitably signifying the small emphasis given it. Four years later, a slight improvement occurred when the effort, called the Military Information Division, was placed under the adjutant general. This activity, with one military officer and one civilian intelligence analyst supported by two assistants and a messenger, was located in a single room. Its mission was to collect information on foreign military capabilities. The Spanish-American War of 1898 caused a minor explosion in the unit when it was increased to eleven officers, ten clerks, two messengers, two rooms, and a budget of $3,640. The intelligence

---

1. Naval developments are admirably portrayed by Jeffrey M. Dorwart in *The Office of Naval Intelligence: The Birth of America's First Intelligence Agency, 1865–1918* (Annapolis: Naval Institute Press, 1979); see also Rhodri Jeffreys-Jones, *American Espionage: From Secret Service to CIA* (New York: Free Press, 1977), pp. 22–25.

work in the War Department was supplemented by some forty National Guard units across the country.[2]

The war of 1898 did not, however, substantially increase either the army's or the navy's intelligence mission. When the inevitable spy scare developed, it was the Secret Service that received a $50,000 appropriation to ferret out Spanish infiltrators in Tampa, the assembly point for American land forces. Although the Military Information Division had opened a file on the Cuban situation as early as 1892, the army was able to find only $45 to hire two private detectives in Tampa.[3] Officers of the Military Information Division did see some action in Cuba, and it was the heroic effort of the division's Andrew S. Rowan, who, in taking a communication from American commander Major General William R. Shafter to Cuban revolutionary Calixto Garcia, laid the basis for Elbert Hubbard's famous 1899 piece, "A Message to Garcia."[4] This achievement aside, the army's intelligence program ranked a distant third, behind the navy and the Secret Service.

Some improvement did occur, on the operational level, with the advent of a terrible little jungle war in the Philippines. The rigors of that insurgency led General Arthur MacArthur, commander of the Division of the Philippines, late in 1900, to create his own Military Information Division. For the first time, the army found itself engaged in the ugly business of counterrevolution, with its necessary reliance on spies, informers, interrogators, and blacklists of civilians.[5] The Philippine agency was the first authentic field office of army intelligence, and its existence brought forth a question that plagued the army for decades: should field intelligence units respond to the orders of their local

2. The official history of Military Intelligence, for all its weaknesses very good on the intricacies of organization, is Bruce W. Bidwell, *History of the Military Intelligence Division, Department of the Army General Staff, 1775–1941* (Frederick, Md.: University Publications of America, 1986). Various drafts of Bidwell's manuscript are in Record Group 319, National Archives, Suitland Records Center. See also Jeffrey-Jones, *American Espionage*, p. 26; G. J. A. O'Toole, *The Encyclopedia of American Intelligence and Espionage* (New York: Facts on File, 1988), pp. 26–28; and the unpaginated introduction to each reel of the National Archives microfilm publication M1440, *Correspondence of the Military Intelligence Division Relating to "Negro Subversion," 1917–1941* (Washington, D.C.: National Archives, 1986).

3. Joan M. Jensen, *Military Surveillance of Civilians in America* (Morristown, N.J.: General Learning Press, 1975), pp. 1, 5–6.

4. Bidwell, *History of Military Intelligence*, p. 61. A photograph of Rowan is in John Patrick Finnegan, *Military Intelligence: A Picture History* (Arlington, Va.: U.S. Army Intelligence and Security Command, 1985), p. 9.

5. On the Philippines, see Brian M. Linn, *The U.S. Army and Counterinsurgency in the Philippine War, 1899–1902* (Chapel Hill: University of North Carolina Press, 1989); and O'Toole, *Encyclopedia of American Intelligence*, p. 27.

commanders or to those of the parent intelligence office in Washington? On the question of policies regarding the collection of information on civilians, as opposed to the perceived needs of the commander for information on threats to his mission, the issue of who controlled the field intelligence units became a major problem over the years. In the case of the Philippines, the local division initially had only a liaison relationship with Washington, but in 1902 it was formally merged with and controlled by the Military Information Division at the Department of War.[6]

While field commanders and their intelligence officers in the Philippines, and in Cuba as well when the army returned to that island in 1906, were learning the value of a systematic intelligence system using agent networks in the civilian population, the army leadership in Washington continued to ignore the intelligence function. In a series of organizational changes involving confusing nomenclature, the general staff restricted its interest in intelligence to the development of maps and orders of battle on potential enemies. Despite the appearance in 1904 of an office with the awkward name Second (Military Information) Division, this unit, manned by six officers and a few clerks, was in no way able to handle an authentic intelligence mission. Nor was anyone in Washington interested in its doing so. By 1908, the Military Information Division had disappeared as a separate entity, having been relegated to committee status within the newly created War College Division. Operations in the Philippines against the Japanese after the war scare of 1907 were terminated, and in 1909 the army's intelligence agents were withdrawn from Cuba. With a world war five years away, the intelligence function of America's military was so thoroughly submerged in the War College as to be unidentifiable.[7]

Nor was any improvement in its status forthcoming. Under General Leonard Wood's 1911 reorganization of the general staff into a four-division structure, the War College continued to be responsible for the collection and dissemination of all military intelligence.[8] Information was being collected, primarily by the military attachés at American embassies around the world who routinely sent messages to Washington. At the receiving end, however, nothing happened to the reports

6. Bidwell, *History of Military Intelligence*, pp. 62–63; Jensen, *Military Surveillance*, p. 6.

7. Bidwell, *History of Military Intelligence*, pp. 76–83; Jensen, *Military Surveillance*, pp. 6–7.

8. Jack C. Lane, *Armed Progressive: General Leonard Wood* (Novato, Calif.: Presidio Press, 1978), p. 169.

because the army lacked even a systematic filing system, to say nothing of a processing capability. Although by 1915 there were ten committees theoretically handling intelligence, no single officer was dedicated to and responsible for analyzing the data that arrived. As an army study put it over forty years later, the intelligence program was on a "disastrous journey down the road toward total extinction."[9]

One man single-handedly changed this situation: Ralph H. Van Deman, recognized by the army as the father of Military Intelligence. Born in Delaware, Ohio, in 1865, and graduated from Harvard College in 1888, Van Deman studied some law and finished medical school before accepting a commission in the infantry in 1891. Assigned to the mapping section of the old Military Information Division in 1897, he did not reach Cuba until after the war in 1898, but he did see action in the Philippines. There he worked in MacArthur's intelligence program, developing a system of undercover agents and informers.[10] In 1904 he was a member of the first class at the Army War College, and subsequent assignments shifted him back and forth between Washington and the Philippines. The latter experience made him the army's most fervent believer in an active intelligence program.[11]

When Major Van Deman returned to Washington in May 1915 for duty with the War College, he began immediately to lobby for the reestablishment of a separate section on military intelligence. Initially he had little success, and it is apparent that his persistence was a source of annoyance to his superiors. On March 2, 1916, he wrote two lengthy memoranda to the head of the War College, one summarizing the sad state of intelligence and the other describing the unfortunate history of the program. Van Deman put it plainly that military intelligence's "personnel and material have been merged and scattered in the War College Division and . . . its functions have ceased to be exercised,"

9. Bidwell, *History of Military Intelligence*, p. 92.

10. Linn, *The Philippine War*, p. 155, mentions Captain Van Deman in the Military Information Division in MacArthur's headquarters in Manila.

11. The best biographical information on Van Deman is contained in Nathan Miller, *Spying for America: The Hidden History of U.S. Intelligence* (New York: Paragon House, 1989), pp. 176–79; William R. Corson, *The Armies of Ignorance: The Rise of the American Intelligence Empire* (New York: Dial Press, 1977), pp. 45–47; O'Toole, *Encyclopedia of American Intelligence*, pp. 461–63; and Marc B. Powe, "A Sketch of a Man and His Times," in Ralph E. Weber, ed., *The Final Memoranda: Major General Ralph H. Van Deman, USA Ret., 1865–1952, Father of U.S. Military Intelligence* (Wilmington, Del.: Scholarly Resources, 1988), pp. ix–xxv. The "final memoranda" are historical accounts written by Van Deman late in his life, and like Bidwell's work, they must be used with care because Van Deman refused to include any mention of his civilian spy system. Nevertheless, *Final Memoranda* is certainly valuable, especially since Van Deman reproduced important documents dealing with official decisions about military intelligence from 1889 to 1915.

noting that the committee system had failed to produce a legitimate intelligence effort. "Does it not seem that the time has come," he asked, "when the General Staff should take steps to correct this condition of affairs?" He recommended the creation of a separate Military Intelligence Division, reporting directly to the army chief of staff, responsible for all military information matters, and freed from other staff duties.[12]

Despite the War College's endorsement of Van Deman's plan, the army chief of staff rejected the idea of creating a separate identity for intelligence in the military bureaucracy. Van Deman was, however, given a free hand, within the War College, in intelligence matters. In April 1916, he was able to see to it that each of the major army commands (called departments) was required to have an intelligence officer on its staff. Under the April order, these officers reported to the chief of staff of their respective departments, but, if necessary, they could be called upon to accept intelligence missions from the national headquarters. Van Deman also established liaison with the investigative units within the Department of State and the Department of Justice, with the Secret Service of the Treasury Department, and with his counterparts in the navy. Before the year was out he was using the title "Officer in Charge of Military Intelligence."[13] Also during 1916, Brigadier General John J. Pershing undertook his unsuccessful incursion into Mexico in search of Pancho Villa. Although no intelligence effort appears to have been conducted from Washington, Pershing appreciated the need for information and appointed a staff officer who used native informants. Reports flowed back to Washington, some of which noted the growth of revolutionary socialism in northern Mexico, along with a fear that it might spread to the United States. By 1917 there was a considerable military presence along the southern border, and these units contained intelligence officers sensitive not only to the threat of raiding bandits but to politics as well.[14]

---

12. Van Deman's two memoranda for the chief of the War College Division, March 2, 1916, are reprinted in Weber, ed., *Final Memoranda*, pp. 103–54.

13. For Van Deman's use of the title, see his December 19, 1916, letter to Naval Intelligence, in Record Group 38, Office of Naval Intelligence, "CAP" file, box 1A (hereafter cited as "CAP" file), National Archives. On Van Deman's relations with army commands, see his memorandum dated July 28, 1916, in file 10560–1–A part III, Record Group 165, Military Intelligence Division, National Archives. See also Bidwell, *History of Military Intelligence*, p. 96, and Weber, ed., *Final Memoranda*, p. xvi.

14. Bidwell, *History of Military Intelligence*, pp. 94–95; Jensen, *Military Surveillance*, p. 8. On November 8, 1916, Secretary of War Newton D. Baker forwarded to President Woodrow Wilson a report from the Southern Department's intelligence officer, who was working with a Mexican informant known as "xyz" (Papers of Newton D. Baker, microfilm reel 1, p. 134, Manuscript Division, Library of Congress).

During the period when military intelligence was fighting for survival, the navy had maintained its intelligence program intact and reasonably well staffed so that the Office of Naval Intelligence had grown into an increasingly sophisticated operation. As early as 1906, navy agents kept suspected Japanese and German operatives under surveillance. Agents reported from around the world, and in October 1915 the navy, recognizing the need for data on threats to its home bases, established an Information Service in the Naval Defense Districts. Each geographical headquarters had an intelligence officer, an aide for information, and with this system the navy was prepared to launch a genuine intelligence effort when the United States entered World War I.[15]

That the army leadership had virtually no inclination to support an intelligence program is demonstrated clearly by the fact that when the United States declared war against Germany on April 6, 1917, Van Deman's activity, still submerged in the War College, remained unable, as one officer put it, "to execute any of its fundamental intelligence responsibilities in a proper manner."[16] Again, with his superior's approval, Van Deman took his case directly to the chief of staff, only to be dismissed with the opinion that when U.S. troops got to France the Allies would surely have plenty of information on the enemy awaiting them. Finally, the army chief told Van Deman not to bother him further with his appeals. According to Van Deman's own account, these orders prohibited his approaching the secretary of war on the matter, which is precisely what he did.[17]

In keeping with the protocol of his profession, he acted surreptitiously. One of his back channels to Secretary of War Newton D. Baker resulted from a fortuitous assignment, which no doubt Van Deman had resisted because it took him away from his intellience desk. At Baker's request, novelist Gertrude Atherton had visited a number of army training camps, and while she was in Washington Van Deman was detailed to escort her. In their conversation, she expressed considerable appreciation for the work of the British secret service in the war effort, and Van Deman seized upon the opportunity to tell of his futile efforts, apparently in considerable detail. "She became quite excited," Van Deman recalled, "and said that she should certainly report this matter to

---

15. Dorwart, *Office of Naval Intelligence*, pp. 87–103. For the navy's coordination with Van Deman in 1916 on such intriguing matters as "liquid fire" and disappearing ink, neither of which ever amounted to much, see the "CAP" file, boxes 1A and 1B. For the work of navy secret agent Robert L. Pruitt against the Japanese in the United States, see box 7.

16. Bidwell, *History of Military Intelligence*, p. 99.

17. Weber, ed., *Final Memoranda*, p. 21.

the Secretary of War that very day." After learning that the superintendent of the Washington police and Baker habitually took breakfast at the
same club, Van Deman used his established liaison with the district law
enforcement system to have the superintendent also contact the secretary of war on behalf of army intelligence.[18]

The result was an order from the chief of staff on May 3, 1917, directing
the creation of a Military Intelligence Section within the War College.
The mission of this unit was described as "military espionage," "counter-
espionage," and cooperation with the Allies' intelligence services "in
connection with military intelligence work in the United States and with
our forces in the field, either at home or abroad."[19] Although Van
Deman would have preferred the status of a separate division for his
work, the connection with the War College was the best he could get at
the time, and the mission statement was broad enough to cover what he
had in mind. Moreover, the position in the War College allowed Van
Deman some cover under a sympathetic superior who gave him free rein
while insulating him from an antagonistic chief of staff who resented Van
Deman's maneuvering.

Major Van Deman's section was established immediately, assuming
responsibility for "secret service work," along with the map room and
the "photograph gallery." His staff consisted of himself, Captain Alexander B. Coxe, who became his secretary, one retired officer, and two
clerks. Initially, his budget amounted to only $25,000, but Van Deman's
transformation of this small endeavor was astounding. Within six weeks
he obtained $500,000 from Congress, which he spent through "confi-
dential vouchers" to avoid publicity. He arranged the transfer of another
$100,000 from the quartermaster general, which he used to pay infor-
mants. In October, Congress gave him another half a million. That
amount was doubled for the following year, and when the war concluded
in November 1918, Van Deman's brainchild had over a million dollars
unexpended. Staffing increased similarly, and at its peak the Washington office of Military Intelligence alone had 282 officers and 1,159
civilians.[20]

While directing the army's spy program, Van Deman never gave up on

18. Ibid., p. 22; Joan M. Jensen, *The Price of Vigilance* (Chicago: Rand McNally, 1968),
pp. 118–19. Miller, in *Spying for America*, pp. 192–93, rejects the Atherton story and
suggests that the real pressure on the secretary of war to aid Van Deman came from Claude
M. Dansey, the British intelligence chief in the United States.

19. Quoted in Bidwell, *History of Military Intelligence*, p. 113.

20. U.S. Army, General Staff, Military Intelligence Division, *The Functions of the
Military Intelligence Division, U.S. General Staff* (Washington, D.C.: Military Intelligence Division, 1918), pp. 2–3; Bidwell, *History of Military Intelligence*, pp. 110–12.

his administrative goal of a clear and unique slot for Military Intelligence on the general staff, and he continued to pressure the chief of staff for separate divisional status for his group. He was turned down repeatedly, but he did achieve, on June 28, 1917, full authority over all intelligence officers in the field. This control was important because the geographical spread of the department officers gave him agents across the nation.[21] This order only sanctified a reporting process already establishd by Van Deman, for by that time department officers were following his instructions to contact the local agents of the Department of Justice, acquire copies of their reports on "Socialist activities," and forward them to Washington.[22]

Equally important, the field units at last had an office in Washington that welcomed information gathered by whatever means, and Van Deman had the authority to require them to run specific missions selected by him. Information was fast in arriving. One of the earliest reports came from the intelligence officer of the Central Department, headquartered in Chicago, who transmitted a report that on July 16, 1917, an army lieutenant at Camp Nichols in Kansas City had been invited, by virtue of his previous work as a police detective in that city, to accompany the local authorities on a raid of the meeting hall of the Agricultural Workers Organization, a branch of the Industrial Workers of the World (IWW). The raid resulted in the confiscation of several loaded revolvers, what appeared to be burglary tools, and "three suit cases of letters and records." The lieutenant reported that he was reviewing the evidence in association with the Kansas City police and the local Secret Service agent. He added that, while a detective, he had made a special study of "these so-called Industrial Workers" and in 1913 had arrested more than four hundred of them.[23]

When Van Deman, by July a lieutenant colonel, learned of the lieutenant's participation in the Kansas City raid, he ordered the Central Department intelligence officer to have the seized material forwarded to him. Encouraged by this interest in Washington, the Camp Nichols officer volunteered his own analysis of the IWW for Van Deman's review.

21. Bidwell, *History of Military Intelligence*, pp. 113–15.
22. Department intelligence officer, Fort Sam Houston, to chief of MI, June 22, 1917, in Randolph Boehm, ed., *U.S. Military Intelligence Reports: Surveillance of Radicals in the United States, 1917–1941* (Frederick, Md.: University Publications of America, 1984), reel 1, p. 350. This collection of thirty-four reels of microfilm, averaging over a thousand pages per reel, represents a significant portion of the investigative files of Military Intelligence from Record Group 165 of the National Archives (hereafter cited as MI Microfilm).
23. Ralph E. Truman to department intelligence officer, Chicago, July 16, 1917, MI Microfilm, reel 2, pp. 28–29.

"Ninety-five per cent of their members," he said, "are foreign born, being the off-scouring of the entire world—anarchists at heart. They defy law and order, and are against any form of government." The remainder he termed "thieves, thugs, highwaymen, burglars, murderers, and ex-convicts."[24]

Van Deman's early interest in the IWW and other radical movements is apparent from the attention he paid to this minor raid in Kansas City, which resulted in a $100 fine for each of the ten radicals arrested and their expulsion from the city. What is not obvious is the origin of his interest. Nothing in his autobiographical writings suggests any concern for American politics, and indeed, he had been out of the country a great deal until 1915. A rather obvious interpretation is that his service in the Philippines had made an interest in the affairs of civilians a matter of routine. There he had faced an insurgency rooted in the civilian population and had resorted to the techniques of counterintelligence in an attempt to find and suppress disloyal citizens.

As appealing as that explanation may be, it bases Van Deman's attitudes and actions solely on his personal experience. It may be instead that he acted as part of a larger phenomenon, for he was not the only Ivy League gentleman to become alarmed at the level of radicalism in the United States. Naval Intelligence was dominated by such men, as were many of the volunteer organizations that came forward to assist the government. By the end of the war, literally hundreds of thousands of upper-middle-class men and women were working to fight radicalism in the name of patriotism. Nor was Van Deman's Military Intelligence Section the only agency involved in spying on and repressing the American left. The three decades before the American entry into World War I had seen a demand for strikebreakers and labor spies that had created a booming private detective industry. The fledgling Bureau of Investigation in the Department of Justice found a new mission in hunting down radicals during the war, and in the months immediately following the conflict the attorney general gambled his political future on pursuing the Red menace.

Yet Van Deman's decision to oppose the left is intriguing because, as the founder of the modern army intelligence function, he set its course for over fifty years. A professional espionage program offered him ample missions without focusing on ideology. He could have limited his domestic work to countering the activities of suspected enemy agents and

24. Van Deman to department intelligence officer, Chicago, July 28, 1917, ibid., reel 2, p. 24; Truman to department intelligence officer, July 30, 1917, ibid., pp. 26–27.

sympathizers and could even have included ethnicity as an indicator of pro-German inclinations without undertaking a massive campaign against fundamental civil liberties. Instead, he put the army on a path of antiradicalism that eventually came close to destroying Military Intelligence, and he also took on the radicals in a vendetta that extended long after the end of his official relationship with the organization he created.

These were not tolerant years, no matter how many reforms the Progressive Era had achieved, and the established classes had become increasingly seized by fear of cultural catastrophe. Calls for the eugenic elimination of the unfit and the restriction of immigration grew especially loud, and lynch law and vigilante justice were common. Van Deman might have taken another path, but it is not surprising that he chose the one he did. It may be, moreover, that the emergency of the war would have resulted in the creation of an organization like Military Intelligence without his intervention, and any hard-boiled intelligence chief probably would have reached the same estimate of the situation that he did and recognized the same threats. In the spring of 1917 those threats were formidable and obvious to anyone charged with countering challenges to the military and the war effort.

To say, as is now generally accepted, that the Central Powers had a sloppy propaganda campaign and a poorly developed intelligence operation in the United States would have been unthinkable in 1917. The historic fact that not a single case brought under the Espionage Act of World War I was for spying was certainly not known in 1917. What was obvious was that both German and British agents had operated openly in this country before our entry into the war and had done so legally because there was no law against clandestine intrigue.[25] Van Deman knew the German spies were here, and he soon caught one.

Lather Witcke, traveling under the name Pablo Waberski, was a twenty-two-year-old German spy working in Mexico when Van Deman's men first detected him. He had talked about sabotage and even claimed credit for the famous Black Tom Island explosion in New Jersey, and an army agent's search of his luggage had revealed coded documents.

25. Phillip Knightley, *The Second Oldest Profession: Spies and Spying in the 20th Century* (New York: Norton, 1987), pp. 36–37. For information on continuing British activity in the United States, see a February 21, 1921, memorandum from J. Edgar Hoover to Military Intelligence, subject: "British Espionage in the United States," in Theodore Kornweibel, Jr., ed., *Federal Surveillance of Afro-Americans (1917–1925): The First World War, the Red Scare, and the Garvey Movement* (Frederick, Md.: University Publications of America, 1986), reel 22, pp. 559–73. These twenty-five reels of microfilm contain documents from several federal investigative agencies, including the Bureau of Investigation of the Department of Justice, the State Department, Military Intelligence, and the navy (hereafter cited as Surveillance of Afro-Americans Microfilm).

When he crossed the border in early 1918, at Nogales, Arizona, Van Deman's men took him into custody and whisked him off to Fort Sam Houston. The materials in his possession proved to be his credentials as a German agent, along with orders for other Germans to provide assistance and funds. With Military Intelligence officers as the prosecution's chief witnesses, the army gave Witcke a secret trial before a military tribunal at Fort Sam Houston and sentenced him to death. When the case was appealed to President Woodrow Wilson, the Justice Department opposed the execution, partly on the grounds that Witcke had committed no crime in this country. Probably out of fear that having the army administer justice in espionage cases was a bad precedent, Wilson commuted the sentence.[26]

Labor unrest, whether or not it was instigated by the Germans, clearly provided aid and comfort for the enemy, and many Americans no doubt agreed with the authors of *The German Secret Service in America*, who wrote in 1918 that the "anarchist socialist, and I.W.W. element" had caused enough trouble "to qualify them as allies, if not actual servants of the Kaiser."[27] Could any rational person whose country was involved in a desperate struggle fail to be outraged over the activities of the IWW's "Rebel Girl," Elizabeth Gurley Flynn? Her pamphlet *Sabotage* certainly sounded inflammatory, and in the emergency no one considered the subtitle, *The Conscious Withdrawal of our Workers' Industrial Efficiency*. Sabotage did not mean slowdown. Sabotage was sabotage.[28]

26. The fullest account of the Witcke case is in Henry Landau, *The Enemy Within: The Inside Story of German Sabotage in America* (New York: G. P. Putnam's Sons, 1937), pp. 112–28. Landau indicates that Military Intelligence, the Bureau of Investigation, and the British secret service had agents in Mexico who watched for Industrial Workers of the World activity and draft evaders as well as German spies. A photograph of Witcke is opposite p. 102. See also Jensen, *Price of Vigilance*, pp. 225, 232, 261; Weber, ed., *Final Memoranda*, p. 37; Bidwell, *History of Military Intelligence*, pp. 169–70. A copy of General Order No. 32, June 4, 1920, which gives the history of the case and implements Wilson's May 27, 1920, commutation to life imprisonment at hard labor, is in the Alexander B. Coxe, Sr., Papers, J. Y. Joyner Library, East Carolina University, Greenville, N.C. The document has the spy's name as Lather Witcke, and that is the spelling I have adopted. Van Deman, in his memoirs, has it as Luther Witke, Jr., and Bidwell calls him Lother Witzke. Landau has it Lothar Witzke, a usage adopted by O'Toole in *Encyclopedia of American Intelligence*, pp. 500–01, and by Miller, *Spying for America*, 195–96. Jensen uses Waberski, as does Edmund M. Morgan in "Court-Martial Jurisdiction over Non-Military Persons under the Articles of War," *Minnesota Law Review* 4 (January 1920): 79–116. Witcke was confined in the federal penitentiary at Leavenworth, Kansas, and released on September 26, 1923. He returned to Germany, where he received the Iron Cross.

27. John P. Jones and Paul M. Hollister, *The German Secret Service in America, 1914–1918* (Boston: Small, Maynard, 1918), p. 189.

28. Elizabeth Gurley Flynn's *Sabotage* (Cleveland: IWW Publishing Bureau, 1916) can be found in MI Microfilm, reel 1, pp. 103–35. Despite her definition of sabotage as "either

Though it now seems reasonable, so long after the panic and paranoia of 1917, to agree with the historian who determined that the IWW was not a "real menace" and "did not represent any serious chink in the democratic armor," such an objective assessment could have been made by few federal officials at the time.[29] The IWW was generally held responsible for the labor violence that had swept the country in recent years, resulting in what two authors have termed "the bloodiest and most violent labor history of any industrial nation in the world."[30] Nor did it matter to the patriot of 1917 that most of this violence was spontaneous and little of it inspired by anarchism. The few examples of anarchist action, especially Alexander Berkman's attack on Henry Clay Frick during the Homestead strike of 1892 and Leon Czolgosz's assassination of President William McKinley in 1901, were spectacular enough to blame the anarchists (and the socialists and the IWW, who were all linked in the public mind) for the continued violence. Out West there had been ugly confrontations between the IWW and vigilantes, notably in Everett and Centralia, Washington, in late 1916. By July 1917 federal troops were stationed in Arizona, Montana, Washington, and Oregon, for fear that labor violence would disrupt the production of copper and lumber vital to the war effort.

Additionally, the anarchist Berkman, the "Red King," was still very active. After serving fourteen years in prison for his attempt on Frick's life, he began publishing a magazine with the notorious title the *Blast*, the first issue of which appeared on January 15, 1916. Emma Goldman, the "Red Queen," whose name had come up in both the Frick and McKinley shootings, was also very energetic with her magazine *Mother Earth*. Other frightening publications in New York included the well-known *Masses*, along with *Revolt*, and, in Spanish, *Voluntad*. In Chicago there was the *Alarm* and out of Los Angeles the Spanish *Regeneracion*. The *Blast* died for lack of funds before U.S. entry into the war, after which the federal government moved quickly to suppress the others.

---

to slacken up or interfere with the quantity, or to botch in your skill and interfere with the quality" and not "physical violence," lines such as "sabotage is to this class struggle what the guerrilla warfare is to the battle" were clearly inflammatory. One IWW leader later regretted the "careless use of the word" (Ralph Chaplin, *Wobbly: The Rough-and-Tumble Story of an American Radical* [Chicago: University of Chicago Press, 1948], p. 203).

29. Robert K. Murray, *Red Scare: A Study in National Hysteria, 1919–1920* (Minneapolis: University of Minnesota Press, 1955), p. 31.

30. Philip Taft and Philip Ross, "American Labor Violence: Its Causes, Character, and Outcome," in Roger Lane and John J. Turner, Jr., eds., *Riot, Rout, and Tumult: Readings in American Social and Political Violence* (New York: University Press of America, 1984), p. 219.

Berkman and Goldman were arrested on June 15, 1917, in the New York office of *Mother Earth.* Charged with speaking against the war and the draft, each was fined $10,000 and sentenced to two years' imprisonment, after which they were deported to Russia.[31]

Van Deman and his successors in Military Intelligence developed an abiding interest in these two anarchists. Even after their deportation, the army followed them around the world for the rest of their lives. In late 1917, Van Deman was not at all convinced that they had been silenced by mere incarceration, and he accepted at face value a report from the Pinkerton detective agency that Goldman was behind a secret New York society called "the Guillotine," which was determined to kill the president, federal attorneys, and state officials. Although this plot evaporated, as did other leads from Pinkerton, Van Deman's interest in these leading anarchists never wavered.[32]

Even without knowledge of such secret reports, an alarmed public had endured a series of recent instances of blind violence. The terrible dynamiting of the *Los Angeles Times* building in 1910 was followed by smaller incidents in later years that suggested a pattern of German-radical-anarchism gone wild. An anarchist blew himself up when his bomb went off accidentally on July 4, 1914. There were two terrible days in July 1915, less than two months after the sinking of the *Lusitania,* when Eric Meunta, a Columbia University professor of German who claimed that he wanted to show the country the danger of explosives, detonated a small device in the U.S. Capitol. On the following day, in an effort to take the family of John Pierpont Morgan hostage until the shipment of munitions to the Allies ceased, he shot the famous financier. Neither the perpetrator's connection with Germany nor any motive other than the one he stated was ever established. He committed suicide in jail.[33]

In October of the same year, the New York police's Bomb Squad caught a German agent with hundreds of pounds of explosives and four

31. Thomas J. Tunney, *Throttled! The Detection of the German and Anarchist Bomb Plotters as Told to Paul Merrick Hollister* (Boston: Small, Maynard, 1919), pp. 251–75. Among the materials on New York radicals in MI Microfilm, reel 4, pp. 109–213, is a national list of subscribers to *Mother Earth.*
32. William A. Pinkerton to Van Deman, December 10, 1917, MI Microfilm, reel 7, p. 440.
33. Morgan recovered from his wounds. When arrested, Meunta gave his name as Jack Holt (Landau, *Enemy Within,* pp. 101–2). See also Tunney, *Throttled,* pp. 184–212, and U.S. Senate, Report and Hearings of the Subcommittee on the Judiciary, 65th Cong., 1st sess., document no. 62, *Brewing and Liquor Interests and German and Bolshevik Propaganda,* 3 vols. (Washington, D.C.: U.S. Government Printing Office, 1919), 2: 2670–71 (hereafter cited as Overman Hearings).

assembled mines. The arresting officer testified that each "infernal machine" was ready, with "the firing pins and clockwork and rifle cartridges all fixed in place." The would-be saboteur, Robert Fay, was sentenced to eight years in the Atlanta federal prison, escaped, and was recaptured in Spain. In December the same New York team caught a German agent code-named Triple-X, who had placed a number of bombs on ships, although most of these were ineffective. For lack of any other law, those arrested in these plots were tried for failure to give the required notification that they were shipping explosives through interstate commerce. After the war, the head of the New York Bomb Squad told his sensational story to a U.S. Senate investigating committee. Although he admitted that he felt the famous explosion in the summer of 1916 at the Black Tom Island munitions depot might well have been an accident, his account was certainly testimony to the panic that gripped this country at least a year before the United States declared war.[34]

Another sensational bombing came on July 22, 1916, when the San Francisco Preparedness Parade was hit by an explosion that killed ten and wounded forty. Subsequently, Thomas Mooney, his wife, and three others were arrested, and Mooney was sentenced to death. A left-wing labor organizer, Mooney was regarded by many contemporaries as having been railroaded, and his name became a rallying cry for the left in general. After his sentence was commuted to life imprisonment, his cause remained active until his release in 1939, and throughout that period Mooney rallies were always of interest to Military Intelligence.[35] To Van Deman, support for Mooney represented disloyalty and was cause for investigation. He acquired photostatic copies of all the Mooney material confiscated by the police and had operatives attend numerous Mooney defense rallies. One who did so was volunteer agent C–289, working for the intelligence officer of the Western Department in San Francisco. C–289 reported on an April 17, 1918, "Mooney Mass Meeting" at the San Francisco Civic Center Auditorium. The two principal speakers at this well-attended meeting were the venerable labor spokeswoman Mother Jones and the Irish nationalist Hannah Sheehy-Skeffington.[36]

34. See the testimony of Inspector Thomas J. Tunney, January 21, 1919, in Overman Hearings, 2: 2670–77, and Landau, *Enemy Within*, pp. 36–51.

35. On Mooney, see Richard H. Frost, *The Mooney Case* (Stanford: Stanford University Press, 1968).

36. C–289, intelligence report, San Francisco, April 17, 1918, MI Microfilm, reel 1, p. 701. Mooney material can be found throughout the Military Intelligence files, but a substantial portion is in reel 1, pp. 458–932.

Irish-Americans were viewed as a definite threat because of their susceptibility to anti-British propaganda. His work with British intelligence since 1916 convinced Van Deman that the Germans were providing guns to the Sinn Fein in the United States. James Larkin, founder of the Irish Citizen Army, had been in this country since 1914, but it was not until 1919 that he was arrested by the New York police and imprisoned for criminal syndicalism. Van Deman was concerned because in some critical industries with severe labor problems the work force was largely Irish. Thus in places such as Butte, Montana, Sinn Fein, noted one student of the American Irish, became a "code word" for an "Irish-IWW-German conspiracy." Even though the IWW came very late to the Butte dispute, the organization was generally regarded as the source of the copper industry's problems. And since the workers were Irish, and the Irish hated the British and were pro-German, it all fit neatly into a web of subversion. As a Department of Labor mediator in Butte wired the secretary of labor in early July 1917: "If there are not any U.S. secret service men here, they should be to deal with question of German influence."[37]

Another ethnic group regarded with suspicion and hostility was the East Indians or, as everyone referred to them, the Hindus. Apparently Muslim nationalism in India went unnoticed in the United States. The basis for the "Hindu Plot" was the belief that the anti-British Indians were pro-German. Specifically, the 1915 conspiracy involved guns and ammunition purchased with German money in New York and shipped to San Francisco, where they were loaded on the *Annie Larsen*, which was to transfer the illegal cargo to the *Maverick* in the South Seas for shipment to India. When the two ships failed to rendezvous, the *Annie Larsen* returned to the United States and was seized on July 1, 1915. Twenty-nine Germans and Indians were convicted in San Francisco in a trial that lasted until the spring of 1918. The case was further sensationalized when one of the leaders on trial was shot and killed in the courtroom by a colleague, apparently over an internal dispute involving the misappropriation of funds for the cause of Indian nationalism.[38]

By 1915 there were around seven thousand Indians in the United

37. W. H. Rodgers to William B. Wilson, July 2, 1917, in Record Group 60, Glasser Files, box 3, National Archives. See also David M. Emmons, *The Butte Irish: Class and Ethnicity in an American Mining Town, 1875–1925* (Urbana: University of Illinois Press, 1989), pp. 377–79, and Jeffreys-Jones, *American Espionage*, p. 117.

38. Landau, *Enemy Within*, pp. 28–33. See also Emerson Hough, *The Web* (Chicago: Reilly and Lee, 1919), pp. 104–5; Tunney, *Throttled*, pp. 69–107; and Jeffreys-Jones, *American Espionage*, pp. 107–16.

States, of whom about one-third were Muslim and even more were Sikhs. They were mostly laborers in California and suffered the discrimination that state afforded all Asians. Some of them were certainly nationalists and anti-British; the major revolutionary group was called the Hindustan Gadar party. Other organizations included the Friends of Freedom for India and the India Home Rule League of America, which published *Young India* and other pro-India, anti-British material. By late 1917, the Indians in America were one of the ethnic groups in which army intelligence officers had a keen interest. The New York branch of Military Intelligence had the local police arrest the nationalist leader Dr. Chandra H. Chakravarty on the grounds that the Germans had given him money.[39]

Van Deman was building his organization as spring faded into summer in 1917, when a threat occurred to which he was unable to respond. The East St. Louis race riot began on July 2 and left forty-eight dead. The only federal intelligence presence in the area was a lone agent from the Department of Justice's Bureau of Investigation who tried to track down rumors that weapons were being stockpiled.[40] Military Intelligence was not yet capable of reacting rapidly to sudden flare-ups, and it had no capability to go undercover in black areas. Van Deman, however, was convinced that American blacks, like the Irish and the Indians, were easy prey for German agents, and he began to devote considerable attention to gauging the sentiment and movements of blacks.

One other area warranted Van Deman's concern as he estimated the threat facing the army in 1917: resistance to the draft. The opposition of a number of groups to conscription had led the Department of Justice to expect widespread disorders on June 5, 1917, when the first mass registration was held. Thousands of volunteers assisted in a security watch. The day passed quietly, however, except for an Irish-American demonstration in Butte. Nevertheless, the military establishment grew extremely concerned about draft evaders.[41] Along with the "slackers,"

---

39. Overman Hearings, 2: 2674, 2677–79. For another file on the Hindus, see the Lusk Committee Papers, L0039, box 1, folder 12, New York State Archives, Albany. On discrimination against Asians, see Ronald Takaki, *Strangers from a Different Shore: A History of Asian Americans* (Boston: Little, Brown, 1989), pp. 295–98.

40. On the riot, see Elliott M. Rudwick, *The Race Riot at East St. Louis, July 2, 1917* (Carbondale: Southern Illinois University Press, 1964). The role of the Bureau of Investigation is included in the congressional investigation into the riot, along with National Guard reports, in Rudwick, ed., *The East St. Louis Race Riot of 1917* (Frederick, Md.: University Publications of America, 1985), on microfilm.

41. John W. Chambers II, *To Raise an Army: The Draft Comes to Modern America* (New York: Free Press, 1987), p. 211.

as they came to be called, Van Deman was concerned about the Socialists and pacifists. He reasoned that in insisting on defending the civil right of a person conscientiously to refuse military service, these groups were encouraging resistance to the draft.

All these together seemed a large threat to Van Deman in the summer of 1917. The enemies were varied: Socialists, pacifists, supporters of pacifists, Germans, German-Americans, Americans suspected of being pro-German, Americans suspected of being neutral, the IWW, black activists, and labor agitators active in too many sensitive industries. By the end of the summer, naval agents had completed a major investigation of the Sperry Gyroscope Company in New York and were planning to arrest the numerous aliens employed there. The West Virginia coal fields were tense again, and the governor worried that because his National Guard had been called into federal service, he had no protection against a threatened walkout by thirty thousand miners. Oil field organizers were calling for strikes in Texas and Louisiana, and by early November troops were dispatched to those states for guard duty.[42] Soldiers had already been sent to Arizona and Montana, where the crucial copper industry was thought to be endangered by the Irish-IWW-German conspiracy, and to the Northwest to protect the lumber supply needed to produce the military's aircraft.

To meet these threats, Van Deman assembled a sizable intelligence network. Larger by far than the Secret Service and the Office of Naval Intelligence, it rivaled the Bureau of Investigation, the forerunner of the Federal Bureau of Investigation. The army had manpower, and out of the millions eligible for military service, thousands willingly accepted the assignment to investigate and fight the radical threat.

42. See Glasser Files, boxes 6 and 7, on tension in the coal and oil fields. The navy's lengthy Sperry case is in "CAP" file, box 1B. At the same time the navy had developed a keen interest in the nature of "Mother Keebaugh's Army and Navy Club" in Dallas, Texas; see Record Group 38, Office of Naval Intelligence, "Suspect" file, box 3, National Archives.

CHAPTER 2

The Structure of Military Intelligence

In organizing his new intelligence agency in May 1917, Ralph Van Deman relied heavily on advice from the British. Acquiring both the name, Military Intelligence (MI), and his organizational chart from them, he even, for a time, used their spellings. The British functional system for mission designation involved the initials MI, followed by a number specifying each section. MI5, for example, denoted the British counterespionage program.[1] Under Van Deman's Americanization of this model, MI1 handled administration, and MI2 collected foreign military intelligence, prepared "the current estimate of the strategic situation," and supported the war effort in Europe. Initially, "contra-espionage" was divided into three sections, with MI3 responsible for "contra-espionage in the military service" and conscientious objectors in the army. MI4 controlled "contra-espionage outside the military service in the United States," which is to say domestic intelligence. MI5 worked on "contra-espionage abroad," with over half its resources dedicated to Latin America. Eventually, MI3 and MI5 disappeared, their functions transferred to MI4, which became the Negative Section and later Branch. MI6 handled translations; MI7, Graphics, reproduced maps and censored films for the troops. MI8 was the highly secret Codes and Ciphers Section.[2]

The Plant Protection Section, initially MI3K, was a special case. Technically, its Plant Protection Service, created in July 1917, was a separate government agency involving only civilian agents guarding war-related industries. But the service's mission dovetailed so nicely with that of the Negative Branch that the two were almost indistinguishable. Within less than a year after its creation, the service had offices adjacent to those of

---

1. Ralph E. Weber, ed., *The Final Memoranda: Major General Ralph H. Van Deman, USA Ret., 1865–1952, Father of U.S. Military Intelligence* (Wilmington, Del.: Scholarly Resources, 1988), p. 23; Bruce W. Bidwell, *History of the Military Intelligence Division, Department of the Army General Staff, 1775–1941* (Federick, Md.: University of Publications of America, 1986), pp. 122–23.

2. See the organizational charts in Record Group 165, Military Intelligence Division, 10560–377, National Archives.

Van Deman and worked directly with his staff. By the end of the war, the Plant Protection Service had 372 employees, 331 of them agents. This effort, it has been said, was "in reality an undercover intelligence organization and not . . . just a civilian guard service." The IWW was a special target for its covert operations, and the service's specialty was infiltrating unions. It was more than willing to report any suspicious person or activity it came across.[3]

Van Deman's concept of intelligence involved both positive and negative poles. Positive, a term still used by the intelligence community, referred to useful information about the enemy, while negative intelligence meant opposing the enemy's effort to use undercover agents to learn about or to harm one's own side. Negative intelligence has not survived in the glossary of espionage, but its general purpose is best summed up in the current use of the word *counterintelligence*. It is an error, however, to view negative intelligence as merely the prevention of enemy espionage or sabotage. Fighting foreign spies was the theoretical mission of negative intelligence, but that unit, and to a remarkable extent the whole of the army intelligence establishment, was consistently more concerned with countering a revolution from the left. The fundamental orientation of negative intelligence became antiradicalism, as a Military Intelligence officer made clear during his interrogation of a former officer from czarist Russia. Living in the United States under the name Andrew P. Anthony, the Russian was one of many arrested by the army and other federal and state agencies following a series of bombings in the spring of 1919. Part of the transcript of his interrogation reads:

Q. What was your rank?
A. 1st Lieutenant.
Q. You were connected, I believe with the Russian Military Intelligence System.
A. Is it confidential is it?
Q. Yes, everything you say will be considered confidential.
A. In that first year I was engaged in internal revolutionary investigation.
Q. That corresponds to what we call counter espionage?
A. Exactly.[4]

3. Bidwell, *History of Military Intelligence*, pp. 187, 207. The Plant Protection Service was well under way by late summer of 1917, and its reports are spread throughout the files of Military Intelligence. For a sample of the reports of Agent 101, see Randolph Boehm, ed., *U.S. Military Intelligence Reports: Surveillance of Radicals in the United States, 1917–1941* (Frederick, Md.: University Publications of America, 1984), reel 2, p. 488 (hereafter cited as MI Microfilm). The voluminous and fascinating files of the Plant Protection Section, amounting to a hundred feet or more, are at the Suitland Records Center of the National Archives, Record Group 165, entries 104–8.
4. The interrogation is part of an intelligence report submitted by Lieutenant Donald C. Van Buren, June 12, 1919, MI Microfilm, reel 14, pp. 774–82.

Negative intelligence, counterespionage, countersubversion, and counterrevolution all meant the same: spying on American radicals. Once Van Deman had focused on the left, he understood that to counter that threat, with its insidious methods of propaganda and manipulation, the negative function must become a true domestic intelligence system, watching everywhere for signs of enemy activity, no matter how subtle. Accordingly, the Negative Branch had sections for passport control, censorship, tracing German money flowing to American radicals, morale, graft and fraud, "Counter-Propaganda: Publications, Moving Pictures, etc.," and "Counter-Propaganda: Pacifists, Religious Sects, Agitators, Negro Subversion." There were also specific desks for "Labor," "Plant Protection," and "I.W.W. Sabotage." By 1920, MI4 had a "Foreign Influence Section." One of its functions was the "study of revolutionary movements."[5]

As much as Van Deman might ponder organizational charts for Military Intelligence, his real difficulty started at the top: however structured, the agency needed the security of an independent status within the army general staff. Until that was achieved, Military Intelligence could never be assured personnel, money, missions, or respect. Van Deman dreamed of heading a Military Intelligence Division and becoming a peer on the general staff. He resubmitted his request for organizational upgrading in January 1918, only to have it rejected by the chief of staff.[6] Some progress occurred the following month, when the Military Intelligence Section of the War College became the Military Intelligence Branch of the Executive Division of the general staff. This new designation did not mean that MI was a branch in the sense that one might hold a commission in the infantry, artillery, or signal corps. Van Deman had no ability to offer commissions, and one of his earliest problems was recruiting officers in the rapidly expanding army.

Regular army commissions were extremely difficult to obtain, and Van Deman never had more than half a dozen regular officers working for

5. Records reflecting the evolving structure of the Negative Branch during World War I are in Record Group 165, Military Intelligence Division, 10560–1–A and 10560–51/4, National Archives. The 1920 charts are in Richard D. Challener, ed., *United States Military Intelligence, 1919–1927*, 30 vols. (New York: Garland, 1978), vol. 13, opposite pp. 3721, 3725. A useful, if defensive, description of the missions of MI, along with other charts, is Marlborough Churchill, "The Military Intelligence Division, General Staff," *Journal of U.S. Artillery* 52 (April 1920): 293–315. A reprint of this article can be found in the Alexander B. Coxe, Sr., Papers, J. Y. Joyner Library, East Carolina University, Greenville, N.C.

6. Acting secretary, general staff, memorandum for chief, War College Division, January 4, 1918, in Record Group 165, MID, 10560–230/1, National Archives.

him. Commissions in the National Army or in the Officer Reserve Corps were far more available, but still Van Deman had to depend on borrowing slots from other branches.[7] He had no problem finding people who desired to work with him in the exciting world of rooting out spies, saboteurs, slackers, and Socialists, but he had to keep them on a voluntary basis, promising them commissions as they became available. In this fashion he secured the services of Nicholas Biddle to head the New York office of Military Intelligence. Biddle served for three months as a volunteer, only to learn that his application for a commission in the signal corps had been rejected. Van Deman had to ask Felix Frankfurter, a special assistant to the secretary of war, to intervene, after which Biddle got his commission. Another officer for whom Van Deman also secured a commission was the young cryptographic genius Herbert O. Yardley, who headed Van Deman's Codes and Ciphers Section and who, after the war, went on to create the famous Black Chamber in the State Department.[8]

At its greatest strength when the war ended, Military Intelligence carried only 427 commissioned officers on its official rolls. Most of these officers worked in the home office in Washington, D.C. The others, called special intelligence officers, were spread out in branches in key cities. The largest component was with Biddle in New York City, where he employed 25, along with more than 50 special agents with the rank of sergeant. Additional commissioned officers at department headquarters and at many subordinate units were not counted as belonging to Van Deman. Although the army now had far more agents than ever before, there were nowhere near enough to do the job of national surveillance that Van Deman demanded. Civilian help was essential, either on the payroll or as volunteers. As a result, the majority of the clerical personnel and secret agents in Van Deman's office and in his branches were civilians. Intelligence headquarters in Washington had nearly a thousand civilians employed on Armistice Day, and the New York branch had

7. Bidwell, *History of Military Intelligence*, p. 126. Marc B. Powe, in Weber, ed., *Final Memoranda*, p. xviii, suggests that Van Deman could grant commissions in the National Army, but he may have this ability confused with Van Deman's unfulfilled request for such authority.

8. Bidwell, *History of Military Intelligence*, p. 127, describes Frankfurter as Van Deman's "close personal friend." If such a relationship did exist, it could not possibly have survived the war. See also Weber, *Final Memoranda*, pp. xviii–xix; and U.S. Army, *The History of the Counter Intelligence Corps in the United States Army, 1917–1950 (with Limited Tabular Data to 1960)*, 30 vols. (Baltimore: U.S. Army Intelligence Center, 1959), 3:69. This work is available in Record Group 319, National Archives (hereafter cited as CIC History). For accounts of the practice of serving as a volunteer before receiving a commission, see Record Group 165, MID, 10560–589.

86, of whom 51 were investigators.[9] The army's intelligence mission was worldwide, and not all of these people were employed in spying on the American left, but roughly two-thirds of the total force assigned to Van Deman were in the Negative Branch, whose primary function was countering the threat from radicals. At its peak in the war, that branch had 202 officers, 60 investigators, 54 volunteers waiting for commissions, and 605 clerks. Moreover, the office directed the work of thousands of officers and enlisted men outside of Washington.[10]

There were two categories of intelligence officers in the field. The greater number were on the staffs of particular army units, from the large department headquarters down to the various camps and installations. The continental United States was divided into six departments, reflecting their geographical locations: the Eastern Department was headquartered in Boston; the Northeastern in Governor's Island in New York Harbor; the Southeastern in Charleston; the Central in Chicago; the Southern at Fort Sam Houston in Texas; and the Western at the Presidio in San Francisco. Each department was further divided into districts, the headquarters of which had an intelligence unit that controlled the posts and camps within its area. The staffs of each of the forty-two army divisions also had intelligence officers, as did all major posts and camps. In addition, intelligence officers were attached to the several postal censorship stations, to the headquarters of the fourteen Plant Protection Service districts, and at the embarkation sites in Hoboken, New Jersey, and Newport News, Virginia. The officer training corps at colleges and universities had intelligence officers as well.[11]

In addition to these field units, with their dual mission of responding both to local commanders and to the Washington office of Military Intelligence, Van Deman developed a second category directly controlled by him and unrelated to any other army command. These branch offices, led by special intelligence officers, were set up in major cities, beginning with New York in July 1917. Philadelphia followed in November, and by mid-1918 offices were in place in St. Louis, Seattle, Pittsburgh, and New Orleans. New York was the largest, accounting for about half the total branch office staff of 45 officers, 80 noncommissioned

9. CIC History, 3:58. In Record Group 165, MID, see E. F. McCarron, memorandum for Lieutenant Colonel McKenny, February 4, 1920, 10560 (no further designation) and "Organization and Functions of the Negative Branch, M.I.D.," August 24, 1921, 10560–489.

10. Typed document entitled "Military Intelligence Division," n.d., Record Group 165, MID, 10560–1–A Part II.

11. Ibid.; Bidwell, History of Military Intelligence, p. 129.

investigators, and 120 civilians. In addition to these sites, Washington dispatched officers to particularly troubled areas, where their temporary duty sometimes became virtually permanent. Despite the technicality of the chain of command that separated them, the intelligence officers of the department headquarters and the special officers of the branches had similar functions and identical reporting requirements.[12]

The quality of reporting from the smaller field units seems to have varied considerably, no doubt depending on the attitude of the local commander toward intelligence, on the competence of the junior officer he appointed, and on how many other tasks were assigned. Although Van Deman insisted that intelligence work required "special qualifications and men of the utmost integrity," the positions were subject to rapid turnover as officers were sent overseas to the war. At the departmental level and below, the commanding officers who made the staff appointments often regarded intelligence work as no more than a frill. Systematic training for intelligence officers did not begin until the end of the war, when regular in-service lectures were established and a course on intelligence was added at the General Staff College.[13] Many of these so-called intelligence officers did nothing beyond respond to official requests for information, and then their activities were limited to brief checks with the local police. Others energetically developed their own networks of undercover agents both on and off their posts.

In addition to his directly controlled branches and his more or less directly controlled field units, Van Deman created two other groups. The first was a truly covert agency whose existence Van Deman kept secret from all but his executive and financial officers. Living in and operating out of a private residence in southeast Washington, the unnamed element consisted mostly of men selected from the city's police force, commanded by a former New York police captain. This group wore civilian clothes and handled sensitive work for Van Deman in the nation's capital.[14] It seemed natural to recruit policemen, and on August

12. The list of branch offices is as it appears in Bidwell, *History of Military Intelligence,* p. 126. "Military Intelligence Division" adds St. Paul, but this branch never seems to have developed. Other lists are longer and regard the department intelligence offices at Chicago, San Francisco, and San Antonio as branches. That Van Deman himself did so (Weber, ed., *Final Memoranda,* p. 33) suggests that he had a high degree of control over these department officers and that they functioned as branches. See also CIC History, 3:59–60.

13. Van Deman to Major General Kuhn, April 24, 1918, Record Group 165, MID, 10560–27/1, National Archives. See also G. B. Perkins, memorandum for Colonel Masteller, June 29, 1918, 10560–160/2, ibid.

14. Weber, ed., *Final Memoranda,* p. 33.

13, 1917, the army spy chief used that concept in developing the Corps of Intelligence Police. At first designated only for overseas duty, where the idea seems to have originated from General Pershing's staff, the corps consisted of 50 former policemen with foreign language skills. In November 1917, Van Deman expanded its strength by 250, all assigned to investigative duty within the United States, mostly in Washington and New York. Eventually there were 750 in France and 550 at home. In New York, the corps' office at 240 Centre Street was separate from the Military Intelligence branch established in room 805 at 302 Broadway, but the corps' investigations were controlled by the branch chief. Called "inspectors," the intelligence police carried the military rank of sergeant and wore civilian clothes.[15]

The head of the New York branch, Nicholas Biddle, after getting his commission as a major and later colonel in the signal corps, served for the duration of the war as chief of the largest military intelligence group outside of Washington. A Harvard graduate, Biddle was a prominent banker in New York, had been the trustee of the William Astor estate, and, when Van Deman found him, was a special deputy police commissioner supervising the Bomb Squad, which had been organized in 1914.[16] Biddle's assistant and successor, Captain John B. Trevor, also a Harvard graduate, was an attorney and had been a trustee of the American Museum of Natural History since 1908. He and the branch's propaganda analyst, Archibald E. Stevenson, were members of the elite Union League Club in New York. Both carried their investigations of the American left well beyond World War I.[17]

15. Bidwell, *History of Military Intelligence*, pp. 127–28. For a sample of the letterhead of the New York corps' stationery, see MI Microfilm, reel 6, p. 138. Richard Polenberg, in *Fighting Faiths: The Abrams Case, the Supreme Court, and Free Speech* (New York: Viking, 1987), pp. 60–61, says that the Corps of Intelligence Police in New York was actually the Bomb Squad, which had been transferred en masse to MI.

16. Weber, ed., *Final Memoranda*, p. 44; Rhodri Jeffreys-Jones, *American Espionage: From Secret Service to CIA* (New York: Free Press, 1977), p. 111; CIC History, 3:69; Thomas J. Tunney, *Throttled! The Detection of the German and Anarchist Bomb Plotters as Told to Paul Merrick Hollister* (Boston: Small, Maynard,1919), p. 70; Polenberg, *Fighting Faiths*, p. 61; *Who Was Who*, 1:92. For evidence that Biddle cooperated with Van Deman while still a deputy police commissioner, see Biddle to Van Deman, July 27, 1917, MI Microfilm, reel 2, p. 861.

17. See *Who Was Who*, 3:862, for Trevor; 4:904, for Stevenson. Photographs of Biddle and Trevor are in Tunney, *Throttled*, opposite pp. 4, 268. This volume, written while the war was on, is romantic sensationalism about German agents and mad anarchist bombers. Still, with its concentration on thrilling cases before the United States entered the war, it is interesting. See also Tunney's testimony in U.S. Senate, Report and Hearings of the Subcommittee on the Judiciary of the United States Senate, 65th Cong., 1st sess., document no. 62, *Brewing and Liquor Interests and German and Bolshevik Propaganda*, 3 vols. (Washington, D.C.: U.S. Government Printing Office), 2:2669–90.

When Chief of Staff Hugh L. Scott retired in May 1918, Van Deman had high hopes that the new chief, Peyton C. March, would be sympathetic to the needs of Military Intelligence. He was, but not to Van Deman personally. When the authorization for the long-awaited Military Intelligence Division, headed by a brigadier general, came down in August, Van Deman had already been shipped off to France. Historian Joan M. Jensen has expressed the opinion that the Department of Justice's concern over the scope and methods of Van Deman's army agency must have forced Secretary of War Baker to remove him.[18] Attorney General Thomas W. Gregory certainly was concerned about the army's usurpation of his department's perogatives and would become more so near the end of the war, but he seems to have had a genuine admiration for Van Deman. As late as April 26, 1918, just before Van Deman was exiled from Washington, Gregory wrote Baker that "we are all especially impressed with Colonel Van Deman and his work."[19] Moreover, there is considerable evidence that Van Deman had an excellent relationship with Baker and his key assistants.

The official army version, that Van Deman's involvement in general staff politics and his constant finagling for the advancement of Military Intelligence cost him his job, seems to be correct.[20] In his letters, Van Deman, always referred to the chief of staff as his nemesis, and he confided the same feeling to Baker's private secretary, who had gone to France as an intelligence officer in March 1919. The young officer, Ralph Hayes, gave the secretary of war the following appraisal of Van Deman's situation: "He understands, of course, that the C. of S. is hostile to him, but does not know the reason, if there is a specific reason. As he looks upon it, he has pretty completely failed in the work at which he has spent twenty years or more. The evidence of it to him are his being supplanted as Chief early in the war, the failure to receive any advancement during the war, and his being sent off to Europe without any orders."[21] All that Hayes wrote was true. Van Deman had been sent to Europe with only vague orders to coordinate with the Allies on intelligence, and it was six months before he had anything to do. It was a disaster for Van Deman professionally; his name was pushed down some forty spaces on the promotion list, and he did not get his first star for nearly a decade. Despite appeals by Hayes and others for Baker's

18. Joan M. Jensen, *The Price of Vigilance* (Chicago: Rand McNally, 1968), p. 124.
19. Gregory to Baker, April 26, 1918, Papers of Newton D. Baker, microfilm reel 4, p. 338, Manuscript Division, Library of Congress.
20. CIC History, 1:31; Bidwell, *History of Military Intelligence*, pp. 116–17.
21. Hayes to Baker, March 4, 1919, Baker Papers, reel 7, p. 395.

intervention on Van Deman's behalf, the secretary stood fast on his principle of not interfering in internal army matters.[22]

Van Deman's successor was Lieutenant Colonel Marlborough Churchill, another Harvard graduate and an artillery officer. When Military Intelligence finally became a formal division of the general staff in August 1918, Churchill jumped to the temporary rank of brigadier general. He was surprised and perhaps a little embarrassed by his appointment. At one time he had been assigned to the staff of Colonel Dennis E. Nolan, Pershing's intelligence chief in France, but he had found no joy in that work and had soon requested a more active assignment. He regarded himself as an amateur in the field of intelligence and expressed tremendous admiration for Van Deman, whom he hoped would be allowed to return to the United States and "go on with the work here."[23] Less than a month after his promotion to brigadier general, Churchill wrote Van Deman, whom he called the "creator" of the Military Intelligence Division, "It is perfectly clear in my mind that I am sitting here, at the head of *your* service and that I am wearing if not your stars, at least the stars of M.I.D." He thought the "logical thing" was to bring Van Deman "back to take the helm again," but he noted that the chief of staff would not agree.[24]

As unhappy as he was, Van Deman had to accept his situation. He toured the front and compared notes with his counterparts in the Allied forces and was so bored that he began keeping a diary. Staying in touch with Churchill, he sent back suggestions on passport control, censorship, and training.[25] At the end of the war, Van Deman was asked to remain in Europe to handle security for the peace conference, an assignment for which he immediately set up a Negative Intelligence Department. Churchill was sincere in calling Van Deman the creator of

22. Documents reflecting other attempts to have Van Deman returned to his post in Washington are in the appendixes of Weber, ed., *Final Memoranda*.

23. Churchill to Nolan, June 4, 1918, reprinted, ibid., p. 157. For a sketch of Churchill's career, see G. J. A. O'Toole, *Encyclopedia of American Intelligence and Espionage* (New York: Facts on File, 1988), pp. 114–15; for Nolan, ibid., p. 329.

24. Churchill to Van Deman, September 16, 1918, Record Group 165, MID, 10560–235, National Archives. On the same day, Churchill wrote Alexander Coxe, former MID executive officer then on his way to France: "If you can do anything to have Van Deman come back and take hold here, do it. I mean every word I wrote in the letter to him" (Coxe Papers).

25. Several of Van Deman's letters from France are in Weber, ed., *Final Memoranda*, pp. 158–91; others can be found in Record Group 165, MID, 10560–490, National Archives. The diary became the basis of the biographical statements that are the heart of *Final Memoranda*. The manuscript version, with the title "Memoirs of Major General R. H. Van Deman," is in the U.S. Army Intelligence Center and School Library, Fort Huachuca, Arizona.

the Military Intelligence Division, reporting that his predecessor had "performed miracles in building up an intelligence service which is as good as anything which I saw in England or in France."[26] Despite his absence, the agency remained Van Deman's creation. The new division's mission statement provided for the collection of both positive and negative intelligence, as well as authorization to continue its censorship activities and cooperation with other intelligence agencies. If it had been Secretary Baker's idea to restrain Military Intelligence by removing Van Deman, he failed to follow through and monitor the conduct of Marlborough Churchill, who pursued American radicals as energetically as had his predecessor.

The Office of Naval Intelligence had been far superior to the army's intelligence effort before the war, but Van Deman's efforts soon reversed the situation. The chief of Naval Intelligence, Roger Welles, admitted the growth of Military Intelligence as early as July 1917, when Assistant Secretary of the Navy Franklin D. Roosevelt requested help for an acquaintance looking for a position as a translator. Welles had no opening and referred Roosevelt to the army, which he said had "a large appropriation for collecting and disseminating information and are just starting to work in earnest."[27] By September 1917, the navy's intelligence headquarters in Washington, D.C., had a staff of seventy, which directed an intelligence network that, like the army's, had both centrally controlled branch offices and more locally oriented intelligence officers. It had eight branches in major port cities involving altogether about five hundred people. The New York branch was the largest, located first at 15 Wall Street and later at 288 Fourth Street. In charge of this secret office was Lieutenant Commander Spencer D. Eddy, yet another Harvard alumnus and New York socialite.[28]

Local aides for information were attached to the headquarters of the

26. Quoted in Weber, ed., *Final Memoranda*, p. 157. Van Deman was not allowed back to Washington until the summer of 1919, and then only after Secretary Baker intervened personally on his behalf. At Van Deman's request, his comrade Alexander Coxe made a personal appeal to Baker, through Ralph Hayes. Afraid that once again he and Van Deman had gone out of general staff channels, Coxe kept careful records of the entire affair. See Van Deman's July 24, 1919, cable to Coxe, with Coxe's undated note on the bottom and reverse; see also Coxe's July 31, 1919, confidential memorandum for the record, both in Coxe Papers. Van Deman left France on August 14, 1919.

27. Welles to Roosevelt, July 6, 1917, in "ONI: Welles file," Assistant Secretary of Navy Papers, Franklin D. Roosevelt Library, Hyde Park, N.Y.

28. Record Group 38, Office of Naval Intelligence, "CAP" file, box 7, National Archives; Jeffrey M. Dorwart, *The Office of Naval Intelligence: The Birth of America's First Intelligence Agency, 1865–1918* (Annapolis: Naval Institute Press, 1979), p. 109. A photograph of Eddy is in Tunney, *Throttled*, opposite p. 248.

thirteen naval districts around the country. The Atlantic coast had aides in Boston, Newport, New York City, Philadelphia, Baltimore, Norfolk, Charleston, and Key West. An aide in New Orleans covered the entire Gulf Coast, and his counterpart in Chicago handled the Great Lakes, Mississippi River, and Midwest areas. On the Pacific Coast, aides were headquartered in San Francisco and the Puget Sound area. The aide for information at the Seventh Naval District headquarters in Key West, for example, had a large staff, including nineteen investigators. From there he maintained liaison with Military Intelligence, local police, customs, and the Department of Justice. He also ran a huge network of informants in 117 Florida cities and towns, with eighty confidential sources in Miami, thirty-seven in Tampa, and thirty-nine in Key West. [29]

Naval Intelligence inspected every ship entering the country, a task for which New York had four hundred men and New Orleans nearly as many. Although its agency was smaller than the army's, the navy intelligence mission had a somewhat tighter focus, centered around port security. If it did not always adhere strictly to that mission and went off on various tangents, the navy could limit its concern to the coasts and large ports. Within those areas it concentrated on suppliers of critical equipment and on the danger of labor disputes disrupting the docks. A recent analysis of Naval Intelligence found some problems of coordination between the Washington-controlled branches and the several aides for information. [30]

That study, after noting the navy's "traditional disdain" for army intelligence, concluded that Van Deman's intelligence effort in World War I outstripped the navy's in "size and efficiency." [31] Overall, the army and the navy cooperated, certainly at the highest levels, but it was inevitable that their agents in the field would sometimes trip over one another, resulting in complaints and countercharges. Faced with the army's growing supremacy in combating subversion, the navy demanded control over at least a piece of the action. In the summer of 1918, Churchill and the Department of Justice agreed that the navy could "have" the Marine Transport Workers, an IWW affiliate. Churchill ordered his "Department and Special Intelligence Officers, and Plant

29. Aid [sic] for Information, "Chart of Seventh Naval District, 1918," in "CAP" file, box 6.

30. Dorwart, *Naval Intelligence*, pp. 103–15. For a concise statement of the navy's concern about the IWW, see the Lusk Committee Papers, L0040, Box 1, folder 20, New York State Archives, Albany. For evidence that Naval Intelligence had informants placed in the highest levels of the IWW, see MI Microfilm, reel 6, p. 235. Naval documents use "aide" and "aid"; Dorwart prefers "aid" (p. 103).

31. Dowart, *Naval Intelligence*, p. 116.

Protection Agents" to cease their efforts to penetrate that union and to cooperate fully with the navy. The analysis of information from the navy's undercover operations was not finished until December 23, 1918, after the war was over. This was also the case for similar studies being conducted by the army. The lengthy report entitled "Investigation of the Marine Transport Workers and the Alleged Threatened Combination Between Them and the Bolsheviki and Sinn Feiners" summarized the harsh methods the navy had used against the IWW.[32]

Like Military Intelligence, the Office of Naval Intelligence was dominated by Ivy League graduates. Another Harvard man who took an interest in intelligence was Assistant Secretary of the Navy Franklin D. Roosevelt, and his dabbling in the spy business was a matter of some concern to the navy professionals. Once they accused Roosevelt's private secretary, Louis M. Howe, of trying to operate his own informant network. Despite his annoying "hands-on" approach, Roosevelt was close to old Harvard friends in intelligence. He made several contributions, most notably in setting up a Naval Reserve Force used for intelligence purposes. Although the amateurs recruited by Roosevelt and others could be given to excess in their patriotic zeal, it was these volunteers in both the navy's and the army's intelligence services who made up the heart of the domestic spy apparatus in World War I.[33]

Middle-class America poured its soul into the war effort on the home front. Flanders was far away, but spies, saboteurs, slackers, Socialists, pacifists, and neutrals were right around the corner. Professional Americans vied with each other in signing members into their superpatriotic societies and vigilance committees. H. C. Peterson and Gilbert C. Fite, in their classic *Opponents of War*, present a fascinating and flamboyant list of such organizations: "the American Defense Society, the National Security League, the American Protective League, the Home Defense League, the Liberty League, the Knights of Liberty, the American Rights League, the All-Allied Anti-German League, the Anti-Yellow Dog League, the American Anti-Anarchy Association, the Boy Spies of America, the Sedition Slammers, and the Terrible Threateners."[34] The first two of these were important, but the third was paramount.

---

32. The navy's report is in MI Microfilm, reel 8, pp. 212–67; "CAP" file, box 8; and in Record Group 60, Glasser Files, box 5, National Archives.

33. Dorwart, *Naval Intelligence*, p. 113. The Assistant Secretary of Navy Papers in the FDR Library show that Roosevelt received confidential navy reports on labor, socialism, and terrorism and that on occasion he gave investigative assignments to Naval Intelligence.

34. H.C. Peterson and Gilbert C. Fite, *Opponents of War, 1917–1918* (Seattle: University of Washington Press, 1957), p. 18.

The American Defense Society, formed in 1915 and led by Elon H. Hooker, named Theodore Roosevelt as its honorary president. Its office was located on One Madison Avenue, and its permanent aim was the "repression of the preaching of foreign ideals." The society opposed immigration and stood for "Americanization," a strong merchant marine, universal military training, and sound money. In the summer of 1917 the group created the American Vigilance Patrol, the purpose of which was to harass and "arrest" radical street speakers. In the fall it took out an advertisement seeking information on German spies. When Biddle in New York saw this solicitation, he wrote Van Deman: "We are to have another Secret Service," adding that "the power of these volunteer organizations to do harm is tremendous." He urged that steps be taken to "curb or control their activities."[35] As it turned out, Van Deman had trouble with such groups only when they were not under his authority.

The National Security League, headed by S. Stanwood Menken and later by Colonel Charles E. Lydecker, was also headquartered in New York. It had been founded in 1914 to urge preparedness for the day America entered the war. The group, along with the American Defense Society, caused George Creel, head of the government's Committee for Public Information, no end of trouble by charging that he was soft on Germans and pacifists. In Creel's opinion, the chauvinistic organization's patriotism was "a thing of screams, violence and extremes, and their savage intolerances had the burn of acid."[36]

Not included in Peterson and Fite's list was the older National Civic Federation, founded in 1901 by Ralph M. Easley and dedicated to suppressing socialism. Among its board members were William Howard Taft, Andrew Carnegie, and Samuel Gompers. The National Civic Federation used informants to spy on radicals, passing the information on to Military Intelligence.[37] Easley also founded the League for Na-

35. Quoted in Jensen, *Price of Vigilance*, p. 97; and William R. Corson, *The Armies of Ignorance: The Rise of the American Intelligence Empire* (New York: Dial Press, 1977), p. 58.

36. Quoted in Peterson and Fite, *Opponents of War*, p. 18. See also Walton E. Bean, "George Creel and His Critics: A Study of the Attacks on the Committee on Public Information" (Ph.D. dissertation, University of California at Berkeley, 1941); and Robert K. Murray, *Red Scare: A Study in National Hysteria, 1919–1920* (Minneapolis: University of Minnesota Press, 1955), pp. 85–88. Some organizational material on the National Security League is in the Assistant Secretary of Navy Papers, FDR Library. See also Robert D. Ward, "The Origin and Activities of the National Security League, 1914–1919," *Mississippi Valley Historical Review* 47 (June 1960): 51–65.

37. Easley to Churchill, October 31, 1918, MI Microfilm, reel 34, p. 201. See also Steve Golin, *The Fragile Bridge: Paterson Silk Strike, 1913* (Philadelphia: Temple University

tional Unity. Other efforts at suppression were supported by the several state councils of national defense, some of which engaged in outright vigilantism. Minnesota created the Minnesota Commission of Public Safety, a loyalty league that was an official agency enforcing the state's tough antisedition law. The Lone Star State had the Texas Loyalty Rangers, and Arizona its Citizens' Protective League and Workmen's Loyalty League.[38] That the fight against Germany included a struggle against domestic radicalism and that private organizations had to lead that fight was nowhere better expressed than by the New York State Association Opposed to Woman Suffrage. In November 1917 it voted itself out of existence in order to form a new group that would "conduct a militant campaign against socialism, against pacifism, and against all forms of pro-Germanism."[39]

The largest and most active of the patriotic organizations was the American Protective League (APL). The basic mission of this private group that acquired official status as an auxiliary of the Department of Justice was to provide manpower for investigations by the federal intelligence community. Professional concerns about employing amateurs such as Biddle's early complaint were overruled by a generally perceived need for public support and involvement. The Department of Justice, the navy, and the army each used volunteers provided with credentials, and each recognized the desirability of having them structured in a chain of command and reporting. Van Deman's intelligence officer in the Western Department had organized his supporters into a Volunteer Intelligence Corps a thousand strong. The Minute Men in and around Seattle had nearly three times that number. In short order, however, the energetic leaders of the APL came to dominate the private volunteer spy industry and to force other groups to merge with it. Both the army and

Press, 1988), pp. 77–78, 83; Bean, "George Creel," p. 210; and Murray, *Red Scare*, p. 85. The full story of the federation and its transition to covert operations against the radicals is in Marguerite Green, *The National Civic Federation and the American Labor Movement, 1900–1925* (Washington, D.C.: Catholic University of America Press, 1956); see esp. chap. 8.

38. The state councils of national defense and the efforts of some to curb vigilantism are covered in William J. Breen, *Uncle Sam at Home: Civilian Mobilization, Wartime Federalism, and the Council of National Defense* (Westport, Conn.: Greenwood Press, 1984). See also Peterson and Fite, *Opponents of War*, pp. 17–18; Jensen, *Price of Vigilance*, p. 63; and Joan M. Jensen, *Military Surveillance of Civilians in America* (Morristown, N.J.: General Learning Press, 1975), p. 13. On the Minnesota situation, see David Paul Nord, "Hothouse Socialism: Minneapolis, 1910–1925," in Donald T. Critchlow, ed., *Socialism in the Heartland: The Midwestern Experience, 1900–1925* (Notre Dame: University of Notre Dame Press, 1986), pp. 133–66.

39. *New York Times*, November 16, 1917.

the navy continued to recruit and certify private individuals as agents, but the APL ruled as the national volunteer spy agency.[40]

Created in Chicago in 1917, just before the United States declared war on Germany, the American Protective League formed a Secret Service Division and offered its services to the Department of Justice. By late June, Justice had formally recognized and endorsed the APL as a "volunteer citizen's organization," in Attorney General Thomas W. Gregory's words, "acting as an auxiliary to this Department and voluntarily working under its general direction."[41] At that time Justice's Bureau of Investigation had about three hundred agents, but the APL had a thousand. Within months it had a quarter of a million.[42]

In the inevitable territorial battles over who would become the national domestic spy agency, the Department of Justice might easily have used its vast resources in the APL to overshadow the work of Military Intelligence. That it did not was largely owing to the APL's natural affinity for the military. In fact, many APL agents received army commissions. For those who remained volunteers, working with the army no doubt gave them a sense of direct contact with the war. Furthermore, the army's attitude and methods were more in tune with those of the APL, some of whose members felt restricted by the legal process that limited Justice's ability to wage the domestic war. The official history of the league shows no defensiveness about its burglaries ("done a thousand times in every city of America") or its other illegal methods. Since the patriots were "after the guilty alone," the innocent could not disapprove of these means. There was "no time to mince matters or to pass fine phrases when the land was full of dangerous enemies in disguise."[43] The enthusiasm with which these patriots relished their relationship with Military Intelligence is obvious: "It was whispers that 'M.I.D.' heard— the whispers of perfidious men, communicating one with the other, plotting against the peace of America, the dignity of our Government,

40. On MI's Volunteer Intelligence Corps, see Jensen, *Price of Vigilance*, pp. 122–24. Late in the war, Churchill suggested that the Committee on Public Information's famous Four-Minute Men could be used even more effectively as propaganda agents and could report to MI "'bad spots' as far as loyalty," J. S. Buhler, memorandum for Major Brown, October 18, 1918, Record Group 165, 10560–172/1, National Archives. For sample volunteer agent reports to MI, see MI Microfilm, reel 4, p. 973, and reel 8, p. 642.

41. Gregory's letter of September 21, 1918, restating the government's relationship with the APL, is printed in full in the APL's magazine, *Spy Glass*, September 21, 1918, available in Record Group 65, Bureau of Investigation, APL, box 12, National Archives.

42. The definitive history of the APL is Jensen, *Price of Vigilance*. The official history, Emerson Hough, *The Web* (Chicago: Reilly and Lee, 1919), is well worth reading for its illumination of the hysteria of the times.

43. Hough, *The Web*, p. 163.

the sacredness of our flag, the safety of American lives and property."
Their appreciation for the dark world of negative intelligence was
equally subtle: "All the deeds that can come from base and sordid
motives, from low, degenerate and perverted minds, all the misguided
phenomena of human avarice and hate and eagerness to destroy and
kill—such were the pictures on the walls of 'M.I.D.'"[44]

In certain areas, especially the West, where patriots thought the
government was too lenient on the IWW, the league preferred to work
with Military Intelligence, sometimes against the Department of
Justice.[45] According to Churchill's testimony a year after the war ended,
the APL had been "placed at the disposal" of Military Intelligence. This
relationship was part of the national mission the APL had acquired by the
time it moved its headquarters from Chicago to Washington, D.C., in
November 1917. One of its three national directors, Charles Daniel
Frey, was commissioned a captain in the army and assigned to MI to
handle liaison. Within six months, this function had become a separate
section of the Negative Branch, and by the end of the war it had a staff of
nearly forty people.[46]

The principal task the APL performed for the army was to conduct
"character and loyalty investigations." Military Intelligence relied heavily on this effort, which if handled by the army would have severely
drained its manpower. All candidates for a military commission were
covered, as well as officers already in the military who were under
consideration for "some confidential or important service." The APL
routinely investigated workers in the Red Cross, Young Men's Christian
Association, Salvation Army, and other relief and service organizations
before the military gave them permission to travel overseas. Military
Intelligence required APL agents to interview a minimum of three
people before submitting a loyalty report. In addition to these tasks, the
APL also performed "special investigations of individuals directed by
Military Intelligence." These missions ranged from surveillance of particular people in areas where MI lacked sufficient manpower to the
covert penetration of leftist groups. The league realized that its civilian
membership gave it "unusual opportunities for the investigation of

44. Ibid., pp. 11–12.
45. Jensen, *Price of Vigilance*, pp. 226–30. Jensen cites another case, in Michigan, when
the APL and the Bureau of Investigation "subverted the authority of the United States
Attorney, the federal official to whom they should have been subordinate" (p. 33).
46. Hough, *The Web*, p. 45; Bidwell, *History of Military Intelligence*, pp. 189–90;
Jensen, *Price of Vigilance*, pp. 86–87; and typed lecture by Churchill, "The Military
Intelligence Division, War Department, General Staff," September 4, 1919, in Record
Group 165, MID, 10560–328/110, National Archives.

radical organizations of all kinds." As its original historian said, the APL had "a busy mind and a long arm."[47]

MI assigned a staggering number of cases to the APL. "It is not uncommon," APL headquarters noted just before the war ended, "to receive five hundred reports in a day for Military Intelligence alone."[48] Ultimately, the league claimed to have handled over 3 million cases for the army. Of those about half a million were special investigations involving "counter-espionage matters, German propaganda, deserters, slackers . . . made at the direct request of the heads of the different sections of the Military Intelligence Division at Washington." Twenty-five thousand cases involved undercover operations against radical organizations. The clear emphasis on work for the army was equally evident in tabulations from APL state units. The Philadelphia office reported conducting 50 cases for the navy, 4,250 for the Department of Justice, and 13,477 for Military Intelligence. These were not the APL's only clients; in the City of Brotherly Love it investigated more than 100 charges of hoarding, waste, and profiteering for the Food and Fuel administrations.[49]

Relations at the local level between MI agents and the APL appear to have been cordial, expressing a reciprocal arrangement that accomplished work for MI and gave the APL volunteers identity and a sense of contributing. In at least one instance when a Military Intelligence investigation threatened to conflict with an ongoing operation by the APL, the army backed off and gave the league its head. Certainly local intelligence officers felt entirely comfortable in giving specific case assignments directly to the neighborhood APL chief. APL agents were supplied with Bureau of Investigation and MI reporting forms, and thousands of both wound up in the army's files.[50]

Given the zeal with which league operatives undertook this enormous

47. Hough, *The Web*, pp. 12, 46. See the *Spy Glass* for October 19 and November 4, 1918, Record Group 65, Bureau of Investigation, APL, box 12 (National Archives): for a color-coded report format used by the APL's New York division in its work for MI: "yellow for commission cases, green for overseas civilian service and rose-colored for special investigations." The investigations of individuals for MI went into that agency's PF file series. For a good view of their contents, see Theodore Kornweibel, Jr., ed., *Federal Surveillance of Afro-Americans (1917–1925): The First World War, the Red Scare, and the Garvey Movement* (Frederick, Md.: University Publications of America, 1986), reel 23; here the cooperation between Van Deman and the APL is very clear.

48. *Spy Glass*, October 19, 1918, Record Group 65, Bureau of Investigation, APL, box 12, National Archives.

49. Hough, *The Web*, pp. 46, 211–12.

50. For samples of reports reflecting these various activities and relationships, see MI Microfilm, reel 4, pp. 453–54, reel 5, pp. 97–99, 121, reel 6, pp. 220, 226, reel 33, pp. 410–11.

investigative load, they were bound to make mistakes, and at times they were simply sloppy. Washington instructed army intelligence officers that when they needed help in cases "requiring professional skill" they were to go to the Bureau of Investigation instead of the APL.[51] The navy's aide for information in the Twelfth Naval District on the West Coast became extremely unhappy when the APL falsely accused an officer of drunken philandering and of harboring pro-German sentiments. The APL agents, the aide said, were "of scant moral worth" and were "activated by mean motives." He further concluded that the naval intelligence agents at the San Pedro Submarine Base, along with agents at the branch offices in Los Angeles and San Francisco, had been deluded by the APL and had participated in an investigation that was "not a credit to the service." Summarizing the situation for the director of Naval Intelligence just after the war ended, he suggested that reliance on the APL and other volunteers had been a mistake because "the voluntary 'Protective Leagues'" did "much more harm than good. Thousands of persons have been falsely reported upon and recorded as suspects by having their names placed in the files of these organizations." In an obvious criticism of Military Intelligence and the Department of Justice, he noted that "these errors have not been committed only by the voluntary organizations, but by many of the Federal Departments."[52]

Military Intelligence never ceased relying on the APL to conduct background investigations, but it did tighten control over the final decision of suitability in the case of commissioned officers. At the end of the war, however, the Negative Branch's chief concern with the APL was in improving the speed with which APL agents completed their reports.[53] Despite the unavoidable issues of the timeliness and quality of APL work, in many areas Military Intelligence virtually incorporated it into the army structure. For intelligence officers in places such as Chicago, the league had become indispensable. After the war, when the Department of Justice wished to terminate the phenomenon it had unleashed, the army was the APL's strongest supporter. The Negative Branch had learned the value of patriotic civilian informers and had created contacts with the ultraconservative community that would continue for two decades.

51. "Statement of Functions, Scope, Organization, and Procedures of M.I.4," n.d., Record Group 165, MID, 10560–589/1, National Archives.

52. Aide for information, Twelfth Naval District, to director of Naval Intelligence, December 17, 1918, "CAP" file, box 6.

53. *Spy Glass*, October 19, 1918, Record Group 65, Bureau of Investigation, APL, box 12, National Archives.

CHAPTER 3

The Early Intelligence Community

At the onset of World War I not a single federal agency
had any substantial investigative capability, and the
modern concept of an intelligence community did not
exist. The intelligence efforts of the Secret Service, the Bureau of
Investigation, the army, and the navy were small and uncoordinated.
Not only did these agencies mushroom during the war, but new federal
bureaus appeared, many with intelligence departments. Interagency
rivalry became particularly bitter, first between the Department of
Justice and the Secret Service of the Treasury Department, and later
between Justice and Military Intelligence. Before examining the army's
place in the emerging federal intelligence community, however, the
question of its relationship with private detective agencies and the local
police requires examination.

In the generation before the war, most investigative work had been
handled by the private sector, and the domestic spy industry was very
large because of the high demand for information on labor activists.
Some companies preferred to develop their own intelligence forces, as
the textile industry in New Jersey and Massachusetts had done by 1914
with its "confidential corps" in the plants watching for "anything that
might be of a seditious nature." Most other firms relied on established
detective agencies for guards and to penetrate labor organizations.[1]

By 1917 there were nearly three hundred detective agencies across the
country investigating labor activity. Chicago had fifty-eight agencies,
and New York had nearly three times that number.[2] Only a few offered

1. For information on private labor espionage, see Sidney Howard, *The Labor Spy* (New
York: Republic Printing Co., 1924). For specific industries, see David J. Goldberg, *A Tale
of Three Cities: Labor Organization and Protest in Paterson, Passaic, and Lawrence,
1916–1921* (New Brunswick: Rutgers University Press, 1989), p. 12, and Steve Golin, *The
Fragile Bridge: Paterson Silk Strike, 1913* (Philadelphia: Temple University Press, 1988),
pp. 79, 92.
2. On private detectives, see Frank Morn, *"The Eye That Never Sleeps": A History of
the Pinkerton National Detective Agency* (Bloomington: Indiana University Press, 1982),
pp. 169, 174–78; and Rhodri Jeffreys-Jones, *American Espionage: From Secret Service to
CIA* (New York: Free Press, 1977), pp. 20–21.

national coverage. The Pinkertons were the nation's biggest and best known, and the founder's sons had created the Pinkerton National Detective Agency, with Robert A. Pinkerton heading the effort out of New York and William A. in charge in Chicago. By the turn of the century, however, the Pinkertons were tainted by their violent antilabor record and by rumors after 1898 that they had taken assignments for the Spanish. A serious challenge to the traditional supremacy of the Pinkertons had developed from the Burns Detective Agency, founded in 1910 by former Secret Service agent William J. Burns. He became so famous that in the early 1920s he headed the Department of Justice's Bureau of Investigation before J. Edgar Hoover took control. By 1915 Burns had twenty offices in the United States and one in London. The Thiel Detective Service Company, founded in 1873, was also capable of providing a national service. Thiel was very active in labor disputes and conducted a successful long-term undercover operation in the oil fields of Oklahoma, where two agents had achieved senior positions in the IWW. One of them was in charge of the monies in the IWW's legal defense fund.[3]

The Pinkertons' unsavory record in industrial disputes led Congress in 1893 to outlaw the hiring of private detectives by any federal department. In World War I, however, the demand for professional operatives was so great and the private agencies so available that Military Intelligence deliberately violated the law. The clearest case of such a use involved the Northern Information Bureau, founded in 1903 by L. W. Boyce in Minneapolis, which was employed chiefly by the large grain and lumber companies. By 1916 Boyce had concluded that the IWW was "a serious menace to the growth and prosperity of the business of Minneapolis" and that it was "unpatriotic, and anti-American, pro-German and everything that was bad."[4] Boyce initially funded the investigation himself, placing two agents in the inner circles of the Minneapolis IWW. Soon the Pillsbury Flour Mills Company and other large firms began to underwrite the effort, paying up to $50 per month for Boyce's reports.

3. Mid-Continent Oil & Gas Association to Van Deman, March 21, 1918, in Randolph Boehm, ed., *U.S. Military Intelligence Reports: Surveillance of Radicals in the United States, 1917–1941* (Frederick, Md.: University Publications of America, 1984), reel 6, pp. 244–45 (hereafter cited as MI Microfilm). For the three largest firms, Pinkerton, Burns, and Thiel, taken together, Howard, in *Labor Spy*, p. 17, gives the unbelievable figures of 135,000 operatives, over a hundred offices, "10,000 local branches," and a "combined annual income of $65,000,000."

4. See two letters, L. W. Boyce to Fitzhugh Burns, both dated September 27, 1918, in MI Microfilm, reel 12, pp. 955–61.

By 1918 Boyce's bureau had six agents, one of whom was a woman, supplying daily reports from within the IWW. Claiming that his operatives' salary of five dollars and more a day was above scale, he offered the army a deal at four dollars. Boyce also told the army that he had attempted to work with the Department of Justice and the American Protective League, "but that relationship has not been entirely satisfactory." He promised that he could provide good information "regarding the I.W.W. Organization, the radical Socialist element, the Mooney Defense League, and we also have an operator who is a member of the Non-partisan League." The local army intelligence representative wanted very much to use Boyce's agents. He suggested that they be enrolled in the Corps of Intelligence Police or be given credentials for their protection should they be arrested in a police or Bureau of Investigation raid on the IWW group they had joined. He noted that it was imperative that a plant hold a workingman's job because "any man who is foot loose and has money in his pocket would be immediately suspected of being a spy for the employers or for the Department of Justice."[5]

Marlborough Churchill hesitated to make such a deal with a private investigative company. When he checked with the Bureau of Investigation, he was assured that "the employment of detective agencies by the Government is prohibited by statute." His senior officers also thought the plan a bad idea, and Biddle in New York concurred with Edmund Leigh, head of the Plant Protection Service, on the dangers of private detectives who had a vested interest in causing trouble. After a month's consideration, and despite the advice of his people, Churchill decided to approve the arrangement. On October 29, 1918, he authorized his intelligence officer in St. Paul to hire "John Fisher, operative for Northern Information Bureau, St. Paul, Minn., at the rate of $4.50 per day. This to be drawn upon the lump credit now at your disposal for this purpose."[6]

Another source obvious to any federal agent searching for leads was the local police. By 1917, fear of the IWW dynamiters had led most major cities to create details similar to New York's Bomb Squad. The former chief of that unit, the famous Thomas J. Tunney, was very helpful in establishing MI's relationships with police departments. He was assigned to travel around the country to policemen's conventions and

5. Burns to director of MI, October 19, 1918, ibid., reel 12, pp. 946–47.
6. Director of MI to intelligence officer, St. Paul, October 29, 1918, ibid., reel 12, p. 940. The harsh criticism of private firms by Churchill's staff is in a folder marked "Detective Agencies, Private," General Correspondence, Plant Protection Section, Record Group 165, entry 104, National Archives, Suitland.

create avenues of coordination. In New York, MI and the Bomb Squad, which changed its name to Bomb and Neutrality Squad and then to Neutrality Squad, had a very close relationship, especially when Tunney went back to the police force and resumed command of the Neutrality Squad in early 1918. By that time, he was less concerned about Germans than about the IWW and "radical groups of Russians in New York City." In Chicago, relations with the army were so good that police officers sometimes made their reports on radicals using the department intelligence officer's reporting forms.[7]

Local coordination, whether with the APL, the police, or private detectives, was only part of the story. World War I brought a surprisingly large number of federal agencies into the arena of domestic intelligence where none had been before. Military Intelligence had to have a relationship good or bad, with each of these. A June 12, 1918, army memorandum listed the following national and international agencies as sources for the Negative Branch:

> M.I.4 receives all reports from military attachés throughout the world, relating to counter-espionage; all reports, Bureau of Investigation, Department of Justice; postal censorship comments from postal censor stations throughout the United States; all information received by War Trades Intelligence; all applications for passports and visas; information gathered by Naval Intelligence; information relating to counter-espionage within the United States, collected by the State Department and persons in the consular service throughout the world; a mass of information from British Intelligence and British censorship; the French Second Bureau of the General Staff; occasional information from the Italian Intelligence and other intelligence services of the Allies; reports of the Plant Protection Section; . . . newspapers throughout the United States; and from a large number of other sources of a confidential nature.[8]

If anything, this claim was understated. The army's intelligence units throughout Europe enabled it to coordinate with foreign governments in following American radicals abroad and to mount operations against them. The best relations were with the British, no doubt because of the remarkably free hand they were allowed in pursuing their enemies in the United States. Domestically, MI4 coordinated with some agencies not on the list. The Intelligence Service of the U.S. Food Administration, for example, reported to Van Deman on its efforts to suppress

7. Tunney to Fuller Potter, January 5, 1918, MI Microfilm, reel 33, p. 396; and Tunney to Corps of Intelligence Police, April 8, 1918, reel 8, p. 650.

8. "The Military Intelligence Branch, Executive Division, General Staff," June 12, 1918, Record Group 165, MID, 10560–49, National Archives.

violations of food regulations and told of rumors of "German money for the purpose of fomenting what might be termed a revolution." The Secret Service and Police Section of the U.S. Railroad Administration forwarded information on suspicious shipments. Should any further data be required to suggest that the United States loved the world of secrets and spies, there was the Intelligence Department of the Young Men's Christian Association.[9]

The War Trade Board investigated businesses thought to be German-controlled or dealing with the Germans so its work was of great interest to MI. The Bureau of War Trade Intelligence had a number of special agents, headed by Paul Fuller, Jr., who had organized an intelligence branch in the Department of Commerce shortly before the United States entered the war. The status of that organization was recognized by the larger investigative agencies, which gave it a place on the postal censorship committee and its subgroups around the country. The relationship clearly was not always pleasant because in 1918 army agents were so concerned about the politics of the war trade representative on the postal review panel in Nogales that they had him removed.[10]

One omission on the Negative Branch's list of cooperating agencies is particularly interesting. The Secret Service of the Department of the Treasury was the nation's oldest investigative agency, and its sleuthing was so legendary that the public referred to all federal investigators as secret service agents. The emergency of the war precipitated a huge fight in the federal bureaucracy over which agency would acquire the lucrative mission of spying on the civilian population. The primary combatants were William G. McAdoo, secretary of the treasury, and Attorney General Thomas W. Gregory. By the second half of 1917, it was obvious to any concerned observer that the counterintelligence and counterrevolutionary effort in the United States would be better served by a central intelligence agency. Many thought it should be headed by a

9. On the Food Administration, see James Miles to Van Deman, March 14, 1918, MI Microfilm, reel 8, pp. 693–95; and Joan M. Jensen, *The Price of Vigilance* (Chicago: Rand McNally, 1968), pp. 91–92. MI carried on a considerable correspondence with the YMCA, which had operatives on army posts and with troops abroad; see MI Microfilm, reel 2, pp. 224–31; reel 3, pp. 138, 416. For an overview of the world of domestic intelligence, see Richard Polenberg, *Fighting Faiths: The Abrams Case, the Supreme Court, and Free Speech* (New York: Viking, 1987), pp. 154–96.

10. U.S. Senate, Report and Hearings of the Subcommittee on the Judiciary, 65th Cong., 1st sess., document no. 62, *Brewing and Liquor Interests and German and Bolshevik Propaganda*, 3 vols. (Washington, D.C.: U.S. Government Printing Office, 1919), 2:2807; Bruce W. Bidwell, *History of the Military Intelligence Division, Department of the Army General Staff, 1775–1941* (Frederick, Md.: University Publications of America, 1986), p. 194; and James R. Mock, *Censorship, 1917* (Princeton: Princeton University Press, 1941), pp. 58–59.

chief who reported to the president and directed the efforts of all other investigative units. Treasury's Secret Service supported that concept, as did the press, the Pinkerton agency, and the National Security League. That idea, however, was too simple to appease the other agencies that did not wish to see their roles diminished. The agreement concluded by early 1918 gave Treasury no role in counterintelligence, while the Departments of Justice, State, Army, and Navy shared the mission.

The bad blood between the Bureau of Investigation and the Secret Service afforded Ralph Van Deman an opportunity to observe that since Military Intelligence was already receiving and filing reports from the other agencies, it might be wise to designate the army as the official clearinghouse for domestic intelligence. Against the wishes of the Secret Service, the heads of the several spy groups approved that plan. Senator George E. Chamberlain of Oregon asked Van Deman on April 19, 1918, the obvious question about the compromise: "Is it not a duplication of work to have so many intelligence departments in the different branches of the Government?" Van Deman responded:

> It possibly is, Mr. Chairman. If we had started out with one secret service organization and that organization had been in existence for years and was working smoothly, we probably would be able to handle investigations in this country better than now, but to try to form such an organization now would mean slowing up the whole work for months, or perhaps a year, before you could get into operation. By close cooperation—the use of the telephone and telegraph, etc.—I think we are able to handle the work with very little duplication. You would have duplication even with a single organization. I feel that we are getting along now with practically no useless duplication.[11]

Although the Secret Service opposed the clearinghouse concept as an unacceptable alternative to its proposal that there be a master agency, it also appears that because of its animosity toward the Department of Justice, the Treasury supported the expansion of Military Intelligence as a counter to the power of the Bureau of Investigation. Finally, though it is clear that the military benefited from the Justice-Treasury imbroglio, some credit must be given to Van Deman for his ability and forcefulness in carving out and maintaining a major role for the army.[12]

11. U.S. Senate, Committee on Military Affairs, 65th Cong., 2d sess., *Hearings, Extending Jurisdiction of Military Tribunals* (Washington, D.C.: U.S. Government Printing Office, 1918), pp. 38–39 (hereafter cited as Military Tribunal Hearings).

12. The best study of the struggle between Justice and Treasury, not a small part of which was the latter's anger over the APL's persistent habit of carrying badges identifying its members as Secret Service men, is Jensen's *Price of Vigilance*. The conflict is a prominent subtheme throughout, but for the role of the army, see pp. 55, 101–4. See also William R. Corson, *The Armies of Ignorance: The Rise of the American Intelligence Empire* (New York: Dial Press, 1977), pp. 58–59; and Ralph E. Weber, ed., *The Final Memo-*

In the nineteenth century the Department of Justice had used a variety of agents, including private detectives and men on loan from the Secret Service. The prohibition on employing Pinkertons was followed in 1908 by a law forbidding the department to use the Secret Service. The next year Justice created the Bureau of Investigation to supplement the work of U.S. marshals and attorneys. Congress funded the bureau in 1910 to investigate violations of the Mann Act, which had been designed to suppress the "white slave traffic" of prostitution. Once the war began in 1914, the bureau grew steadily in order to enforce the neutrality laws, to reach three hundred agents by mid-1917; its wartime strength peaked at about fifteen hundred.[13]

Van Deman had met with Department of Justice officials as soon as he got command of MI in May. By early July 1917 he moved to establish close ties with A. Bruce Bielaski, chief of the Bureau of Investigation, sending him a flood of requests for information. One of his earliest queries regarded Victor L. Berger, Socialist congressman from Milwaukee, and Albert M. Todd, head of the Public Ownership League of America in Kalamazoo. "I know you have something on Berger," Van Deman told Bielaski, "but you may not have Mr. Todd. If not, will you have him looked up for me?"[14] Van Deman appears to have taken his clearinghouse function seriously, making sure that State, Navy, and Justice all received copies of reports sent to him. The bureau was always his largest supplier of information, and the MI files contain volumes of carbons of the bureau's Form One.[15]

randa: Major General Ralph H. Van Deman, USA Ret., 1865–1952, Father of U.S. Military Intelligence (Wilmington, Del.: Scholarly Resources, 1988), p. 27.

13. Jensen, *Price of Vigilance*, p. 155.

14. Van Deman to Bielaski, July 6, 1917, MI Microfilm, reel 3, p. 240. Before becoming president of the Public Ownership League of America from 1916 to 1922, as well as a member of the American Civil Liberties Union and the League for Industrial Democracy, Todd had been the Prohibition party's nominee for governor of Michigan in 1894 and a member of the United States House of Representatives from 1897 to 1899. See his profile in *Who Was Who in America*, 1:1243.

15. On Van Deman's early coordination with the Department of Justice and other agencies, see Military Tribunal Hearings, p. 38. Bureau of Investigation reports appear throughout the MI Microfilm, but reels 16–18 consist entirely of bureau bulletins for 1920–21. For an example of Van Deman's routing service, see his February 15, 1918, memorandum to Bielaski, forwarding an Elizabeth Gurley Flynn letter confiscated by the postal censorship authorities (reel 1, p. 438). After leaving the Bureau of Investigation in early 1919, Bielaski became a corporate attorney. In 1922, he was kidnapped by Mexican bandits and effected his own escape. Later, as a federal prohibition agent, he created controversy when he used government funds to operate a speakeasy as a sting operation. He left government service in 1927 and died in 1964 (*New York Times*, February 20, 1964; Robert Rice, "Annals of Crime," *New Yorker* 26 [September 23, 1950]: 84–109). Beyond the standard coordination, Bielaski had a special tie to Military Intelligence. His sister, the

Churchill always credited Van Deman with maintaining "harmony at the top." He reported in September 1918 that "due to the excellent foundation laid by Van Deman, the spirit of cooperation between MID and DJ, ONI and the State Department remains excellent."[16] The vehicle for liaison was a weekly meeting, every Wednesday afternoon, in the office of John Lord O'Brian, special assistant to the attorney general and head of Justice's War Emergency Division. There the chiefs of the Bureau of Investigation, Military Intelligence, Naval Intelligence, and the State Department's secret service discussed their cases and conflicts. Despite Churchill's claim about harmony, clashes were inevitable.

Justice was naturally jealous of its domestic mission and clearly had the legal high ground when it observed, as it did occasionally, that the army had no authority to raid the homes and offices of civilians or to arrest civilians, no matter how radical. In February 1918, Van Deman and Bielaski argued over MI's relationship with the Slovenian Republican Alliance and other Slavic groups in the United States. Anxious to show their Americanism and avoid harassment, the Slavs had requested Military Intelligence identification cards. Justice resented this encroachment on its presumed monopoly in the civilian arena. Two months later tensions were doubly strained when Van Deman, with the support of a handful of alarmed congressmen, threatened to steal the entire show from the Department of Justice by having enemy aliens and seditious Americans tried in military tribunals instead of civilian courts.

The Senate Committee on Military Affairs heard testimony on a bill that would have subjected to court-martial those who spread "false statements and propaganda" or in any way hindered the war effort. Wheeler P. Bloodgood, a Milwaukee lawyer and member of the ex-

fiesty Alice K. Bielaski, supervised the civilian clerical staff of the Negative Branch. See her memorandum for Wrisley Brown, November 10, 1919, in Alexander B. Coxe, Sr., Papers, J. Y. Joyner Library, East Carolina University, Greenville, N.C. Another sister, Ruth Bielaski Shipley, became the director of the State Department's passport office and kept many radicals from traveling abroad. See Herbert Mitgang, *Dangerous Dossiers: Exposing the Secret War against America's Greatest Authors* (New York: Donald I. Fine, 1988), pp. 116–18. A brother, Frank B. Bielaski, was director of investigations for the Office of Strategic Services in 1945 when he raided the office of the magazine *Amerasia*, a case made famous by Wisconsin Senator Joseph McCarthy in 1950 (*New York Times*, April 6, 1961). For all the Bielaski siblings, see the article on their father, Alexander Bielaski, in *Minutes of the Baltimore Annual Conference, Methodist Episcopal Church*, 1927, pp. 397–99, available at the Commission on Archives and History, United Methodist Church, Baltimore Conference, Baltimore.

16. Memorandum "K," attached to Churchill to Van Deman, September 16, 1918, in Record Group 165, MID, 10560–235/1, National Archives; Churchill lecture, "The Military Intelligence Division," September 4, 1919, 10560–328/110, ibid.

ecutive committee of the Wisconsin Loyalty League (100,000 members in 350 chapters), and very sensitive about the reelection of the Socialist Berger, opened the hearings with testimony on April 17. Bloodgood had visited army camps from Texas to Oregon and was astounded at the level of Socialist propaganda charging Wall Street with responsibility for the war. His efforts to have the Justice Department crack down on such sedition had proved fruitless, despite the private support of Assistant Attorney General Charles Warren.

After a day's recess, Military Intelligence followed Bloodgood with even more sensational testimony. Leading off was Nicholas Biddle's private secretary, Norman H. White, who also expressed his concern about the inability of the Department of Justice to address "every conceivable kind of propaganda instituted, not only by Germans, but by . . . the Swiss, the people from Holland, people from South America and every conceivable country on the earth, including Norway and Sweden."[17] The 20,000 aliens from enemy countries he estimated to live in New York became "20,000 Spies" in the *New York Times* headline.[18] To fight this threat, the military had to have the power to arrest, as White knew from personal experience: "I have taken a man in the middle of the night with three bombs in his room. I have no power to arrest him. I have no power to search him." In such cases, Military Intelligence had to wait for the civilian authorities to open their offices before the captive could be handed over to a lengthy bureaucratic process that usually resulted in the saboteur's release on bail. Decisive action and the right for military agents to protect themselves demanded that they be given police powers. "The Department of Justice has got all it can handle," White said, "with prosecutions under the smuggling act, the Mann Act, and a thousand other things." He asked, "Why should the military arm be subservient to another arm of the service which is already overloaded with work?"[19]

Van Deman's statement was considerably less sensational than his subordinate's but directly on the point: "We have got to have summary justice in order to meet the kind of thing we are up against in this country. . . . The ordinary courts . . . are tied up with form and red tape

---

17. Military Tribunal Hearings, p. 32. A photograph of White is in Thomas J. Tunney, *Throttled! The Detection of the German and Anarchist Bomb Plotters as Told to Paul Merrick Hollister* (Boston: Small, Maynard, 1919), opposite p. 180.

18. *New York Times*, April 20, 1918. The public's confusion over the multitude of intelligence agencies is demonstrated in this article. White identified himself in the hearings as "engaged in secret-service work for the Government in the Military Intelligence Section," so the *Times* dubbed him "a Secret Service man."

19. Military Tribunal Hearings, pp. 32–36.

and law which they can not get around." Civil courts, he added, required more evidence than would a military tribunal. "It is most difficult," he complained, "to get the evidence." Besides, in England and France the military already had such jurisdiction. As long as the courts allowed due process for critics of the war, Van Deman suggested, the already high level of vigilantism among an outraged public would continue: "The destruction of property and the killing of innocent people and the citizens of the country . . . is getting worse rather than better."[20]

Captain Edward McCauley, the assistant director of Naval Intelligence, who handled domestic operations, also testified on the proposal to have spies and subversives tried by court-martial. He reinforced Van Deman's point about evidence: "Naval and military men are apt to consider things as legal evidence, even with the advice of lawyers, that perhaps civilians would not consider sufficient to condemn a man in court." When asked what particular propaganda concerned the navy, he named newspapers, pamphlets, and fliers that were "opposed to the administration, against the country, and pacifists' propaganda."[21]

John F. McGee, a judge and an important member of the Minnesota Commission of Public Safety, happened to be in Washington on other business and came forward to advise the Senate committee. He testified that his commission's "secret service" had uncovered a good deal of information on Socialists, pacifists, the IWW, and "the treasonable Nonpartisan League."[22] Even though "scores of cases" were referred to the Department of Justice for action, the results had been disappointing; "a ghastly failure," he called it, "from the beginning." The Bureau of Investigation, he said, had no more than four agents covering Minnesota and the Dakotas, with not a single representative in all of the Mesabi Range, which produced more than 75 percent of the nation's iron ore. Local officials were also weak, McGee complained. In his part of the country, the children of German immigrants still spoke the language of the old country in parochial schools. In sedition cases, many state and local prosecutors found it impossible "to draw a jury of which a large part of the membership was not equally guilty with the defendant." District attorneys, he said, "faint when they have to go up against a real fight. They have no stomach for it. They do not want to antagonize the disloyal elements."[23]

20. Ibid., pp. 40–45.
21. Ibid., p. 46.
22. The Farmers National Nonpartisan League, strongest in North Dakota, did not take this and other slanderous statements by McGee quietly; after consideration of the military tribunal bill was dropped, the committee stayed in session to hear the radical agrarians' defense. Military Intelligence, however, shared McGee's view of the league.
23. Military Tribunal Hearings, pp. 49–56.

McGee, too, feared that without summary justice administered by the military "we are going to have the Klu-Klux [sic] Klan multiplied a thousand times in the country, and lynching parties without number unless the law is enforced." Becoming even more heated, he insisted that "our modern civilization is on the verge of destruction." In his opinion, at the onset of the war "firing squads ought to have been organized everywhere . . . working full time." Since they had not been, they should be created immediately and "work overtime in order to make up for lost time." [24]

Despite White's assertion that "we are practically a military Nation," bringing civilians up for summary judgment before the army smacked too much of Prussianism, a favorite word of the time to describe what Americans were fighting. Moreover, the complaint of an overloaded Justice Department was never supported by any additional evidence, and an announcement from President Wilson that he opposed the measure was all it took to end these proceedings. In the heat of this brief but bitter contest, Charles Warren resigned, amid speculation that he had been fired, to embark on a brilliant career as a legal scholar and Pulitzer Prize-winning historian. For his part, Attorney General Gregory issued a stinging repudiation of Warren's involvement with the military tribunal proposal. [25]

Gregory also lashed out at White of Military Intelligence. No doubt spurred by the performance before Congress, the New York APL, on April 23, sent Gregory a report on White, claiming that he had "launched into a scathing denunciation of the men in the Department of Justice and of their methods in too leniently dealing with German suspects." Even worse, as White "paced up and down the room like a tiger," he "severely criticized Attorney General Gregory, saying that the latter did not want to have these cases pushed. He also said that Mr. Gregory's wife was a German." Gregory protested directly to Secretary of War Baker, calling White's comment about his wife "infamous," and adding: "So many complaints have come to me as to this man's intemperate and false statements and insinuations that I feel it to be my duty to call your attention to it so that you may determine whether or not he shall continue as a member of your Intelligence Division." [26]

24. Ibid., pp. 56–57.

25. Jensen, *Price of Vigilance*, pp. 12–22, 106–9. President Wilson's letter to Senator Chamberlain, in which he called the military tribunal bill unconstitutional and "altogether inconsistent with the spirit and practice of America," is reprinted in the *New York Times*, April 23, 1918. A letter from Gregory repudiating Warren is in the same story.

26. The APL report on White is W. T. Carothers to Charles DeWoody, April 23, 1918,

Despite the argument over civilian versus military control, army intelligence continued to investigate and interrogate suspects, turning them over to federal or local authorities at their leisure. The attorney general's office was genuinely concerned, as a June 19, 1918, internal memorandum said, that "the Office of Military Intelligence has definitely decided to supplant the investigation services of the Department of Justice throughout the country."[27] It is small wonder that Churchill, who had joined the agency in early June 1918, appreciated the harmony that Van Deman had developed between the agencies. Until the end of the war, only six months away, the new director of Military Intelligence was in fairly constant difficulty with the attorney general. The particular hot spot was the mining town of Butte, Montana, and the issues were the alleged leniency of the Department of Justice and the army's illegal use of the arrest power. Van Deman had begun to get reports of a difficult situation in Butte early in 1918, and the awful troubles in that violence-ridden city are described elsewhere. Those disorders had an important influence at the national level. Shortly after taking over Military Intelligence, Churchill received a disturbing telegram from his agent in Butte that the U.S. attorney, Burton K. Wheeler, "by reason of his personal political affiliations with I.W.W., socialists, shin fenners and non-partisan league . . . is not handling espionage, seditious and disaffecting matters." Federal judge George M. Bourquin was guilty of lack of enthusiasm, the wire said, and was "not in tune with time, holds himself judicial recluse in attitude of not permitting war hysteria influence to enter judicial chamber and in few cases before leans too far on side of mercy."[28]

The judge had been the subject of MI reports for months after he announced his intention to give draft evaders only a day in jail.[29] The printers of seditious literature calling for strikes were placed under a

attached to Gregory to Baker, April 26, 1918, in Papers of Newton D. Baker, microfilm reel 4, pp. 338–39, Manuscript Division, Library of Congress. Baker's answer has not been found, but White's voluntary connection with MI seems to have been severed. Since Van Deman was relieved of his command of MI and left for Europe on June 1, the question of whether Gregory's April 26 complaint to Baker was the cause of the intelligence chief's removal is a natural one. Gregory's letter, however, contained only praise for Van Deman, and no evidence, beyond this chronological proximity, has been found to link Van Deman's exit to either the military tribunals gambit or the White episode.

27. Quoted in Jensen, *Price of Vigilance*, p. 124.

28. Telegram, Knabenshue, San Francisco, to Milstaff, Washington, June 4, 1918, MI Microfilm, reel 2, pp. 390–92.

29. Gund, untitled memorandum, February 9, 1918, ibid., reel 2, pp. 329–30; department intelligence officer, San Francisco, to director of MI, October 4, 1918, ibid., pp. 362–63.

bond of $10,000 by most judges, but in Butte they got off for $500. When Bourquin, in dismissing the case against an IWW slacker, harangued the sheriff for making the arrest at the request of the local Bureau of Investigation agent, the sheriff asserted that he would no longer round up idle men. MI reported to Churchill that in Butte among patriotic Americans "a very high feeling is spreading," and there was talk of "a coat of tar and feathers" for the judge.[30]

Churchill wanted both Wheeler and Bourquin out, and he took the extraordinary step of forwarding his intelligence officer's unedited complaints about them to the Justice Department, recommending that they be removed or transferred. Justice's O'Brian responded that the problem, to the extent there was one, seemed to rest only with the judge, who could not be removed. Churchill then directed the intelligence officer of the Western Department to send more agents to the area because "people around Butte appear to be suspicious of the local Department of Justice officials." He reasoned that part of Justice's problem was involvement in Butte politics, and since his men were not connected locally, citizens "would have more confidence in a representative of the Military Intelligence."[31]

This encouragement from Washington and an increasingly tense situation with the miners inspired the intelligence officer in Spokane to direct his subordinate in Butte to begin arresting those calling for a strike. In issuing the order, the Spokane office invoked the authority of the Department of Justice, but it is unclear what coordination, if any, took place between MI and Justice. Certainly none occurred in Washington. MI raided the IWW in the Butte area, seized its records, and took scores of people into custody. When Bureau of Investigation agents reported to Washington that these men were being placed in the jails of various local sheriffs without any charges, the attorney general protested to the secretary of war.[32]

The fallout from the attorney general's complaint was so severe that Churchill had to accept restrictions on his domestic intelligence program. "As a matter of principle," he wrote Van Deman, "we have agreed to consult DJ before embarking on anything new in the realm of the civil

---

30. District intelligence officer, Butte, to chief of MI, September 13, 1918, ibid., reel 2, p. 364. For more on Judge Bourquin's link to the IWW and the Nonpartisan League, see William Preston, Jr., *Aliens and Dissenters: Federal Suppression of Radicals, 1903–1933* (Cambridge, Mass.: Harvard University Press, 1963), p. 111.

31. Chief of MI to intelligence officer, Western Department, July 9, 1918, MI Microfilm, reel 2, p. 384; O'Brian to Churchill, June 19, 1918, ibid., pp. 385–86.

32. The records from Butte are in MI Microfilm, reel 11, pp. 407–556.

population." He ordered the head of his Negative Branch to work on improving relations with Justice and expressed an interest in "curbing the ambitions" of his domestic intelligence staff, but, he added, "it is delicate ground."[33] The Butte situation had escaped Churchill's control, however, and the army continued to make arrests. The local Bureau of Investigation agent wired Bielaski, his chief in Washington, that the troops were "making *many* indiscriminate arrests in Butte without any process." He called the arrests "illegal and unjustifiable" and said they "merely serve to increase feeling[s] of unrest among laboring class." The army was getting in the way of the representatives of the Department of Labor who were attempting to mediate the dispute, the agent maintained. If the troops were not called off, he said, their actions "may cause further and serious trouble [in] Butte and interfere with production of copper."[34]

These wholesale and patently illegal arrests brought Attorney General Gregory thundering down on the army. Churchill, knowing he was in trouble, wired the commanding general of the Western Department in San Francisco for information. He was assured that the troops understood that they had no authority to make arrests and had merely "detained certain persons in discharge of their duty as assistants to local authorities. . . ." The western command's telegram added that "this report is another part of malicious propaganda being circulated by radical element in effort to discredit military."[35]

When the official report of the military's action came to Secretary Baker, it made no mention of intelligence agents, citing only the arrests made by troops guarding the mines. Claiming that the detentions were not arrests, without elaborating, the report stressed the violence committed by the agitators, "interfering with, uttering threats, threatening bodily violence to peaceful law abiding citizens going to and from mine." Furthermore, the army argued, there was "no time to secure formal warrants or comply with legal technicalities." Moreover, the explanation went, the Bureau of Investigation agents had been informed verbally about the detentions "until such agents refused to longer handle such cases." The trouble had been caused "by large turbulent lawless element

33. Memorandum "K," Churchill to Van Deman, September 16, 1918, Record Group 165, 10560–235/1, National Archives.
34. Department of Justice telegram, October 4, 1918, MI notation 10110–903/24, in Record Group 60, Glasser Files, box 4, National Archives.
35. Telegrams, Churchill to commanding general, Western Department, October 4, 1918, and Watkins to Milstaff, Washington, October 6, 1918, MI Microfilm, reel 11. pp. 480–81.

of mixed nationalities either I. W. W. or persons affiliated with them."
The "best law abiding and responsible" citizens felt that the army had
"the situation well in hand," and the military's efforts were "endorsed,
approved and commended by them as necessary to avert grave dangerous consequences resulting from mob violence." In calling the detentions "illegal and unjustifiable" and in refusing to accept them for
prosecution, the report concluded, the Department of Justice had lessened respect for the military, while other "adverse reports . . . emanate
from a source which is in sympathy with the I. W. W. element."[36]

The secretary of war accepted this report at face value and quoted a
substantial part of it in his response to the attorney general. He did add
that "clearly the War Department ought not to permit the military to do
anything which cannot be properly backed up by civil process," and he
offered to withdraw the troops from Butte, a proposal designed to take
the steam out of Justice's complaint. He left the door open, however, in
the last line of the letter when he proposed to foster cooperation
between the two departments "by giving instructions to the military
commander there . . . as you may suggest."[37]

Attorney General Gregory took Baker at his word and responded with
a long letter, full of basic lessons in civics. Troops of the United States
Army should be stationed at the mines to guard them, he said, but they
should never make an arrest unless an unauthorized person tried to
enter or committed some act of violence in their presence. To make his
point, he added, "These guards, I repeat, are not police officers."
Gregory then attacked the notion that there was "a distinction between
detention and *arrest.*" Such an argument, he said, was not "tenable, and
the attempt to make it is one of the causes of the present situation." He
stated flatly that "raids must not be made without duly issued search
warrants," and he called attention to the army's inclination to define
sedition "so broadly that a person . . . might well conclude that any
strike in a war industry plant or any promotion or agitation of such a
strike would constitute the grave crime of Treason."[38]

Then Gregory turned to Military Intelligence. He noted that Churchill's agents had "organized at Butte a considerable number of civilians in
espionage work." He let that observation pass "without discussing now
the advisability of or necessity for such action," but he sharply criticized
the agents for making arrests and organizing raids. Army intelligence

36. Militia Bureau to third assistant secretary of war, October 15, 1918, Glasser Files,
box 3.
37. Baker to Gregory, October 14, 1918, ibid.
38. Gregory to Baker, October 23, 1918, ibid.

officers, Gregory said, should turn any information regarding a crime over to the U.S. district attorney. In a veiled reference to the attacks on Wheeler, he insisted that "if the United States Attorney be lacking in the performance of his duties, I assure you that I will administer the appropriate reprimand or discharge as the case may warrant." In no case, however, would Gregory allow an army officer "to substitute his judgment as to whether a federal crime has or has not been committed for the judgment of the United States Attorney." The attorney general denied that his agents had been overly cautious in prosecuting radicals and added that "the impatience of the military officers is essentially due to their impatience at the limitations of the laws themselves and not to any shirking on the part of the federal officials." He admitted that his people might share some responsibility for the remarkably bad relations between the two intelligence agencies in Butte, and he promised that they would be ordered "to cooperate with the military and the local police officials as fully as possible." Gregory wanted the troops to remain but only if Baker defined for "the guard and the Military Intelligence their proper functions respectively in a situation such as exists at Butte."[39]

As important as the Butte case is to understanding the military attitude toward the domestic crisis during the war, it was still a local problem, solved at that level. The intense political and personal differences between agents of the Departments of War and Justice in Butte did not occur in most places. Indeed, while the two were at each other's throats in Butte, in Seattle MI had one of its men on loan to the Bureau of Investigation for work as a double agent against a suspected pro-German. In Chicago the division superintendent of the bureau headed a War Board for coordinating intelligence that included the chief army intelligence officer and his navy counterpart. Relations were so close that the army had advance notice of Justice's raids on radicals in that city.[40] Having several agencies operating in the field not only involved more duplication than Van Deman had admitted to Congress, but it also meant that conflicts were inevitable. The possibility of one agency "uncovering" the operative of another was always present. Generally, at the operational level, however, the agencies developed a reciprocal relationship out of necessity, if nothing else. Though every agency had

---

39. Ibid.
40. F. D. Simmons to Roger S. Day, October 17, 1918, MI Microfilm, reel 6, p. 209. See the "Historical Statement" by Hinton A. Clabaugh, head of the bureau in Chicago, appended to Emerson Hough, *The Web* (Chicago: Reilly and Lee, 1919). For Clabaugh's early coordination with MI, see the telegram from Evans to Van Deman, August 21, 1917, MI Microfilm, reel 4, p. 688. See also Corson, *Armies of Ignorance*, p. 60.

its secrets, the exchange of information that was the heart of the intelligence community was never threatened.

It is important not to overestimate the Department of Justice's complaint about the army's actions in Butte. The attorney general was in a poor position to pose as a defender of civil liberties, especially when the actions of his auxiliary, the American Protective League, are considered. In its famous "slacker raids," that group of officially sanctioned vigilantes arrested and detained tens of thousands of loyal Americans guilty of no greater crime than failing to have their draft registration papers on their persons. These raids, discussed in more detail later, produced considerable outrage, prompting President Wilson to order an investigation in September 1918. Just at the time when the attorney general was cracking down on the illegal work of the military, his chief assistant, John Lord O'Brian, was defending the APL. O'Brian, whose concern for due process was not insignificant, conceded that the bureau had exceeded its authority, and he criticized the use of the APL and soldiers and sailors in the arrests. Ultimately, however, he defended the raids as necessary to the war effort.

Necessary or not, the excesses of the American intelligence community, private, civil, and military, were produced by the perceived emergency of the war and the hysteria that accompanied it. The APL moved to dominate the civilian volunteers, and the Department of Justice, having checked the ambitions of the Secret Service, was determined to contain the army's aggressive Negative Branch. World War I ended before the several issues within the young and ill-defined intelligence community could be resolved. Two and a half weeks after the attorney general lectured the secretary of war on the proper function of the army regarding civilians, the Armistice was signed. Now that there was no longer a military emergency, army intelligence and the APL would end their domestic surveillance—or so it seemed reasonable to presume. Before observing the difficulties in demobilizing America's army of domestic spies, a closer look at the techniques of negative intelligence seems appropriate.

CHAPTER 4

Scope and Methods
of Negative Intelligence

Well before the official creation of the Negative Branch of the Military Intelligence Division, Ralph Van Deman had developed the concept of negative intelligence and put it into practice in his MI4 section. Negative intelligence was simply, as he told Congress, "the looking up of suspected people who are connected with the enemy's operations within our lines; also the stopping of enemy propaganda."[1] Another official statement of the scope of the army's domestic intelligence mission found "hardly a field of human endeavor that is not affected by the war." Consequently, the men working for Van Deman and Churchill had to look for "anything that tends to diminish the ardor, the conviction, the optimism of the people at large." Since the "misbehavior, disloyalty, or indifference of native Americans is as important a material of military intelligence as any other," the conclusion was obvious: "A constant supervision has to be exercised over our civil population."[2]

And so it was. A rule of thumb for the military maintained that only it could recognize the intelligence needed to protect the war effort. Civilians in the APL, the Bureau of Investigation, and the State Department might provide valuable assistance. The press could as well, and Van Deman's office in Washington subscribed to over sixty newspapers, routinely clipping and filing articles, a practice duplicated for local papers by field agents.[3] Crushing an insidious conspiracy, however, required insidious means, and in the Great War the methodology of Military Intelligence and, indeed, of the entire intelligence community, public and private, was surprisingly modern.

1. U.S. Senate, Committee on Military Affairs, 65th Cong., 2d sess.: *Hearings, Extending Jurisdiction of Military Tribunals* (Washington, D.C.: U.S. Government Printing Office, 1918), p. 38.
2. U.S. Army, General Staff, Military Intelligence Division, *The Functions of the Military Intelligence Division, U.S. General Staff* (Washington, D.C.: Military Intelligence Division, 1918), pp. 17–18, 21.
3. Churchill to Marlen E. Pew, July 15, 1918, Record Group 165, MID, 10560–60/7, National Archives.

The invention of the telephone in 1876 was followed shortly by the invention of the wiretap. The criminal community of the mid-1890s had been the first to appreciate the wiretap's benefits, and soon thereafter most states outlawed the practice. During World War I, however, telephonic eavesdropping became a standard practice for the intelligence community. By the summer of 1917 the New York branch of Naval Intelligence was producing transcripts of the telephone conversations of Russian aliens.[4] Other devices for the surreptitious collection of information, though not as compact as those of the electronic age, were also available. Photographic surveillance and the photographing of documents appear to have been well developed. Electronic eavesdropping, or the use of a "bug" as we know it today, was in its infancy, but the early dictagraph sufficed. That instrument could be used alone to pick up conversations in offices and hotel rooms, or it could be attached to a wiretap to record telephone conversations. Van Deman's expert on the "Tel. Tap and Dictagraph Circuit" was Inspector John G. Purdie of Biddle's New York office, who made his services available to other branches, including Plant Protection, when needed.[5]

Techniques of searching were also quite modern. Although the term *body search* does not appear to have been used, suspicious females boarding passenger ships were subjected to a "vaginal examination," and a rectal exploration was used for both sexes. Searches of body cavities were conducted by operatives of the Customs intelligence department on their own initiative or "at the request of either the representative of the Department of Justice[,] Naval Intelligence, [or] military intelligence."[6] Certainly one can assume that female agents searched subjects of their own sex, for, apart from the need for sensitivity obvious even to the most cynical of spy masters, the importance of women in intelligence had not been overlooked. The supersecret Washington, D.C., field office of Military Intelligence had a female agent, identified

4. Record Group 38, ONI, "Suspect" files, box 1, ibid. For more on wiretapping, see Frank Morn, *"The Eye That Never Sleeps": A History of the Pinkerton National Detective Agency* (Bloomington: Indiana University Press, 1982), p. 177; and Joan M. Jensen, *The Price of Vigilance* (Chicago: Rand McNally, 1968), pp. 151–52.
5. The best account of the use of the "electric camera" and the dictagraph is in Emerson Hough, *The Web* (Chicago: Reilly and Lee, 1919), pp. 163–70. For similar methods by the navy, see Jeffrey M. Dorwart, *The Office of Naval Intelligence: The Birth of America's First Intelligence Agency, 1865–1918* (Annapolis: Naval Institute Press, 1979), p. 171. Purdie's telephone tap–dictagraph system required a six-volt battery. His diagram is in the "Dictograph [sic] File," in Record Group 165, General Correspondence, Plant Protection Section, entry 104, National Archives, Suitland.
6. "CAP" file, box 7, Record Group 38, ONI, National Archives.

as "Miss Anna W. Keichline of Bellafonte, Pa., an architect."[7] The state of New York's 1919 investigative effort, the Lusk Committee, had Agent 22, Margaret M. Scully, offer her services as a typist to Emma Goldman, who was awaiting deportation, in an attempt to get close to the anarchist. Scully, who hoped to be an actress, proved entirely unreliable and was fired by Goldman.[8] Military Intelligence's use of reporter Marguerite Harrison was more successful. Her relationship with Goldman in Russia in 1920 ranked her as a "highly esteemed spy" for the army.[9]

Informants and undercover agents were the workhorses of the military's domestic intelligence system. Good intelligence officers took pride in the number of coded agents they acquired. The Plant Protection Service had its own network, and the Morale Section had agents among the troops at every post. The leader of the Pittsburgh branch of Military Intelligence bragged that his "confidential informant #836" was "the friend and adviser of all the leading radicals throughout the United States. He brings to his work not only intelligence and patriotism, but a very thorough knowledge of the theories of the various schools of socialism."[10]

One of Biddle's operatives in New York, Agent 99, gathered such valuable information on "the activities of the Bolsheviki, the I.W.W.'s and anarchists" that his handler refused to share it with other departments for fear of uncovering his plant.[11] Agent 99 provided reports almost daily from early 1918 to July, when he was exposed. Typed poorly but legibly, his products have a fascinating, almost Joycean quality about them. Here is the last portion of his last report, picked up in the middle of a sentence several pages long, with typing errors included, as he is being questioned by one Mary about some missing mail:

> it seems to me that the fellow in charge of the mail had not nerve to come to me, and ask me those kind of questions, or to theothe fellow on whom you have

7. U.S. Army, *The History of the Counter Intelligence Corps in the United States Army, 1917–1950 (with Limited Tabular Data to 1960)*, 30 vols. (Baltimore: U.S. Army Intelligence Center, 1959), 3:66, available in Record Group 319, National Archives (hereafter cited as CIC History).

8. Lusk Committee Papers, L0038, box 1, folder 14, New York State Archives, Albany (hereafter cited as Lusk Files).

9. Alice Wexler, *Emma Goldman in Exile: From the Russian Revolution to the Spanish Civil War* (Boston: Beacon Press, 1989), pp. 33–34. Marguerite Harrison recounted her work for MI, which caused her imprisonment in Russia, in her *There's Always Tomorrow: The Story of a Checkered Life* (New York: Farrar & Rinehart, 1935).

10. Intelligence officer, Pittsburgh, to director of MI, December 23, 1918, in Randolph Boehm, ed., *U.S. Military Intelligence Reports: Surveillance of Radicals in the United States, 1917–1941* (Frederick, Md.: University Publications of America, 1984), reel 12, p. 1030 (hereafter cited as MI Microfilm).

11. Biddle to Van Deman, February 6, 1918, MI Microfilm, reel 33, p. 447.

also the suspicion,anyhow Mary what are you against me,for nothing you are so unpolite,and mean to me? for the last couple of months,you are acting as if I would be some kind of a German-Spy,or any other kind of a Spy,Well she said I can *Do As I Please* and anybody that I do not care much about,and dont like his ways,and if I like to be mean to him, I will be mean to him,and nobvody would stop me from that,so I told her that I dont give a Damn for her ways anyhow,because I know where it comes from,Murray was sitting in a corner and kept on watching all the time on me,my expression and my ways while I was questioned about the Mail,but I kept on purpose cold-bloodet and when she was trough with me, I went back to the Piano and started a real Wobbly song to play,where few of the members joined in the Chorus.(It seems to me that they are preparing to drop me from their list as a member of the I.W.W. but thatr could be done only trough a business meeting,whcih will affect us both,who the other fellow supposed to be, I do not know otherwise everything is quite.[12]

More precise information on this particular IWW local came to Biddle from New York's Neutrality Squad. The local had offices at 74 St. Marks Place, but only eight people were identified as "active members." The Mary who rightly accused Agent 99 of being a spy was Mary Cooper, "Belgian, typewriter." Murray, known only by that name, was a "soap box orator and agitator, American." Others in the group were an executive secretary; officers for publicity, lecturing, finances; a "Hall Secretary"; and an editor for the group's organ, *Labor Defender.* Van Deman always wanted to know the nationality of his suspects, and this IWW section consisted of four Americans, one Belgian, one German, one "Norwegian or Danish," and one Russian Jew.[13]

A secret agent's risk of being revealed as a spy was probably matched by the possibility of being arrested by some other intelligence agency unaware of the operation. Before the war ended, word had spread through the intelligence community of the plight of an operative of the Burns Detective Agency who had been swept up in the mass arrests sponsored by the Department of Justice against the IWW in Chicago in the summer of 1917. That operative, "well up in the councils of the I.W.W.," had been arrested as a true radical and spent eight months in

12. Agent 0–99 to Corps of Intelligence Police, July 4, 1918, ibid., reel 8, pp. 521–30. As J. Edgar Hoover said in 1920, when complaining about delays in paying his sources, "Confidential informants, as a rule, are a rather temperamental lot" (Theodore Kornweibel, Jr., ed., *Federal Surveillance of Afro-Americans (1917–1925): The First World War, the Red Scare, and the Garvey Movement* [Frederick, Md.: University Publications of America, 1986], reel 13, pp. 626–28, hereafter cited as Surveillance of Afro-Americans Microfilm).
13. Thomas Tunney to Corps of Intelligence Police, April 8, 1918, MI Microfilm, reel 8, p. 650.

jail before his agency, "after a great deal of trouble," effected his release. To protect its informants, Military Intelligence had developed the practice of providing them with credentials, even if their status was entirely civilian and voluntary.[14]

Professional undercover work obviously required that an agent be acceptable to the target organization. Van Deman's Morale Section, for example, used "Civil Agent Ludwik Kradyna" to get inside the Russian element in the army at Camp Dix, New Jersey.[15] Army officers and even the plainclothed inspectors of the Corps of Intelligence Police were unsuitable for covert work against largely immigrant groups. Anyone, however, could attend their public functions. When Van Deman spotted an announcement for a radical affair, he sent one of his men because the public was invited. It mattered little, then, who drew the assignment in March 1918 when he ordered, by coded wire, his Chicago intelligence officer to have a "representative attend concert and ball given by the Russian Union of the I.W.W."[16]

Such open coverage was a mainstay in the army's domestic system, and though it was completely obvious, it was used by the entire intelligence community. Although any agent was capable of attending a radical meeting and taking notes, the counterintelligence mentality much preferred to hire a professional stenographer to take down the seditious language verbatim. In New York, William F. Smart, "certified shorthand reporter," made his services available to any interested intelligence agency. For producing two typed copies, he charged sixty cents a page. Van Deman and Churchill also purchased transcripts of the great trials of the day, particularly those of the ıww in Chicago and U.S. Representative Berger in Milwaukee.[17]

Professional stenographers stood out at radical programs, and so, no doubt, did the private detectives and agents from the bureau, the army, the navy, and the local police. In June 1917, before Van Deman was ready to run such operations, a bureau agent accompanied by a stenographer from the U.S. Immigration Service attended a peace rally on the Boston Commons sponsored by the Lettish Socialist Club of Roxbury. More than three thousand people came to hear James Oneal, secretary of the

14. Fitzhugh Burns to director of MI, September 28, 1918, ibid., reel 12, p. 953.

15. Intelligence officer, Camp Dix, to director of MI, November 7, 1918, ibid., reel 34, p. 339.

16. Van Deman to intelligence officer, Central Department, March 23, 1918, ibid., reel 1, p. 160.

17. Lusk Files, L0040, box 1, folder 17. For the Berger trial and references to other transcriptions, see MI Microfilm, reel 3, pp. 968–1067.

Socialist party of Massachusetts. Standing on a bandstand "decorated with two tiny American Flags, and a big RED Banner," he began: "Mr. Chairman, friends, conscripts and secret agents!" [18] At an IWW meeting in Seattle, a speaker called attention to a point by saying, "Now all you secret service men and detectives get out your paper and pencil and put this down." [19] The famous writer Lincoln Steffens, suspect for his radical connections, noted while on a speaking tour in September 1917 that "Federal stenographers have taken down my lectures for some official reading." [20]

Radicals seemed to understand that being spied on was an occupational hazard. The *Washington Post* even announced to the world that Socialist leader Eugene V. Debs was "under strict surveillance by government agents." [21] Accepting these conditions, most leftist organizers saw no necessity in distinguishing which particular government agency, or which corporation for that matter, was spying on them at a particular time. At any large radical meeting there were likely to be agents and stenographers from several organizations. John Reed, the best-known American to witness the Russian Revolution, wrote from Christiania, now Oslo, Norway, in a December 1917 letter intercepted by the State Department, "So I often wander around the city, especially at night, I and my weary spies." [22] His wife, Louise Bryant, on her return from Russia, could not remember if it had been "the naval intelligence or the military intelligence" that had confiscated the papers of a colleague. [23]

There is not a great deal of information on the question of whether the repertoire of either Military Intelligence or the larger intelligence community included the systematic use of violence or torture. Raids by the army alone or in association with other agencies, involving armed

18. The June 12, 1917, Bureau of Investigation report from agent Weiss is in MI Microfilm, reel 1, pp. 369–75.

19. Robert Friedheim, *The Seattle General Strike* (Seattle: University of Washington Press, 1964), p. 11.

20. Steffens to Allen H. Suggett, September 30, 1917, in Ella Winter and Granville Hicks, eds., *The Letters of Lincoln Steffens*, 2 vols. (New York: Harcourt, Brace, 1938), 1:405. In an October 31, 1918, letter to James H. McGill, Steffens confided that he was "afraid of the Military Intelligence" because it had identified him as sympathetic to the "revolutionists" (ibid., 438–39). He was not physically afraid, apparently, but worried that they were responsible for the difficulty he was having in securing a passport. They were.

21. *Washington Post*, June 18, 1918.

22. Quoted in MI's summary of John Reed to Louise Bryant, n.d., MI Microfilm, reel 19, p. 191, included in a general report on Bryant's mail in the winter of 1917–18, pp. 191–93.

23. U.S. Senate, Report and Hearings of the Subcommittee on the Judiciary, 65th Cong., 1st sess., document no. 62, *Brewing and Liquor Interests and German and Bolshevik Propaganda*, 3 vols. (Washington, D.C.: U.S. Government Printing Office, 1919), 3:473.

men who bashed down doors, ransacked offices, confiscated documents, and hauled off radicals for interrogation, were in and of themselves violent acts, yet no raids by federal agents on leftist groups ever resulted in gunfire. Victims of the subsequent interrogations complained of beatings, and it does seem reasonable to believe that the policeman's rubber hose found its way into Military Intelligence, filled as it was with so many former law officers. The subject, however, seems to have been taboo in intelligence reports.[24] There is substantial evidence of brutality at army posts containing America's four thousand conscientious objectors. Sergeants appear to have administered awful, even sadistic, beatings, but the attitude that inspired them came from the officer corps. The camps under the command of General Leonard Wood were the most violent in their treatment of pacifists.[25]

One other form of violence also appears to have been limited to enlisted men. Throughout the war, and afterward, it was not uncommon for off-duty soldiers and sailors to disrupt meetings of anarchists, pacifists, and Socialists. Complaints about this behavior in New York were significant enough just after the war to cause an investigation by Military Intelligence's branch office. Since their agents had been present to take notes, they were asked about the "alleged misconduct of soldiers and sailors at radical meetings." There was nothing to it, they responded: "The anarchists and socialists of this City themselves are entirely responsible for every bit of trouble which has occurred and of which they are complaining." The reports, though clearly prejudiced, do give a fascinating view of the violent clashes in New York.[26]

They began on June 4, 1917, the night before the national draft registration day. The speeches opposing the draft by anarchists Emma Goldman and Alexander Berkman at this meeting resulted in their arrest and conviction. A group of soldiers, in uniform and armed with electric light bulbs, bricks, lemons, and "stink-balls," had moved near the stage

24. The best-documented case of violence in an army interrogation of civilians is in Richard Polenberg, *Fighting Faiths: The Abrams Case, the Supreme Court, and Free Speech* (New York: Viking, 1987), pp. 66–69. In the Red Scare after the war, the Department of Justice was accused of torture and even the death of one suspect, who fell from a window of a federal office in New York. For factual and devastating attacks, see Constantine M. Panunzio, *The Deportation Cases of 1919–1920* (1921; rpt. New York: Da Capo Press, 1970); and R. G. Brown et al., *Illegal Practices of the United States Department of Justice* (1920; rpt. New York: Arno, 1969).

25. These revelations about the mistreatment of conscientious objectors came out a few years after the war and are summarized in H. C. Peterson and Gilbert C. Fite, *Opponents of War, 1917–1918* (Seattle: University of Washington Press, 1957), pp. 126–38.

26. The reports in this and the following paragraphs by Trevor, Stevenson, and two intelligence police sergeants are in MI Microfilm, reel 12, pp. 2–8.

and were interrupting the speakers "with loud voiced remarks." In the middle of Berkman's speech, "a small riot broke out in the part of the gallery occupied by the soldiers, where a free-for-all took place, in which a number of anarchists were beaten up." The speaker receiving the most severe treatment was Joseph Cain, Jr., "a young man of conscriptable age," who opposed the draft. When he shouted, "give me liberty or give me death," the soldiers hit him with a barrage of missiles, "apparently preferring to satisfy Cain's second choice." The fighting continued in the streets after the meeting, and "a number of anarchists were arrested by the soldiers."

Similar incidents occurred throughout the war, by the end of which the troops had found a new symbol against which to rally: the Red flag. The day after the Armistice, five thousand Socialists marched from the People's House of the Rand School of Social Science to Carnegie Hall. "Two American flags and hundreds of red flags were carried by the marchers, and all along the route there was trouble between the socialists and soldiers, sailors, and civilians who objected to the red flags." The police were successful in keeping the military out of the hall, but two weeks later, at Madison Square Garden, where thirteen thousand Socialists gathered, the troops saw Red again. Identified as soldiers and sailors by their uniforms, these men attacked the police denying them entrance to the Garden. A disaster was in the making until a unit of mounted police "charged into them from the rear." Still, some troops did find entry and "promptly adopted more forcible methods of relieving the socialists of their red flags, with the result that small riots were constantly breaking out."

Although it is clear from this fascinating report by the intelligence police that the Socialists were the victims of rioting troops, the sergeant who wrote it had no sympathy for them. The Red flag, he concluded, "invariably rouses men in uniform to action. Those who were beaten up got just about what was coming to them." John B. Trevor had replaced Biddle as head of the New York branch at the end of the war, and he gave the report his full endorsement when forwarding it to Washington. He also included a statement from the chief of his propaganda section, Archibald Stevenson, that substantiated the charge that the Socialists had taunted and insulted the troops. Stevenson had been present at the Carnegie Hall event, and though his job was analyzing Red propaganda, his report reflected his considerable ability as a propagandist for the right. He said he personally witnessed a woman who stalked a soldier "quietly watching the affair from the sidewalk," and when she reached him "she lashed him across the face with a red handkerchief and shouted at the same time, 'Take that, you dirty bastard.'"

Trevor maintained that though such unfortunate incidents were subversive of military discipline, "it would be misleading to assume that these attacks on the so-called socialists are evidence of military brutality." These actions were just and fair treatment of "an element which has endeavored by preaching pacifism and obstruction to the Draft, and even open disloyalty, to make the prosecution of the war more difficult." Trevor understood why soldiers reacted to the insults of traitorous Socialists. Only recently, while being driven to his office, he had passed an obvious radical, "an individual of this character," who made an insulting gesture with his hand and shouted, "G'dwan ye buggers." Trevor's chauffeur wanted to "smash the man up," but Trevor, aware that such action was inappropriate for an officer in uniform, satisfied himself by arresting the culprit and hauling him off to the police.

In the counterpropaganda portion of the Negative Branch's mission, the concepts of a free press and freedom of speech were disregarded. The army was especially concerned that seditious material not reach its troops. To that end, the branch prepared an "Army Index" of books prohibited on posts. The intitial list, consisting of 124 pro-German or antiwar books, generated a heated argument within the Department of War, and the secretary of war reduced the number by 25 percent. Despite continuing concern in the secretariat that other worthy books remained on the army list, no further deletions were made. The *Open Letter to Profiteers*, by the pacifist Scott Nearing, was banned, along with the milliennialist piece *Jesus Is Coming* by William E. Blackstone. The latter, which sold a million copies by 1932, was guilty of advocating turning the other cheek while awaiting the advent. Immigration official Frederic C. Howe's *Why War?*, written in 1916 and dedicated to Woodrow Wilson, was also considered unsuitable. The most famous book on the army's list was the *Review of Review*'s 1918 *Two Thousand Questions and Answers about the War.* George Creel, head of the administration's Committee on Public Information, had made the mistake, he later admitted, of writing a preface to the volume after a quick reading. The American Security League, which hated Creel, pounced on the book as "a masterpiece of Hun propaganda." The book, it seemed, lacked the required statement that Germany alone was responsible for the war. It was also missing, as Creel later put it, "a straight-out condemnation" of German brutality. What would become entirely acceptable revisionist history was treason in 1918. The book was withdrawn, revised, and reissued without Creel's preface. [27]

27. Creel's role in the *Two Thousand Questions* scandal is covered in detail in Walton E. Bean, "George Creel and His Critics: A Study of the Attacks on the Committee on Public

Though the military took its usual excessive approach in book banning, it had no corner on the censorship market during the war. Creel's Committee on Public Information, hated as treasonous by conservatives, was roundly criticized by liberals as too harsh. During the war, the *New York Times* spoke of the "rash, intruding, Creelish hand." Creel's dilemma is instructive of the plight progressives, including the president and the secretary of war, faced when confronted with a war as destructive of principles as it was of lives and property. Creel, a strong supporter of a free press, found himself forced to compromise. Without his moderating hand, however, censorship might have been even tighter. For example, he regarded the army's index as embarrassing and refused to give it public notice.[28]

The requirement for censorship of the mail was as obvious as the need to ban books, and the army and navy were heavily involved in this effort. Congress's joint resolution declaring war on Germany gave the president the authority to censor telegraph, telephone, and cable communications. Wilson parceled this duty out, making the navy responsible for the ocean cables, while the army controlled the telegraph and telephone lines. In the fall of 1917, Wilson established a Censorship Board to handle the mail. The board was composed of Creel and representatives from the army, navy, War Trade Board, and Post Office. Major Douglas MacArthur acted as the first chief military censor before that designation was officially used. After his departure for the war, the head of the Bureau of Insular Affairs represented the army on the Censorship Board until that function passed to Military Intelligence in June 1918. Just as Ralph Van Deman's dream was being realized with the establishment of MI as a separate division of the general staff, his successor, Marlborough Churchill, picked up the duties of chief military censor and War Department representative on the president's Censorship Board.

The board, based in Washington, set policy for an Executive Postal Censorship Committee headquartered in New York City. Below this level were censorship stations at critical ports and several towns on the

Information, 1917–1919" (Ph.D. dissertation, University of California at Berkeley, 1941), pp. 214–32. For the "Army Index," see Bruce W. Bidwell, *History of the Military Intelligence Division, Department of the Army General Staff, 1775–1941* (Frederick, Md.: University Publications of America, 1986), p. 201; and, the best on the subject, James R. Mock, *Censorship, 1917* (Princeton: Princeton University Press, 1941), pp. 159–71.

28. For complaints aginst Creel, see Bean, "Creel and His Critics," pp. 63–121. Stephen Vaughn in *Holding Fast the Inner Lines: Democracy, Nationalism, and the Committee on Public Information* (Chapel Hill: University of North Carolina Press, 1980), p. 238, says that Creel did not see freedom of speech as an absolute right in the war emergency and that his committee's "record was flawed by the crusading zeal of the time."

sensitive Mexican border. Postal censor stations also operated in Puerto Rico and Hawaii, as well as in London, Paris, Havana, and Panama. The composition of the local stations matched that of the national board, and the program called for each representative to submit a list of the kinds of information to be censored and the names of suspects whose mail was to be checked automatically. Although each agency was supposed to look for information peculiar to its needs, the army and navy were the largest users of the system. They wanted data not only on the enemy and the war but also on political and economic matters that seemed, on paper, to be the responsibility of War Trade Intelligence. Even before Churchill took over as censor, the army had reported to the president its interest in "anarchist, socialist, and pacifist groups," as well as "labor disturbances" and "German sympathizers." The new intelligence chief defined his censorship duties broadly, including "the prevention of information, falsehood, propaganda, or other activity tending to depress or misinform our own people."[29]

The censors read the mail and deleted offending material; some letters might be delayed or confiscated. Censorship had two purposes: to suppress information such as the location and strength of military units that might be helpful to the enemy, and to gather data that might be useful to a government agency. Information relating to topics of interest was copied or summarized and provided to the appropriate intelligence agency. Twenty-one broad topics were established, and each had enough subheadings to allow the largely untrained staff to delete or confiscate pretty much whatever caught their attention. Under the topic "Criminal" fell not only sabotage but also strikes and labor agitation. Similarly, "Propaganda" included not only that by Germans but also by Socialists and pacifists. "Anarchists and I.W.W. Activity" was a separate category. As the scholar most expert on the censorship program has said, "To Military Intelligence, nihilists, pacifists and conscientious objectors were almost the same, as far as their mail was concerned."[30] There was a natural competition between the military, which wanted to see everything, and the Post Office's desire to avoid undue delays in mail delivery. The task of checking all the mail was staggering; the list of suspects alone totaled a quarter of a million. The midsized postal censor station in San Antonio and its substations along the Mexican border, for example, in

29. The history, organization, and operation of the postal censorship program was summarized by Churchill in a lengthy memorandum for the chief of staff, August 5, 1918, Record Group 165, MID, 10110-890/15, National Archives, and Record Group 60, Glasser Files, box 9.
30. Mock, *Censorship*, p. 127.

one week late in the war, examined nearly 120,000 pieces of mail, an effort involving 247 people.[31]

The restrictive laws and presidential orders of the war did not give the army police power, but they certainly suggest the climate of hysteria in which Military Intelligence thrived. Immediately upon the declaration of war, a presidential proclamation, based on the 1798 Alien Enemies Act so hated by Jeffersonians, allowed the Department of Justice to round up more than two thousand aliens, who were interned at army posts. The following day the president issued a secret order allowing dismissal of federal employees for disloyal talk. A week later he formed the Committee on Public Information, headed by Creel and having both censorship and propaganda functions. Before the end of the month he gave the army and navy control over wire communications (the navy already monitored the wireless). The Selective Service Act of mid-May made it illegal to obstruct the draft. The Espionage Act of June, aimed at more than spies, punishing any obstruction of the war effort by word or deed, gave mail censorship power to the Post Office. In the fall of 1917 the Trading with the Enemy Act was passed, followed on October 12 by Wilson's creation of the Board of Censorship. The Sabotage Act and the Sedition Act in the spring of 1918 gave the government broad powers to arrest anyone for damaging property, "no matter how essential" to the war effort, and for uttering or printing abusive language or ridicule about the administration. On October 16, 1918, just before the war ended, the Alien Act was passed allowing the secretary of labor to deport radicals who had the misfortune not to be born in this country.[32]

Despite Wilson's progressive reforms and his equally well-known nobility in foreign affairs, protecting civil liberties was not one of his priorities. The litany of repressive laws and regulations highlights the trade-offs Wilson was willing to accept. It is difficult to imagine any other president, either a Lincoln or a Jefferson, who would not have made the same compromises when faced with the country's first world war. When offered a clear opportunity to champion civil liberties, however, Wilson was wishy-washy. Early on he told his attorney general that he thought the concept of ordaining the vigilantes of the American Protective

31. Ibid., pp. 62–72, describes these operations. For examples of Military Intelligence's application of information received through the postal censorship program, see MI Microfilm, reel 2, p. 748; for the navy, "CAP" file, box 2.

32. A good summary of these measures is in Harry N. Scheiber, *The Wilson Administration and Civil Liberties, 1917–1919* (Ithaca: Cornell University Press, 1960), pp. 13–28. See also Donald O. Johnson, *The Challenge to American Freedoms: World War I and the Rise of the American Civil Liberties Union* (Lexington: University of Kentucky Press, 1963), pp. 55–84.

League as federal auxiliaries seemed "very dangerous." Yet he accepted doing so on the basis of manpower needs. On the positive side, he supported the Department of Justice in opposing the military tribunals bill, and in the spring of 1918 he made several statements deploring mob violence against German-Americans.[33]

Wilson's only known criticism of Military Intelligence came on August 27, 1918, when he wrote the secretary of war that he thought the army spies were taking entirely too long in their investigations of YMCA workers who had applied for permission to go abroad. "This tangle of threads," he said, "ought surely to be cut." Baker responded that the reviews were necessary because "some organizations are selecting men whom it would be unwise to send across, and only after investigation by the Military Intelligence can we exercise wise and fair discrimination."[34] Apparently both were unaware that the APL was making the investigations for MI.

The Wilson administration's failure to curb the abuses of its intelligence agencies is made all the more ironic by the genuinely progressive nature of many of its members. Attorney General Gregory is usually cited as a progressive, although not by all; certainly his special assistant O'Brian was. Both Secretary of Labor William B. Wilson and Secretary of War Baker had impeccable progressive credentials. The diminutive Baker, the youngest cabinet member, had a splendid reform record as mayor of Cleveland before he entered the cabinet in early 1916. He had volunteered for the Spanish-American War and been rejected for physical reasons but was philosophically opposed to war, and his work with the League to Enforce Peace and with Oswald Garrison Villard's League to Limit Armaments caused the press to label him, incorrectly, as an ex-pacifist.[35]

Yet Wilson and his cabinet were not out of step with the country in sacrificing civil liberties. As subsequent discussion will show, state legislatures were busily strengthening their antiradical legislation, especially with Red flag laws which forbade displaying the hated color. The Supreme Court clamped down on free speech, formulating the "clear and present danger" concept in the *Schenck* case in March 1919.

33. Scheiber, *Wilson*, pp. 49–50.

34. Woodrow Wilson to Newton D. Baker, August 27, 1918, in Arthur S. Link et al., eds., *Papers of Woodrow Wilson*, vol. 49 (Princeton: Princeton University Press, 1985), 359–60; Baker to the president, August 29, 1918, Papers of Newton D. Baker, microfilm reel 6, p. 226, Manuscript Division, Library of Congress.

35. Daniel R. Beaver, *Newton D. Baker and the American War Effort, 1917–1919* (Lincoln: University of Nebraska Press, 1966), p. 1; C. H. Cramer, *Newton D. Baker: A Biography* (1961; rpt. New York: Garland, 1979), pp. 76–82.

No community was safe from vigilante or mob action, and the hundreds of thousands of volunteer spies for the intelligence agencies attest that ideological purity had become an obsession for many Americans. It is difficult to assess the meaning of this high level of intolerance in a society that had been so reform-minded. Perhaps the late nineteenth-century view of society as an evolving organism still drove many of the progressives and forced them to place the needs of the state above the rights of the individual. Or perhaps American progressivism had a darker, authoritarian side. Progressives demanded morality in public service and in business, and they came to insist upon a morally pure ideology which they intuited could not exist on the left. If foreigners were feared for their religion, their language, their cultural habits, and even the size of their families, they were equally detested for the alien ideologies they brought with them or to which they seemed especially susceptible. Nativism and fear of radicalism were not new to the American scene, but the war exacerbated them to the extent that liberals who defended a radical's civil liberties were themselves oppressed and imprisoned.

This conservative climate of opinion notwithstanding, the present study demands further investigation into the attitude and methods of Baker and especially the reasons for his apparent inability to halt Military Intelligence's extralegal activities. One authority on the subject has concluded that Baker was essentially a prisoner of his bureaucracy and that, though he wanted to end Military Intelligence's fight against sedition at home, he "could never convince his subordinates that this was a proper course." Such criticism as the army did get from Baker and the Department of Justice "merely drove the Military Intelligence underground," waiting until the secretary was abroad to become especially unruly.[36] Another study suggested that Baker's style was not to interfere with the military professionals. The secretary admitted that he was not a hands-on administrator. "The volume of the Department's business," he said, "was too great to permit more detailed personal study except in cases of great importance." Each day he conferred with the army chief of staff, who brought the documents Baker needed to see, after which the chief took the papers away.[37] Unlike senior officials today, he apparently received no regular intelligence briefings, although he did have some meetings with both Van Deman and Churchill.

There is no doubt about Baker's good intentions. One study, generally critical of the Wilson administration, found the secretary of war "always

36. Jensen, *Price of Vigilance*, pp. 124, 224.
37. Cramer, *Baker*, pp. 124–25, 136.

generous and tolerant," describing him as a liberal who was "most sympathetic and generous, not only to [conscientious] objectors, but to the Civil Liberties Bureau."[38] When vigilantes horsewhipped the Ohio reforming minister and pacifist Herbert S. Bigelow in October 1917, Baker was the most outspoken member of the administration in deploring the outrage. The army establishment, and Military Intelligence in particular, put a great deal of pressure on Baker through alarmist reports to harden this attitude. As the war progressed, one of his biographers has noted, the secretary "talked less about civil liberties," and "the war finally blunted Baker's principles," much to the disgust of his old liberal friends such as Villard, who "despised and distrusted him."[39]

Baker's chief assistants who dealt with Military Intelligence also had impressive credentials. Third Assistant Secretary Frederick P. Keppel had been a dean at Columbia University and later became president of the Carnegie Corporation, and Baker's private secretary, Ralph Hayes, had been with him since Cleveland. Felix Frankfurter was headed for the Supreme Court; Walter Lippmann's status as a progressive journalist is well known; and Emmett J. Scott was a prominent black educator at Tuskegee Institute and Howard University. Even if Baker preferred not to know the details, these assistants did, and it is particularly interesting that late in the war his two protégés, Hayes and Lippmann, both received army commissions and served in Military Intelligence. Keppel sent information on pacifists to Van Deman, who promised to put them with "my already extensive file in this connection." Van Deman confided to Frankfurter that Clarence Darrow and "other notorious attorneys" were helping the iww, adding that George Creel was acting on their behalf in Washington.[40] The practice of these assistants, with whom Van Deman corresponded directly and frequently, was to return the documents to him, with a note that Baker had seen them.

Of Baker's assistants, Walter Lippmann had the clearest view of the danger of repression. In the fall of 1917, he prepared for Colonel Edward M. House a strong condemnation of the postal censorship program. Noting that he had "no doctrinaire belief in free speech," he accepted that because of the war "it is necessary to sacrifice some of it." The

38. Johnson, *Challenge*, pp. 26, 53; Peggy Lamson, *Roger Baldwin, Founder of the American Civil Liberties Union: A Portrait* (Boston: Houghton Mifflin, 1976), p. 75.

39. Beaver, *Baker*, pp. 231–39.

40. Van Deman to Frankfurter, January 17, 1918, MI Microfilm, reel 2, p. 477; Van Deman to Keppel, March 1, 1918, ibid., reel 5, p. 168. On Baker's assistants, see Cramer, *Baker*, p. 133; and Ronald Steel, *Walter Lippmann and the American Century* (Boston: Little, Brown, 1980), p. 139.

practice of barring radical newspapers from the mails, however, disturbed Lippmann, and he believed that "the method now being pursued is breaking down the liberal support of the war and is tending to divide the country's articulate opinion into fanatical jingoism and fanatical pacifism." He thought the suppression of the radical papers "gives them an importance that intrinsically they would never have." A proper government, he said, "ought to be contemptuously uninterested in such opinion and ought to suppress only military secrets and advice to break the law."[41]

There is little doubt that Secretary Baker was aware not only of the existence of Military Intelligence but also of the nature of its activities. On August 18, 1917, in a letter to Wilson, he introduced Van Deman as the "Chief of the Intelligence Division (Secret Service) of the Army" and noted that the colonel was investigating an army officer whose loyalty had been questioned. In June 1918, Baker referred to Churchill in a similar letter to the president, and the lack of any further identification makes it obvious that Wilson already knew of Churchill. The documents that have survived show that the cabinet officer had a fairly close relationship with both intelligence leaders. Van Deman sent Baker reports on conditions back in Ohio. He also reported on the activities of the son of Florence Kelley, one of Baker's radical friends. The younger Kelley had spoken out against the government's raid on Scott Nearing's home. On another occasion, Baker told the president about ordering Military Intelligence to undertake investigations of disloyalty in New York's docks, of rumors that soldiers were being gouged by retailers, and of charges of mismanagement in aircraft production. The largest and most complicated investigation Baker initiated involved allegations that he was receiving kickbacks from a construction company.[42]

Aside from these special reports, there were the finished products of Military Intelligence's work that went to the highest levels of government. The function of intelligence included not only the collection and

41. Lippman to House, October 17, 1917, Baker Papers, reel 1, p. 627.
42. Baker to the president, August 18, 1917, Baker Papers, reel 3, p. 308; Baker to the president, June 22, 1918, reel 6, pp. 411–12; Van Deman to Baker, November 23, 1917, reel 2, p. 641; Van Deman, confidential memorandum for the secretary of war, October 6, 1917, reel 2, p. 111; Baker to the president, July 10, 1917, reel 3, p. 374; Baker to the president, July 21, 1918, reel 6, p. 155; Baker to the attorney general, May 8, 1918, reel 4, p. 345; Baker, memorandum, May 17, 1918, reel 4, p. 147. On MI's investigation of the North Atlantic Construction Company, at Baker's orders, see office of MI, New York, to office of MI, War Department, June 5, 1918, reel 4, pp. 141–47, and Churchill, personal memorandum for the secretary of war, June 14, 1918, reel 5, p. 202. After the war, Keppel in a memorandum for the secretary of war, May 10, 1919, put Van Deman and Churchill at the top of his list of those recommended for the Distinguished Service Medal (reel 7, p. 569).

analysis of information but also its dissemination. Reports came to Washington from the field in a variety of forms. Telegrams were frequently sent regarding a specific suspect or event, as were raw intelligence reports from undercover agents. Other submissions involved more formal studies. By the summer of 1918 the larger intelligence offices, the branches and the headquarters of the several departments, were completing regular reports headed "Weekly Report on Socialistic, Anarchistic, I.W.W. and Bolsheviki Activities."[43] The Washington headquarters eventually published a series of reports for its own use, handling so many that before the war ended it was lobbying the chief of staff for its own printing office. These internal documents included a "Daily Report," a "Weekly Report," another weekly report on morale and public opinion, a secret "Weekly Bulletin for Intelligence Officers," and, eventually from the Negative Branch, a "Weekly Situation Survey on Radical and Racial Activities."[44] For higher officials, including the chief of staff, the secretary of war, and the president, Military Intelligence prepared a *Weekly Intelligence Summary* that covered the entire international scene, with particular attention to the war effort.

Although the intelligence summaries were very general, they are of interest because they were widely circulated around Washington. As finished intelligence products, the summaries never discussed the sensitive sources and methods that produced the information, but they were clear on the attitude of the military regarding the domestic picture. The generation of the summaries, obviously necessary to justify the existence of his unit, was an early concern of Van Deman's, and on June 2, 1917, his office produced the first issue. His principal domestic enemies were obvious from his headings, which included "I.W.W.," "Negro Unrest," "Anti-Conscription Activities," and "Socialist Activities." The primary focus of these reports, however, remained the war and the international scene. After the summer of 1917, domestic affairs were not mentioned until the following spring, when a section called "United States, Internal Situation" was added. This portion covered such topics as civilian morale, German propaganda, the IWW, pacifism, the Sinn Fein, Nonpartisan League, Mexican labor, and black unrest. In the fall of

43. These reports make up a considerable portion of the MI Microfilm files; for a sample, see reel 1, p. 156.

44. MI4's "Weekly Situation Surveys" are scattered throughout the MI Microfilm collection. State Department and Bureau of Investigation records in the National Archives have a fairly complete set filed in order. Portions of these, with appropriate archival references, are in Surveillance of Afro-Americans Microfilm, reel 13, pp. 117–299, and reel 17, pp. 351–818.

1918 consecutive pagination was begun in a sophisticated printed format. Domestic coverage ended in early 1919 for reasons soon to be obvious.[45]

Another person high in the Wilson administration, and very familiar with Military Intelligence, was George Creel, powerful head of the Committee on Public Information. The furor over his preface to *Two Thousand Questions* made him vulnerable to the charge of being soft on the Germans, and his connections with leftist writers such as Lincoln Steffens made him at least a parlor red. Creel found working with the intelligence community on the Censorship Board very difficult, recalling that his relations with all the agencies, including the army, were "bitter to the breaking point." Creel made that statement in 1939, when he also recounted his opposition to the American Protective League: "Made up of waiters, bus boys, taxi drivers and clerks, it was an outrageous thing that I attacked openly and repeatedly as a lot of transom peepers and keyhole listeners." Creel very much resented the attacks on him, and his commitment to civil liberties revived after the war emergency. Twenty years after the Armistice he said that "Attorney General Gregory was a vicious old reactionary who spent most of his time trying to prove that I myself, and all my associates were pacifists, pro-Germans, and Bolsheviks." When Creel saw his own dossier compiled by Military Intelligence, he found it "a foot thick and accused me of every treason."[46]

It is certainly no exaggeration to say that Creel and Van Deman did not get along. Finally, to put an end to rumors about treason on his staff, the newsman asked Van Deman to conduct a full investigation of the Committee on Public Information. The result was a fifty-six-page report from Military Intelligence which questioned the loyalty of fourteen members of Creel's staff. A later scholarly examination of the report found that it "revealed that semi-literacy, and that fanatical credulity toward idle rumor and malicious slander, so distressingly characteristic of a certain class of the war-time agents of the Military Intelligence." Creel refused to accept these findings, refuting them in a long report to Churchill in July 1918. He did admit that one of his staff, dismissed before the

45. The weekly intelligence summaries have been published in facsimile form under the title *United States Military Intelligence, 1917–1927*, 30 vols. (New York: Garland, 1978). Accompanied by Richard D. Challener's thorough introductions for each volume, these reports should be of interest to international scholars and anyone concerned with the military mind. There is no doubt that Secretary Baker saw these reports; they were among his papers donated by his estate to the Western Reserve Historical Society in Cleveland, where they are filed as "U.S. War Department, Intelligence Reports, 1917–1921, MS 3490."

46. The quotations from Creel are in Bean, "Creel and His Critics," pp. 84, 236.

investigation, had been "a violent pro-German." This was the historian Hendrick W. Van Loon, not the real threat Van Deman had found: former *Collier's* editor Edgar G. Sisson. A registered Republican, Sisson had voted Progressive in 1912 and 1916, but his real mistake was visiting Russia in late 1917. Overlooking the facts that the president had authorized the trip and that Sisson had come away violently opposed to Lenin's revolution, Military Intelligence seemed to suspect anyone who had any contact with the Bolsheviks.[47] Van Deman would have been aghast, and his worst suspicions confirmed, had he known that during his investigation, Creel had taken the liberty of showing Lincoln Steffens the reports on him generated by Military Intelligence. Steffens was also close to Wilson's adviser Colonel Edward M. House, whose politics and connections also worried Military Intelligence.[48]

There is no evidence that any part of the Wilson administration significantly retarded the expansion of Military Intelligence. There were moments of heated debate and times when critics had to be accommodated. Creel, for all his later protestations, never took on Van Deman directly. Even the attorney general's attempt to restrain the army seems to have been motivated as much by a desire to protect his own territory as to defend a radical's civil liberties. Secretary of War Baker saw the abuses only as isolated, and correctable, incidents. When the war ended, the program Van Deman had set up eighteen months earlier was just reaching its potential. In that period, he and his associates had honed their spying skills, using them in a shadow war against draft resisters, the ıww, and black Americans. Those special targets of the Negative Branch deserve special attention.

47. The analysis of MI's report on the Committee on Public Information is in ibid., pp. 236–37. See also Will Irwin to Churchill, July 10, 1918, Record Group 165, MID, 138–18/1, National Archives. On MI and Sisson, see Vaughn, *Holding Fast*, pp. 195, 252; on Sisson's trip to Russia and his claim that the Germans had underwritten the Bolshevik revolution, see Polenberg, *Fighting Faiths*, pp. 108–9. Sisson's famous documents supporting his claim of German influence are appended to his *One Hundred Red Days: A Personal Chronicle of the Bolshevik Revolution* (New Haven: Yale University Press, 1931). For the finding that the documents were false, see George F. Kennan, "The Sisson Documents," *Journal of Modern History* 28 (June 1956): 130–54. See also Paul A. Goble, "Sisson Documents," in Joseph L. Wieczynski, ed., *The Modern Encyclopedia of Russian and Soviet History*, vol. 35 (Gulf Breeze, Fla.: Academic International Press, 1983), pp. 150–52. For more on Van Loon, see Roy Talbert, Jr., *FDR's Utopian: Arthur Morgan of the TVA* (Jackson: University Press of Mississippi, 1987), p. 45.

48. Steffens to House, May 8, 1918, in Winter and Hicks, eds., *Letters of Steffens*, 1:426–27.

CHAPTER 5

The War Resisters

B ack-to-the-landers and subsistence farming advocates of the early 1970s accepted the word of Scott Nearing as gospel. The simple creed he had expressed in *Living the Good Life* seemed all naturalness and light. More than fifty years earlier, Nearing was regarded by patriotic Americans as a dangerous fanatic preaching the evil message of socialism and pacifism. Although he was one of the few radical leaders of the period who did not serve time in jail, Military Intelligence and the other federal agencies hounded him unmercifully.

Nearing, who had a Ph.D. degree in economics, was in trouble before the United States entered the war. His socialism and reform efforts got him fired from the University of Pennsylvania in 1915 and from the University of Toledo in 1917. The Department of Justice had stenographers attending his speeches as early as March 1916. Van Deman's interest centered around Nearing's association with the Rand School of Social Science in New York and the People's Council of America for Peace and Democracy, of which he was executive chairman. Although some progressives, such as Stanford University's chancellor, David Starr Jordan, were involved in the council, it was dominated by left-wingers. The organizing committee included well-known Socialists Max Eastman, Morris Hillquit, Algernon Lee, Eugene V. Debs, and Victor Berger. The council's crime was pacifism.[1]

---

1. Randolph Boehm, ed., *U.S. Military Intelligence Reports: Surveillance of Radicals in the United States, 1917–1941* (Frederick, Md.: University Publications of America, 1984), reel 4, pp. 742, 1007, reel 5, p. 29 (hereafter cited as MI Microfilm). For material on Nearing, see his *The Making of a Radical: A Political Autobiography* (New York: Harper & Row, 1972); and Stephen J. Whitfield, *Scott Nearing: Apostle of American Radicalism* (New York: Columbia University Press, 1974). See also the entry on Nearing in Bernard K. Johnpoll and Harvey Klehr, eds., *Biographical Dictionary of the American Left* (New York: Greenwood Press, 1986), pp. 289–90. Other information is in U.S. Senate, Report and Hearings of the Subcommittee on the Judiciary, 65th Cong., 1st sess., Document no. 62, *Brewing and Liquor Interests and German and Bolshevik Propaganda*, 3 vols. (Washington, D.C.: U.S. Government Printing Office, 1919), 2:2715; H. C. Peterson and Gilbert C. Fite, *Opponents of War, 1917–1918* (Seattle: University of Washington Press, 1957), pp. 184–85; John W. Chambers II, *To Raise an Army: The Draft Comes to Modern America* (New York: Free Press, 1987), p. 207; and Donald O. Johnson, *The Challenge to American Freedoms: World War I and the Rise of the American Civil Liberties Union* (Lexington: University of Kentucky Press, 1963), p. 22.

Pacifists, an official Military Intelligence publication said, were "so played upon by German agents" and "more or less unwittingly recruited" by them as to represent a "dangerous element."[2] The People's Council was formed in early August 1917, and before the month was out Biddle in New York knew about it. As it happened, in setting up its office the council hired a stenographer who had little stomach for its disgusting pacifism. She promptly reported it to the Department of Justice, which asked her to stay on as an informant. Justice included Biddle from the beginning, and for the three weeks their source remained in place they got a bird's-eye view of the formation of the council.[3]

Van Deman had only to hear that Louis P. Lochner was in the inner circles, as executive secretary, of the People's Council to know this organization was trouble. In mid-August he reminded Bielaski of the Bureau of Investigation that Lochner had been on Henry Ford's unsuccessful Peace Ship and was a "very active peace propagandist." Van Deman, still short of investigators at this early date, urged Bielaski to find out more about the Ford effort and to look for German funds going to Lochner, closing with a plea that sounded more like an order: "Will not your office undertake this at once?"[4] One result was a search by federal agents of Nearing's home, allowing him to claim that in the summer of 1917 he received the "first domiciliary raid of the war."[5] Biddle continued to observe the group's New York headquarters closely and, using his banking connection, was able to secure the council's canceled checks. By fall the army had Nearing and his fellow pacifists well covered.[6]

Department of Justice reports on Nearing carried the notation "Alleged German Suspect," and those of Military Intelligence, in completing the "offense charged" section, accused him of "Neutrality." Because Nearing's group was composed of "reformers of the intellectual and idealist type," Marlborough Churchill regarded it as "the more dangerous in their propaganda."[7] Under Churchill, Military Intelligence continued its persecution of the People's Council. Nearing was indicted by a federal grand jury in 1918 for obstructing the draft with an antiwar pamphlet *The Great Madness,* published by the American Socialist Society of the Rand School. The trial, which did not take place until after

2. U.S. Army, General Staff, Military Intelligence Division, *The Functions of the Military Intelligence Division, U.S. General Staff* (Washington, D.C.: Military Intelligence Division, 1918), p. 16.
3. Biddle to Van Deman, August 29, 1917, MI Microfilm, reel 2, p. 55.
4. Van Deman to Bielaski, August 17, 1917, ibid., reel 4, p. 804.
5. Nearing, *Making of a Radical,* pp. 109–10.
6. Biddle to Van Deman, September 22, 1917, MI Microfilm, reel 4, p. 996.
7. Churchill to intelligence officer, Boston, July 30, 1918, ibid., reel 5, p. 243.

the war, produced the odd result, after thirty hours of jury deliberation, of finding Nearing innocent but fining the publisher $3,000. The army used sterner measures with his California colleague William Short, a Unitarian minister and chairman of the People's Council in San Francisco.

The western group first came to Van Deman's attention in late 1917, when Short sponsored a trip by Nearing to the Pacific Coast. The educator and pacifist took a train across the country, making stops for speeches and getting into trouble with local authorities, especially in Minnesota. In San Francisco, however, the police forced cancellation of the planned meetings, and on November 22 they raided the council's offices. It seems likely that Military Intelligence participated in this raid because the seized materials were taken directly to army headquarters.[8] That, however, was only the beginning. Dismayed by the leisurely pace with which the federal grand jury was deliberating the fate of Short and his staff, Van Deman set in motion, and Churchill completed, a plan to bring this pacifist under military jurisdiction.

As a Unitarian minister, Short had an automatic exemption from the draft, Class 5, Division B. Yet he could hardly be a real minister, Van Deman reasoned, because he was working for the People's Council, which the army devoutly believed to be an organization of draft dodgers connected to the IWW. Churchill summed up the case against Short: "He has been active in opposing the draft, also in connection with the defense of one Thomas Mooney . . . and has made himself generally obnoxious." A visit by one of Churchill's officers to Short's draft board was all it took to change his status to Class 1, Division A, cannon fodder. With the unusual World War I provision that considered a draftee in the military upon receipt of the induction notice, Short had to make a decision fast. He appealed his reclassification, did not appear for induction, and was arrested by the army as a deserter.[9]

In the meantime, Military Intelligence raided the council's San Francisco office once more, this time without the company of the local police or benefit of a search warrant. With the aid of "special agent Ignatius McCarthy of the Department of Labor," army operatives made their surreptitious entry into the office. The records they found included a national membership list and three notebooks in a mysterious short-

8. The largest file on the People's Council is ibid., reel 5, pp. 1–357. See p. 33 for a description of the seized material.

9. The charge against Short was later reduced to draft evasion (ibid., reel 2, p. 443; reel 5, p. 261). For a verbatim account of Short's interrogation at Camp Lewis, see reel 5, pp. 298–309. He was released in early 1919.

hand. In an attempt to hide the raid, the agents "photo-stated" the notebooks and returned the originals to their proper place. Churchill wanted the actual documents, however, and he sent his men on yet another raid. This time the council staff had anticipated them, and no useful materials, especially nothing that would help translate the annoying shorthand, were found. Agent C–351 had to report that he was "unable to confiscate any letters, as the officers of the Council realizing that they are under surveillance were careful not to leave anything about." The civil authorities were apparently a bit concerned about Churchill's high-handed methods, and in September he was told that a search order could be issued only if he stated that he had evidence showing a violation of the Espionage Act. He gladly made this statement, but at the war's end Churchill had not found the conspiracy he imagined.[10]

Short was not the only minister on the West Coast who concerned Van Deman. He was very interested in the Conference of Christian Pacifists of California, and he caused a thorough investigation by the bureau into the Reverend Father Arch Perin of the Episcopal church in San Francisco. Two women of that city were spreading the gossip, picked up by army agents C–302 and U–3–C, that Perin had said he "would neither hang nor allow to be hung an American Flag in or on his Church and would hang a RED ONE first."[11] Other peace organizations carefully monitored by the intelligence community included the Women's International League for Peace and Freedom, founded by Jane Addams in 1915, and the more radical No-Conscription League headed by anarchists Emma Goldman and Alexander Berkman before they were put away for obstructing the draft.[12] Van Deman continued to worry about Goldman, noting in the spring of 1918 that despite her confinement and the banning of her publication, *Mother Earth*, from the mail, she had not ceased her pernicious work. "It might be well," he told her warden, "to place greater restrictions upon her."[13] Military Intelligence never hesitated to advise other agencies, at any level. Shortly after assuming command, Churchill wrote the chief of the U.S. Weather Bureau that one of his employees in Huron, South Dakota, was an IWW member and

10. Ibid., reel 5, pp. 111, 143, 210.

11. All capital letters are in the original, ibid., reel 2, p. 484. MI's interest in black churches and ministers is covered in Chapter 7.

12. Chambers, *To Raise an Army*, p. 207. Richard Drinnon, in *Rebel in Paradise: A Biography of Emma Goldman* (Chicago: University of Chicago Press, 1961), p. 186, calls the No-Conscription League " the nerve center of the resistance to the draft."

13. Van Deman to warden, Federal Penitentiary, Atlanta, April 9, 1918, MI Microfilm, reel 6, p. 173.

"extremely disloyal and unpatriotic." The chief weatherman responded that he had already fired the Wobbly.[14]

Many Americans no doubt agreed with Van Deman's early June 1917 assessment that antidraft agitation "is noted throughout the United States." Socialist propaganda, he reported, preached "continuous active public opposition to war," along with protesting against war taxes and bonds.[15] There was, moreover, alarming antidraft activity in rural areas, where people did not want their sons sent to a foreign war. The most famous of these generally local incidents was the "Green Corn Rebellion" in the Southwest, primarily Oklahoma, where agrarian socialism and traditional animosity to federal revenue agents led to armed resistance and several firefights in the summer of 1917. By the fall, local authorities had crushed that movement.[16]

Such difficulties were compounded by another group whose avowed purpose was to give aid and counsel to war resisters: the National Civil Liberties Bureau (NCLB), which changed its name to the American Civil Liberties Union (ACLU) after the war. Growing out of the American Union Against Militarism, an essentially progressive group, the NCLB was formed as a legal aid society in the spring of 1917, and by the summer it was complaining to President Wilson that a peace parade in Boston had been broken up by soldiers and sailors. In the fall, to separate the antiwar campaign from the cause of civil liberties for draft objectors, the NCLB was given an independent status.[17]

The ACLU has always enjoyed a reputation as a liberal agency, yet in its infancy it was downright radical. In those early years all its clients, a study has revealed, were from the left: "conscientious objectors, socialists, anarchists, communists, syndicalists, and labor unions." The major figure in the movement was Roger Nash Baldwin, a wealthy Mayflower descendant with a Harvard degree in anthropology, who had worked in a settlement house in St. Louis. He was also a Socialist, a

14. Churchill to C.F. Marvin, July 31, 1918, ibid., pp. 24, 92.
15. Richard D. Challener, ed., *United States Military Intelligence, 1919–1927*, 30 vols. (New York: Garland, 1978), *Weekly Intelligence Summary*, June 9, 1917, in vol. 1 (no consecutive pagination for the early issues).
16. James R. Green, *Grass-Roots Socialism: Radical Movements in the Southwest, 1895–1943* (Baton Rouge: Louisiana State University Press, 1978), pp. 354–72. See also "Uncle Sam's Little War in the Arkansas Ozarks," in Peter Karsten, ed., *The Military in America, from the Colonial Era to the Present* (New York: Free Press, 1980), pp. 297–300.
17. Lillian D. Wald et al. to Wilson, August 10, 1917, in Arthur S. Link et al., eds., *Papers of Woodrow Wilson*, vol. 43 (Princeton: Princeton University Press, 1983), pp. 420–24; Chambers, *To Raise an Army*, p. 206; Johnson, *Challenge to American Freedoms*, p. 24.

conscientious objector, and an idealist who thought he could deal rationally with Ralph Van Deman and Nicholas Biddle.[18]

By early 1918, Van Deman had identified Baldwin as the ringleader of a seditious group encouraging resistance to the war. He set Biddle in New York, headquarters of the NCLB, on Baldwin's trail. Biddle's chief assistant on the case was Grant Squires, Madison Avenue attorney, friend of Woodrow Wilson, and burglar. In a desire to be straightforward with the authorities, Baldwin had made an overture, about March 1, by visiting Biddle in his office and providing a review of the aims and purposes of the NCLB. Such a contact by one who was clearly a tool of the Germans only whetted the army's appetite, and on the night of March 6, Biddle and Squires broke into Baldwin's office, stealing publications they found openly displayed. Ten days later Squires had an official interview with Baldwin, during which the latter offered copies of the very documents that had been purloined.[19]

Baldwin erred in taking Secretary of War Baker at his word regarding his promise of fair treatment for conscientious objectors and in failing to understand that policy made at the top is not always implemented in the field.[20] Since he had first approached Biddle and afterward had voluntarily given him all his files, Baldwin persisted in thinking he deserved some cooperation. "If any serious issue is involved, not susceptible of easy adjustment," he told Biddle, "we shall want to take it up with Col. Van Deman." His openness must have astounded the cynics of negative intelligence when he wrote: "As it is important to us to secure promptly the return of the only copy of our minutes we have, I will ask you to be good enough to expedite this inquiry,—not meaning of course to urge any such haste as would inconvenience you in learning every detail of our work. You appreciate that we do not want misunderstanding and further opportunity for criticism a day longer than is absolutely necessary."[21]

18. Johnson, *Challenge to American Freedoms*, p. vi. For Baldwin's background, see pp. 9–14.

19. On the burglary of Baldwin's office, see Grant Squires to Nicholas Biddle, March 16, 1918, MI Microfilm, reel 9, pp. 45–47; and office of MI, New York, to chief of MI, March 22, 1918, pp. 70–71. Military Intelligence interrogated Baldwin several times in March and again in August 1918. For transcripts, see ibid., pp. 9–33, 50–56.

20. Felix Frankfurter advised Baker on the treatment of conscientious objectors in a September 18, 1917, memorandum in Papers of Newton D. Baker, reel 1, pp. 404–6, Manuscript Division, Library of Congress. For Baldwin's negotiations with the office of the secretary of war, see Samuel Walker, *In Defense of American Liberties: A History of the ACLU* (New York: Oxford University Press, 1990), pp. 37–38.

21. Baldwin to Biddle, March 21, 1918, MI Microfilm, reel 9, p. 72.

Understanding between Military Intelligence and a complete civil libertarian such as Baldwin was impossible. From Baldwin's perspective, the NCLB's desire to advise war resisters of their rights and to protect them from unfair treatment was entirely legal, and he felt, from conversations with Keppel in the office of the secretary of war, that the Wilson administration understood. He was prepared to negotiate his methods of making his advice available so as not to persuade into conscientious objection those who otherwise would have fought. He also offered all his publications for review by Military Intelligence. In answer to the charge that his operation was funded by the Germans, he turned over his financial records and challenged Van Deman's accountants to find even $500 from German sources. For his part, Baker never felt he let Baldwin down. After the war, he reported to President Wilson that he was proud of his record in handling conscientious objectors. Had he had the full cooperation of certain camp commanders who failed to adhere to the policy to avoid "all cruel and brutal treatment," he said, he could have reduced even further the number who refused noncombatant service and had to be court-martialed. Even so, he believed the 504 military trials of war resisters in the American army compared favorably to the nearly 6,000 imprisoned by the British. [22]

The army's objections, as summarized by Biddle, were that the NCLB was still associated in the public's mind with the clearly pacifist American Union against Militarism and that Baldwin's work created additional objectors, made bold by the promise of help. Biddle also felt that the army could not tolerate Baldwin's loud complaints about the harsh treatment given objectors in the military camps. Biddle's initial assessment of Baldwin and his group's work became the official view of Military Intelligence: "that this organization serves no good purpose and that their activities should be stopped." [23] Although Military Intelligence kept Baldwin under close surveillance, it is unlikely that Secretary Baker would have allowed any direct move against him. Baldwin's own conscience was his undoing: when he received his draft notice he announced his refusal to serve and was sentenced to a year in prison on October 30, 1918. With time off for good behavior, Baldwin was released on June 19, 1919. The last of his fellow objectors got out on

22. Baker to Woodrow Wilson, July 1, 1919, Baker Papers, reel 9, pp. 156–57.
23. Office of MI, New York, to chief of MI, March 18, 1918, MI Microfilm, reel 9, pp. 76–77. MI's file on Baldwin is pp. 1–77. See also Walter Nelles, *A Liberal in Wartime: The Education of Albert De Silver* (New York: Norton, 1940), p. 146; Johnson, *Challenge to American Liberties*, p. 34; and Walker, *In Defense of American Liberties*, pp. 37–38.

November 27, 1920, just over two years after the conclusion of the war.[24]

Radical agitators who were drafted into the army presented another problem. Local intelligence officers had the responsibility to monitor these individuals and to crush their propaganda. In May 1918 the intelligence office at Camp Lewis, Washington, reported on a typical case, that of Private Edward F. Bassett, late of Butte, Montana, and a "notorious labor agitator who talks but doesn't work." Bassett had tried to avoid military service, claiming his father as a dependent. When this request was denied, Bassett had to report, along with four hundred others, to the train station for transportation to camp. At the depot he attempted to make a speech calling for a democratic army with elected officers. Camp Lewis knew it had a problem and promised Washington in a "Special Weekly Counter-Espionage Report" that Bassett "will be watched by agents of this office."[25]

Bassett typified two characteristics feared by public opinion and the government bureaucracy: he was a radical and a slacker. The latter term, peculiar to World War I, did not necessarily imply any ideology but referred instead to men of draft age who were neither in military service nor otherwise occupied in the war effort: they were slack. Official action intensified in the summer of 1918 when, after an amendment to the draft law, the army provost marshal issued his "Work or Fight" order by which young men "found to be idlers or engaged in non-productive occupations or employments" could lose their deferred classifications.[26] The slacker might have failed to register for the draft, in which case he would have no classification card, or he might have lied in filling out his draft questionnaire, receiving a fraudulent classification. The latter crime required a fairly sophisticated investigation to determine, for example, whether a son was in fact the sole support of his parents. Subjects for such investigations were generally identified from the tips of neighbors who, as one report put it, "have sons in the army and who think the subject should be made to do his duty."[27]

24. Johnson, *Challenge to American Liberties*, pp. 44–48, 53; Chambers, *To Raise an Army*, p. 218; Walker, *In Defense of American Liberties*, pp. 40–41. Baldwin headed the ACLU until 1950 and died in 1981.

25. Intelligence office, Camp Lewis, to chief of MI, May 31, 1918, MI Microfilm, reel 2, p. 393.

26. The amendment and the "Work or Fight" order are in Record Group 165, entry no. 104, Plant Protection Section, General Correspondence, "Department of Justice File," National Archives, Suitland Records Center.

27. Edmund Leigh, Memorandum on Rudolph Graf, July 24, 1918, MI Microfilm, reel

The easiest way to find delinquents was simply to stop them on the street and demand that they produce proper draft registration documents. Such a dragnet procedure, however, required considerable manpower, and in early 1918 the army turned to the American Protective League for aid.[28] Out of this request, endorsed by the attorney general, came the famous "slacker drives" of 1918. The first roundup of slackers occurred in Minneapolis in late March, when a hundred men were arrested by APL agents deputized by local police. Another raid came in May in Philadelphia, when the APL moved against two roadhouses selling liquor to soldiers. Later the APL in that city concentrated on prizefights, where hundreds of indolent young men could be found. By the summer, there were large drives in most major cities. In July in Chicago, for example, some 10,000 APL agents questioned 150,000 men and arrested 16,000 for failure to produce their draft cards.

The most notorious drives, however, came in September in the New York area. Here the military was heavily involved, and, incidentally, the secretary of war was away on his second secret trip to France. Military facilities were used as holding areas for the thousands detained, and an army intelligence officer accompanied each APL team on its sweep. Official policy required that arrests should be made only by the police, but the situation got out of hand, and thousands of loyal citizens were treated roughly by soldiers, sailors, and APL vigilantes.[29] The *New York World* estimated that fifty thousand men had been detained and called the "dragonade" a "monstrous invasion of human rights." The raids spilled into northern New Jersey, where Military Intelligence was very active in taking two thousand slackers.[30] United States Senator William M. Calder of New York reported to his colleagues: "In one place I saw a street car stopped and an armed sailor go into the car and take men out of it, in some cases where they were escorting ladies. Men were stopped in the street. They were taken out of their places of business and crowded into vans, perhaps 50 or 60 packed in like sardines, and sent to the police

7, pp. 113–14.

28. The army provost marshal general's letter to the APL, dated February 7, 1918, is reprinted in the league's organ the *Spy Glass*, October 19, 1918, available in Record Group 65, Bureau of Investigation, APL, box 1, National Archives.

29. The best description of the several slacker drives is in Joan M. Jensen, *The Price of Vigilance* (Chicago: Rand McNally, 1968), pp. 189–218; the account of the Philadelphia raids is in Emerson Hough, *The Web* (Chicago: Reilly and Lee, 1919), pp. 216–17.

30. *New York World*, September 5, 1918; David J. Goldberg, *Tale of Three Cities: Labor Organization and Protest in Paterson, Passaic, and Lawrence, 1916–1921* (New Brunswick: Rutgers University Press, 1989), p. 15.

station houses." Senator Hiram W. Johnson of California was especially incensed: "Where is it that forced along with a sergeant behind him the innocent citizen marches and gets his 'first taste of discipline,' the citizen not arrested by writ, not indeed taken into custody because of aught he has done? Why, it is in the most populous city of the great democracy of the world that behind this citizen strides a sergeant with a bayonet and says, 'Hold up there! Hip, hip, hip!'"[31]

Numerous stories of individual mistreatment soon appeared. One prominent New Yorker, whose name was withheld when Senator Calder read his letter into the record, was having dinner with a young woman in a Brooklyn restaurant when the military police appeared and demanded to see his draft card. He had his business card, his personal card, and his voter registration card, but the draft board had never sent him his papers. Off he went to the Brooklyn station house, where from ten in the evening he stood without food or water until three in the morning, when he was marched over to the Twenty-third Regiment's armory. Again, "neither chairs, drinking water, nor any comforts were provided." Finally, at 4:30 A.M., his partner found him and arranged his release. The next morning he promptly obtained his card, and when he returned to the armory to prove his loyalty he found "a great many unfortunates who were not lucky enough to get off as I had." "In instance after instance," he reported to his senator, "men like myself were refused the use of a telephone to call up their homes; men with families of children were kept there like culprits." This man had two brothers in the military as volunteers, "and it is very hard," he concluded, "to be jeered at on the streets and insulted by local and Government officials, to be dragged and driven from one point to another, when one is entirely innocent, and especially when one has done everything he could to comply with the law and stands ready to serve his country in every way. I have worked on liberty loans and I have done everything I could consistently to help my country, and this is what I get for it."[32]

The notoriety surrounding the New York arrests caught President Wilson's attention, and he ordered the attorney general to make an investigation. The actual inquiry was conducted by John Lord O'Brian, and Gregory's report to the president on September 9, 1918, was cautious. Though he blamed the military, citing an August letter from the secretary of war complaining about the high number of draft delinquents

31. *Congressional Record*, September 5, 1918, 65th Cong., 2d sess., 56:9977–78.
32. Unidentified to William M. Calder, September 5, 1918, ibid., September 6, 1918, p. 10064. For the Senate debate, see pp. 9976–86, 10063–70. See also *New York Times*, September 6–8, 1918.

and requesting assistance from the Department of Justice, he explained that "running down individual cases obviously would have been futile" so "some form of dragnet . . . was absolutely essential." Gregory maintained that his department had never envisioned that either the APL or the military would actually make arrests, only that they would assist in the detention and investigative process. The attorney general took "full and entire responsibility" for the program, but he rebuked the Bureau of Investigation for encouraging both the military and the APL to assume an illegal arrest power. "Besides being unlawful," he told the president, their use "in making arrests was ill-judged, as such men are not generally fitted by training or experience to exercise the discretion required in the circumstances."[33]

This official explanation by the nation's chief law officer found an extenuating circumstance in the fact that the military and APL volunteers "were led into this breach of authority by excess of zeal for the public good."[34] The matter essentially ended there. After an initially stormy debate, the Senate shelved a proposal to have the Military Affairs Committee investigate the "Prussianism" obvious in the slacker drives.[35] The domestic intelligence programs of the Department of Justice, the military, and the APL continued unabated. In fact, Gregory wrote his civilian organization on September 21 offering praise and assurance that "the patriotic and self-sacrificing spirit of its members has won my warmest admiration."[36] Raids by local APL units continued even beyond the end of the war on November 11. As one unit history put it, "having its hand well skilled by this time, the A.P.L. went on vice raids." This fascinating turn, indicative of its moral, progressive base, was most obvious in Philadelphia, San Diego, and New Orleans, where "a general cleaning up" occurred. In Louisiana the APL established a home for wayward girls, and in California it fought vice and bootlegging.[37]

Military Intelligence escaped public censure for its significant role in the New York sweep. Although the *New York Times* had reported the involvement of the "Military Intelligence Bureau," it was the provost marshal, in charge of the draft, and the Justice Department, in charge of the APL, that received the brunt of the criticism.[38] Military Intel-

33. Attorney General Gregory's letter to President Wilson, in *New York Times*, September 12, 1918.

34. Ibid.

35. *New York Times*, September 7, 1918.

36. Gregory's September 21, 1918, letter to the APL is printed in the *Spy Glass* of the same date, available in box 12 of the APL papers in the Bureau of Investigation files.

37. Hough, *The Web*, pp. 216–17, 328–31, 354.

38. *New York Times*, September 6, 1918.

ligence's promotion of unlawful arrests of civilians was obvious to the attorney general, however, and only a few days later he entered into a debate with the secretary of war over the army's similar actions in Butte, Montana, against the IWW. Perhaps his attack on the army was all the more bitter because of the recent complaints directed at his own operations. Yet the attorney general's condemnation of such arrests does sound a bit hollow when one considers that in the famous *Abrams* case, which got under way in New York shortly after the slacker raids, the Department of Justice made no complaint whatever in a matter that began with an arrest by the Corps of Intelligence Police.

Jacob Abrams was one member of a small, impoverished group of Russian aliens who shared a decrepit third-floor apartment on East 104th Street. At another location, these anarchists (plus one Socialist) maintained a small printing operation in a basement. In August 1918 their cause became a protest against the U.S. military intervention in Siberia, just then beginning. They sacrificed all their money to print five thousand copies each of two leaflets: one in English, entitled *The Hypocrisy of the United States and Her Allies*, and the other in Yiddish, headed *Workers—Wake Up*. The first offering attacked President Wilson for appearing to be a friend of Russia while planning "to crush the Russian Revolution." "His shameful, cowardly silence about the intervention in Russia," the flier continued, "reveals the hypocrisy of the plutocratic gang in Washington and vicinity." It ended with a call for worker solidarity against capitalism and for the Bolsheviks. The leaflet in Yiddish was more shrill, urging a general strike to "spit in the face of the false, hypocritic, military propaganda which has fooled you so relentlessly."[39]

Their method of distribution was to throw the leaflets from rooftops into the streets below in working-class neighborhoods or to hand them out at radical meetings. They had distributed most of the leaflets by August 23, 1918, when on that early morning one of their members was busily dispersing them from a fourth-floor hat factory at the corner of Houston and Crosby. Concerned citizens brought copies of the offensive material to the police station, where they were reviewed by a Military Intelligence officer. He dispatched two intelligence police sergeants, who quickly captured the lone propagandist. During an interrogation by Biddle and his men, he confessed the location of his co-conspirators, and there Military Intelligence collared six Russian aliens.

39. The translation of the Yiddish document introduced into court (and quoted here) has been challenged by Richard Polenberg in *Fighting Faiths: The Abrams Case, the Supreme Court, and Free Speech* (New York: Viking, 1987), pp. 52–55.

Abrams, who by virtue of the alphabet gave his name to the case, was at twenty-nine the oldest; Mollie Steimer, the one woman in the group, was the youngest, at twenty-one. After making the arrests, the intelligence police took their captives to the police station, where they were interrogated, in the presence of the sergeants, and charged with a violation of the Sedition Act. The Justice Department made a number of interesting decisions in this case. First, it did not refuse to prosecute because the arrests were performed by the military, as it had done in Butte. Second, it chose to apply the Sedition Act even though the United States was not at war with Russia. It appears that this last decision was made on the basis that the Yiddish leaflet urged "workers in ammunition factories" to strike. The brief October trial is generally regarded as having turned more on the political beliefs of the defendants than on any actual threat they represented to the nation's ability to prosecute the war just ending in Europe. Abrams and two others were given sentences ranging from three to twenty years. Mollie Steimer drew fifteen. It took a year for the appeal to reach the Supreme Court, which upheld the decision.

It was at the Supreme Court, however, that the case gained its notoriety. Rather than just another example of wartime hysteria, the *Abrams* case became the classic statement of the "clear and present danger" concept. Only Justices Oliver Wendell Holmes and Louis D. Brandeis dissented, and it was Holmes's minority opinion that became one of the great statements on First Amendment rights. Although the jurist had used the danger test in the earlier *Schenck* decision, when he had upheld the conviction of Charles T. Schenck for writing a leaflet urging opposition to the draft, Holmes did not see anything clear and present about the threat posed by the Abrams group. The lesson learned, apart from the injustice done the defendants, was that there was little threat, as a famous civil libertarian has said, from "the silly, futile circulars of five obscure and isolated young aliens . . . who hatched their wild scheme in a garret, and carried it out in a cellar." [40]

Yet to Military Intelligence, the Justice Department, a jury, and the majority of the Supreme Court justices, these foreigners did present a danger. In 1918 there was fear everywhere, and Van Deman, Churchill,

40. There is a considerable body of work on the *Abrams* case, but Polenberg's *Fighting Faiths* is the most recent and comprehensive. The garret and cellar comment was made by long-time civil liberties advocate Zechariah Chafee, Jr., in his *Free Speech in the U.S.* (New York: Atheneum, 1969), p. 140. In early 1921, Wilson commuted the sentences to deportation. Abrams was allowed back into the United States for medical treatment in 1952 and died the following year. Mollie Steimer died in Mexico in 1980.

and the men under them were not prepared to argue the legal or moral merits of the war on the home front. Before the war was over, the army had reached a frenzy of negative intelligence paranoia. The Propaganda Section, in many ways the most negative-minded of the Negative Branch, began in October to collect information on "professors in schools, academies, etc., whose loyalty, activities, writings, etc., are under suspicion."[41] Naval Intelligence shared this paranoia, conducting a thorough investigation, including the interception of mail, of the German University League in New York. In that city, the navy placed John Reed under steady surveillance and investigated the IWW whenever possible. At the Charleston shipyard Naval Intelligence forced out a young woman seditious enough to demand equal pay for equal work. Like the army, Naval Intelligence also detained suspects when it seemed necessary. One particular bit of paranoia the two services shared was anti-Semitism. As its best history says, Naval Intelligence became "obsessed with pursuing American Jews."[42]

Military Intelligence's most dedicated anti-Semite was Agent B–1, who started reporting to the New York office in the summer of 1918. B–1 made the average negative intelligence officer seem almost normal; he envisioned ever so plainly "the International German Jewish gang, aiming at world social revolution." B–1's mission was equally clear:

> The aim of this report is to emphasize the necessity of confining by no means the intelligence work at the present time to the Bolsheviki or the I.W.W. Movement as such. Every shade of the socialistic movement, whether disguised under the form of trade unionism or under the pink shirt of the A.F.L. . . . must be watched, must be considered as extremely suspicious to the cause of humanity and civilization, must be the object of the utmost attention of the intelligence staffs, especially now when the whole civilization is on the verge of tottering into the flames of anarchy.[43]

Not only were B–1's reports sent to Washington, but after the war, when Churchill and Van Deman were at the peace conference, they were taken to Paris. B–1's masterpiece was a lengthy analysis entitled

41. J.S. Buhler, memorandum for Major Brown, October 18, 1918, Record Group 165, MID, 10560–172/1, National Archives.

42. Jeffrey M. Dorwart, *The Office of Naval Intelligence: The Birth of America's First Intelligence Agency, 1865–1918* (Annapolis: Naval Institute Press, 1979), pp. 119–20. For the German University League, see Record Group 38, ONI, "CAP" file, box 2, National Archives. For Naval Intelligence's investigation of businessmen thought to be cheating on government contracts, see "Suspect" file, box 8, ibid.

43. The B–1 file is in MI Microfilm, reel 12; see esp. pp. 9–96, 125–29; the quotation is in "Report 8," p. 41.

"Bolshevism and Judaism," which put Jewish bankers in cahoots with Lenin.[44] Before leaving for France, Churchill assigned his staff the task of following up on B–1's theories, noting that the agent was "a special confidential source," whose reports he had found "useful as a means of checking against reports on similar subjects received through our regular channels."[45] Despite the general's endorsement, the staff was remarkably frank in its criticism. The Negative Branch's legal officer found B–1's theories "a jumble of opinions formed by an ill formed, suspicious and biased individual."[46] Captain Carlton J. H. Hayes, a prominent scholar in the field of modern European studies, lodged a "vehement protest" against B–1's belief that the entire labor movement was radical. Hayes noted that "trade unionism is legal, not illegal," and launched into a spirited defense of the American Federation of Labor. He concluded that B–1's anti-Semitism was "only another sign of the raving tendency of a fanatical if not of a disordered brain."[47] The Negative Branch wanted to bring in B–1 for examination and analysis. The person on the hot seat was Colonel John M. Dunn, acting director of Military Intelligence while Churchill was in Paris. In a memorandum for the chief of the Negative Branch, Dunn refused to divulge B–1's identity, stated his own "impression" that B–1 was "likely to be somewhat biased in his opinion of the Jews," and shrewdly added his notice of Churchill's comment about finding the reports useful. Dunn thus gracefully sent his staff the message to ignore but not to criticize the general's bizarre source.[48]

With the end of the war, the problem of draft resisters and slackers evaporated, but that did not mean that the Negative Branch could be any less vigilant. Pacifists were, after all, merely one of the threats faced by America, and B–1's conspiratorial view was only an extreme version of the paranoia shared by most Military Intelligence officers. They saw a web of subversion dedicated to the destruction of industrial capitalism and the American way of life. If MI4 had fought the pacifists ruthlessly, it had been equally harsh on radical unions. Even Carlton J. H. Hayes, in his attack on B–1, had acknowledged, "I am

44. "Bolshevism and Judaism," ibid., pp. 92–95. On February 20, 1919, the intelligence officer at Camp A. A. Humphreys in Virginia, in a letter to the director of the Military Intelligence Division, on the subject "Bolshevism; Its Relation to Religion," emphasized "the proneness of the Jew who has abandoned the religion of his fathers to be swayed to the extreme radical side of the social program" (reel 13, p. 646).
45. Churchill, memorandum for Masteller, November 30, 1918, ibid., reel 12, p. 85.
46. Grosvenor, memorandum for Dunn, December 20, 1918, ibid., pp. 127–28.
47. Hayes, memorandum for Brown, December 19, 1918, ibid., pp. 125–26.
48. Dunn, memorandum for Masteller, December 24, 1918, ibid., p. 129.

not opposed to having the intelligence staffs keep a close watch on all radical labor movements—in fact, I am convinced that it is a military duty so to do."[49] Van Deman's fear of labor radicals had begun early. By the summer of 1917, the army was part of a national effort to root out and destroy the ıww.

49. Hayes, memorandum for Brown, December 19, 1918, ibid., pp. 125–26.

CHAPTER 6

The Industrial Workers
of the World

When World War I ended, the Wilson administration faced the bugaboo of Bolshevism, but in the spring of 1917 the main enemy on the left was the Industrial Workers of the World—the IWW, the Wobblies. Historians still debate the exact meaning of that radical labor movement. Some argue that it was a native revolution born in the bitter fights in the mining and timber territories of the Northwest. Others have stressed the role of European immigrants, who introduced the ideas and strategies of anarchism and syndicalism.[1] Like Bolshevism, the term *syndicalism* has largely disappeared from the American vocabulary. For the first three decades of this century, however, it was a dynamite word. The fear that it engendered among decent, God-fearing, property-owning Americans was so great that *syndicalist law* became the generic term for any measure designed to suppress leftist agitation. The best-known syndicalist organization in the United States in 1917 was the IWW, and its policies defined the meaning of syndicalism: one big union, sabotage, direct action, the general strike, workers' control of the means of production, and a new social order.[2]

Created in 1905, with its headquarters in Chicago, and led by one-eyed William D. "Big Bill" Haywood, the IWW was no stranger to the Wilson administration. The president had ordered a federal investiga-

1. To my mind, Melvyn Dubofsky's *We Shall Be All: A History of the Industrial Workers of the World* (Chicago: Quadrangle Books, 1969), is a very fine study, but it has been criticized by Salvatore Salerno, in *Red November, Black November: Culture and Community in the Industrial Workers of the World* (Albany: State University of New York Press, 1989), for maintaining the "myth of frontier origins"; see pp. 45–67. Anne Huber Tripp, in *The I.W.W. and the Paterson Silk Strike of 1913* (Urbana: University of Illinois Press, 1987), sees the IWW as a response to "the A.F.L.'s disregard of western workers and its refusal to support industrial organization" (p. 3).

2. A good definition of syndicalism is contained in Bruce Nelson's *Workers on the Waterfront: Seamen, Longshoremen, and Unionism in the 1930s* (Urbana: University of Illinois Press, 1988), pp. 6–10. Nelson says that syndicalism was largely crushed in World War I, but he sees a resurgence in the 1930s in the maritime labor movement on the West Coast.

tion of Wobbly activity in California in 1915, but no prosecutions resulted. Two years later the war emergency intensified Washington's concern about the IWW's effect on industrial production. The IWW dismissed both sides in the "capitalist slaughterfest," but its strikes were seen by the nation as aid to the enemy, no doubt funded by the Germans. The Appalachian coal fields and the eastern textile industry were of concern to the administration, but it saw the real IWW threat in the critical western forests and mines.[3] The resulting federal suppression of the IWW was so severe that some analysts have seen it as an overt Wilsonian conspiracy. To maintain, as one frequently cited scholar has, that "by September, 1917, the Wilson Cabinet had determined to crush the I.W.W., using both the Army and the Justice Department in its attack," is to suggest somewhat more solidarity than the Democratic administration ever achieved.[4] Moreover, the attack on the IWW and other radicals was not just a federal program but included widespread state and local repression, often characterized by vigilante violence.[5]

Nevertheless, the fairly independent decisions made by federal agencies ended the IWW's effectiveness. The Justice Department tied up its energy and money in long court cases that put IWW leaders in jail or forced them to flee. Liberals in the Labor Department worked to steal the Wobblies' thunder through mediation and reform, and its immigration officials deported the most odious aliens. The army was deployed to protect crucial industries and, once unleashed, became the most reactionary element in the federal effort during the war.

Secretary of War Baker had initially resisted the notion of using soldiers for strike duty. In the spring of 1917, when asked to send troops against the IWW in the Arizona copper mines, he responded, "This is clearly *not* a case for troops, but for justice and good sense."[6] He agreed with his assistant Felix Frankfurter that, though the IWW was a radical

3. Dubofsky, *We Shall Be All*, p. 404; Ralph Chaplin, *Wobbly: The Rough-and-Tumble Story of an American Radical* (Chicago: University of Chicago Press, 1948), p. 19.

4. Harry N. Scheiber, *The Wilson Administration and Civil Liberties, 1917–1919* (Ithaca: Cornell University Press, 1960), p. 48. This theme is repeated in Dubofsky, *We Shall Be All*, in a chapter suggestively titled "Decision in Washington, 1917–1918," but nowhere is a specific and joint agreement to crush the IWW identified. See pp. 398–422.

5. John W. Chamber's conclusion, in *To Raise an Army: The Draft Comes to Modern America* (New York: Free Press, 1987), p. 208, that the repression of pacifists and draft resisters "was too widespread and varied to be centrally directed or conspiratorial" seems equally applicable to the IWW and other radicals. It is true, however, that the easy manner in which officials from different federal departments associated the word *suppress* with the IWW does suggest a national policy. At any rate, the perceived need to suppress certainly existed at every level.

6. Quoted in Dubofsky, *We Shall Be All*, p. 400.

and dangerous group, it was "probably very small." The solution, Frankfurter felt, was to focus on the unskilled workers ignored by the American Federation of Labor and give them an option to the IWW, whose violent methods most workers saw as counterproductive. "The Government must distinguish," he said, "between radicalism in the labor movement and the destructive policies of the I.W.W." and "must in some way seek to utilize the leaders of such movements and not repress them or drive their following into methods of violence." Baker was so impressed with Frankfurter's analysis that he loaned him to the Department of Labor, where he served as the secretary of the president's commission on labor during the war.[7]

Baker's attitude was typical of his progressive, peaceful inclinations, but, as so often was the case in the war, the crisis forced him to adopt harsher policies. As it turned out, he had to use troops, and he relinquished his own and the president's authority when he instructed local commanders to respond immediately to requests for assistance. Baker anticipated trouble in the Mesabi Range in Minnesota with its valuable iron deposits. In late April 1917, he coordinated an effort that resulted in the dispatch of two labor mediators and a Bureau of Investigation special agent. This situation was resolved peacefully, but it was followed by extraordinary events in Arizona, Montana, and Washington.

Van Deman identified copper production as a vulnerable part of the defense arsenal in his early analyses. His June 9 weekly summary for Baker and Wilson had an alarming and grossly exaggerated description of IWW activities in the copper districts. His informants, he said, indicated that the IWW controlled 60 percent of the miners in Arizona and was "spreading with rapidity throughout the copper districts of Utah." He offered no basis for his claim that "money from unknown sources has been freely supplied," nor did he provide any evidence to support his contentions that "the I.W.W. are preaching strong opposition to war" and "arms and munitions are reported to be cached in various locations." Equally unsubstantiated was his alarming report that "enemy agents are known not to be alien to this increased hostile activity" and were "endeavoring to stir up trouble in the mining camps." At the same time, Van Deman reported rapid IWW organization in the western oil fields,

7. Frankfurter, memorandum for the secretary of war, September 4, 1917, Papers of Newton D. Baker, microfilm reel 1, p. 401, Manuscript Division, Library of Congress. Baker's recommendation of Frankfurter to Labor is in Baker to the president, September 1, 1917, reel 3, p. 328. Frankfurter's role on the labor commission is covered in Dubofsky, We Shall Be All, pp. 415–22.

concluding that "acts of *sabotage* leading to curtailment of supplies may be expected." Two weeks later, he renewed his sensational reports on Arizona, noting that the army's contract for 45 million pounds of copper was endangered by ıww activity. He also observed that though most miners were foreigners, representing "more than 50 nationalities," it was the Austrians who "appear to dominate and in some mines outnumber all other employees many times over." It logically followed, to the paranoid spy master, that "it is among this Austrian element that the I.W.W. agitation is taking place."[8]

These exaggerations notwithstanding, Van Deman was correct in predicting major trouble. Arizona was a political mess, caught in a disputed election in November 1916 that was not resolved until late the following year. Both the Democrat, pro-labor George W. P. Hunt, and the Republican, Thomas E. Campbell, had themselves sworn in, and each addressed the legislature. Campbell, who had won the election by thirty votes, was declared governor by a lower court. Hunt, who, until the Campbell interregnum, had been the new state's first and only governor, regained the chair at the end of the year when the state supreme court ruled in his favor. During this period, a number of loyalty leagues had been formed to fight the ıww menace, and Campbell clamored for federal troops, though Hunt did not want them in Arizona.[9]

Despite Secretary Baker's early reluctance to use them, troops were available. The Southern Department, headquartered at Fort Sam Houston, maintained a high state of readiness because of continuing border clashes with Mexican rebels, whose activities had hardly diminished after Pershing's punitive expedition ended. Sam Houston's department intelligence officer kept Van Deman informed, but at this early date there were few agents to field. Baker dispatched Lieutenant Colonel James J. Hornbrook, a cavalry officer, to Arizona to observe and report to the adjutant general in Washington. In late June, Hornbrook concluded that "troops would expedite production [of copper] but cannot be justified on ground of disorder."[10]

That situation changed drastically, and Hornbrook's daily telegrams to Washington described an increasingly tense environment. On July 5,

8. Richard D. Challener, ed., *United States Military Intelligence, 1917–1927*, 30 vols. (New York: Garland, 1978), *Weekly Intelligence Summary*, June 9 and 22, 1917.
9. The best collection of documents on the Arizona labor situation is in Record Group 60, Glasser Files, box 3, National Archives. For the political situation in Arizona, see Marshall Trimble, *Arizona: A Panoramic History of a Frontier State* (Garden City, N.Y.: Doubleday, 1977), pp. 354–55.
10. Hornbrook's message was relayed by telegram, Hawker to adjutant general, July 1, 1917, Glasser Files, box 3.

Troop D of the Seventeenth Cavalry deployed to the copper mines. On July 12, Hornbrook wired: "Posse of thousand men gathered up about eleven hundred undesirable strikers today and deported them. One deputy was killed and two strikers. Everything orderly."[11] That was the famous Bisbee deportation. Two days earlier, a smaller dress rehearsal had occurred upstate in Jerome. The Jerome Loyalty League, organized on July 3, had rounded up nearly seventy strikers (and some private detectives who had gone too deep in their cover) on July 10 and shipped them by railroad cattle car across the California line. There they were met by vigilantes, who held them for three days before shipping them back to Arizona.[12]

No doubt made bold by the lack of any state or federal response to the Jerome action, the loyal citizens of Bisbee took to arms against the ɪww two days later. The sheriff, former Rough Rider, former Arizona Ranger, and gunfighter Harry Wheeler, deputized a small army which arrested nearly twelve hundred strikers, corralled them in a baseball park, and marched them to the train station, where they were loaded onto cattle cars. The train, provided free by a patriotic railroad company, transported them to Columbus, New Mexico. When officials there refused the unusual shipment, they went on to Hermanas, a tiny depot in the desert. There they were abandoned in the wasteland with no provisions.[13]

Immediately upon news of the Jerome deportation, Van Deman began serious coordination with the Department of Justice, asking Bruce Bielaski, chief of the Bureau of Investigation, to find out if the Arizona ɪww had received funds from German sources.[14] After the

11. Hornbrook to adjutant general, July 12, 1917, ibid.

12. Dubofsky, *We Shall Be All*, p. 384; Robert L. Tyler, *Rebels of the Woods: The IWW in the Pacific Northwest* (Eugene: University of Oregon Press, 1967), p. 121; H. C. Peterson and Gilbert C. Fite, *Opponents of War, 1917–1918* (Seattle: University of Washington Press, 1957), p. 53; Joan M. Jensen, *The Price of Vigilance* (Chicago: Rand McNally, 1968), p. 63. I have not been able to determine the precise number deported from Jerome. Peterson says sixty-seven, Jensen sixty-five; perhaps it depends on how one counts the private detectives.

13. The best account of the Bisbee deportation is in Dubofsky, *We Shall Be All*, pp. 385–87. In an unpaged photographic section, he includes three pictures of the exit from Bisbee. According to Peterson and Fite, *Opponents of War*, p. 54, one vigilante and only one striker were killed. See also Tyler, *Rebels of the Woods*, p. 120; Jensen, *Price of Vigilance*, pp. 63–64; Chaplin, *Wobbly*, p. 211; and Joseph R. Conlin, *Big Bill Haywood and the Radical Union Movement* (Syracuse: Syracuse University Press, 1969), p. 179. The army count of the Bisbee deportees was 1,186.

14. Van Deman to Bielaski, July 10, 1917, in Randolph Boehm, ed., *U.S. Military Intelligence Reports: Surveillance of Radicals in the United States, 1917–1941* (Frederick, Md.: University Publications of America, 1984), reel 1, p. 456 (hereafter cited as MI Microfilm).

Bisbee incident, the secretary of war ordered the army to take the stranded deportees into protective custody rather than allow them to perish in the desert. Once the army had them, disposal became a problem. All of the strikers except the nationals of the Central Powers, whom Van Deman ordered detained for further interrogation (with disappointing results), were discreetly released in small groups over a period of several weeks.[15] Federal troops stayed on duty at various mining camps in Arizona, with most of the activity centered around Globe, from July 1917 to 1919. They were housed in barracks built at the expense of the mining companies, all too suggestive of which side they were on. Although Frankfurter's labor commission managed to restore a semblance of stability, the Arizona copper fields remained a hotbed of labor agitation, always on the verge of a strike.

By the fall of 1917, Van Deman had developed his intelligence operation to the point that he had agents in the field reporting directly to him. The following spring he furnished the Justice Department with a list of the names of the "I.W.W.s" deported from Bisbee, and by then his agents had identified the real threat in that state as none other than the controversial governor. Hunt had been declared the winner of the 1916 election in late 1917, and powerful forces, among them Military Intelligence, wanted to make sure that he lost in November 1918. They were convinced that Hunt was a member of the IWW. The Thiel Detective Agency furnished Van Deman a picture of Hunt with "two of the most radical I.W.W.'s our Western country has had to deal with." The department intelligence officer in Chicago, the aggressive Major Thomas B. Crockett, was convinced that "Governor Hunt is an Honorary Member of the I.W.W.," and he believed in the existence of a fabled letter from Hunt to Big Bill Haywood wherein he accepted membership. Crockett searched diligently for the document when he participated in a raid on the IWW headquarters in Chicago but never located it. Crockett's informant was Eugene Fox, an official with the El Paso and Southwestern Railroad, the company that provided the IWW a free ride out of Bisbee.[16]

Van Deman was also in possession of a lengthy diatribe, dated April 13, 1918, against Hunt from an informant, now unknown but clearly

15. McCain, telegram to commanding general, Southern Department, August 9, 1917, in Glasser Files, box 3; Dubofsky, *We Shall Be All*, p. 387.

16. Van Deman to intelligence officer, Southern Department, April 4, 1918, MI Microfilm, reel 1, p. 428; Crockett, memorandum for Reichman, May 3, 1918, reel 8, p. 927; Charles N. Watkins to R. G. Watkins, May 23, 1918, reel 8, p. 925. See also Dubofsky, *We Shall Be All*, p. 386.

heavily involved in Arizona politics. For years, the informant said, Hunt had "lunged into the most radical advocacy of things all sane men abhor. Many have charged this to political ambition; others to degeneracy, about which many rumors afloat." The report accused the Democrat of "filling all his appointments with the pro-German agitators and I.W.W., and the feeling in the state is . . . that Hunt must be lynched." He concluded that "the most ordinary deduction would be that Hunt is either an employe[e] of the German government or is duped by employees of the German government and hopes to lead a revolution on behalf of the I.W.W.s."[17]

When Churchill replaced Van Deman in June 1918, he continued the attack on Hunt, ordering the Southern Department to "institute a discreet and confidential investigation of Governor Hunt, tending to show . . . his connection with the I.W.W. and his encouragement of them and their methods." Churchill hoped to get enough evidence to have the Justice Department convict Hunt under the same law that had just been used successfully against the iww in Chicago, namely obstructing the war effort. "It is needless to say," he added, "that a matter of this character would have to be conducted with extreme discretion and secrecy."[18] One would think so: on the job less than two months, Churchill was already plotting against a duly (well, almost duly) elected governor of a state of the Union.

The Justice Department by this time had spent a year investigating the iww in Arizona, and it had never proved that Hunt was a member. What it did find was that the governor had tremendous opposition from the mining companies and considerable support from labor. Military Intelligence concluded that Hunt's iww connection must be "deeply concealed on his part" and eventually shelved the case. The rationale of the department intelligence officer who recommended to Churchill that the investigation be postponed indefinitely was that an attack on Hunt could inflame his Mexican supporters, who might withdraw their labor from the war effort. "It is particularly desirable," he said, "that those Mexicans be prevented from leaving the United States. The result of a general exodus upon their part would be very serious."[19] Although

---

17. The army's copy of the anti-Hunt statement, dated April 13, 1918, has no heading and is unsigned; see MI Microfilm, reel 1, pp. 75–80.

18. Churchill to intelligence officer, Southern Department, ibid., reel 8, p. 912.

19. Department intelligence officer, Fort Sam Houston, to director of MI, September 19, 1918, ibid., reel 8, p. 907. This message enclosed William Utley's report on Hunt, pp. 908–10.

Churchill backed off from direct persecution of Hunt, he kept his agents active in Arizona beyond the end of the war.

Whatever Military Intelligence's opinion of Hunt, he seems to have been in good standing with the Wilson administration. During the part of 1917 when he was not governor, he served as a commissioner on the president's conciliation panel that solved the strike; the following year he was mentioned as a possible governor of Puerto Rico. Instead, Hunt was nominated by Wilson to be minister to Siam. Informally and confidentially, the army furnished information to the State Department in an attempt to prevent the appointment. The particular datum that had surfaced by this time was an April 5, 1917, letter from Hunt to an alleged IWW organizer. The letter had been stolen by a "field detective," probably from a private firm, and given to Military Intelligence in 1918. The letter itself was not particularly radical. Hunt said there were three things "essential for the preservation of our Country"—a free press, free speech, and free schools. He complained that the mining companies controlled the press in Arizona, free speech had been curtailed, and the Rockefeller and Carnegie foundations controlled education. He rambled rather incoherently about businessmen who applauded the Red flag in Russia (he was writing before the Bolshevik coup d'état) and imprisoned those who carried a similar flag in Arizona.[20] Despite the army's interference, the diplomatic appointment won Senate confirmation, and Hunt served in Siam until October 1921, after which he returned to the governor's chair from 1923 to 1928 and from 1931 to 1933. He died the following year.[21]

Copper was also a source of trouble in Butte, Montana. Violence had been a part of the labor history of that area for years, and by World War I the repressive tactics of the Anaconda Copper Mining Company, aided by the Burns Detective Agency and martial law under the state militia, had smashed the union and forced an open shop. Work was open to any miner with a record sufficiently clean to obtain his "rustling card," a licensing system that served effectively as a blacklist.[22] By mid-1917 the copper district was polarized between the miners on one hand and the

20. Brown, memorandum for McCain, May 3, 1920, ibid., reel 8, p. 895. The letter in question, pp. 896–98, is on executive letterhead and is so poorly typed as to suggest that the governor did it himself. Presumably a forger would have typed it perfectly and made it clearly incriminating.

21. A biographical sketch of Hunt, a rancher with an eighth grade education, a friend of prison reform, and an opponent of capital punishment, is in *Who Was Who*, 1:608.

22. For a description of the rustling card system, see Secretary of Labor William B. Wilson to Secretary of War Baker, August 21, 1917, Glasser Files, box 3.

company, the governor and his militia, and the APL, controlled by the company, on the other. Tensions were especially high after the disaster on June 8, 1917, when two hundred miners lost their lives in an explosion at the Speculator Mine.[23]

Within a week after the Speculator blast a strike was on, and shortly thereafter IWW agitator Frank H. Little came up from Bisbee, Arizona, to organize the miners. In the wee morning hours of August 1, masked men dragged Little from his rooming house and lynched him. His body, discovered hanging from a railroad trestle, had pinned to it a placard, about five by nine inches, with this message:

OTHERS TAKE
NOTICE!
FIRST AND LAST
WARNING

3–7–77

———

———

L - D - C - S - S - W -

The *L* on the last line had a circle around it, suggesting that it stood for Little, with the other initials indicating those scheduled for similar treatment. William F. Dunn, editor of the pro-labor *Butte Daily Bulletin*, and several colleagues subsequently received duplicates of the 3–7–77 card. The three numbers were easily recognized by Butte old-timers as the symbol of Montana vigilantes almost half a century earlier: three feet by seven feet by seventy-seven inches, the dimensions of a grave.[24]

Despite this tragedy, Butte remained relatively quiet after giving the martyred Little the biggest funeral in the town's history. Following Van Deman's suggestion about the German origin of IWW monetary support, the Department of Justice's agent worked closely with the APL and company detectives but was unable to find any evidence of "enemy influence in the present labor difficulties in the copper mines of Butte

23. For a contemporary account, fascinating and prejudiced, see George R. Tompkins, *The Truth about Butte* (Butte: Century Printing Co., 1917). Of Governor Samuel V. Stewart, Tompkins said, "for downright belly-crawling sycophancy and slavish pandering to the dictates of corporate greed he stands without a peer, absolutely" (pp. 28–29).

24. The Bureau of Investigation's report on the lynching is in MI Microfilm, reel 2, pp. 167–71. A picture of the placard is in Tompkins, *The Truth about Butte*, p. 43. See also Jensen, *Price of Vigilance*, p. 69, and Dubofsky, *We Shall Be All*, p. 392.

and elsewhere throughout the State."[25] The workers were equally unsuccessful in gaining redress of their grievances. Despite the pleas of the secretary of war, the secretary of labor, and Jeannette Rankin, the first woman member of the U.S. House of Representatives, the copper company refused to stop using the rustling card.[26] Although the 1917 strike ended peacefully and the production of copper, now protected by federal troops, was not threatened, Van Deman watched the reports from Butte with increasing concern. By early 1918 he was convinced that federal judge George M. Bourquin and U.S. attorney Burton K. Wheeler were extremely lax in their treatment of slackers, a concern that eventually got Churchill into trouble in Washington.[27]

The tension in Butte nearly came to a head on St. Patrick's Day, when the Pearse Connolly Club, "composed of I.W.W.'s and pro-Germans," held a parade against the orders of the mayor. Troops under the command of Major Omar N. Bradley, the "GI's General" of the next world war, placed a machine gun downtown and helped the local police arrest over a hundred marchers. After that, Van Deman opened a direct correspondence with Governor Samuel V. Stewart, warning him of "a very serious outbreak within the next thirty days." Stewart agreed that Butte was "a seething volcano and there is apt to be trouble at any time."[28]

With Churchill's subsequent and significant increase in Military Intelligence activities in Butte, it seems likely that to make their prediction of a strike come true, the army's undercover agents were prepared to provoke one. In Butte the army's intelligence officer, not under the command of Bradley's guards, was First Lieutenant Will H. Germer. His superior was Captain J. H. Dengel, in charge of the intelligence office in Spokane, Washington, who in turn was under the supervision of the department intelligence officer at the headquarters of the Western Department in San Francisco, directly responsible to Churchill. Normally these channels were followed, but in a crisis situation Germer or Dengel had the authority to contact Churchill's office in Washington immediately.

Operationally, Dengel ran the army's intelligence network in the

25. Bureau of Investigation agent E.W. Byrn, Jr., report, July 11, 1917, MI Microfilm, reel 2, p. 188.

26. Secretary of labor to secretary of war, August 21, 1917, Glasser Files, box 3.

27. The earliest concern about Montana federal officials appears in a February 9, 1918, digest of reports entitled "Memorandum," MI Microfilm, reel 2, pp. 329–30.

28. Van Deman to Stewart, April 6, 1918, ibid., p. 399; Stewart to Van Deman, April 13, 1918, p. 397. For the use of Bradley's troops, see Glasser Files, box 4.

Northwest. By July 1918 it had become clear to him that, despite the IWW's apparent lack of activity in mining and timber, the organization was strong and working underground. Accordingly, he initiated the arrest in Spokane of several suspected IWW members, who were prosecuted under the city's criminal syndicalism ordinance. In mid-August, when mail intercepts suggested that the Butte IWW was about to resume agitation, Dengel ordered Germer to pick up Joe Kennedy, a prominent IWW leader, and he grew increasingly concerned when Germer failed to do so.[29] The Spokane intelligence officer became particularly perturbed after interrogating W. E. Hall, "the personal emissary of William D. Haywood," who had just returned from Butte. Hall was on his way to Seattle with "a trunk full of literature" when Dengel grabbed him in Spokane on August 20.

Hall confessed that "he had been sent from Chicago by Haywood" to urge a general strike "with the object of obstructing the production of government war materials in the mining and lumber districts," thereby forcing the government to release "all Class War prisoners." Found on Hall's person, on tissue paper rolled into a tiny ball, was "the original draft of the call for a general strike." This "strike order" urged action on behalf of "all political and economic prisoners," mentioning, among others, Tom Mooney and Haywood's hundred IWW members recently convicted in Chicago. The authenticity of the strike order has been questioned. IWW attorneys at the time argued that the real author of the call was a Pinkerton detective, a claim substantiated by the Thiel Agency. When Military Intelligence chased down the Pinkerton operative in Seattle, he denied the authorship and any role in agitating for the strike. A prominent labor historian has suggested "that Haywood should have ordered such an action seems ludicrous," noting that neither the Department of Justice nor the Department of Labor had uncovered any sentiment for such a political strike.[30]

---

29. The Butte situation caused a heated exchange between the secretary of war and the attorney general and is therefore particularly well documented. Dengel's lengthy account of his actions was prepared on November 8, 1918, and is in MI Microfilm, reel 9, pp. 831–41; unless otherwise noted, the quotations below come from this illuminating document. A useful summary of most other relative documents was prepared by the War Department on October 10, 1918 (reel 11, pp. 413–24). The actual documents, including a copy of Tompkins's The Truth about Butte, can be found in two large files: reel 2, pp. 126–425, and reel 11, pp. 407–556. A smaller file on Joe Kennedy is in reel 11, pp. 383–406. The Negative Branch's concern about Butte in the summer of 1918 was strengthened by its July 17 interrogation of Edward F. Bassett, the IWW member from Butte who had been inducted into the army (reel 2, p. 370). Transcripted copies of many of these documents are in the Glasser Files.

30. Dubofsky, We Shall Be All, pp. 450–51.

Dengel, however, was thoroughly convinced that the conspiracy "emanated from Chicago undoubtedly" and that Butte was chosen as the tactical headquarters because "they were apparently reasonably sure of less interference." He continued to arrest iww members in Spokane, and his concern about Butte increased when he began to discover, courtesy of the Post Office, letters from that city, postmarked August 20, that contained mimeographed copies of the strike circular. Despite repeated telegrams to Germer, the radical Kennedy was still at large. Notifying Churchill of his intention to take action, Dengel dispatched secret agent C–371 to Butte. Immediately upon his arrival on August 23, C–371 supervised a raid on iww headquarters and the arrest of Kennedy and others. Additional raids and arrests occurred the following day.

Meanwhile, Dengel's other main spy, C–758, had been ordered to Butte, not by the army but in the context of his undercover role as a "trusted member" of the Spokane iww. He informed his radical masters that the police were on to him in that city and was sent to Butte "with instructions to urge an immediate strike." The army was now in a position both to cause and to crush the walkout. With Kennedy and the other leaders in jail, C–758 returned to Spokane and fetched the iww's attorney, who arranged for their release on what the army thought was absurdly low bonds. While Dengel continued to direct arrests in Spokane, Kennedy called a strike in Butte for September 10. At least that was the meaning Dengel took from Kennedy's wires to iww head-quarters throughout the West, from Seattle to Jerome: "Peterson's trial comes up September 10, 1918."

It is apparent that Germer's reluctance to make arrests in Butte stemmed from his unhappy relations with Department of Justice officials there, who did not share Dengel's sense of urgency. When the call for a strike was pushed back to September 12, Germer went to Churchill for advice, wiring: "Shall I use military here and hold leaders and partici-pants as military prisoners?" Churchill, just then embroiled in the con-troversy over the army's illegal arrest of thousands of slackers in New York, responded, "Consult and co-operate with U.S. Attorney at Butte in handling I.W.W. conspirators."[31]

Germer had already made such an attempt with no satisfactory end. On September 9, he had taken to the Bureau of Investigation's agent a wire from Dengel ordering that "Kennedy should be taken immediately and other ringleaders regardless of bond and held as hostage." The

---

31. Germer telegram to Milstaff, Washington, September 11, 1918, MI Microfilm, reel 11, p. 500; Churchill to intelligence officer, Butte, September 11, 1918, p. 501.

Justice agent, E. W. Byrn, Jr., told Germer that the method was "at decided variance with my conception of the law and the policy of this Government." He informed Washington that he could not cooperate with Germer "for the reason that the Military Intelligence acts in many cases without the slightest regard to the law, and this office cannot by cooperating with the Military Intelligence countenance any such action." When Bielaski, pushed by Churchill in Washington, asked for details on the approaching strike, Byrn told him the army was merely crying wolf, noting that the strike so far had failed to materialize and adding that "Military Intelligence this section seems inclined to take action [on] I.W.W. matters hastily and in cases where law does not justify action."[32]

Even when the strike actually came on September 13, Byrn told his Washington chief that it had "not assumed dangerous proportions and operation of mines not seriously hampered." He reported that of nearly twenty thousand miners, only a few hundred had joined the strike. That morning Byrn met with Germer and reached an agreement for a joint bureau-army "quiet investigation" to secure information for the federal attorney. "It was clearly understood in this conference," Byrn later reported, "that no action of any sort was to be taken by this office, the Military Intelligence office, or the United States Attorney's office until further conference was had."

There are no orders in this remarkably complete record requiring Germer to violate this understanding with the Department of Justice. Presumably he was under considerable pressure from Dengel's two operatives to take immediate action. Summoning Major Bradley, the town police, and gunmen from the copper company, Germer made quick plans for a massive roundup in which any man found with two or more strike circulars would be arrested. On the night of September 13, these forces raided the headquarters of the Metal Mine Workers' Union and, in the same building, the printing plant and editorial offices of the *Daily Bulletin*. There Bradley personally pulled sufficient linotype from the melting pot to reproduce with the aid of a rival printer, an exact copy of the strike call. Posting a guard around the building with instructions to allow no one to enter, Bradley led his men of the Fourteenth Infantry to Finlander Hall, location of the IWW headquarters, where he disarmed one man and arrested all he found.[33]

Bradley's men had also been instructed to look for slackers, and they

---

32. Copies of agent Byrn's reports to Bielaski, including and commenting on the Dengel wire and relations with Military Intelligence, ibid., pp. 439–53.

33. In its investigation, the bureau took official statements from civilian volunteers who accompanied Bradley. A particularly detailed report is in ibid., pp. 462–65.

seem to have brought in a great many properly registered men who were released. As a result, only thirty-eight names appeared on the police blotter as having been arrested by soldiers. Dengel claimed that another twenty-four, "all leaders and radicals, agitators," were arrested by Military Intelligence. Justice agent Byrn was furious, particularly when, the following morning, Bradley's pickets refused to allow him to enter the buildings they guarded. He wired Washington that he feared "that the raids will serve to make effective the I.W.W. strike, which, by itself, could not have lasted long or been successful." He knew instinctively that Germer had led the action, but when confronted, the Military Intelligence officer denied any participation, and the local police acknowledged that they were unable to recall Germer's presence. There was no mistaking Bradley's guards, however, and Byrn had the major hauled up to the federal district attorney's office "for an interview." This was Byrn's first bit of luck: Bradley, "a West Point man, an officer and a gentleman, who would not falsify for any man or thing," told the truth. Germer had instigated the raids, and, yes, upon reflection, the army's action was illegal. Bradley agreed to return the two buildings under military control to their rightful owners. He also told the Department of Justice officials that he had no idea upon whose authority the raids had been made. Certainly there was no federal authority, and the county district attorney also disavowed the arrests. The police bookings for those arrested carried the notation, "Held for the Council of Defense."[34]

In the ensuing investigations by Justice and the army, one particular bit of incriminating information developed about Germer. On the night the strike began, a man named Eugene Carroll was killed. One rumor had it that Carroll had been murdered by a copper company gunman; another made him an undercover policeman shot while attempting to arrest a man for pro-German talk. Some days later, in a conversation with one of Byrn's subordinates about the possibility that the killing might inflame the workers, Germer said, "I don't think it will amount to much—if it does, we'll kill some more."[35] No official investigation ever followed up on that statement, and perhaps Germer did not mean it as it sounds, but it does indicate the attitude behind the army's actions in the Northwest.

The lieutenant made one other bit of history before the strike ended. He was the only Military Intelligence officer, at least the only one in

---

34. Byrn, report, September 23, 1918, ibid., pp. 429–38. On the arrests, see agent D. H. Dickason's report, September 17, 1918, pp. 459–60.
35. Dickason, report, September 19, 1918, ibid., pp. 449–50.

uniform, to address an IWW assembly. A week after the beginning of the strike, Germer, the assistant federal attorney, and other officials responded to a request from Local 800 that they appear before a mass meeting. Germer spoke first, promising to forward the workers' demands (for an eight-hour day, release of prisoners, and an end to harassment and the rustling card) and urging them to return to work until a Labor Department representative arrived to hammer out a settlement. Germer's comments were translated into German, Italian, and Spanish. He understood the last two well enough to know that his comments were conveyed correctly. An obliging Pinkerton agent monitored the German translation for him. Germer felt that his effort at reconciliation was betrayed two days later when at another meeting, attended by three military spies, the IWW voted to continue to strike.[36]

Federal attorney Wheeler was unavailable for the mass meeting, having left for Washington to protest Military Intelligence's provocative actions. No doubt hoping to calm the situation, the army pulled out Bradley's infantry and replaced it with United States Guards. The arrests continued, however, and in the last half of September nearly a hundred were incarcerated, many by soldiers acting on their own, unaccompanied by police officers. In most cases, no formal charges were filed against those detained by the army. Byrn complained bitterly to Bielaski, and, with Wheeler in Washington, the stage was set for the unpleasant exchange between Secretary of War Baker and Attorney General Gregory, which was described previously.[37]

By this time Thomas Barker, representing Felix Frankfurter's Labor Department group, had arrived in Butte. He was followed on October 1 by Churchill's highest-ranking army intelligence officer in the region, Captain Rolin G. Watkins, acting intelligence officer at the department's headquarters in San Francisco. Watkins exonerated Germer and downplayed the arrests, apparently with the concurrence of the Labor Department. The army introduced its argument, supported by Secretary of War Baker, that the detentions were technically not arrests, and when Baker threatened to withdraw his troops, the attorney general, after a bitter denunciation of Military Intelligence and the arrests, let the matter drop.[38]

---

36. Germer's reports to Churchill on these meetings are dated September 22 and 23, 1918; ibid., pp. 485–97.

37. Bureau agent-in-charge Byrn reported these arrests to Washington on October 4, ibid., p. 425. Secretary of war to attorney general, October 14, 1918; and attorney general to secretary of war, October 23, 1918, in Glasser Files, box 3.

38. Watkins's initial report was an October 2, 1918, wire to Churchill in which he quoted

Wheeler, in Washington, seeing that no action would be taken against Germer, turned in his resignation. He later won four terms in the U.S. Senate and served as Robert M. La Follette's running mate on the Progressive ticket in 1924. After the war, Germer stayed in Butte to fight the rising tide of radicalism, and Bradley's career obviously never suffered from his part in the Butte affair. The army won an additional victory on October 7, 1918, when Judge Bourquin, in an uncharacteristic decision, allowed the extradiction of Joe Kennedy and three others to Spokane, where they had been indicted on conspiracy charges. The Department of Justice extracted its pound of flesh in these hearings when it forced the exposure of two of Military Intelligence's "best operatives," no doubt C–371 and C–758, who Justice thought were actually agents of the copper company.[39]

The IWW's threat to timber production in the Northwest had been identified well before Dengel's arrival in Spokane in the late spring of 1918, and it is only fair to observe that he inherited a widely held belief that the mission of the army in that area was to smash the radical movement. In the summer of 1917 the governor of the state of Washington, along with U.S. Senator Miles Poindexter, supported by the attorney general of the United States, had literally begged the secretary of war not to remove the federal troops from that state. The military, the governor told Baker, had already made "a large number of arrests" and was keeping the strikers under guard.

In agreeing to maintain the units in Washington, the War Department was blunt about their role, using forms of the verb *to suppress* with the greatest of ease. The assistant secretary of war wrote Attorney General Gregory that in response to his request "the troops in the State of Washington at present engaged in suppressing the activities of the

the Labor representative: "Copper production would have been stopped not once or twice but many times had it not been for able assistance given Department of Labor by Germer" (MI Microfilm, reel 11, pp. 483–84). His final report is quoted in Baker's letter of October 14, 1918, to Gregory, Glasser Files, box 3. Watkins claimed that the "best law abiding and responsible element . . . endorsed, approved and commended" the army's actions "as necessary to avert dangerous consequences." The cabinet controversy is detailed in Chapter 3.

39. Watkins, telegram to Milstaff, Washington, October 7, 1918, MI Microfilm, reel 11, p, 391. The army-Justice conflict in Butte was always clouded by local politics and the close connection between the copper company and the APL. Federal troops remained in Butte until early 1921. The final Military Intelligence report from there is dated January 3 of that year, and the last information on a key individual came that summer, when the army noted that William F. Dunn, who had edited the *Daily Bulletin* raided by Bradley and had sailed for Russia in the spring, had been arrested by the Germans for lacking a passport (p. 407). For 1920 army reports from Butte, see reel 18, pp. 234–87. The withdrawal of troops and the last MI reports are described in Glasser Files, box 3.

Industrial Workers of the World" would remain until the state got its militia organized. Two weeks later, the army's adjutant general informed Senator Poindexter that his request to the president for "the retention of Federal Troops for the suppression of the activities of the Industrial Workers of the World" was being honored.[40] In fact, the army's actions in 1917 went beyond Washington, spreading into Idaho and Oregon. Cooperating with state authorities and vigilantes, the military not only arrested strikers but held them in detention camps as prisoners of war without charges or benefit of counsel. The reasons behind such extraordinary methods, well before Military Intelligence was in the field, related to a direct threat against the war effort. Lumbermen were on strike, and without them the army would never get the millions of board feet required to construct thousands of airplanes.[41]

Problems with the construction of aircraft ultimately became the secretary of war's biggest headache, but the threat of the IWW to timber was eliminated very early through a set of unique organizations: the Spruce Production Division and the Loyal Legion of Loggers and Lumbermen, both created by Colonel Brice P. Disque of the Army Signal Corps. The Spruce Division was an official army unit containing more than twenty-five thousand soldier-loggers working at civilian pay. The civilian lumberjacks of the 4Ls, as the Loyal Legion was known, were recruited by a hundred army officers who administered an oath in which the loggers promised to produce lumber for airplanes and ships and to "stamp out any sedition." As a civilian organization, the 4Ls was both a company union and a vigilante group, and it effectively removed the IWW from the lumber industry.[42]

According to Churchill, who came to appreciate Disque's success in avoiding strikes, two strategies were employed by his colleague: "very stringent and drastic action . . . against the ring leaders . . . putting them in jail where they belong," followed by specific improvements in working conditions for the rank and file. For muscle in the woods, Disque used agents of the American Protective League, private detectives supplied by the Lumbermen's Association, and, when they became

40. William M. Ingraham to attorney general, July 30, 1917, and H. P. McCain to Miles Poindexter, August 15, 1918, in Glasser Files, box 6.
41. Dubofsky, *We Shall Be All*, p. 403; Tyler, *Rebels of the Woods*, pp. 95, 129–33.
42. The intelligence officer of the Western Department told Churchill on July 26, 1918, that he kept the Loyal Legion's 26 intelligence officers and 125 field agents hard at work: "The moment a dangerous or active I.W.W. raises his head, he is incarcerated" (MI Microfilm, reel 9, p. 954). See also Tyler, *Rebels of the Woods*, pp. 103–15; William Pencak, *For God and Country: The American Legion, 1919–1941* (Boston: Northeastern University Press, 1989), p. 150. The 4Ls lasted until 1935.

available, operatives from Military Intellgence.[43] Since the squadrons of the Spruce Production Division were scattered throughout the great forests of the Northwest, Churchill urged his intelligence officer in Portland to make doubly certain "as to the completeness of the Counter Espionage organization" among them. "It is considered highly important," he said, "that an internal and under cover system be operated." His particular interest was in discovering sabotage, especially after an April incident at a sawmill near South Aberdeen, Washington, where eight railroad spikes were so carefully concealed in a hemlock log that they avoided detection until the bandsaw hit them. Such incidents were rare, however, and Portland reported that most of the local Wobblies had come down with the "bull horrors," a paralysis produced by fear of the authorities, "due to the vigorous manner in which they are caught up upon the least evidence of law-breaking."[44]

Another hot spot of radical activity in the Northwest was Seattle, where the army and the navy cooperated with the Minute Men Division of the APL and the stern administration of Mayor Ole Hanson to crush the radical threat to that important port. As Camp Lewis, outside Seattle, mushroomed with draftees in the fall of 1917, the situation was so desperate that Colonel M.E. Saville's military police were authorized to operate off the post. Saville himself was given a letter of introduction, on January 15, 1918, from the commander of the Ninety-first Division describing him as "in charge of the task of suppressing prevalent seditious activities in the Northwest." Saville saw more than a threat to timber. "Sabotage was openly advocated in the streets of Seattle," he reported, and supplies on the docks, including "millions of dollars worth of foodstuffs," were liable to destruction by the IWW, as was construction in the shipyards. Not only was the IWW attempting to organize his soldiers, but the city was being "terrorized by thugs who beat up, outraged, and, in some cases, mutilated more than 300 respectable women." Seattle was in control of "a vice ring, a pro-German ring and an I.W.W. ring with interests interwoven and backed by political, finan-

43. Churchill to intelligence officer, Southern Department, September 11, 1918, MI Microfilm, reel 6, p. 254; Harold M. Hyman, *To Try Men's Souls: Loyalty Tests In American History* (Berkeley: University of California Press, 1959), p. 308; Bruce W. Bidwell, *History of the Military Intelligence Division, Department of the Army General Staff, 1775–1941* (Frederick, Md.: University Publications of America, 1986), p. 193.

44. Churchill's call for undercover work in the Spruce Production Division is in his letter to George Gund, intelligence officer, Portland District, Western Department, August 7, 1918, MI Microfilm. reel 9, p. 116. A log-spiking incident is reported in Plant Protection to chief of MI, April 29, 1918, reel 7, p. 264. The "bull horrors" analysis is in intelligence officer, Portland, to chief of MI, June 22, 1918, reel 3, p. 428.

cial and religious elements of great strength." His appraisal also pointed out that the U.S. attorney was "not equal to the task"; the local police were "sub-servient to the vice ring . . . controlled by certain powerful pro-German and I.W.W. influences"; and the "Bureau of Investigation officials were lamentably weak." Saville had the makings of a first-class negative intelligence officer.[45]

By early 1918, both the army and the navy agreed that the IWW in the Seattle area had been brought under control. Concentrating on the waterfront, the navy had eliminated "the great number of I.W.W.'s and alien enemies with which it was infested and contaminated." Particularly helpful in this regard had the been the work of the Minute Men, "a political counter-irritant against the socialistic agitation of the I.W.W.'s." In the navy's opinion, the ability of both the U.S. attorney's office and the Bureau of Investigation to respond to radicalism had improved. The navy also appreciated the assistance of the Immigration Service in "holding for deportation certain undesirables" and the Post Office's help in "excluding from the mails certain I.W.W. socialistic and other disreputable printed matter." The result of these combined efforts, including the stationing of army guards on the waterfront, was that "the strength of those opposed to our Federal Government is weakening and I.W.W.ism and Bolshevikism are less rampant." In this investigative fury, some twelve thousand Minute Men were running a thousand cases a month, and Seattle's biggest problem was how to house the thousands who had been arrested.[46]

Whether or not Dengel was correct in his analysis that the trial of the IWW leaders in Chicago was the cause of the renewed labor troubles in August 1918, it is certainly true that the systematic arrest of so many Wobblies put that once powerful organization on the defensive. The resulting trials, one historian has concluded, changed the very nature of the IWW, forcing it to become "a legal organization concerned as much with the defense of civil liberties as it was with winning higher wages, shorter hours, or a new and better world."[47] Although the arrests made by the military in the Northwest were certainly important to this transformation, it was the famous September 1917 sweep by the Department of Justice that netted the critical leadership of the IWW. Those leaders, located in Chicago, were all too aware of the intelligence

45. Commanding officer; 316th Trains Headquarters and Military Police, to Commanding officer, 91st Division, March 30, 1918, in Glasser Files, box 6.
46. The navy's report on Seattle, dated February 28, 1918, is in ibid. On the Minute Men, see Jensen, *Price of Vigilance*, p. 127.
47. Dubofsky, *We Shall Be All*, p. 444.

community's interest in them. "We were already being shadowed," one of them recalled, "night and day by federal and city 'gumshoes.' More and more stool pigeons and spies were in attendance at I.W.W. gatherings." When the raids came, no one was surprised. On September 5, 1917, federal agents "swarmed down upon every I.W.W. union and branch office in the nation" hoping to find evidence of German influence.[48]

In Chicago more than 150 radicals were arrested in raids in which the local army intelligence chief participated and were charged with violating the Espionage Act. They were in jail when news was received of the Bolshevik coup d'état in November 1917. Their preliminary hearings were held before federal judge Kenesaw Mountain Landis on December 15, 1917. Charges against some (including Elizabeth Gurley Flynn and her lover Carlo Tresca) were dropped, and the others, about a hundred, were released on bond. The trial began on April 1, 1918, and lasted until the end of August. Van Deman wanted the army to have "all the information it can possibly obtain in regard to the activities of the I.W.W. and kindred organizations" and ordered a transcript of the trial "as essential to the prosecution of this work." He reported to the Bureau of Investigation that he fully expected the iww to initiate "destructive activities against various industries throughout the country" starting on May 1.[49]

After the completion of the Chicago trial and during the Butte crisis, the army's Western Department increased its demands for intelligence reports on the iww. All units were instructed to "secure evidence of the general conspiracy and of the connection between local trouble-makers and those operating in other districts." In Utah the army helped form a "public safety committee," which it directed in arresting and interrogating iww activists. In Nevada other intelligence officers choked off a strike demanding the release of "class warfare prisoners" by arresting the instigators, who were found with "six half-sticks of dynamite." By the end of the war, intelligence units in the West were forwarding weekly

48. Chaplin, *Wobbly*, pp. 214, 220.

49. Van Deman to intelligence officer, Central Department, June 1, 1918, MI Microfilm, reel 5, p. 412; Van Deman to Bielaski, March 2, 1918, reel 2, p. 279. Haywood and his key lieutenants got thirty years in Leavenworth, and the organization was fined over $2 million. IWW editor Chaplin's detailed account of the trial is in *Wobbly*, pp. 220–324. See also Dubofsky, *We Shall Be All*, pp. 423–44, and Conlin, *Haywood*, pp. 177–78. In 1919, out of jail while his case was on appeal, Haywood skipped bail and fled to Russia. President Warren G. Harding commuted the others' sentences in 1923. Military Intelligence's thick dossier on Haywood extends, in MI Microfilm, from reel 5, p. 392, to reel 6, p. 114, and includes the transcripts of *U.S.* v. *Haywood, et al.*

summaries on the "I. W. W. Situation" to Washington.[50] A few days after the Armistice, Naval Intelligence finished its report on iww activity on the two coasts, the Gulf, and the Great Lakes. This fairly sophisticated analysis serves as a handy evaluation of the action of the "various investigative departments of the Government" in meeting the radical threat. New York was "quiet"; Boston, "shut down tight"; Baltimore and Norfolk, "semi-dormant"; and Florida, "fairly rid of I.W.W. agitation." In the Great Lakes area, the situation was "well in hand," and "regulations along the Pacific coast seem to be so stringent that Marine Transport Workers and I.W.W.s are not allowed even to hold meetings."

Such complete success, the navy concluded, had been achieved through the conscientious application of three proven methods: informants, raids, and detention of leaders. Because there were spies "in the ranks of the organization itself," plans were revealed and leaders identified. The subsequent arrest of these officers was critical because "it has been demonstrated time and again that if the leaders are removed, the organization crumbles." Raids served two purposes. First, confiscated material was extremely important in securing convictions of those arrested, especially since "the threat of physical violence which the I.W.W. holds over its members" made testimony unlikely. Beyond providing evidence, there was a raid's "unquestionable moral[e] effect," the bull horrors disease, caused by a "strong fear of governmental investigation and action." Not only was the operation of a target disrupted, but "raids have always been followed by a noticeable falling off in the active membership and a suspension of propaganda activities."[51] In short, repression worked.

The special and rough treatment given the iww does not mean that the military failed to monitor other left-wing groups. All radicals, "no matter to what party or belief they may belong," the navy said in its report, "join in a concerted movement against what they term 'the oppression of the Capitalist system.'" Churchill continued Van Deman's interest in Socialist Victor Berger, the U.S. representative from Milwaukee imprisoned and evicted from Congress for his views on the war,

50. The Western Department's instructions on intelligence reporting, along with a summary of conditions in the Northwest, are in department intelligence officer to all intelligence officers, September 28, 1918, Glasser Files, box 7. The resulting reports are in MI Microfilm, reel 12, pp. 773–878. All intelligence units, including the Plant Protection Service, watched the IWW. The least activity occurred in the Southeast.

51. The navy's report on the IWW is in MI Microfilm, reel 8, pp. 211–77; Glasser Files, box 5; and Record Group 38, Office of Naval Intelligence, "CAP" file, box 8, National Archives.

and pressed the Justice Department for sterner action against him.[52] Military Intelligence was well represented at the Socialist national convention in New York in early May 1918, and reports on each session were dispatched to Van Deman. By that time he had extensive files on the Socialist leaders, and at the local level his agents penetrated their organizations.[53]

The year 1918 brought a new threat: almost imperceptibly, the subject of army intelligence reports changed from "IWW" to "IWW and Bolsheviki."[54] It was a fairly simple task to work the Leninists into the traditional threat scenario based on German manipulation. Lenin, or Lenine, as his name was often spelled in 1918, had been sent to Russia by the Germans, and when he took power he immediately closed down the eastern front. The connection to the United States was that Lenin's right-hand man, Leon Trotsky, or Trotzky, had lived in this country for a short time in early 1917, editing the radical propaganda organ *Novy Mir* until the abdication of the czar started him on his return to Russia.

American radicals were thrilled by the Bolshevik triumph in Russia, and left-wing journalistic and academic circles were naturally fascinated. After the American participation in the Allied intervention in Russia, followed by the Siberian expedition, there was increasing criticism of Wilson's policy. Making good their revolution in Russia and increasing their propaganda in the United States, the "Bolsheviki" became major targets of negative intelligence. On August 19, 1918, Churchill gave Biddle in New York the following advice on discriminating between the "two kinds of Bolsheviki sympathizers": "There is one kind—the more 'radical'—who in the name of democracy or historic socialism ad[m]ires the Soviet Government in Russia. This kind is ignorant of the pro-German machinations of Lenine and Trotzky and is doubtless sincere, though from our standpoint, mistaken. . . . There is another kind of Bolsheviki sympathiser, however, who is drawn from I.W.W., Socialist Labor, Anarchist, or German elements and simply uses the American policy towards Russia as an excuse and opportunity for opposing the

52. The main collection of material on Berger in MI Microfilm runs from reel 2, p. 968, to reel 3, p. 334, and includes a transcript of his trial. On October 28, 1918, John Lord O'Brian promised Churchill that "additional prosecutions of Berger" were forthcoming (reel 3, p. 30).
53. Eugene V. Debs's file is in MI Microfilm, reel 7, pp. 150–257. For Military Intelligence's penetration of the Young People's Socialist League, see reel 3, pp. 948–49.
54. The Plant Protection Service developed a large file on the "Bolsheviki," but many of the reports have the unusual subject of "Slavonic Races" or "Slavonic Activities," in Record Group 165, entry no. 104, Plant Protection Section, General Correspondence, "Bolsheviki," National Archives, Suitland Records Center.

war." Churchill worried about both kinds, and he told Biddle that "espionage should be employed at all Bolsheviki meetings."[55]

The most frightening thought was that with their propaganda the Russian revolutionaries would rekindle the radicalism the authorities were just eliminating. In late 1918, it became apparent to Military Intelligence that, with the iww all but dead, it was "more probable that danger lies in the Bolshevist idea." In carrying out Churchill's orders, Biddle began to concentrate on Russian organizations, concluding, "It will be a blessing to this Department when we shall be able to handle these societies as straight revolutionary organizations, enemies of this country and its interests."[56] Before examining the fascinating story of the nation's response to the Bolsheviki in the Red Scare after the war, one last internal threat from the war years must be examined. Van Deman also feared black Americans' response to German and radical propaganda. His methods against the black community started Military Intelligence down an intriguing path that for a brief period made the agency seem almost moderate.

55. Chief of MI to Biddle, August 19, 1918, MI Microfilm, reel 10, pp. 153–54.
56. Biddle to director of MI, September 6, 1918, ibid., reel 34, p. 115.

CHAPTER 7

Black Americans

In early July 1917, East St. Louis experienced the war's most serious race riot, leaving nearly fifty people dead and a federalized Illinois National Guard in control. In August black soldiers rioted in Houston, and thirteen of the mutineers were hanged in December, with others awaiting execution. In such a climate, Ralph Van Deman identified "Negro Unrest" as an early topic in the intelligence summaries he prepared for the Wilson administration. He naturally saw the German hand behind the rioting. In June he had reported "an anti-government attitude on the part of isolated groups among the negro population . . . which would tend to indicate German activity." At the same time, he told the improbable story that German agents were posing as sewing machine salesmen and, upon gaining access to black homes, spreading the propaganda "that this country is not theirs and that they should not fight for it."[1] Shortly thereafter, Military Intelligence opened a new file for a new subject, "Negro Subversion," making the first entry on August 13. An early item noted "several incidents of where colored men had attempted to make appointments with white women." Although these overtures were rebuffed, as each woman "very properly called the negro down for his presumption," they were taken as indicators of "a general unrest among the colored people."[2]

1. Richard D. Challener, ed., *United States Military Intelligence, 1917–1927*, 30 vols. (New York: Garland, 1978), *Weekly Intelligence Summary*, June 9, 1917. This summary is in vol. 1, in which the summaries are paged separately.
2. The Military Intelligence files on black Americans are available in two microfilm publications. By far the cheapest is National Archives, *Correspondence of the Military Intelligence Division Relating to "Negro Subversion," 1917–1941*, microfilm project number M1440 (Washington, D.C.: National Archives, 1986), six reels from the army's investigative files. Theodore Kornweibel, Jr., ed., *Federal Surveillance of Afro-Americans (1917–1925): The First World War, the Red Scare, and the Garvey Movement* (Frederick, Md.: University Publications of America, 1986), has twenty-five reels, containing not only the documents in the National Archives version, but also additional army material as well as substantial collections from other federal agencies, especially the Bureau of Investigation and the State Department. Hereafter, these two are cited as Negro Subversion Microfilm and Surveillance of Afro-Americans Microfilm. For the last, a thorough printed guide is of great assistance to researchers. The Glasser Files, in Record Group 60, National Archives, also have important material on black history, and the incidents cited above come from an October 19, 1917, "Memorandum re Colored Situation" in box 6. Box 4 has

After the riot in East St. Louis and the one shortly thereafter in Chester, Pennsylvania, Van Deman continued to insist that "at the bottom of the negro unrest German influence is unquestionable." He expected "violence of a serious nature." [3] In September he told Biddle in New York that "the negro question is more than tense just now, and it behooves us to find out all we can as to conditions." On at least one occasion in the fall, he discussed the race problem with Secretary of War Baker, following it up with a report from his "colored agent that we have had employed for some time to keep his eye on negro agitation." In January, Bielaski of the Bureau of Investigation sent Van Deman information on the "local colored situation," noting that he would take no action because he understood that Military Intelligence was "making a rather extensive investigation of this matter." [4]

Black American soldiers, segregated in the Ninety-second Division and the Ninety-third Division (provisional), served their country faithfully in World War I. Constituting 10 percent of the population, they provided 13 percent of the men under arms. [5] In a society as overtly racist as the United States was at the time, there were bound to be problems. The most notorious case happened in March 1918 at Camp Funston, Kansas, home of the Ninety-second Division. Initially the incident was minor enough: a black sergeant protested the discrimination of a local theater. The difficulty arose when the Ninety-second's white commander, Major General Charles C. Ballou, decided to issue a policy statement. In Bulletin Number 35, he allowed that though the sergeant was within his rights in visiting a theater, he was "guilty of the greater wrong in doing *anything* no matter how *legally* correct, that will provoke race animosity." He urged his men to sacrifice their "personal pride and gratification" in the interest of the war effort. Noting that "white men

documents regarding the East St. Louis riot, as does the University Publications of America's 1985 microfilm project entitled *The East St. Louis Race Riot of 1917*. The editor of that work, Elliott Rudwick, is author of *Race Riot at East St. Louis, July 2, 1917* (Carbondale: Southern Illinois University Press, 1964). For Houston, see Robert V. Haynes, *A Night of Violence: The Houston Race Riot of 1917* (Baton Rouge: Louisiana State University Press, 1976).

3. Challener, ed., *Military Intelligence, Weekly Intelligence Summary*, August 11, 1917, in vol. 1.

4. Van Deman to Biddle, September 11, 1917, Negro Subversion Microfilm, reel 1, p. 370. Van Deman refers to his conversation with Baker in his memorandum for Keppel, December 14, 1917, reel 1, p. 665. See also Bielaski to Van Deman, January 11, 1918, reel 1, p. 756; Surveillance of Afro-Americans Microfilm, reel 19, pp. 321–26, 447–48, 454–55.

5. Nearly two hundred thousand blacks were in the army, many relegated to the most onerous labor. Almost all of the forty-two thousand black combat troops saw action in France. See Bernard C. Nalty, *Strength for the Fight: A History of Black Americans in the Military* (New York: Free Press, 1986), p. 111.

made the Division and they can break it just as easily if it becomes a trouble maker," he ordered his troops to "avoid every situation that can give rise to racial ill-will. Attend quietly and faithfully to your duties, and don't go where your presence is not desired." Despite an outraged black press that called for his removal, Ballou retained command and led the Ninety-second to the Argonne.[6]

Racial problems also occurred at the several training camps that had received units of both races. The most general cause of discontent had to do with the recreational facilities provided by the Knights of Columbus and, more extensively, by the Young Men's Christian Association. The Catholic organization appears to have welcomed everyone, but the YMCA "huts" were strictly segregated. Although technically the YMCA facilities were under the authority of the organization's national directors, the effort on behalf of blacks was led by Jesse E. Mooreland, international secretary of the Colored Men's Department of the YMCA. Attached to the association's War Work Council in Washington, the black leader supervised the "field secretaries" of his race, including some fifty in Europe, who ran the programs for the military.[7]

At the basic level, the recreation huts offered lonely soldiers a place to buy a postage stamp, have a snack, or read a magazine. Because opportunities for idle soldiers at remote training sites were severely limited, competition for what was frequently only a tent was fierce.[8] Facilities for whites, at home and in France, were given priority, and bitter feelings occurred when blacks were ejected from those for whites only. On posts that did have huts operated by black YMCA secretaries, Military Intelligence frequently found the dreaded "colored agitator." Cooperating closely with William G. Low, Jr., chief of the YMCA's Intelligence Department, the army found several cases, especially at South Carolina's Camp Sevier and Camp Jackson, when black YMCA workers "caused considerable dissension" by opposing segregation. After a case in which "colored agitators" at Camp Devens, near Boston, entered the barracks without permission, Low suggested that all black visitors be required to

6. HQ 92nd Division, Camp Funston, Bulletin No. 35, March 28, 1918, Negro Subversion Microfilm, reel 2, p. 123; see also pp. 111–35; Surveillance of Afro-Americans Microfilm, reel 19, pp. 555–67; Nalty, *Strength for the Fight,* p. 113.

7. The YMCA intelligence bureau performed an extensive investigation of Mooreland for Military Intelligence. See Surveillance of Afro-Americans, reel 23, pp. 85–138.

8. The secretary of war's policy of limiting recreation activities to the efforts by the Knights of Columbus and the YMCA is dated September 22, 1917, Papers of Newton D. Baker, microfilm reel 2, p. 569, Library of Congress, Manuscript Division. All of the racial incidents involved the YMCA. The Young Men's Hebrew Association worked through the YMCA.

report to the YMCA before being allowed to talk to the men. Van Deman, in an unusual refusal to bow to paranoia, rejected the proposal as impractical unless white visitors were similarly controlled. When Low asked if the National Association for the Advancement of Colored People (NAACP) journal, the *Crisis*, should be banned from the huts, Van Deman readily agreed.[9] Both aspects of the YMCA program, segregation and sedition, remained problems for the army. After the war, the YMCA espionage chief reported to Military Intelligence that "control over its negro work has not been satisfactory to this office." He was particularly unhappy with Mooreland, whom he said was "under the influence of the DuBois faction."[10]

Similar to his view of the industrial labor problem, Van Deman's assumption that blacks could be easily seduced by Germans changed toward the end of the war to a belief that the Socialists were wooing blacks for the Red revolution. The strategy Van Deman employed against American blacks was, however, somewhat different from the strong-arm methods he used to suppress the IWW. This slightly gentler approach may well have been the result of leadership by the secretary of war. Baker had a genuine commitment, obvious in his large correspondence with philanthropist and race reformer George Foster Peabody, to decent treatment for black soldiers.[11] This is not to say that the secretary was so radical as to end segregation in the service, and he generally bowed to pressure, especially from the president, to move a white officer chafing under an assignment to a black unit. But he did appoint as his special assistant the black educator Emmett J. Scott. This official at Tuskegee, who had been Booker T. Washington's aide and after the war became the chief financial officer of Howard University, handled the sensitive issue of race for the War Department. Scott received hundreds of complaints from black soldiers, many of which he referred to Military Intelligence for investigation. He maintained close ties with Van Deman and Churchill.[12]

9. Low to Van Deman, April 27, 1918, Negro Subversion Microfilm, reel 2, p. 224; Van Deman to Low, May 11, 1918, p. 225; Low to Van Deman, May 2, 1918, pp. 228–29; Van Deman to Low, May 6, 1918, p. 230. See also Low to Van Deman, June 5, 1918, reel 3, p. 138; Dunn to Low, November 30, 1918, reel 4, p. 3.

10. Low to Dunn, December 16, 1918, ibid., reel 4, pp. 7–8; Low to Dunn, January 4, 1919, p. 9.

11. Baker shared with Peabody copies of Military Intelligence reports concerning black troops. See Peabody to Baker, February 19, 1919, Baker Papers, reel 8, p. 158. Correspondence with Peabody is throughout the Baker Papers.

12. Nalty, *Strength for the Fight*, p. 111. After the war, Scott wrote *Scott's Official History of the American Negro in the World War* (1919; rpt. New York: Arno Press, 1969). A sketch in Rayford W. Long and Michael R. Winston, eds., *Dictionary of American Negro*

The black agent whom Van Deman mentioned in his letter to Secretary Baker was Major Walter H. Loving of the Philippine Constabulary, who served Military Intelligence faithfully for nearly three years. Whereas other units, especially the Southern Department, were able to develop black agents, Loving ran a national program, funded secretly by Van Deman, from a private office in Washington. Van Deman told Biddle in New York to "put every possible confidence in Loving and rely upon his work." Loving was, in Churchill's words, "one of the best types of 'white man's negro.'"[13] After opening his office, with a secretary and a telephone, in the fall of 1917, Loving spent January and February traveling around the nation setting up an "information chain" of volunteer black sources, "all men of means," and scheduling patriotic speeches by Roscoe Conkling Simmons.[14] Shortly thereafter, Van Deman sent the major a confidential memorandum praising him for "the prompt and efficient measures . . . taken to suppress the dangerous propaganda among the colored people in Harlem." May found Loving investigating the field secretaries of the black YMCA, thought to be serving as distribution agents for the *Crisis* on army posts. About the same time, Van Deman instructed him to go to St. Louis, where the black newspaper *Argus* was "exploiting" stories on discrimination and lynching. Van Deman ordered Loving to secure "a change of the tone and character of editorials of this paper so far as they relate to the negro question."[15]

The head of Military Intelligence firmly believed that complaints

Biography (New York: Norton, 1982), pp. 549–51, describes him in the War Department as "an effective go-between but not a leader." Surveillance of Afro-Americans Microfilm, reel 22, contains many of the complaints sent to Scott, who was himself mentioned in an army investigation of BOULE, a black secret collegiate society that briefly came under suspicion (reel 21, pp. 398–400). Scott was also the subject of minor Bureau of Investigation scrutiny for "Alleged Activities among the Negroes," reel 10, p. 1321.

13. Van Deman to Biddle, March 18, 1918, Negro Subversion Microfilm, reel 2, p. 39; Surveillance of Afro-Americans, reel 19, p. 524. Churchill's appraisal of Loving is in a memorandum for the chief of staff, August 20, 1919, Negro Subversion Microfilm, reel 5, p. 1028, and Glasser Files, box 8. For references to other blacks recruited by MI, see Ralph E. Weber, ed., *The Final Memoranda: Major General Ralph H. Van Deman, USA Ret., 1865–1952, Father of U.S. Military Intelligence* (Wilmington, Del.: Scholarly Resources, 1988), pp. 33–34; and U.S. Army, *The History of the Counter Intelligence Corps in the United States Army, 1917–1950 (with Limited Tabular Data to 1960)*, 30 vols. (Baltimore: U.S. Army Intelligence Center, 1959), 3:73, in Record Group 319, National Archives.

14. Loving to Van Deman, November 23, 1917, Negro Subversion Microfilm, reel 1, p. 576. See also pp. 763, 774, 838, 840. In Surveillance of Afro-Americans Microfilm, see reel 19, pp. 458–647.

15. Van Deman to Loving, April 22, 1918, Negro Subversion Microfilm, reel 2, p. 73; Van Deman to Loving, May 13, 1918, p. 547; Van Deman to Loving, May 16, 1918, p. 289; Loving to chief of MI, May 30, 1918, p. 293. In Surveillance of Afro-American Microfilm, the *Crisis* material is in reel 19, pp. 625–80; the *Argus* is pp. 684–705.

about lynching damaged the defense interests of the United States. On August 4, 1917, Kelly Miller, the dean of the College of Arts and Sciences at Howard University, wrote an open letter on the subject to President Wilson. Entitled *The Disgrace of Democracy*, it was a vigorous attack on lynching: "The vainglorious boast of Anglo-Saxon superiority will no longer avail to justify these outrages." When Van Deman saw the letter printed as a pamphlet, he was shocked. He told Loving that Miller's "intelligence and the authority with which he speaks can have but one effect, that of stimulating adverse propaganda among the negroes." Loving interviewed the offending dean and reported a change in behavior, but Miller, citing his contributions to the national cause, was as upset as Van Deman. "I confess," he told Loving, "that I am somewhat surprised and disappointed on finding myself under surveillance by the Intelligence Department." Reports on Miller continued, and when he went on a speaking tour before black soldiers, YMCA agents monitored him.[16]

Another of Van Deman's earliest sources, although hardly an agent, was Robert R. Moton, Booker T. Washington's successor at Tuskegee Institute. Though Moton earnestly desired confidentiality, he occasionally supplied information on radicalism and war resistance. Baker probably referred Moton to Van Deman, as the cabinet officer and the black leader appear to have been friends. From Moton, Van Deman got the name of Dr. C. V. Roman of Nashville, who also sent him information, which he shared with Frankfurter in Baker's office.[17] It is not surprising that the military should have enlisted the aid of conservative blacks to maintain domestic stability during the war, but it does seem somewhat unusual that Van Deman also developed a dialogue with younger and more active spokesmen, especially one so outspoken as W. E. B. Du Bois.

Du Bois saw the war as an opportunity for his "talented tenth," and in his initial patriotic support he went so far as to accept government censorship in return for modest progress. The relationship between Du Bois and Van Deman was strange. Early in their acquaintance, Van

16. Van Deman to Loving, February 28, 1918, Negro Subversion Microfilm, reel 1, pp. 806–7; Miller to Loving, March 8, 1918, pp. 809–10. Miller's *Disgrace of Democracy: Open Letter to President Woodrow Wilson* (Washington, D.C.: n.p., 1917) is in Negro Subversion Microfilm, reel 1, pp. 337–46. The Department of Justice was also suspicious of Miller, and its file on him contains another copy of *Disgrace of Democracy*; Surveillance of Afro-Americans Microfilm, reel 11, pp. 877–901; the army material is in reel 19, pp. 466–89.

17. Moton to Van Deman, September 12, 1917, Negro Subversion Microfilm, reel 1, p. 416; Van Deman to Moton, September 18, 1917, p. 417. In Surveillance of Afro-Americans Microfilm, see reel 19, pp. 338–44.

Deman worked to find an army commission for a young black graduate of Harvard referred to him by Du Bois. As he learned more about black activism, however, Van Deman grew suspicious of the editor of the *Crisis*, and he appears to have maintained the contact primarily as a means of gaining information.[18] Van Deman ordered the *Crisis* off army posts and had his agents and the Bureau of Investigation make a thorough investigation of it. Churchill, who joined Military Intelligence just when it turned on Du Bois, urged Charles H. Studin, whom the NAACP appointed to censor the *Crisis*, to "make a special effort to eliminate all matter that may render the paper liable to suppression in the future." Military Intelligence "can not tolerate," the new intelligence chief said, "carping and bitter utterances likely to foment disaffection and destroy the morale of our people."[19]

This harsh attitude toward Du Bois's journal is confusing because it was owned and controlled by the National Association for the Advancement of Colored People, and just at the time Van Deman initiated the crackdown on the *Crisis*, he brought the white chairman of the board of the NAACP into his office. The motives that led the father of negative intelligence to make such an open gesture of goodwill are lost, but the principle of co-optation was not one that he had used before or would again. Perhaps the appointment was made only after pressure from Scott and Baker. At any rate, the brief career of Major Joel E. Spingarn in Military Intelligence was a whirlwind of activity and enthusiasm. Commissioned in the infantry after schooling with the First Reserve Officers' Training Corps, Spingarn arrived at the Negative Branch on May 17, 1918. With a primary mission, like everyone else in the branch, to work on "Bolsheviki; I. W. W. etc.," his specialty was "Negro Subversion." He worked closely with Emmett Scott in the secretary's office and hoped to organize a "counter espionage system among colored people themselves." His specific accomplishments included appearing before Congress to urge the passage of an antilynching bill; recruiting at least one black officer, Lieutenant T. Montgomery Gregory, for domestic negative intelligence; securing a formal agreement with Du Bois for the censorship of the *Crisis*; and assisting black leaders in their appeal for the

18. Negro Subversion Microfilm, reel 1, pp. 437–48, 455–56; Surveillance of Afro-American Microfilm, reel 19, pp. 347–64. For Du Bois's disillusionment over the treatment of blacks, see Nalty, *Strength for the Fight*, pp. 107, 114.

19. Churchill to Studin, June 3, 1918, Negro Subversion Microfilm, reel 2, p. 295. On Du Bois's willingness to accept censorship, see his letter to Emmett Scott of March 24, 1918, reel 2, pp. 150–51. Scott referred the matter to Van Deman. For Du Bois's complaint about unfairness to black troops, see p. 316. See also Surveillance of Afro-American Microfilm, reel 19, pp. 625–80.

return to active duty of the highest-ranking black army officer, Colonel Charles Young.[20]

Spingarn's position as a negative intelligence officer required him to investigate the NAACP, which he headed. In the former capacity he made a formal request to NAACP secretary John R. Shillady for a list of the leaders of the national association and its branches. At that time the NAACP had 117 active branches with 32,000 members, and it anticipated that an ongoing membership drive would increase that number by several thousand. The response, addressed to him at Military Intelligence, bore his name and military rank on the letterhead as chairman. The stationery also carried the NAACP's purpose: "to make 11,000,000 Americans physically free from peonage, mentally free from ignorance, politically free from disfranchisement, and socially free from insult."[21]

The case of Colonel Young became a major cause for concerned blacks when the physical examination for his colonelcy revealed hypertension. Despite the promotion board's recommendation that Young be retained on active service, the medical report resulted in his being placed on inactive status, assigned to the Ohio National Guard. Since Ohio was one of the states left with no guard units, Young had nothing to do. In June 1918, to make a case for his physical fitness, he traveled the five hundred miles from Wilberforce to Washington on horseback (and a quarter of it on foot). Despite Scott's aid in arranging an interview with Secretary Baker and a recommendation from General John J. Pershing that Young be given command of a "colored regiment," no assignment resulted. Many black leaders believed that the forced retirement of the West Point graduate was based on racism, not on medical grounds. Their concerted effort to have him given a command resulted in his return to active duty just five days before the Armistice.[22]

20. Spingarn, memorandum for Churchill, June 10, 1918, in Negro Subversion Microfilm, reel 2, pp. 609–11, and Surveillance of Afro-Americans Microfilm, reel 19, pp. 727–30. In addition to being one of the white leaders of the NAACP, Spingarn was a poet, a former professor of comparative literature at Columbia University, and owner of the *Amenia* (New York) *Times*. He died in 1939 (*Who Was Who*, 1:1164).

21. Shillady to Spingarn, June 19, 1918, Negro Subversion Microfilm, reel 3, p. 12. In Surveillance of Afro-Americans Microfilm, information on the NAACP is in reel 19, pp. 802–47.

22. The Baker Papers have a good deal of information on the Young case. See especially Young to Pershing, September 9, 1918, reel 6, p. 338, which has Pershing's handwritten endorsement to Baker and also attaches Young's itinerary from Ohio to Washington. See also "Memorandum on the Case of Colonel Charles Young," n.d., Negro Subversion Microfilm, reel 2, pp. 639–41, which contains synopses of Young's service record and the medical report. A sketch of Young is in Long and Winston, eds., *Dictionary of American Negro Biography*, pp. 677–79. His photograph is in John Patrick Finnegan, *Military Intelligence: A Picture History* (Arlington, Va.: U.S. Army Intelligence and Security

Spingarn's biggest success came in the third week of June, when he arranged a conference in Washington for "editors of the colored newspapers and other leaders of the colored race." Secretary Baker claimed credit for the concept of such a meeting, and funding came from Creel's Committee on Public Information. Baker afterward told President Wilson, "I had the conference called in order that I might in a very authoritative way deny and disprove some rumors afloat in the country to the effect that negro soldiers were being badly treated in France and were being exposed in places of special danger in order to save the lives of white soldiers." [23] Du Bois worked closely with Spingarn in setting up the conference and also in the effort to recruit blacks for Military Intelligence, to which Du Bois claimed he had been offered a captain's commission. The black editor hoped that creating a black presence in negative intelligence would mean "that when the question of unrest among Negroes arises, these men would be able to point out to the government why the unrest existed and offer a remedy." [24]

Churchill saw the editors' conference as a countermeasure to William Monroe Trotter's radical Colored Liberty Congress, scheduled to meet in Washington from June 24 to June 27. The intelligence chief regarded Trotter's movement as a menace, and he intrigued to have it killed. Churchill was furious when Trotter got wind of the army's opposition and publicized it in his *Guardian*. [25] After this jerky start, Spingarn and Du Bois's three-day conference began on June 19. Thirty-one editors and ten other prominent blacks, including Moton of Tuskegee and Archibald H. Grimke, former U.S. consul to Santo Domingo, attended the meeting in the Interior Building with Scott presiding. The gathering featured speeches by numerous administration officials, including Secretary Baker, Creel, and Assistant Secretary of the Navy Franklin D. Roose-

---

Command, 1985), p. 9. See also Nalty, *Strength for the Fight*, pp. 110–11. Young was posted to Liberia after the war and died in Nigeria in 1922; speakers at a memorial service in New York included Franklin D. Roosevelt, Spingarn, and Du Bois.

23. Baker to the president, July 1, 1918, Baker Papers, reel 6, p. 135.

24. Quoted in Loving, memorandum for Masteller, Negro Subversion Microfilm, reel 2, pp. 323–24; the date "5/2/19" is in pencil at the top. Loving refers to an April 27, 1919, speech by Du Bois in which the editor claimed that when he went to France, at Spingarn's urging, to see firsthand the conditions under which black soldiers fought, Military Intelligence kept him under surveillance.

25. Churchill to intelligence officer, Northeastern Department, July 12, 1918, Negro Subversion Microfilm, reel 2, p. 592; Churchill to same, July 13, p. 587; intelligence officer, Northeastern Department, to chief of MI, July 15, 1918, pp. 593–94. Trotter, who got along with neither Booker T. Washington nor Du Bois, is considered by his biographer to be "one of the twentieth century's first important Negro leaders in the militant tradition" (Long and Winston, eds., *Dictionary of American Negro Biography*, pp. 603–5).

velt. Spingarn felt that "perhaps no other incident created so much enthusiasm" as the reports of three French officers who spoke on "the treatment accorded to African troops in France." Spingarn had wanted the conferees to be able "to let off steam," and in that respect he judged the meeting a success, reporting to Churchill that "every phase of the negro problem was discussed."[26]

The most heated session featured Moton, who reported that judging from a tour of southern states, "he had never known so much unrest among his people." The chief cause, he believed, was the continued lynchings, which were "producing a dangerous feeling among the colored people of the country." Although other grievances were aired, among them "the refusal of the Red Cross to employ colored nurses, the refusal of the government bureaus to employ colored stenographers . . . the discrimination against negroes in travel, [and] the treatment of Colonel Young," the paramount complaint was the failure of the federal government "to protect colored people against lynching."[27] Du Bois drew the task of preparing a list of fourteen particular complaints, along with a message for the Creel Committee to pass to the president. The fourteen points began with a call for national legislation on lynching, followed by requests for black nurses and physicians in the military and for additional training and promotion for black officers. Equity along racial lines in assigning stevedore and sanitation duty was requested, as well as improvement in the way the white press reported black news. Other items dealt with Colonel Young's request for active duty, a loan for "the Negro Republic of Liberia," and clemency for the remaining soldiers sentenced to death for the Houston incident. A final point requested unspecified action on the "condition of travel among colored people," the closest the group came to a call for an end to Jim Crow segregation. No mention was made of removing the barriers that prevented blacks from voting.[28]

In an "Address to the Committee on Public Information," the editors maintained that "German propaganda among us is powerless, but the apparent indifference of our own Government may be dangerous." Counting seventy-one lynchings since the entrance of the United States into the war, including four women, and noting that "not a single person has been punished for lynching a Negro," the report concluded that "Federal intervention to suppress lynching is imperative." Citing the

26. Spingarn to Churchill, June 22, 1918, Negro Subversion Microfilm, reel 2, pp. 618–20.
27. Quoted in ibid.
28. The "Bill of Particulars" is in Negro Subversion Microfilm, reel 2, pp. 628–29.

lack of opportunity in government service, the analysis went on to recommend a presidential order ending "first-class fares and third-class accommodation and frequent other embarrassing discriminations" on the government-controlled railroads. Portions of the appealing conclusion bear repeating:

> The American Negro does not expect to have the whole Negro problem settled immediately; he is not seeking to hold-up a striving country and a distracted world by pushing irrelevant personal grievances as a price of loyalty . . .; but he is today compelled to ask for that minimum of consideration which will enable him to be an efficient fighter for victory, namely:
> (1) Better conditions of public travel
> (2) The acceptance of help where help is needed regardless of the color of the helper
> (3) The immediate suppression of lynching.[29]

Three days after Military Intelligence's black conference ended, the Colored Liberty Congress convened, and its criticism was direct. In attendance was Major Loving, who reported that the group "bitterly condemned" Emmett Scott for involving relatively few black editors in his meeting. Although Scott had invited Trotter, he had chosen not to come after Churchill's interference; others were "indignant and think themselves slighted" over their omission.[30] The Negative Branch prepared excerpts from the addresses at the congress in which the speakers emphasized the issues of segregation and disfranchisement. Trotter, after expressing loyalty to the flag that his father had fought to save, said, "When I walk down Pennsylvania Avenue and see Old Glory flying over so many jim crow places, I hang my head in shame for disgrace." A black attorney from Oklahoma, who had three sons in France, testified, "We are going to win this war, and when we win, I want the black fingers that are pulling the triggers to kill the Hun to be able to make a cross on the ballot." A delegate from "the dark and bloody ground" of Kentucky, who spoke of loving his country as he did his God, maintained, "If I thought that God Almighty wanted the white men of this nation to have all the good things and the colored the bad, I would willingly return to him this life as a precious gift."[31]

Though Churchill was no doubt distressed by such language, the

29. "Address to the Committee on Public Information," ibid., pp. 622–24.
30. Loving to chief of MI, July 1, 1918, ibid., reel 2, p. 591.
31. "Excerpts from Addresses at Colored Liberty Congress," ibid., reel 2, p. 589. For records on the Liberty Congress and Spingarn's conference, including a list of attendees, see ibid., reel 2, pp. 587–627; Surveillance of Afro-Americans Microfilm, reel 19, pp. 714–78.

conference planned by Spingarn apparently worked an amazing transformation in the intelligence commander. By June 1918 this man, who, like Van Deman, had consistently misread the American left as pro-German, had become virtually a reformer in race relations. He understood clearly what all students in survey courses of American history are now required to learn: that "for more than ten years educated negroes have been divided between two schools of thought." He correctly cited, in a memorandum for the chief of staff, those two camps as that established by Booker T. Washington, which stressed "the negro's need of industrial training and economic power," and a more recent one "represented by W. E. B. Du Bois, emphasizing the direct demand for civil and political rights." The reaction against "Dr. Washington's more conciliatory attitude," Churchill told his chief, "would have taken place even if we had not declared war against Germany; it is due to a consciousness of their inferior status on the part of large masses of negroes, for the first time in American history." Though some of the unrest "may be due to the interposition of German agents in isolated cases," he concluded that "the real causes are more fundamental." Noting that the primary grievance of blacks was lynching, he took the unprecedented action of endorsing the entire agenda from the editors' conference because "immediate attention to these fourteen complaints would stimulate negro morale to an extraordinary degree." His memorandum came back from the chief of staff stamped "Noted," and any start toward racial reform in the military was tabled for thirty years.[32]

After his conference, Spingarn testified before Congress on an antilynching bill, and, though the measure was stalled, movement continued in the executive branch. On July 1, 1918, the secretary of war wrote President Wilson a strong letter beginning: "I have been much disturbed and my anxiety is growing at the situation in this country among the negroes. The reports of the Military Intelligence Branch . . . indicate more unrest among them than has existed before for years." The conference had "resulted in a very helpful understanding," and he expected that "the negro press is going to be sounder," but Baker felt that a clear antilynching statement from the president was required. He wanted Wilson to point out "the unpatriotic character of these acts of brutality and injustice" and to urge the states to "search out and prosecute the offenders." He also suggested that the Department of Justice be ordered to assist in such investigations.[33]

32. Churchill, memorandum for the chief of staff, June (illegible) 1918, Negro Subversion Microfilm, reel 2, p. 621.
33. Baker to Wilson, July 1, 1918, Baker Papers, reel 6, p. 135.

Wilson had received a similar request from Moton and other black leaders, and he indicated an intention to make such a public statement, but when none was forthcoming over the next two weeks, Military Intelligence took action. Spingarn no doubt drafted the document, but it was Churchill's signature that forwarded to the chief of staff a letter which he proposed that the secretary of war send to the president. The letter asked Wilson to make a public call for the "immediate cessation of lynching," and Baker signed it without change.[34] On July 26 the Committee on Public Information released a formal statement from the White House. "There have been many lynchings," Wilson said, "and every one of them has been a blow at the heart of ordered law and humane justice." He asked, "How shall we commend democracy to the acceptance of other peoples, if we disgrace our own?"[35]

It is, of course, testimony to the racial conservatism of the Wilson administration that so much effort was required before he would make a simple statement deploring mob violence. And when he did, it was just that—mere moralizing. He did not unleash the Bureau of Investigation, as Baker had recommended, but instead urged the governors to "make an end to this disgraceful evil." It was certainly no civil rights act, but it was all that black Americans got. Perhaps the strangest aspect of this all too modest achievement was the intriguing role of Military Intelligence.

By the middle of July, Spingarn was busily at work in the Negative Branch organizing a "separate sub-section on negro subversion, which will be in charge of some of the ablest leaders of the colored people." He anticipated "a great deal of constructive work in countering unrest and disloyal propaganda."[36] Two weeks later he was ordered to France, and plans for the subsection were scrapped. Officially, the army explained that a decision had been made "to restrict military intelligence in the colored field entirely to colored troops."[37] Spingarn's sudden departure, following his apparent success, is jarring, especially in view of the fact that Churchill never implemented any such restriction on the scope of his unit's investigations. Something dreadful had happened in his relationship with Spingarn, resulting in the latter's immediate shipment overseas.

34. Churchill, memorandum for the chief of staff, July 19, 1918, Negro Subversion Microfilm, reel 2, p. 666; Baker to Wilson, July 19, 1918, p. 664. See Surveillance of Afro-Americans Microfilm, reel 19, pp. 779–90.

35. The press release with Wilson's July 25, 1918, statement is in Negro Subversion Microfilm, reel 2, pp. 671–72.

36. Spingarn to John Geary, July 16, 1918, ibid., reel 2, p. 571.

37. Spingarn to Scott, August 1, 1918, ibid., reel 2, p. 680.

There is no clue in the archives as to the reasons for Spingarn's precipitous removal. It seems to have caught him by surprise. Churchill, for his part, could not associate the word *formerly* with Spingarn's name soon enough, reporting his ouster a day before it technically occurred. [38] A year later, when Secretary Baker received a complaint that Spingarn had called for a general strike by southern blacks, the Negative Branch drafted a reply for the secretary which claimed that Spingarn's work in Military Intelligence "did not prove satisfactory." [39] Just before he was summarily relieved, Spingarn had finished a highly enthusiastic press release entitled "Editors' Conference Yields Big Results," which Churchill stopped as unnecessary. The piece contained no grounds for dismissal, merely waxing happily about the president's antilynching statement and the army's plans to accept black nurses. The document, which ended with a note that "Colonel Young may soon be called to active duty," was self-serving with its repeated statements about the success of the conference, and it may indeed have been unnecessary, but it was not insubordinate. [40]

Churchill may have held Spingarn responsible for the leak about the plans to torpedo Trotter's conference, or Spingarn's association with Du Bois may have caused his ouster. As a disciple of the late Booker T. Washington, Emmett Scott would not have appreciated Spingarn's overtures to Du Bois. Loving, too, and for the same reason, had never trusted Spingarn. In his investigative reports he always noted the white reformer's link to the NAACP and the *Crisis* in thinly disguised negative wording. Loving had also expressed a very low opinion of the editors' conference arranged by Du Bois and Spingarn. Whatever the cause, Spingarn was off to France, and while there he met Du Bois, who visited Europe after the Armistice, a rendezvous carefully noted by Loving. Perhaps Churchill had reached the conclusion, not officially expressed until 1919, that the NAACP was "urging the colored people to insist upon equality and to resort to force." Spingarn's leadership of such a dangerous organization would have certainly made him unwelcome in the Negative Branch. [41]

38. Churchill to Scott, August 2, 1918, ibid., reel 3, p. 271.

39. It is not clear that Baker signed the letter to Senator William F. Kirby; the copy in ibid., reel 5, p. 744, is unsigned and dated only July 1919. After service in France, Spingarn was discharged on April 5, 1919.

40. Spingarn's draft release, dated July 29, 1918, ibid., reel 2, pp. 678–81.

41. See Loving's reports, ibid., pp. 293, 323, 591. The view of the NAACP as dangerous is contained in a report to Churchill called "The Negro Situation," dated August 15, 1919, in Glasser Files, box 8. Spingarn had attempted to distance himself from the NAACP, sending in his resignation on July 6, 1918. When the board did not act on it, he repeated his

For a while after Spingarn's exit, Churchill made a display of sending information on black civilians to Scott in the secretary's office, with the note that Military Intelligence no longer had an interest in the matter. In fact, Loving's confidential mission continued for another year, well after the end of the war. In addition to Loving's work, Churchill charged his Morale Branch, formerly a section of the Negative Branch, with making a special study of the problems of the black soldier. On the whole, and given the times, Military Intelligence seems to have made an honest effort to handle unrest by improving conditions for blacks in the army. On December 30, 1918, for example, the Negative Branch reported to Scott that "the conditions as regards colored soldiers at Camp Sevier are not yet all that they should be, but there is evidence of some improvement having been made as a result of our efforts." Specifically, the Military Police and the white noncommissioned officers in charge of the labor battalions had been ordered "that they should, under all circumstances, handle and treat the colored soldier in the same way as the white soldier."[42] Even before the war was over Churchill's white officer in charge of black morale had suggested to the YMCA's intelligence chief that his agency remove the "For Whites Only" signs at the recreation huts. Although separate huts were to be maintained, the segregation was to be more subtle, handled by unit designation.[43] Nevertheless, there was still a shortage of huts available for blacks.

Cosmetic changes and even an attempt to end the abuse by white sergeants were hardly enough to pacify soldiers or civilians when they continued to be subject to lynch law. In late 1918, after the lynching of a black uniformed soldier in Kentucky and of two brothers and two sisters in Alabama, Loving reported to Churchill that racial unrest seemed to have increased since the Armistice. Black papers across the country, he said, were asking, "What will be the negro's reward for helping to win the war for democracy?" Loving felt that the disappointing answer had created a situation in which "not since the East St. Louis riot have the colored people been so worked up as they are today," and he very much feared a repeat of that violence. Loving's operatives were covering mass

desire to quit, noting, "I feel myself wholly out of sympathy with the attitude of some of the directors" (Surveillance of Afro-Americans Microfilm, reel 19, p. 811). His relief from intelligence may have helped restore his relations with the NAACP; he remained its chairman for another year and later held other offices with the association.

42. Masteller to Scott, December 30, 1918, Negro Subversion Microfilm, reel 4, p. 516.

43. Cutler to Low, September 26, 1918, ibid., reel 3, p. 416. The printed guide to Surveillance of Afro-Americans Microfilm lists the various reports on camp conditions separately by location.

protest meetings and attempting to defuse the situation, but he was plainly worried.[44]

Large-scale violence did not occur in the winter of 1918–19, and Churchill's Morale Branch had time to finish its study "The Negro in the Army." This report, compiled by Major James E. Cutler, was completed on December 23, 1918, and was based on the results of a questionnaire completed by the intelligence officers at forty-six military installations. Cutler also relied on Loving's reports on army camps and on similar evaluations supplied by a black minister, Charles H. Williams, who as field secretary for the Federal Council of Chuches' Committee on Welfare of Negro Soldiers had inspected twenty-five camps.

Williams continued his inspections until February 1919, and he made several specific recommendations in his thorough final report. He called for a "change in the atmosphere" regarding the treatment of black soldiers by white officers and for more black officers, chaplains, and sergeants. The civilian also suggested that the educational programs for immigrants be extended to blacks, and he wanted a recreation officer appointed at each camp, along with the construction of suitable "hostess houses" where black soldiers could receive guests. That last point was of considerable importance because on the segregated posts there were no restroom facilities for black women, except where the YMCA provided them.[45]

Cutler's study, which agreed with Williams's findings in many respects, stressed the unhappiness of northern blacks, who, when sent to southern posts, found themselves in a hostile environment. He also identified the conduct of the Military Police as a problem.[46] More revealing than the results of his survey was the secret bulletin that covered the questionnaire Cutler sent to camp intelligence officers. Cutler's analysis of the sociological problems faced by blacks in the military betrayed his traditional racial views. The typical black from civilian life, he said, was "seldom so accustomed to personal cleanliness

44. Loving to director of MI, Negro Subversion Microfilm, reel 4, pp. 763–64; Surveillance of Afro-Americans Microfilm, reel 20, pp. 900–908.

45. Williams's reports are in Negro Subversion Microfilm, reel 6, pp. 1136–1293; see printed guide to Surveillance of Afro-Americans Microfilm. While completing his report in early 1919, Williams was "Physical Director" of the athletic association at Hampton Institute (Surveillance of Afro-Americans Microfilm, reel 19, p. 65). Scott termed his work "painstaking and well planned," and Cutler regarded him as "competent and reliable" and "a qualified colored man" (reel 22, pp. 1160–67).

46. Cutler's report is a December 23, 1918, memorandum for the director of MI, Negro Subversion Microfilm, reel 4, pp. 797–816; Surveillance of Afro-Americans Microfilm, reel 20, pp. 988–1001.

or general sanitation. The mere requirement of having to take a bath may seem an intolerable burden." A black had "not the least sense of what discipline means" because he had "been accustomed to take life very easily and to work now and then when he got around to it." Generally illiterate, "in every way more isolated than the white man," and "more gullible . . . , his habitual easy-going docility may prove either an asset or a liability."[47]

No doubt Cutler regarded himself as a liberal on the race question, since he desired "that colored troops should have every possible chance, within their domain, that white troops have in theirs. In a word, Separation *but* Equal Opportunity." Cutler's views were entirely in line with those of the secretary of war, who had announced two months earlier that it was his policy "to avoid the mixing of colored and white men in the same organization."[48] Every Military Intelligence analysis that addressed the point reaffirmed the wisdom of segregated units. The reform they urged was an increase in the number of black commissioned and noncommissioned officers. That was the world of Wilsonian America. No better testimony could be had of Military Intelligence's inability to grasp the real problem than the racial practices in the very building housing Churchill's headquarters. The numerous black women who worked in that six-story structure, mostly cleaning ladies and messengers, had access to only one restroom on the first floor. Five black typists working on the sixth, however, were so impressed with their role in making the world safe for democracy that they protested the matter of restrooms to Emmett Scott.[49] He queried Churchill. After having made so many investigations of other units regarding allegations of mistreatment of blacks, Churchill now had to look into his own. He shot back to Scott word that "other arrangements have been made."[50]

In the spring of 1919 Cutler made another report on the need for improvement in the treatment of blacks in the army and for greater opportunity for training and promotion. On May 9, 1919, Churchill forwarded Cutler's memorandum to the chief of staff, noting once again the "seriousness of the negro question" and that "all officers do not carry out the spirit of the War Department policy with respect to a square deal for the negro."[51] There seems little doubt that despite its severe limita-

47. MI3 bulletin for intelligence officers, No. 31, October 21, 1918, Negro Subversion Microfilm, reel 4, pp. 824–26.
48. Quoted in ibid., p. 826.
49. Juanita M. Curtis et al., to Scott, October 26, 1918, ibid., p. 48.
50. Churchill to Scott, November 13, 1918, ibid., p. 50.
51. Churchill, memorandum for chief of staff, May 9, 1919, ibid., p. 933. Cutler's study is a memorandum for Churchill, May 9, 1919, pp. 927–28.

tions in understanding the racial issue, Military Intelligence was well ahead of the rest of the army and of the average white citizen. Like other calls for civil rights reform, however, those of Churchill's division went unheeded.

In the summer of 1919 the explosion that Loving had feared came with a vengeance. The major was putting the finishing touches on his final report and preparing to return to the Philippines when the nation's capital erupted. There had been hints of trouble: a fight with sailors buying liquor from blacks in Charleston started a two-day riot in May, leaving three dead; on July 1 a racial disturbance in Longview, Texas, killed five. Mayhem came to the nation's capital on Saturday night, July 19, when, after sensational press accounts of black assaults on white women, a gang of two hundred soldiers and sailors tried to lynch a black man. During four nights of rioting, with armed blacks and whites traveling about in cars, Washington became a free-fire zone. Six were killed and hundreds wounded. A week later, on July 27, Chicago saw even greater violence in, as Military Intelligence said, a "Race War" that killed thirty-eight people. In late September, troops had to suppress a riot in Omaha, and just days later other units were called to Elaine, Arkansas.[52]

Despite the demobilization then well under way, 1919 was also the year of the Red Scare, and, thanks to that paranoia, Military Intelligence was already rearming by the time the race riots began. Churchill gave special authority for the use of volunteer investigators, former members of the American Protective League, in Omaha and Chicago. In Washington, the Department of Justice was finally moved to hire a black special agent for undercover work in the district, but the Bureau of Investigation continued to rely on Military Intelligence for assistance.[53] Cutler saw four reasons for the disorder in Washington: "long continued propaganda . . . urging the colored people to insist upon equality"; resentment by black veterans over their treatment in the army; "attacks upon white women by colored men"; and a poorly prepared local police

52. The Charleston incident is reported in Glasser Files, box 6; Washington, box 8; Chicago, box 4, including the "Report of the Coroner's Jury on the Race Riots"; Omaha, box 5; and Arkansas, box 3. In Negro Subversion Microfilm, Chicago is reel 5, pp. 877–80, 922; Omaha, reel 6, pp. 133–40; Arkansas, reel 6, pp. 168–72. See Surveillance of Afro-Americans Microfilm, reel 21, pp. 443–601, 750–807, for riot material. See also William M. Tuttle, Jr., *Race Riot: Chicago in the Red Summer of 1919* (New York: Atheneum, 1972).

53. Henry G. Sebastian, memorandum for Coxe, August 9, 1919, Negro Subversion Microfilm, reel 5, p. 1018, and Glasser Files, box 6.

force.[54] Loving, who submitted his "Final Report on Negro Subversion" on August 6, had been profoundly altered by the riots. "The Negro has finally decided," he said, "that he has endured all that he can endure. He has decided to strike back."[55]

Loving's fifteen-page, single-spaced report is a fascinating summary of the impact of the war on American blacks. He expressed alarm that the "torch of socialism" had been taken up by bright young blacks since 1915, and he predicted that "the time is not far distant when greater numbers of Negroes will be converted to Socialistic doctrines" so ably expounded by New York black radicals Chandler Owen and A. Philip Randolph. Noting that in the past two years black membership in the IWW had increased from a neglible number to several thousand, Loving thought that the American Federation of Labor's history of discrimination against blacks would make it difficult for that union "to overcome the suspicion in which it is now held by Negro workmen."[56]

Although Loving regarded the Universal Negro Improvement Association as "too young as yet to give it any special significance," he thought the dynamic leadership of Marcus Garvey worthy of continued surveillance by Military Intelligence. The Negative Branch's interest in Garvey had begun in late 1918, apparently initiated by an inquiry from the British intelligence service. Loving and Biddle monitored his movements, a stenographer covered his meetings, and the postal censors checked his mail. Bureau of Investigation agents began making reports on him about the same time.[57] On December 9, Scott summoned Garvey to his office, where he cautioned him against "disrupting the unity of purpose which should exist between the racial groups." Garvey, Scott advised Military Intelligence, "should not be seriously regarded."[58]

54. Cutler, memorandum for the director of MI, July 23, 1919, Negro Subversion Microfilm, reel 5, p. 853.
55. Loving to director of MI, August 6, 1919, Negro Subversion Microfilm, reel 5, pp. 1001–15; also in Surveillance of Afro-Americans Microfilm, reel 21, pp. 613–39 (hereafter cited as Loving Report).
56. Loving Report.
57. The army dossier on Garvey, which includes material from the Bureau of Investigation, is in Negro Subversion Microfilm, reel 4, pp. 78–299, with additional material on reel 6, pp. 1–112, 204–11, 408–68. In Surveillance of Afro-Americans Microfilm, see reel 20, pp. 360–548; for navy material on Garvey, reel 23, pp. 683–707. For stenographic records of other Garvey speeches, see Lusk Committee Papers, L0038, box 2, folder 1, New York State Archives, Albany; for other information, including photographs, L0039, box 1, folder 18.
58. Scott, memorandum for the director of MI, December 11, 1918, Negro Subversion Microfilm, reel 4, pp. 108–9.

Churchill thought otherwise, and surveillance of Garvey continued until 1921. When Loving queried John E. Bruce, a publisher of black literature, about an alleged connection with Garvey, the former reporter retorted, "Please do not insult me by linking my name with any movement, plan, scheme, plot or enterprise with which Marcus Garvey is identified." Instead, he said, "put me down as a 100% 'Merican, red hot republican, and a shouting methodist."[59]

Loving contented himself with a short entry on the NAACP, noting that "among its founders and members are some of the most prominent white men of America." He cited Spingarn, mentioning his former connection with Military Intelligence, and Oswald Garrison Villard, "one of its principal financial backers." He estimated the 1919 membership at 50,000. More interesting to Loving was a recently formed black veterans' organization, the League for Democracy, which he thought would certainly have 150,000 members. He blamed "the short sighted and narrow minded policy of some of the high ranking white officers of the 92nd Division" and the "incompetence and brutality of some of the white officers" of the labor battalions for making this group "a veritable hornets nest of radicals." Since the league welcomed all veterans, regardless of former rank, and encouraged "political alliances with any other radical element," he recommended that the intelligence community give it "the closest scrutiny." He also urged that a full-time black agent be maintained in Harlem, the location of 100,000 blacks and "a hot bed of radicalism which requires continual vigilance on the part of the government."[60]

His analysis of the causes of the recent riots was far different from Cutler's. Even with the long-standing grievances against lynching, disfranchisement, and segregation, Loving said, "it required the awakened spirit of the Negro soldier returning from France full of bitter resentment to set the spark that has released the pent up feelings of the masses." The "insidious propaganda and prejudice" that black soldiers had felt at the hands of white Americans in France was all the "more galling" when compared to their "free social intermingling" with the French. Loving also observed that blacks were bitterly aware of the "confidential circular sent out from the American Army" attempting to have the French limit their tradition of racial acceptance.

At home, Loving saw black civilians equally discontented during the war: "While colored soldiers were shedding their blood in France, their

59. Bruce to Loving, January 13, 1919, ibid., pp. 129–30.
60. Loving Report. Quotations in the following two paragraphs are from this source.

brothers at home were being lynched and burned at the stake. Prejudice flourished as never before." Even the social and economic gains blacks had made during the war worked against them, for when working-class whites returned from France they found blacks on their jobs and in their neighborhoods. The black veteran, however, did not cower before the white backlash: "Defense of himself against German whites," Loving observed, was "quickly shifted to defense of himself against American whites." He considered segregated housing, "whether voluntary or involuntary," a "menace to public safety." In a tactical analysis that should have appealed to the military, he noted that during a disturbance the separated communities became "hostile alien territory," where innocent whites were endangered in black neighborhoods and vice versa.

Major Cutler, whom Churchill considered "an absolutely impartial expert in sociology," gave Loving's final report deep study. Although he noted that his black colleague had "changed his viewpoint somewhat," he nevertheless considered it "a conservative and judicious statement by a colored man." He agreed that during the war the call for black participation in Liberty Loan drives and the cry for "patriotic cooperation" had produced an expectation of "a modification, or possibly removal, of some of the discrimination of which they complain." The situation was so alarming, Cutler said, that even the trusted Loving had come to feel that "agitation and the strongest pressure that the colored people can muster, short of actual hostilities, is now their only recourse." This militancy, he added, "probably typifies the attitude of a considerable proportion of the more thoughtful and substantial negro citizens." Speaking as a sociologist, he thought that the present crisis "may mark the beginning of what usually happens when a people native to the temperate [sic] zone comes in contact with a people native to the tropical zone." Appreciating the successful work of the Urban League in "minimizing the after-effects of the East St. Louis riots and promoting better race relations," he thought the tension might be relieved if "proper ways" could be found to end lynching and to modify "certain 'Jim Crow' regulations so that their enforcement would strike less harshly those for whom these restrictions are not primarily intended."[61]

After pressure from his New York branch, Churchill gave serious

---

61. Churchill's memorandum to the chief of staff, August 20, 1919, Negro Subversion Microfilm, reel 5, p. 1028, and Glasser Files, box 8, includes Cutler's comments on Loving's analysis. Loving's final report somehow fell into the hands of the British secret service, which continued to express a keen interest in American race relations until early 1922; see Negro Subversion Microfilm, reel 6, pp. 231, 525–32; Surveillance of Afro-Americans Microfilm, reel 21, pp. 830–40.

consideration to hiring the Harlem agent recommended by Loving. He had the funds formerly used for Loving's program, and the operative was willing to work for three dollars a day, well under the going rate. Yet Churchill's division, and the entire military, faced tremendous cutbacks, and in the end he had higher priorities on his list of domestic threats. Both Cutler and Loving were demobilized in August, and the latter returned to the Philippines, where he was conductor of the Constabulary Band.[62] After their departure, only occasional reports came in from field units. Along with monitoring Garvey, the army also watched the foreign travels of Jack Johnson, "Negro Ex champ," who had fled because of legal troubles in the United States. When Johnson came to Mexico in 1919 to give exhibition fights, the Fort Sam Houston intelligence office sent excited accounts of his telling the Mexicans how much better they were "than the D—— American Gringoes."[63]

The army's attitude toward Garvey and Johnson was typical of the results of its grappling for a way to resolve the domestic threat of black unrest. Only the negative aspects survived. There is no evidence that Military Intelligence's attempt to improve conditions for blacks in the army and in American society had any lasting significance. The racial reforms recommended by the Negative Branch were forgotten, and as Military Intelligence continued to shrivel within the peacetime army, "Negro Subversion" became a neglected topic. Most of the information the army received on the subject in the early 1920s came from the Department of Justice.

Despite the lack of any marked progress in civil rights, the terrible summer of 1919 was not repeated for over twenty years. When the social tensions of the 1930s returned the army's attention to black Americans, it was entirely focused on the threat of their being subverted by a foreign power. There was, however, that brief period, from the spring of 1918 to the fall of 1919, when Military Intelligence, relative to contemporary white opinion, was just a tiny bit to the left on the race question.

---

62. On the dismantling of Loving's program, see Negro Subversion Microfilm, reel 5, pp. 1016–20, 1030–33; Surveillance of Afro-Americans Microfilm, reel 21, pp. 613–39.

63. John J. Gallagher to department intelligence officer, Fort Sam Houston, August 18, 1919, Negro Subversion Microfilm, reel 6, p. 221. The army, navy, and Departments of State and Justice all followed Johnson's movements, usually referring to him as the "well known negro pugilist" and frequently calling him a traitor. In Surveillance of Afro-Americans Microfilm, see the army file in reel 23, pp. 185–206; for the Justice material, reel 10, pp. 968–75; for army-State cooperation in trying to capture Johnson, who wanted to turn himself in, see reel 18, pp. 155–96, 712–41.

CHAPTER 8

War's End

The work of the Military Intelligence," the secretary of war told President Wilson two days after the Armistice, "will continue." Baker had a more specific outcome in mind with that remark, but it did sum up the permanence the division had achieved in the army's hierarchy. Indeed, General Pershing in France had made his chief intelligence officer a part of his general staff, with the designation G–2, beginning a nomenclature that has continued to the present. Baker used the stability of Military Intelligence to justify granting the president's wish that his friend Grant Squires, the volunteer spy who had burglarized the offices of the National Civil Liberties Bureau, be granted a commission as an intelligence officer.[1]

Baker made Squires an exception to the freeze he had just placed on commissions. Not another one of the volunteers seems to have been treated similarly as the order of the day was a major reduction in force and a year-long demobilization process. Marlborough Churchill prepared a form letter releasing the other volunteers, whose hopes for commissions were dashed by the coming of peace. On November 13, he read the statement aloud to the twenty-nine amateur sleuths in his Washington office, and he intended that volunteers across the country would be separated from their association with army intelligence.[2]

The secretary of war's goal was to reduce the military to no more than 325,000 men by June 1919 and to shrink the intelligence staff in similarly drastic proportions. The plant protection program disappeared, and the Negative Branch was reduced to 27 officers and 31 civilian clerks and stenographers. By the demobilization deadline, the entire Military Intelligence Division had dropped by over a thousand to a mere 274, including all officers, enlisted men, and civilian employees. The branch in New York, the biggest, saw the largest cuts. Within three months after the Armistice, its force of officers was reduced from 25 to 7, its intel-

---

1. Baker to Wilson, November 13, 1918, responding to Wilson's of November 12, Papers of Newton D. Baker, microfilm reel 6, p. 245, Manuscript Division, Library of Congress.
2. Churchill's form letter, November 13, 1918, releasing volunteers and the list of those in Washington who heard it read are in 10560 (not further designated), Record Group 165, MID, National Archives.

ligence police from 51 to 21, and its civilians from 86 to 37. The entire Corps of Intelligence Police technically disappeared in 1920 when the National Defense Act failed to include any staffing authorization. In a paper shuffle, the army was able to keep a remnant of the corps by shifting 45 sergeants from the Detached Enlisted Men's List to serve as intelligence police at the headquarters of the corps areas, the new designation for what had formerly been called departments. By 1934 there were only 15 enlisted men serving in that capacity.[3]

Naval Intelligence went through a similar demobilization, reducing its complement of three hundred reserve officers in November 1918 to twenty-four in 1920. Like the army, the navy did not immediately withdraw from domestic intelligence. Its report on radical influence among dock workers was not finished until over a month after the end of the war, and during that winter navy agents in Pittsburgh kept a close eye on a strike at General Electric and watched conditions in the navy yards very closely. Generally, however, the navy's collection of information was pretty much limited to maintaining liaison with the Department of Justice. In May 1919 a new director of Naval Intelligence, Albert P. Niblack, took the navy completely out of what he called "gumshoe methods."[4]

On February 1, 1919, Churchill's division lost its location in the Hooe Building at 1330 F Street and was moved to a "temporary structure," Unit A at Sixth and B. Squires complained bitterly to the president about the vulnerability of the army's valuable dossiers in that firetrap. A fortnight later the division announced that because of the "rapid demo-

3. U.S. Army, *The History of the Counter Intelligence Corps in the United States Army, 1917–1950 (with Limited Tabular Data to 1960),* 30 vols. (Baltimore: U.S. Army Intelligence Center, 1959), 4:2–3, 16, in Record Group 319, National Archives (hereafter cited as CIC History). Bruce W. Bidwell, *History of the Military Intelligence Division, Department of the Army General Staff, 1775–1941* (Frederick, Md.: University Publications of America, 1986), pp. 252, 257, 364–75; undated, typed manuscript, "Military Intelligence Division," Record Group 165, MID, 10560–1–A Part II, National Archives; see also a manpower chart showing a roughly 50 percent reduction by February 16, 1919, in 10560–489. For Edmund Leigh's unsuccessful attempt to keep the Plant Protection Section alive, see Bertha Campbell, memorandum for file, July 19, 1919, Alexander B. Coxe, Sr., Papers, J. Y. Joyner Library, East Carolina University, Greenville, N.C.

4. Jeffrey M. Dorwart, *The Office of Naval Intelligence: The Birth of America's First Intelligence Agency, 1865–1918* (Annapolis: Naval Institute Press, 1979), pp. 139–40. For the strike in Pittsburgh, see the "Suspect" file in Record Group 38, Naval Intelligence, box 12, National Archives. The December 23, 1918, report, "Investigation of the Marine Transport Workers and the Alleged Threatened Combination between Them and the Bolsheviki and the Sinn Feiners," is in ibid., "CAP" file, box 8; Record Group 60, Glasser Files, box 5; and Randolph Boehm, ed., *U.S. Military Intelligence Reports: Surveillance of Radicals in the United States, 1917–1941* (Frederick, Md.: University Publications of America, 1984), reel 8, pp. 212–67 (hereafter cited as MI Microfilm).

bilization," the handsomely printed *Supplement of the Work and Activities of the Military Intelligence Division* would cease to appear.[5] The diminished intelligence capacity of the army was so obvious that in March a Washington reporter referred to the "lame ducks of the distintegrating Bureau of Military Intelligence."[6]

Only a month before, Churchill had been reprimanded by the attorney general over the illegal arrests in Butte, and he seemed more than willing to watch his command wither away. With evident relief, he told his intelligence officers in a widely distributed "circular letter" of November 20, 1918, that "the emergency no longer exists that required . . . investigations among the civil population." He gave a specific order to "undertake no new investigations." Graft and fraud cases involving military contracts were to continue, but "all unfinished disloyalty and enemy activity cases" were to be turned over to the Department of Justice. He further ordered that the "documentary evidence," the identification cards and other credentials, given to civilian investigators were to be called in and forwarded to him. "Transmit these instructions to all your subordinates," he demanded, "and insist on prompt compliance therewith." Military Intelligence was out of the business of spying on civilians.[7]

In the heat of the Red Scare, partisans of Military Intelligence later blamed Secretary Baker for curtailing the army's fight against domestic subversion. Churchill insisted, however, that he alone had made the decision, after checking with the chief of staff, and that "the Secretary of War never knew anything about the issuing of the order of November . . . until long after." He considered his action "not only expedient but proper," claiming to have recognized the necessity of restraining a Military Intelligence "full of young, enthusiastic officers, scattered all over the country and in every military unit." He felt that the continued application of espionage and "police methods in the investigation of individuals, along lines made prominent by their political beliefs," would have become "a scandal and a menace to our form of government."

5. John M. Dunn, memorandum for Captain Fields, February 12, 1919, Record Group 165, MID, 10560–209/1; and Dunn, memorandum for file, January 25, 1919, 10560–169/4, National Archives. Secretary of War Baker described the strength reductions in a June 14, 1919, letter to Isaac Siegel, 10560–265/2, ibid. Squires's complaint is in Squires to Wilson, January 30, 1919, in Arthur S. Link et al., eds., *Papers of Woodrow Wilson*, vol. 54 (Princeton: Princeton University Press, 1986), 396–98.

6. Quoted in Rhodri Jeffreys-Jones, *American Espionage: From Secret Service to CIA* (New York: Free Press, 1977), pp. 22–25.

7. Churchill to all intelligence officers in the United States, November 20, 1918, Record Group 165, MID, 10560–277, National Archives.

When "the Army does not obey the law," he said in a striking admission of the illegality of his agency's acts, "tyranny, oppression and militarism, in its worst sense, will result."[8]

Despite the preciseness of Churchill's order, however, work in the field did not end immediately. Some intelligence officers in low-intensity areas, such as the headquarters of the Southeastern department in Charleston, quickly reported that "all pending cases among the civilian population were turned over to the Department of Justice and our operatives discharged."[9] Others, faced with continued radical activity, were slower in their response, all the more so perhaps because they knew that Churchill was not available to enforce his mandate. Within two weeks of his order, he placed the Military Intelligence Division in the hands of his assistant Colonel John M. Dunn and left the country to attend the peace conference in Paris. He did not return until the following spring.

In Spokane, the energetic Dengel reported promptly that he was releasing his civilian operatives on November 30, noting that their work had resulted in considerable disorder among factions within radical organizations. That sanguine estimate was dashed a few days later when he received a report that the infamous IWW attorney George F. Vanderveer was claiming new strength for the Wobblies as a result of increasing unemployment associated with the demobilization. He found it particularly alarming that Vanderveer knew that "the Army Intelligence Department was being disbanded and had withdrawn the stool-pigeons from the field." Undercover investigations in the Northwest were reinstated.[10]

Other units reported instances of surveillance continuing into December. Suspected Socialists in Pittsburgh were shadowed by army agents, and a former intelligence officer at the Air Service Depot in Garden City, New York, paid for an informant's investigation of "Bolshevist leaders" with funds siphoned from the camp newspaper. In New Orleans, a Military Intelligence officer masqueraded as a reporter to attend a meeting "at Kolb's notorious and pro-German restaurant" of "a group of men who refer to themselves as 'Social Workers.'" Here the

8. Churchill to Trevor, January 16, 1920, MI Microfilm, reel 15, pp. 886–89; see also Churchill to chief of staff, July 3, 1919, Record Group 165, MID, 10560–277/10, National Archives.

9. Intelligence officer, Southeastern Department, to director of MI, December 24, 1918, MI Microfilm, reel 12, p. 1029.

10. District intelligence officer, Spokane, to director of MI, November 26, 1918, ibid., reel 9, pp. 863–64; district intelligence officer, Spokane, to intelligence officer, Western Department, December 3, 1918, pp. 857–58.

agent encountered and interviewed Harry L. Hopkins, then a Red Cross worker and later a key member of Franklin D. Roosevelt's New Deal. Suspicious of Hopkins's interest in the Bolshevik revolution, the agent concluded that "Hopkins is all right . . . and probably spoke without a due consideration of his choice of words." The New Orleans officer informed Washington of his plans to continue his investigation, "with a view to finding out who the Bolshevists sympathizers are, and who are their associates."[11]

The chief foot-dragger was Major Thomas B. Crockett, intelligence officer for the Central Department in Chicago. The first dodge he used was to request a clarification of the cease-fire order. When informed emphatically that he was included, he strengthened his already close ties with the American Protective League, with which he enjoyed a special relationship because he had been an assistant to founder Albert M. Briggs. On December 12, he requested from the APL's state inspector in Wisconsin the names, addresses, and activities of members of "Radical organizations in your territory." There was no danger of exposing his domestic spy work, he told Washington on December 28, because his "investigations of radical associations, agencies and individuals are conducted strictly 'under cover.'" Filtering his network through the APL, he boasted, meant that most of his informants were unaware of their connection to the army. As 1919 opened, Crockett still had agents attending radical meetings.[12]

The field was confused, and what Churchill had regarded as a simple order had resulted in "every office of every department in every district," as the Seattle intelligence officer put it, having "a different policy." To address this problem, Seattle circulated in mid-December a list titled "Suggestions for I. W. W.-Bolsheviki Investigators." Under the heading "Don'ts for I. W. W." was an appeal to refrain from publicly recognizing the menace since "they depend upon publicity for their very existence." The army was advised to cease disrupting meetings and raiding IWW halls because "unlawful action toward them" provided a "plausible excuse for claim of persecution." Similarly, arrests were dis-

---

11. The target in Pittsburgh was William Thurston Brown of Ferrer Colony, a progressive school in Stelton, New Jersey (intelligence officer, Pittsburgh, to acting director of MI, December 11, 1918, ibid., reel 8, p. 303). For Garden City, see Harry C. Lear to Captain Johnson, December 3, 1918, reel 11, p. 920. On Harry Hopkins, see intelligence officer, New Orleans, to acting director of MI, January 31, 1919, reel 12, pp. 969–73.

12. Department intelligence officer, Chicago, to H. H. Seaman, December 12, 1918, ibid., reel 12, p. 1009; department intelligence officer, Chicago, to director of MI, December 30, 1918, p. 1028; Joan M. Jensen, *The Price of Vigilance* (Chicago: Rand McNally, 1968), pp. 243–44.

couraged except for specific offenses and only when convictions were certain. Under "What To Do," Seattle urged a uniform policy for all army investigators and a centralized approach to investigations that would end the present "disconnected system" wherein each unit identified its own targets and ran its own cases relatively unsupervised. Positive tactics included increased censorship of radical publications, a counter-propaganda educational campaign through the Department of Labor, and the deportation of radicals under the recent October 16 law that allowed the expulsion of "Alien agitators." Seattle was opposed to the use of private detectives as informants because they "like the I. W. W.'s are dependent upon labor agitation for their existence." Instead, that office recommended employing "intelligent, conscientious, well-paid operatives who are willing to make such work and study a permanent undertaking." Such measures were needed, the Seattle chief concluded, because "the I. W. W., the Bolsheviki, the radical socialists and, on some issues, the A. F. of L. have joined," and the Northwest was faced with increasing "advocacy of sedition, revolution and sabotage."[13]

As 1919 opened, army units around the country echoed Seattle's call for, as San Francisco put it, "a uniform and well considered line of action." Most applauded the idea of a counterpropaganda campaign. San Francisco also noted one other special concern for most units. Except for Washington's branches in major cities, all other intelligence offices had a local commander to whom they had to respond. The commanding general of the Western Department, for example, wanted as "full information as possible on the development of the I. W. W. and its plans" so as to respond swiftly to a strike or insurrection. His intelligence office saw its duty to "continue to make every possible effort to secure such information," orders from the Military Intelligence Division in Washington notwithstanding. It was equally clear to San Francisco, and probably to most other offices, that the "only means of any great value" to acquire useful data was "the inside informant." With enough money and "extreme finesse," spies could be placed in the "inner circles" of radical organizations.[14]

In New York, where Biddle was in the process of turning over command to Captain John B. Trevor, Military Intelligence was no less active when the war ended, and the branch office seems to have enjoyed an

13. Office of MI, Seattle, to director of MI, December 13, 1918, MI Microfilm, reel 12, pp. 1036–38.

14. Department intelligence officer, San Francisco, to director of MI, January 10, 1919, ibid., reel 12, pp. 1016–17. Responses from other units to the Seattle letter are spread throughout reel 12.

exception to the no-spying rule. On November 28, an agent and a stenographer from that office attended a meeting of the Russian branch of the Socialist party and found the remarks of Morris Zucker so offensive that they turned their report over to the federal attorney. After army operatives testified before a grand jury, Zucker was indicted and subsequently sentenced to fifteen years for violation of the Espionage Act. In Washington, the Negative Branch concluded that the Zucker case had demonstrated "that the arrangement for the New York Office of Military Intelligence to cover all radical meetings is not in vain, and that the wheels of justice continue to turn in spite of the Armistice."[15]

In mid-November, Archibald E. Stevenson, civilian volunteer and chief of the propaganda section of the New York office, submitted an alarming report on the spread of Bolshevism. The "German Proletariat," he said, was "following the footsteps of its Russian comrades," and all of eastern Europe presented "the same spectacle of upheaval." He worried that "the poison of the Bolshevist" might well "flow over the borders of the Central Powers into Italy and France." He felt that "the congested and industrial districts" in the United States were equally vulnerable. In New York alone he reported there were 4 million persons who were either foreign-born or the children of immigrants, and of these half a million could not speak English. Most disconcerting to him was that the foreign-language press serving that population had "almost without exception . . . carried the message that the war is a capitalist enterprise and inimical to the interests of the Proletariat." Like the Seattle analyst, Stevenson believed the various radical groups were ending their differences and joining in common cause. By his count, "ten to fifteen revolutionary meetings per week" were being held in New York, and the flow of reports into his office proved "without question that there is an organized conspiracy to overthrow the present form of the American government." To meet this threat, Stevenson proposed that Military Intelligence give its files on radicalism to the New York attorney general and urge him to "institute a thoroughgoing investigation of Bolsheviki and allied subjects" and subpoena "all persons known to be connected in any way with the revolutionary activities."[16]

When Biddle forwarded Stevenson's plan to Washington, acting director Dunn flatly rejected it. He thought the proposed state investigation

15. Particulars on the Zucker case and the statement about the arrangements for the New York office are in *Supplement of the Work and Activities of the Military Intelligence Division*, which has March 8, 1919, stamped on it, but which covers the period for mid-January, ibid., reel 13, pp. 662–72.
16. Stevenson to Biddle, November 12, 1918, ibid., reel 12, pp. 1004–7.

would be too "protracted and somewhat vague in purpose." That a federal agency should seek help from a state official on a matter "essentially *national* in scope" was both "impolitic and unwarranted." Furthermore, there "would be too great a risk of Military Intelligence becoming identified publicly with repressive measures in the realm of politics."[17] Far from reprimanding Stevenson for his presumption, however, Dunn gave him a "marked commendation for his valuable study," telling Biddle that the propaganda specialist should be "encouraged to continue a close observation of the movement and its agents." Stevenson stayed on the job, and on December 30 he submitted his "Report of Radical Movement[s] and Propaganda; Part I: Syndicalism and Socialism."[18] Stevenson was sharply critical of the IWW and other radical organizations, but his particular concern was the intellectual support given these groups by the National Civil Liberties Bureau.

When his army office had cooperated with the Department of Justice in a raid on that headquarters in late August 1918, it had found letters showing the "intimate relationship" between the NCLB and the IWW. It had also uncovered evidence proving to Stevenson's easily persuaded mind that high-ranking administration officials, particularly George Creel and Colonel Edward M. House, had used their influence with the president on behalf of Roger Baldwin's civil libertarian organization. Stevenson found another cornerstone of the radical structure in New York's Rand School of Social Science. Here, well-known radicals such as Algernon Lee, Scott Nearing, and Morris Hillquit were aided and abetted by subversive academics. In the latter group, Stevenson named John Dewey, Henry W. L. Dana, and Charles A. Beard. "The intelligence and energy of these men," he observed, "should not be underestimated," for their purpose was "to excite the interest and emotions of the masses of the people."[19]

Such reports had alarmed Dunn to the point that he took for granted that Military Intelligence's national espionage network against radicalism would continue despite the November 20 order. He interpreted messages from Churchill in Paris as being in agreement. Under Dunn's direction, one of the last issues of the *Supplement* was devoted to "Negative Intelligence within the Civil Population: Radical Propaganda." Noting with pleasure the convictions of IWW leaders and other radicals across the country, this printed publication also reported with

17. Acting director of MI to Biddle, November 29, 1918, ibid., reel 11, pp. 818–19.
18. Stevenson's December 30, 1918, report, ibid., reel 13, pp. 440–96.
19. Ibid., p. 496.

obvious approval that uniformed soldiers and sailors were continuing to break up radical meetings. In its national survey, the analysis asserted that the American Federation of Labor in Seattle was thoroughly revolutionary and that "Bolshevism thrives among the Jews and Letts and Russians." The *Supplement* also reported Eugene V. Debs's famous statement, "I am a Bolshevist with every drop of blood in my body."[20] Meanwhile, in New York, the agents working for Trevor and Stevenson continued to report on radical meetings.

Another intelligence program maintained after the Armistice was the high-yield effort of the Postal Censorship Committee. In February 1919 the army's representative on the section in Seattle completed a long report entitled "A World Wave of Anarchy," to which was attached the names and addresses of hundreds of radicals. Birth control advocate Margaret Sanger was included as a "Radical Socialist," as were Lincoln Steffens and Roger Baldwin. On this international list were six Canadians, nine Japanese, four Salvadorians, and one Siamese.[21] Not to be outdone, the army agent in charge of press censorship in New York compiled in May a list of radical newspapers and the names of over two hundred people "interested in Socialist, Anarchist and Bolshevist Propaganda."[22]

The agents of Military Intelligence were stationed around the world by November 1918, and their ability to monitor the international radical movement was extraordinary. Late in that year Carl Sandburg tripped into their net. Sandburg was working for the Newspaper Enterprise Association and had left New York on October 1. Army intelligence agents picked up his trail in Christiania, Norway, where he was obsered collecting a great deal of Russian propaganda which he proposed to bring back to the United States. That alone was guaranteed to make him a suspect, but Sandburg compounded his error by agreeing to carry on his person two bank drafts totaling $10,000, which he was supposed to deliver to Santeri Nuorteva, the Finnish Bolshevik representative in New York. Before departing with the money and printed materials, he left behind with the naval attaché in Christiania four crates of films

20. *Supplement of the Work and Activities of the Military Intelligence Division,* ibid., reel 13, pp. 662–72.

21. Military representative, Postal Censorship Committee, Seattle, to director of MI, February 14, 1919, ibid., reel 13, pp. 500–593.

22. New York Postal Censorship, "Memorandum on Bolshevist, Anarchist and Socialist Newspapers in the United States, with a Partial List of Individuals and Organizations Engaged in Bolshevist and Anarchist Propaganda, and an Appendix of Foreign Newspapers Engaged in Bolshevist and Anarchist Propaganda," May 3, 1919, ibid., reel 14, pp. 614–65.

prepared by the Russians. He asked the navy to send these to Washington, where he hoped to get George Creel's permission to have them released.[23]

It was a simple matter for Military Intelligence to cable New York about Sandburg's mission as a Bolshevik courier, and Captain Trevor was waiting for him in New York. Sailing on the SS *Bergensfjord,* Sandburg reached New York on Christmas Day. It was not to be a happy holiday season for him: Trevor arrested him as soon as he stepped off the boat. Facing charges for violating the Trading with the Enemy Act even though the United States was not at war with Norway, Finland, or Russia, the source of the money, Sandburg was initially subjected to a three-hour interrogation by Trevor and representatives from the customs service, the federal attorney's office, and the British secret service. In that session and a subsequent one on December 27, Sandburg refused to reveal either the source or the intended recipient of the funds. At this point, the other agencies appear to have bowed out of the process, leaving the poet to the tender mercies of Military Intelligence. Trevor kept him in suspense for weeks, and as late as January 17, 1919, Sandburg still expected to be indicted, writing that if he went to trial the issue would be whether or not he had "read American theory and practice of democracy clearer than the military and naval intelligence officers." By the end of the month, Sandburg was ready to make a deal. In return for having the charges dropped, he signed a statement to the effect that he had voluntarily turned over the literature to Military Intelligence and the Department of Justice.[24]

It took an appeal to George Creel and Newton Baker and three months for Sandburg to get his Bolshevik propaganda back. There was never an accounting of the money, which caused bitter complaints from Nuorteva. The intelligence officer of the northeastern military department had requested a considerable amount of data from Nuorteva on his organization's plans and purposes, and on January 22, the Finnish radical told Military Intelligence that he saw "some incongruity between the desire of your department to have statements from me . . .

23. MI4, Christiania, cable to Milstaff, Washington, December 16, 1918, ibid., reel 9, pp. 736–37; acting director of MI to Biddle, December 18, 1918, reel 2, p. 50. Part of the Sandburg case is discussed in Herbert Mitgang, *Dangerous Dossiers: Exposing the Secret War against America's Greatest Authors* (New York: Donald I. Fine, 1988), pp. 88–89.

24. Sandburg to Sam T. Hughes, January 17, 1919, in Herbert Mitgang, ed., *The Letters of Carl Sandburg* (New York: Harcourt, Brace and World, 1968), pp. 147–48. Sandburg was clearly worried about his predicament and referred to it several times in his personal correspondence (ibid., pp. 145–49). The statement he signed on January 28, 1919, is on p. 149.

and steps taken to prevent me from getting possession of funds belonging to me which would be employed in giving out such information."[25] For a year Nuorteva tried unsuccessfully to find the $10,000, and Military Intelligence, customs, the alien property custodian's office, and the U.S. district attorney all systematically denied any knowledge of its whereabouts.

The extreme paranoia and xenophobia of the New York branch was not shared by all Military Intelligence officers. Under the acting directorship of Colonel Dunn, Carlton J. H. Hayes offered a sane and academic interpretation of domestic events. By January 1919 he had taken on the task of attempting to discredit the outlandish and racist reports coming from Agent B–1 in New York. B–1, Hayes observed, did not know the difference between a Menshevik and a Bolshevik. At one point Hayes complained, "It is astonishing that in so brief a report there can be so many blunders, misapprehensions, mistakes, and errors. The report is absolutely of no value."[26] Hayes was hardly averse to collecting domestic intelligence, and in a January 13 letter, prepared for Dunn's signature, he called for "information concerning all nationalistic propaganda," not just that of the Bolshevists. "Meetings of Jews or of Italians or of Jugo-Slavs," he said, by way of example, "should be reported whenever practicable." Hayes differed from the rest of the intelligence community, however, in his disinterest in collecting such information for "any charge of disloyalty or any purpose of prosecution." He wanted the data "to keep our officers in Paris and the Department here fully informed of the reaction of various groups in America to the peace negotiations."[27]

Hayes was the exception. Despite his warnings, the extremism boiling out of New York soon scalded the reputation of Military Intelligence. Archibald Stevenson got himself called as an expert witness before Congress. Stevenson was no ordinary bigot, and his political influence was significant. As a New York attorney, he had begun a private study of German and Irish nationalists, along with pacifists, as early as 1915, and in 1917 he assumed the chair of the subcommittee on aliens of the city's Committee on National Defense. His other source of power lay in the well-to-do Union League Club within which he had organized a Propa-

25. Nuorteva to intelligence officer, Northeastern Department, January 22, 1919, Lusk Committee Papers, L0033, box 1, folder 43, New York State Archives, Albany. For documents related to Nuorteva's attempt to find the money, see MI Microfilm, reel 9, pp. 692–728, and reel 14, pp. 142–45, 551.

26. Hayes, memorandum for Brown, January 25, 1919, MI Microfilm, reel 12, p. 147.

27. Acting director of MI to Geary, MI microfilm, reel 13, p. 371.

ganda League. After a brief stint as a volunteer with the Bureau of Investigation, he found his home with Military Intelligence, carrying a card with the seal of the War Department and the signature of General Churchill identifying him as special agent 650. By October 1918 he was running Biddle's propaganda section, and within a few months he had earned a reputation in some circles as the man most feared by the radicals. Civil libertarian Roger Baldwin considered him a "son of a bitch."[28]

During the war, the custodian of alien property, A. Mitchell Palmer, had alleged that German brewers in the United States were purchasing newspapers to fight prohibition and to propagandize on behalf of the Central Powers. "The organized liquor traffic," he had charged, "is a vicious interest because it has been unpatriotic, because it as been pro-German in its sympathies and its conduct."[29] In September 1918 the Senate authorized its subcommittee on the judiciary, chaired by North Carolina Democrat Lee S. Overman, to investigate the alcohol industry and German propaganda. The military was heavily involved with Overman from the beginning; its chief counsel was Major E. Lowry Humes, on loan from the judge advocate general's office. Early testimony on German propaganda came from Captain George G. Lester of Military Intelligence, but the nature of the investigation began to change on January 21, when New York policeman and former army agent Thomas J. Tunney began to testify. Tunney's well-rehearsed account of his exploits against German bombers and Hindu plotters led him naturally into a discussion of the machinations of the anarchists Berkman and Goldman. At that point, Major Humes opened a discussion of the postwar activities of American Bolsheviks.[30]

The next witness was Archibald E. Stevenson. He presented his view of the "interlocking relation" that connected German sympathizers, pacifists, and radicals. Henry Ford's famous Peace Ship, for example, was inspired by a German agent and led by radicals. He noted that much of the propaganda took place on university campuses, where it was

28. Stevenson's description of his activities is in U.S. Senate, Report and Hearings of the Subcommittee on the Judiciary, 65th Cong., 1st sess., document no. 62, *Brewing and Liquor Interests and German and Bolshevik Propaganda*, 3 vols. (Washington, D.C.: U.S. Government Printing Office, 1919), 2:2690–91, 2785 (hereafter cited as Overman Hearings). On Baldwin and Stevenson, see Peggy Lamson, *Roger Baldwin: Founder of the American Civil Liberties Union, A Portrait* (Boston: Houghton Mifflin, 1976), pp. 82–83, 85. Stevenson's claim of causing fear in radicals in cited in Robert K. Murray, *Red Scare: A Study in National Hysteria, 1919–1920* (Minneapolis: University of Minnesota, 1955), p. 98. His career is outlined in *Who Was Who*, 4:904.

29. Quoted in Overman Hearings, 3:5.

30. Tunney's testimony is in ibid., 2:2670–90.

ГОЛОС ТРУЖЕННИКА

No. 1. CHICAGO, ILL., NOVEMBER 2nd, 1918 No. 1.

DID YOU RING SIR?

DID'NT I TELL YU TO THROW THAT CAT OUT?!!

Attention Workers!

Under the pretext of patriotism, playing upon the hysteria they have created, the agents of the capitalist class through their courts are railroading hundreds of members of the working class to capitalist prisons. One hundred members of the I. W. W. after a farcical trial at Chicago have been sent to prison for terms ranging from one to twenty years, their sole crime being that of attempting to educate and organize the members of their class. Tom Mooney in the death cell at San Quentin, the result of a capitalist frame-up and lack of economic action on the part of the organization of which he is a member.

Eugene V. Debs has been sentenced to ten years because in a speech at Canton, Ohio, he indorsed the I. W. W. and said he did not believe in war. Rose Pastor Stokes has been sentenced to ten years for opposing the war and taking sides with the working class.

Hundreds of members are in jail at Sacramento, Stockton, Fresno, Spokane, Omaha and many other places, suffering harsh treatment, though convicted of no crime. Members of the working class are tarred and feathered, shot and hanged with impunity and no one punished for these crimes.

HOW LONG ARE THE WORKERS GOING TO STAND FOR THIS?

Workers, 20,000 miners in Pennsylvania and 6,000 miners in Montana have struck as a protest against the acts of the capitalist class and demand that all class war prisoners be released. Workers, have you the courage to back up this protest by a

GENERAL STRIKE UNTIL OCTOBER 1.

Economic might is the only power the capitalist will recognize. Use your power NOW, and compel the agents of the capitalists to stop their assaults and jailings of your fellow workers.

HAYWOOD, MOONEY AND DEBS

And all Class War Prisoners MUST and SHALL be released from jail! Down tools until all are released. YOU may be next! Courage, fellows, and DO IT NOW!

International Ptg. Co., Butte, Mont.

Above: The Voice of the Laborer, from the files of Military Intelligence. Left: A strike call, collected by Military Intelligence in Seattle in 1918.

Left: George Creel, chairman of the Committee on Public Information, aboard the USS *George Washington* enroute to Paris, 1918. *Below:* Van Deman shares information with one of his contacts in the office of the secretary of war.

January 17, 1918.

Mr. Felix Frankfurter,
Room 225, War Department,
Washington, D. C.

Dear Mr. Frankfurter:-

A report from San Francisco says that H. F. Doree, head of the I. W.W.'s in Chicago while Haywood is in jail, has written his radical colleagues in San Francisco that Roger Baldwin in New York has secretly organised men like Frank Walsh, Clarence Darrow, and other notorious attorneys, who in their turn have enlisted the aid of certain influential politicians. These persons, according to the report, are to go to Washington, and through the help of George Creel will secure an interview with the President for the purpose of stopping the "persecution" of the I.W.W. Doree, the report adds, has stated with elation that Attorney General Gregory has already corresponded with Walsh and has promised to denounce these unfair attacks on the I.W.W.

This, in view of Professor Parker's talk with you, is submitted for your information and guidance.

Very sincerely,

R. H. VAN DEMAN

Colonel, General Staff,
Chief, Military Intelligence Section.

By

Major, U.S.R.

ch

TELEGRAM

Paris,
Dated July 18,
Recd. July 19, 10:37 a.m.

CODE

Milstaff,

Washington.

No. 689, July 18.

Robert Minor sailed for American July 15
aboard S/S TOURAINE. He should be watched.

VAN DEMAN

M O T T

mep

Office of the Chief of Staff

GE TO
GOVERNMENT RATE.

Code

WAR DEPARTMENT TELEGRAM.

OFFICIAL BUSINESS

Capt. Schmuck

OFFICE CHIEF OF STAFF
MIL. INT. BRANCH—
EXECUTIVE DIVISION
APR 3 10110 -13 1918
WAR DEPARTMENT

WASHINGTON. March 23d, 1918.

Intelligence Officer,
     Central Department,
          Chicago, Ill.
#6 - 78 D, March 4-8.
Have representative attend, concert, and ball, given by, the Russian
Union, of the, I. W. W. Saturday March 23d, eight P. M. at, West,
Side Auditorium Racine, and Taylor, Street, Chicago.

Van Deman

NH

Top left: Secretary of War Newton D. Baker, 1918. *Top right:* Ralph H. Van Deman orders continued surveillance of the radical cartoonist who escaped his trap in France, 1919. *Above:* A typical surveillance order.

Right: Brigadier General
Marlborough Churchill, first
director of the Military
Intelligence Division, in his
Paris office, 1919. *Below:*
Military Intelligence prepares
to arrest Carl Sandberg.

10110-92
M. I. 11.

December 18, 1918.

From: Acting Director of Military Intelligence.

To: Lt. Col. Nicholas Biddle, 302 Broadway, New York City.

Subject: Carl Sandberg.

Attention Captain Whytook.

1. A cablegram from Christiania dated December 16th informs
us that the above left for the United States on the S/S Bergensfjord December 14th. He is said to be in possession of two
drafts of $5,000 each, drawn on Browning and Company and the Irving
National Bank of New York City but payable to Santeri Nuortova.
These drafts are paid for by United States and Swedish currency
and by a Norwegian agent of Gruzenborg named Jorgen Dahl. Dahl
gave another name and address.

2. While in the United States Sandberg is said to have left
with a Naval Attache for transmission to this country to Naval
Intelligence four packages of Bolshevik propaganda films staged
in Russia. These he hopes to have released in Washington through
the influence of George Creel and others. Sandberg refused to
divulge the source of the funds which he has, likewise his connections, yet he had ostensibly been conferring with the Legation.

3. The above is forwarded for your information and is
supplementary to previous letters sent to you concerning Sandberg.

J. M. Dunn,
Colonel, General Staff,
Acting Director of Military Intelligence.

BY:

J. S. Moore,
Captain, U. S. A.

rs

Top: Colonel Ralph H. Van Deman, the father of Military Intelligence, in his Paris office, 1919. *Above:* Van Deman (seated, in uniform) and members of the Current Diplomatic and Political Correspondence Section of the American mission to the Paris peace conference, March 1919.

The files of Military Intelligence contain a wealth of radical literature from the Great Depression.

FIGHT! DON'T STARVE — ORGANIZE!

NEWARK- N J. 4921.31

Demands For
Unemployment Insurance
MADE UPON THE UNITED STATES CONGRESS

Price 5c

Ludwig C. A. K. Martens, a primary target of Military Intelligence in 1919, speaks in Chicago.

SOCIALIST MASS MEETING!

Sunday Afternoon
May 25th, 2:30 o'clock

K.P.HALL

11037 Michigan Avenue

═══SPEAKER═══

A. L. MARTENS

Official representative in the United States of the Russian Soviet Government. The Man with 200 MILLION DOLLARS TO SPEND and no customers.

The Truth, the whole truth and nothing but the truth about Russia.

Members of the National Executive Committee of the Socialist Party will also speak.

Admission 10c   Admission 10c

Union Print Shop, 11415 Michigan Ave.   530

Survey of
Americanism

BULLETIN

PUBLISHED BY

Better America Federation

HEADQUARTERS: LOS ANGELES: 356 SOUTH BROADWAY, PHONE MICHIGAN 9371

Authoritative
Data - Reprint
OFFICE CHIEF OF STAFF
MIL. INTEL. DIV.
1932
WAR DEPARTMENT

Vol. 13   NOVEMBER 1, 1932   No. 7

COMMUNISTS STAGING MOBILIZATION REHEARSAL FOR WORLD REVOLUTION

From Daily Worker, Official Communist Organ

Directives for National Hunger March
(October 24, 1932.)

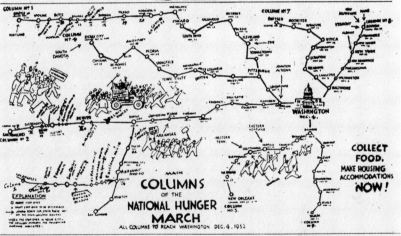

COLUMNS OF THE NATIONAL HUNGER MARCH
ALL COLUMNS TO REACH WASHINGTON DEC. 4, 1932

COLLECT FOOD, MAKE HOUSING ACCOMMODATIONS NOW!

Qualifications of Delegates.

In election of delegates, consideration must be given to the following qualifications:
a) Activity in struggles against unemployment;
b) Age and ability to stand strain of march;
c) Capacity to participate in the many activities connected with the march itself and with the mobilization of workers for support of the struggles that will arise during and after the march.

All delegates to the Hunger March must be registered immediately after their election and registration must be forwarded to the National Committee.

Column and other division captains shall allow only registered delegates to participate and shall therefore check up to see that all who enter the march are duly registered.

Routes and Itinerary.

The march will proceed in eight main columns. Consult map and where necessary write for details to the National Committee. Delegations from towns not on the main routes shall join the columns at the point nearest to them.

Agitational Material and Supplies.

The National Committee will take steps to supply leaflets; posters; stickers; buttons; collection lists and stamps, etc.

We will also begin publication of a National Magazine which is to be sold in the course of preparation and on the march. In addition all locals are urged to secure sufficient supplies of other authorized literature and publications such as the Daily Worker, Labor Unity, etc. All material issued by the National Committee will be forwarded in due time.

(Concluded on Page 2.)

READ PAGES FIVE AND SIX BEFORE YOU VOTE. PASS ALONG THE INFORMATION THEREIN CONTAINED.

One of the Bonus March flyers picked up by Military Intelligence agents in 1932.

Support the Right of the Rank and
File to Meet on the Hill

VETERANS!

Join The Parade

ON FRIDAY

OF THE RANK AND FILE!

*Assemble at 15th Street and Constitution Ave.
at 10 a. m.*

**This Petition will be read on the Capitol
Grounds to all the Veterans and presented to
Congress by a Committee of the Rank and File.**

SUPPORT AND JOIN THE PARADE!

SUPPORT THESE DEMANDS:

1. CONGRESS MUST NOT ADJOURN UNTIL THE BONUS
   IS GRANTED IN FULL TO EVERY VETERAN.
2. The $100,000 appropriated as a loan to get us out of Wash-
   ington must be given instead to shelter and feed the veterans
   in Washington.
3. That the Rank and File be allowed to present this petition
   the way the masses want it presented.

PETITION BY THE RANK AND FILE OF THE BONUS

MARCHERS TO 72ND CONGRESS AND THE MASSES

OF THE PEOPLE OF THE U. S.

SUPPORT THE PICKETING ON THE HILL!

A private spy group provided information to Military Intelligence in the 1930s.

spread, as a senator prompted, by "professors who subscribe to these dangerous and destructive and anarchistic organizations." Stevenson readily agreed that there were "a very large number" of such seditious faculty, mostly "professors of sociology, economics, and history." Then he added, "I have here a 'Who's Who,' that I prepared, giving a brief biographical sketch of them." The nation's first blacklist was about to be revealed by a representative of Military Intelligence.[31]

Senator Overman almost did not allow it; radical propaganda, some of his colleagues observed, was not within the committee's purview. In the end the temptation was too great, and the list was entered into the record and given to the waiting reporters. It began with Jane Addams, the famous founder of Hull House and an outspoken peace activist. Tenth on the list, following Roger Baldwin, was historian Charles A. Beard, cited as a member of the Intercollegiate Socialist Society and lecturer at the Rand School of Social Science. He was kept company by other notorious radicals such as the IWW's Elizabeth Gurley Flynn, socialist Morris Hillquit, and the radical Frederic C. Howe, commissioner of immigration in New York. Other notables included all-around reformer David Starr Jordan, chancellor of Stanford University; Louis P. Lochner, leader of the Ford peace effort; the pacifist Scott Nearing; Socialist presidential candidate Eugene V. Debs; and Oswald Garrison Villard, liberal editor of the *Nation*.[32] It was the afternoon of Thursday, January 23, 1919.

The *New York Times* called the list a "who's who in pacifism and radicalism" and eagerly solicited responses from the honorees. Some were in jail, some unavailable, and some on government business. One of those most eager to respond was Charles Beard, who may have been the first to utter the phrase that has echoed through the witch-hunts of the twentieth century: "I am not and never have been. . . ." Beard used those words in a letter to Senator Overman denying that he was a pacifist, stating that he "had never belonged to Mr. Wilson's sweet neutrality band." He was not, he said, "too proud to fight."[33]

31. Stevenson's appearance is recorded in ibid., pp. 2690–2785. His observation on the Ford peace mission is on p. 2713; on professors, p. 2709.
32. The list given to the Senate is in ibid., pp. 2782–85; the *New York Times* printed it on January 25, 1919.
33. Quoted in *New York Times*, January 26, 1919. For more on Beard's controversial views during World War I, see H. C. Peterson and Gilbert C. Fite, *Opponents of War, 1917–1918* (Seattle: University of Washington Press, 1957), pp. 103–4; Mary Beard, *The Making of Charles Beard: An Interpretation* (New York: Exposition Press, 1955), p. 22; Ellen Nore, *Charles A. Beard: An Intellectual Biography* (Carbondale: Southern Illinois University Press, 1983), p. 84.

Both the Senate and the Department of War were deluged with protests similar to Beard's. Professor Lindsay T. Damon of Brown University exclaimed in a dramatic appearance before the subcommittee, "Can I make myself clear? I am boiling with indignation that Mr. Stevenson ever used my name at all." After deliberating in a closed session, Overman appeased the irate scholar with a formal statement, in an early use of a term that was to become all too familiar, that he was not "in any way un-American."[34] On the Monday following the appearance of the list, Secretary of War Baker issued a statement disavowing Stevenson, saying that he "had never been an officer or an employe[e] of the Military Intelligence Division." He cited his personal disdain for classifications of the political beliefs of individuals and noted that in Stevenson's catalog there were the "names of people of great distinction, exalted purity of purpose, and lifelong devotion to the highest interest of America and of mankind." He singled out Jane Addams for particular praise, claiming that her name lent "dignity and greatness to any list." He insisted that the army did not "censor the opinions of the people of the United States" and that it had "no authority to classify such opinions."[35]

For his part, Overman was offended at the criticism of his committee suggested in Baker's comments, and he produced for the press the very letter from Military Intelligence that offered Stevenson as a witness. There is no doubt that Baker was incorrect in his assessment of the limits on Military Intelligence as well as Stevenson's status. Not only was the army deeply involved in the classification of civilian opinions, but Stevenson certainly had more than an informal relationship with Military Intelligence. His appearance before the Senate had been approved by Trevor in New York and Dunn in Washington. Yet despite vigorous rejoinders by both Stevenson and Overman, the secretary's disclaimer defused any additional public criticism of Military Intelligence.[36]

Much to the dismay of Overman, Baker ordered a ban on any further appearances before Congress by agents from Military Intelligence. Furious over this "muzzling order," and no doubt somewhat embarrassed by his lack of authority to investigate radicalism in the first place, Overman got a new resolution from the Senate empowering him to study

34. Overman Hearings, 2:2787–95; for the defense of others on Stevenson's list, see pp. 2841–42, 2857–61.

35. Baker's entire letter is quoted in the *New York Times*, January 28, 1919, and in Link et al., eds., *Wilson Papers*, 54:398.

36. *New York Times*, January 29, 1919; Overman Hearings, 2:2785. Baker's mail showed approval of, as one writer said, his "vigorous repudiation of Stevenson's . . . cowardly and inexcusable list" (William Hard to Baker, January 29, 1919, Baker Papers, reel 7, p. 375). Paul V. Kellog, editor of the *Survey*, told Baker that his action had "again put American liberals in your debt" (p. 557).

Bolshevik propaganda. He conducted these hearings in February and March, and they included some fascinating testimony from Americans who had witnessed firsthand the "reign of terror" in Russia, proving to his satisfaction that "the Bolshevik guards . . . rape and ravish and despoil women at will." Not all the witnesses accommodated Overman's passion so thoroughly. The progressive Raymond Robins, who had led the American Red Cross mission in Russia, tried to deemphasize the hysteria about the revolution. The most provocative witnesses were John Reed and his wife, Louise Bryant, both of whom got off to a very bad start with the subcommittee when they refused to be sworn.[37]

By virtue of his book, *Ten Days That Shook the World* and the motion picture *Reds,* John Reed is probably the best known of the many Americans who were enthralled with the Russian Revolution. A Harvard graduate and, along with Walter Lippmann, a protégé of the muckraker Lincoln Steffens, Reed was, in the words of Naval Intelligence, "a harmless Greenwich Village radical up until the time he was given the opportunity to visit foreign countries as a magazine and newspaper correspondent." He admired Pancho Villa in Mexico, but he found his fate in Russia with Trotsky and Lenin. Van Deman had followed Reed's activities since early 1918, and Churchill thought him a dangerous pro-German Bolshevik and "one of the cleverest smugglers of papers that has come into this country."[38] Reed was watched closely through the cooperative efforts of the State Department, the army, and the navy, all of which became especially alarmed in April 1918, when Reed booked passage on the *Bergensfjord,* the same ship used by Sandburg but on a different date, in Christiania for his return to the United States. Knowing that he had checked packages containing Bolshevik material, the State Department asked the navy to intercept him in New York and confiscate the documents. Not only did the navy take his material, but he was held for an eight-hour interrogation during which his skin was tested for invisible writing. Afterward, he was kept under the surveillance of operative 204–B–8.[39]

37. The Overman Hearings are in three volumes, with the first two paged consecutively. The third volume focuses on Russia and begins with a reprint of Tunney's and Stevenson's testimony and the famous list. The "reign of terror" comment is in 3:54; the rape report, 47; Robins's testimony, 763–896, 1007–32; that of Reed and Bryant, 466–601. In response to further pressure for Military Intelligence documents, Baker eventually agreed to show them to the subcommittee privately (2:2856–57, 2863–66).

38. Churchill to R. W. Flournoy, Jr., September 16, 1918, Record Group 38, Naval Intelligence, "Suspect" file, box 10, National Archives.

39. Although indicted several times for his writings in the *Masses,* Reed was never convicted. When refused a passport to return to Russia, he escaped under cover. Differences over strategy eventually made him unwelcome in Russia, where he died in 1920. Bertram D. Wolfe provides a good biographical sketch of Reed in his introduction to the

In addition to gagging the army, Baker ordered an immediate cessation of all domestic intelligence activities by the military. The initial ban went out as soon as the Stevenson story hit the newspapers, with a longer order following on January 29. The war had generated "the observation of radicalism," the latter document began, and with peace "the emergency which required this observation no longer exists." The instructions were specific: "The Military Intelligence Division may not properly conduct espionage among the civilian population even to inquire into the political or economic beliefs or activities of individuals or groups of individuals whether they be Anarchists, Socialists, I.W.W.'s, Bolshevists, or members of some special ethnic group." Under these restrictions, Military Intelligence was allowed to investigate radicalism in the army and, to remain current on the subject, to peruse newspapers "and other available data." In addition, army agents were to collect any radical leaflets and other material that came to their attention. In the largest caveat, they could accept "such information as may come to hand from volunteer informants." Finally, Washington still desired information on "the several foreign language groups" to determine the effect of their nationalism on the Paris peace conference. Nevertheless, the prohibition was clear enough: "Officers, agents and Intelligence police will not attend meetings or . . . conduct espionage to obtain this information."[40]

Unlike Churchill's attempt to turn off negative intelligence back in November, the January restrictions were quite effective. In Chicago, Crockett's last report from an agent following "dangerous anarchists" was dated January 25, and when he forwarded it to Washington, he promised to take no further action. His volunteer informants, however, continued to provide intelligence. In New York, Trevor was so chastised he declined to share information with the police, although he did accept communications from them. The technique he developed was to follow radical meetings by observing announcements in the newspaper and

1960 Vintage Books edition of *Ten Days That Shook the World*. See also Robert A Rosenstone, *Romantic Revolutionary: A Biography of John Reed* (New York: Knopf, 1975). The MI dossier on Reed, including several intercepted letters from Russia, is in MI Microfilm, reel 33, pp. 728–833. The navy's extensive file is in "Suspect," box 10.

40. The January 29, 1919, order, which was an expansion of the "brief instructions" four days earlier, is in acting director of MI to intelligence officer, Old Hickory Powder Plant, Nashville, MI Microfilm, reel 4, pp. 650–51. Although cited frequently in communications from the field, the January 25 ban on domestic spying has not been located. Responses from numerous units make it clear that this letter ordered the cessation of, as the New Orleans branch put it, "all efforts to obtain information concerning radical movements, except in the military forces" (intelligence officer, New Orleans, to director of MI, January 27, 1919, reel 12, p. 968).

then notify the Bureau of Investigation, hoping that its agents would attend and provide him a report. When Washington spotted a reference to Stevenson's December analysis in one of Trevor's letters, a caution was issued on "the use of Mr. Stevenson's material." In places such as Gary, Indiana, plagued by labor violence and radical activity, Military Intelligence virtually shut down its operation. After two queries to Arizona, where infiltration and the use of informants were standard tactics against the iww, all intelligence work in that state ceased. Dunn, in Washington, was so mindful of the gag order that, citing the Stevenson case, he declined a request for information from a former associate who was out of the army and working for a "very efficient secret service" operated by businessmen in Cleveland. Plant Protection, not demobilized until June, quoted the January restrictions in its refusal to honor a similar request from Raymond E. Horn in Pittsburgh, who had organized the Federal Service Bureau, a private concern "made up of Ex-Government agents and O.N.I. officials." To market his industrial spy services, Horn had acquired the former offices of Naval Intelligence, including the furniture, and had a sailor in uniform guarding the door.[41]

Churchill later told Trevor that had he been available during the Overman hearings, he could have interceded with the secretary of war and saved both Military Intelligence and Stevenson from Baker's wrath. In his view, Baker had been forced to act with "insufficient information," and Stevenson was the victim of an "unintentional injustice." Grant Squires expressed a similar opinion to Woodrow Wilson, claiming that Baker's denial of Stevenson put Military Intelligence in "a false position." He wondered if Wilson "would approve had you been present."[42] At any rate, and in a reversal of the episodes during the war when Baker had been in Europe leaving the army unrestrained, both Van Deman and Churchill were in Paris, and there was no one to deal with the secretary.

Baker had originally intended to go to Paris as part of the American delegation, and he had assembled a large entourage, including Churchill. These plans changed at the last minute because of the unexpected

41. For Chicago, MI Microfilm, reel 10, pp. 82–84, 468–69; New York, reel 12, pp. 177–78; Washington, reel 10, pp. 75–79. For Arizona, Record Group 60, Glasser Files, box 3, National Archives. For Pittsburgh, Record Group 165, Suitland, Plant Protection Section, entry 104, General Correspondence. On not using Stevenson's material, Theodore Kornweibel, Jr., ed., *Federal Surveillance of Afro-Americans (1917–1925): The First World War, the Red Scare, and the Garvey Movement* (Frederick, Md.: University Publications of America, 1986), reel 19, p. 805.

42. Churchill to Trevor, January 16, 1920, MI Microfilm, reel 15, pp. 888–89; Squires to Wilson, January 30, 1919, in Link, et al., eds., *Wilson Papers*, 54:396–98.

resignation of Secretary of the Treasury William McAdoo, who was worn out, as Baker said, from "the terrible burdens" of his work. Baker apparently volunteered to stay behind, although there is no doubt that he wished it could have been otherwise.[43] For reasons never fully explained, Churchill and the rest of Baker's military group went on to Paris, arriving there in mid-December 1918, just after the president. Although embarrassed and criticized about the "aggregation of useless military people" at the peace conference, Baker allowed Churchill to stay.[44] Van Deman, who had been in France since the previous June, had created a position for himself as head of negative intelligence for the conference, but Churchill was a definite supernumerary. Baker had expected that his director of Military Intelligence would be used by General Tasker H. Bliss, a fully credentialed commissioner plenipotentiary, to gather and analyze information, but the general had little use for spies and rejected Churchill's services on the grounds that "the maintenance of so large a separate establishment" would be unfair to his fellow commissioners.[45]

The entire American delegation had a staff of well over a thousand official members, including several intelligence offices. Colonel House had a personal staff of over fifty, and had brought along the Inquiry as well.[46] Van Deman, with his secret negative branch, had fifty-six people, mostly intelligence police, working for him. Churchill, eventually given the innocuous title of military liaison and coordinating officer, had

43. Baker to Wilson, November 23, 1918, Baker Papers, reel 6, p. 266.
44. Baker's papers in the Library of Congress contain considerable correspondence from Paris, with the most informative coming from generals Tasker H. Bliss and F. J. Kernan and from MI Lieutenant Ralph Hayes, formerly Baker's personal secretary, attached to Churchill's office in Paris. The comment on the overabundance of military personnel at the peace conference is in a letter from Baker to Hayes, January 7, 1919, reel 7, p. 360. Another frequent correspondent with the secretary was Walter Lippmann. Technically a captain in MI working for Van Deman on counterpropaganda, Lippmann regarded his commission merely as a convenience and operated independently in France, writing directly to Baker and House. See Bidwell, *History of Military Intelligence*, pp. 157–58; Ronald Steel, *Walter Lippmann and the American Century* (Boston: Little, Brown, 1980), pp. 141–54. Alexander Coxe's diary, in his papers at East Carolina University, also has material on MI in France.
45. Baker to Kernan, January 30, 1919, Baker Papers, reel 7, p. 554.
46. The Inquiry was a think tank, set up in late 1917 in New York and headed by House, planning for a postwar Europe. Baker loaned Lippmann to the effort, and the young reporter kept his connection with the group while he was with Military Intelligence in France. At the peace conference, the Inquiry had agents in the field reporting on conditions. See "The Inquiry; Report of Progress to December 15, 1917," Baker Papers, reel 2, pp. 205–9; and a 1918 "Report on the Inquiry, Its Scope and Method," reel 5, pp. 46–67. For Lippmann's role, see Steel, *Walter Lippmann*, pp. 128–54.

a staff of a dozen or more.[47] Just as Military Intelligence in the United States had turned after the Armistice to face the threat of Bolshevism, Van Deman had done the same in Europe. On November 13, 1918, he sent a secret coded wire to Churchill noting "the evident attempt of Boshevists and affiliated elements to bring about widespread trouble" and urging a clampdown on passports to keep American radicals out of Europe. "The whole matter," he said in his typical fashion, "should be kept as quiet as possible."[48]

Churchill's arrival in France reinforced Van Deman's view, and the former used his authority to speed up the delivery of New York's Bolshevism reports to Paris. On January 22, 1919, Churchill wired Dunn that no one at the peace conference "realizes that there is a Bolshevik movement in the United States." Churchill said he considered "this question the most important now under consideration," and he overrode Dunn's concern, based on Carlton Hayes's critique, about the limited value of the reports on Bolshevism.[49] Fear of the Red tide was by no means limited to American Military Intelligence. In March 1919, Allied commander General Ferdinand Foch recommended to the peace conference's Council of Four (the Big Four: Woodrow Wilson, David Lloyd George, Georges Clemenceau, and Vittorio Orlando) that he be given an army to crush Bolshevism in eastern Europe. In a remarkably astute analysis, Tasker Bliss opposed Foch's plan, claiming that the problem was not Bolshevism, a word he had tired of hearing, but that of a people whose circumstances were so wretched that they accepted revolution as their only hope. He proposed that measures be taken to improve conditions rather "than to kill the discontented people." "I believe that much of the existing discontent could be relieved by the immediate declaration of peace; by lifting the blockade; by feeding the people; . . . and by getting them again into the habit of working instead of fighting. I believe that Bolshevism is growing simply because of our delay in doing these things."[50]

47. Organizational charts and rosters for the American Commission in Paris are in Baker Papers, reel 7.

48. Van Deman's November 13, 1918, cablegram to Churchill is reprinted, along with a follow-up letter of the same date, in Ralph E. Weber, ed., *The Final Memoranda: Major General Ralph H. Van Deman, USA Ret., 1865–1952, Father of Military Intelligence* (Wilmington, Del.: Scholarly Resources, 1988), pp. 172–74.

49. Churchill, cable to Milstaff, Washington, January 22, 1919, MI Microfilm, reel 12, pp. 146–52. "The Spread and Present State of Extreme Radical Labor Movement in the United States," sent to Churchill in Paris, is in reel 13, pp. 625–45.

50. "Remarks of General Bliss at the Meeting of the Council of Four," March 27, 1919, attached to Bliss to secretary of war, April 3, 1919, in Baker Papers, reel 6, pp. 635–37.

Another American who shared Bliss's soft approach to Bolshevism was William C. Bullitt of the Current Intelligence Department of the American delegation. In February 1919, Bullitt made his famous trip to Russia, accompanied by the leftist writer Lincoln Steffens. His resulting positive report on conditions under the Reds was anathema to hardliners. On April 11, Van Deman wrote Bullitt a long letter refuting each claim of success for Lenin's regime and each call for moderation. "Why should existing society lend moral support," he asked, "to an organization which, by its very nature, must destroy it or cease to exist?"[51] Disillusioned with the peace conference, Bullitt soon resigned and went to London, as Van Deman told Churchill, to consort "with the radical socialistic element." There Military Intelligence kept him under close surveillance. Although he said he liked Bullitt personally, Van Deman thought him "a disappointed and 'disgruntled' man and such a chap is always likely to be dangerous if he is smart and Bullitt is that."[52]

While Bullitt was in Russia, Van Deman faced another case of an American radical in Europe. Despite the combined efforts of both Military and Naval Intelligence to keep Robert Minor from getting a passport, his possession of press credentials was sufficient for George Creel to intercede. The most famous of radical cartoonists, Minor was the son of a Texas judge who first came to the attention of the intelligence community in late 1917 when he worked in the defense of Tom Mooney. The navy, whose Agent "C" tailed Minor in San Francisco, told Van Deman that he was "one of the leading crooks of the I. W. W. crowd" and a "dangerous enemy to the United States; a greater enemy than any German spy . . . through his slanderous attacks."[53] Van Deman's reports from half a dozen agents in San Franciso showed Minor connected with all the leading anarchists, free lovers, and Hindu and Japanese radicals. Mail intercepts revealed a correspondence with Lenin and

51. Van Deman to Bullitt, April 11, 1919, reprinted in Weber, ed., *Final Memoranda*, pp. 162–64.
52. Van Deman to Churchill, June 6, 1919, ibid., pp. 93–95. Van Deman felt completely justified in his opinion of Bullitt when, in 1923, the liberal married Louise Bryant, widow of John Reed. He took Bullitt's 1934 appointment as the first U.S. ambassador to the Soviet Union rather sanguinely, claiming that the diplomat "finally discovered what the Communist International really stands for" (ibid., p. 89). On Bullitt's marriage to Bryant, which did not last, see Beatrice Farnsworth, *William C. Bullitt and the Soviet Union* (Bloomington: Indiana University Press, 1967), pp. 72–73.
53. Edward McCauley to Van Deman, January 10, 1918, MI Microfilm, reel 7, p. 730; officer-in-charge, branch office of Naval Intelligence, San Francisco, to director of Naval Intelligence, March 18, 1918, pp. 666–67.

other senior Russians. Agent 59 considered him "nothing but a disreputable 'pimp' who would like to live off the blood money of women."[54]

Leaving the United States in March 1918, Minor sailed, appropriately, on the *Bergensfjord* for Christiania. He went to Russia, where he worked on Lenin's propaganda staff, editing a newspaper for distribution to Allied soldiers at Archangel. When the Spartacist radicals gained control of parts of Germany in early 1919, he was dispatched to Düsseldorf to join them and continue his propaganda against the American and British forces of occupation. Before Minor's arrival, however, Military Intelligence had penetrated the Düsseldorf radicals using a second lieutenant, code named Siegfried, who posed as an American deserter. In Düsseldorf, Minor wrote a pamphlet entitled *Why American Soldiers Are in Europe*, six thousand copies of which went to Siegfried. Though many of Minor's colleagues were arrested by the British secret service and Düsseldorf was retaken by German troops, Minor remained at large, traveling to Berlin and later to Koblenz. Van Deman desired very much to bring Minor before a court-martial and, no doubt, a firing squad. He planned to have reporter Marguerite Harrison lure him across the bridge at Koblenz and into the American zone. That strategy failed, but in early June the French Sûreté found Minor right under Van Deman's nose in Paris working with striking railway employees.[55]

It did not take Van Deman long to gain custody of the American. Van Deman had Minor placed in a solitary cell in the military prison at Koblenz and charged with a "Violation of the Laws of War." Specifically, Minor was accused of writing pamphlets "for the purpose of creating

54. Department intelligence officer, San Francisco, to director of MI, June 12, 1919, MI Microfilm, reel 7, pp. 692–96.

55. The army's large file on Minor includes a good deal of material from the navy and the Department of Justice, MI Microfilm, reel 7, pp. 444–912. For Van Deman's plan to capture Minor, see Weber, ed., *Final Memoranda*, pp. 84–85, 95–96; CIC History, 4: 12–14. His assistant at this time, and the only other officer aware of the intended trap, was Captain Ogden Mills, later Herbert Hoover's secretary of the treasury. Marguerite Harrison, in *There's Always Tomorrow: The Story of a Checkered Life* (New York: Farrar & Rinehart, 1935), does not mention the trap but does describe her mission to find evidence to use against Minor in his trial (pp. 196–99). See also Nathan Miller, *Spying for America: The Hidden History of U.S. Intelligence* (New York: Paragon House, 1989), pp. 206–9. The case is also covered in the thin biography of Minor, who remained a high-ranking Communist all his life, Joseph North, *Robert Minor: Artist and Crusader: An Informal Biography* (New York: International Publishers, 1956), pp. 114–16. For Steffens's connection with Minor's release, see Lincoln Steffens, *The Autobiography of Lincoln Steffens*, 2 vols. (New York: Harcourt, Brace, 1933), 2:841–43. The best treatment of Minor as a cartoonist is a chapter, with samples of his work, in Richard Fitzgerald, *Art and Politics: Cartoonists of the Masses and Liberator* (Westport, Conn.: Greenwood Press, 1973).

unrest, dissatisfaction, defection, revolt and mutiny." Whether Minor was sentenced to death, as his biographer claims, he was certainly in a great deal of trouble by the time his friend Lincoln Steffens found him. Using his influence with Colonel House, to Van Deman's eternal disgust, Steffens arranged for Minor's release. The case became something of a cause célèbre for the press, which did not like the idea of the military arresting one of its own, no matter how radical he might be. Minor's father appealed to House, a fellow Texan, and to Secretary Baker. The Senate passed a resolution requiring a report from the Department of War on the treatment of Minor. When Minor sailed for home on July 15, Van Deman wired Washington that "he should be watched."[56] Army agents in New York met him at the pier and followed him for several hours until they noticed a similar team from Justice tailing the same target. After extracting a promise of a complete Justice report, the military ended its surveillance. Both agencies maintained a strong interest in Minor; the army's last item on him was dated February 12, 1921. A few months later, J. Edgar Hoover, special assistant to the attorney general, reviewed the evidence against the radical cartoonist but decided not to prosecute.[57]

Van Deman returned to the United States in the summer of 1919, and though he later advised and lectured at the Military Intelligence Division, he never regained his command. Churchill had preceded him, arriving in Washington in late March. What he found there was not comforting. Bielaski had resigned from the Bureau of Investigation in February, shortly after reducing the number of his agents to the prewar level. Within a month the number of Justice agents in Chicago declined from fifty to fifteen. After ordering the American Protective League to disband and closing down his War Emergency Division, Attorney General Gregory had submitted his own resignation in January, effective upon the appointment of a successor.[58]

By the first of February 1919 not only was Military Intelligence no longer actively investigating radicals, but a drastically reduced Department of Justice was without leadership. With the American Protective League disbanded, neither agency had the services of the hundreds of thousands of volunteers who had spied so energetically during the war. The staff of the Negative Intelligence Branch, to whom paranoia had

56. Van Deman to Milstaff, Washington, July 18, 1919, MI Microfilm, reel 7, p. 548.
57. Hoover used MI and ONI material to create a large file on Minor; see National Archives, microfilm project M1085, *Investigative Case Files of the Bureau of Investigation, 1908–1922* (Washington, D.C.: National Archives, 1983), reel 925, file 202600–166.
58. Jensen, *Price of Vigilance*, pp. 246–47, 260–62.

become a way of life, had to be alarmed. Suppose the Reds in America succeeded in using the tactics of their Russian brothers in organizing soviets within trade unions and the military? Suppose a major American city was hit with a general strike? How could the military, hamstrung by the dictates of its civilian leadership, respond to such a crisis? In fact, that drama was only days away from being played out in Seattle, the first major test of the army's new restrictive policy on negative intelligence.

CHAPTER 9

Military Intelligence Remobilized

The ever-vigilant Captain Dengel in Spokane was the first to spot the signs of renewed trouble in Seattle, and his method of discovery was certainly unusual. At four o'clock on the morning of October 16, 1918, Spokane police, acting on a suicide report, entered a hotel room and found a woman "in bed, nude, with a man other than her husband." Desperate to protect her reputation and her chances for a favorable divorce, the woman told the police that "she would divulge information which would prove of great value to the government." Her husband, it turned out, was the area's leading attorney for the Industrial Workers of the World, and she was his confidential secretary. Informing Dengel that within weeks forty thousand Seattle shipyard workers would be walking out in an IWW strike, the woman eventually provided sensitive documents to Military Intelligence and entered the field as an agent provocateur, "sowing seed[s] of dissension" as far away as Butte.[1]

Though Dengel was demobilized before the strike began, Military Intelligence continued to watch what Carlton J. H. Hayes called "the storm-centre . . . in the Northwest." On January 20, Hayes concurred in the recommendation for the insertion of an "expert investigator who has the necessary scholastic backing and scientific training" to tour the West from Bisbee to Seattle and assist in "the shaping of labor policies affecting the Military Intelligence Division." Such an agent, Hayes added, should also be "thoroughly familiar with the policies of M.I.D." so he could advise operatives in the field about the information required by Washington.[2]

1. Intelligence officer, Spokane, to department intelligence officer, October 16, 1918, in Randolph Boehm, ed., *U.S. Military Intelligence Reports: Surveillance of Radicals in the United States, 1917–1941* (Frederick, Md.: University Publications of America, 1984), reel 9, pp. 873–74 (hereafter cited as MI Microfilm); telegram, San Francisco to Milstaff, Washington, October 27, 1918, reel 9, p. 875. The woman's name never appears in the record. For other information on labor activity in Seattle in the fall of 1918, including transcripts of speeches, see reel 34, pp. 440–98.

2. Hayes, memorandum for Dunn, January 20, 1919, MI Microfilm, p. 826.

Hayes's plan came too late. On the next day, thirty-five thousand Seattle shipyard workers struck over wages and hours. On January 22, 1919, the Central Labor Council, the umbrella organization for all Seattle unions, set February 6 as the date for a general strike as a show of solidarity. In the interim, Military Intelligence began to receive reports that "Soldiers, Sailors and Workingmen's Councils" were being created.[3] On February 5, Mayor Ole Hanson telegraphed the secretary of war that he expected his city to be completely shut down in a strike directed not against Seattle but against the government of the United States. "Will you furnish troops?" he asked. "Wire quick." Governor Ernest Lister informed Baker in the second of two telegrams that "tomorrow Seattle and Tacoma will be left in darkness without transportation or communications." Both Baker and the secretary of the navy promised to give the governor "whatever assistance may be found necessary."[4]

The entire Military Intelligence structure of the Western Department, from the headquarters in San Francisco down to Will Germer in Butte, was in a major crisis. Churchill was across the Atlantic, and, as a result of the January restrictions, the MI office in Seattle had been told to "discontinue the I.W.W. investigation" and to close up shop. At the same time, the department commander, Major General John F. Morrison, had been ordered to Seattle and was demanding information on the nature of the enemy. Faced with what appeared to be a genuine revolution, the Seattle intelligence officer opted to stay in business, notifying his Washington and San Francisco superiors that he intended to "continue to cover the strike."[5] The following day he informed them that he had obtained the services of Professor Hans J. Hoff, a Russian-language expert from the Military Censorship Committee, who had consented to attend meetings of the Union of Russian Workers in Seattle.[6] At the

3. Office of MI, Seattle, telegram to director of MI, January 21, 1919, ibid., reel 6, pp. 701–2; office of MI, Seattle, to director of MI, January 30, 1919, p. 549. The earliest reference in the MI files to "soldiers and working men's committees" is in a November 20, 1918, cable from Portland, Oregon, reel 9, p. 830.

4. Hanson to Baker, February 5, 1919; Lister to Baker, February 5, 1919; chief of staff to Morrison, February 6, 1919. These and other requests for and approval of the use of troops, along with several important documents from MI, are in Record Group 60, Glasser Files, box 6, National Archives.

5. Office of MI, Seattle, telegram to director of MI, February 4, 1919, MI Microfilm, reel 6, pp. 517–18.

6. Office of MI, Seattle, to director of MI, February 5, 1919, ibid., p. 511. Hoff, said to translate in fifteen languages, worked not only for Postal Censorship and Military Intelligence, but also for the Seattle Minute Men and Naval Intelligence. After teaching at the universities of Washington and Minnesota, he was at Bethany College in Kansas in 1939, when, four days after World War II started, he volunteered his services once again to Military Intelligence. His file is in Record Group 165, MID, entry 66, National Archives.

same time, he requested additional agents from Camp Lewis who could speak Finnish, Russian, and Swedish. "Request you forward instructions," the Seattle office told Washington, "whether the I.W.W., radical, and strike situation work is to be discontinued or whether we are to cover these fully, including supervision of mails."[7]

When the day of the strike came, Seattle complained to Washington that "no instructions have been received," adding that, on its own authority, the office had borrowed fifteen men from the intelligence unit at Camp Lewis. Heavily armed agitators from Butte were reported in Seattle, where the sixty thousand strikers were wearing red. Most disconcerting of all was that the "striker's tag" was seen on veterans, some still in uniform.[8] Naval Intelligence quoted one former sailor as saying, "While serving in the Navy, I came to Seattle to suppress the I.W.W. movement, but now I am with them, and believe me they are O.K. and they have the only dope." The Seattle aide for information reported that "a number of I.W.W., Bolshevist and radical meetings are taking place every week, but very seldom the English language is used."[9] The department intelligence officer in San Francisco notified Washington that he was leaving for Seattle, adding his presumption that, with troops being deployed, "the instructions covering investigations of radical movements" were lifted.[10] Only after a direct order from Washington to "keep absolutely out of strike situation" was the mobilization of Military Intelligence in the Northwest halted. On February 9, the area's chief intelligence officer responded that he was in compliance, that information collection would be limited to liaison with "other investigating agencies," and army agents would "absolutely refrain from all investigation or espionage." Even Germer in Butte was "being instructed as to policy."[11]

As it turned out, the great Seattle general strike was not all that general. The workers maintained essential services, and with troops in place by the afternoon of February 6 and the tough action of Mayor Hanson in using volunteer policemen, the strike was over in five days, and the soldiers were removed on February 15. The mayor, having achieved national attention for his stand, left on a lecture circuit to warn

7. Office of MI, Seattle, telegram to Milstaff, Washington, February 5, 1919, MI Microfilm, reel 6, pp. 515–16.

8. Office of MI, Seattle, telegram to director of MI, February 6, 1919, ibid., pp. 468–70.

9. Driss Benane to aide for information, February 4, 1919, ibid., pp. 446–47.

10. Office of MI, San Francisco, telegram to Milstaff, Washington, February 6, 1919, ibid., p. 464. The entire file on Seattle in MI Microfilm is on reel 6, pp. 428–826; see esp. pp. 438–39, 461–74, 511–18, 659.

11. Fisher telegram to director of MI, February 9, 1919, in Glasser, box 6.

the country against the Bolshevik menace. Several dozen aliens were detained in the arrests and were later shipped in a sealed train, the "Red Special," that bypassed Butte, where three hundred ıww members threatened to attack it, to Ellis Island for deportation. By the fourteenth, General Morrison had reached Butte, where he wired Washington that the "situation here is serious." He recommended "the prompt deportation of undesirable aliens, mostly Finns and Irish."[12]

It was not until February 19 that Washington got around to slapping Seattle's hand for its short revival of espionage at home. The office's actions, acting director Dunn said, "raises doubt as to whether you had received a copy of the Instructions" of late January. To be sure, he enclosed copies of the orders outlawing such surveillance. In particular, he called the use of Professor Hoff as an operative "clearly at variance both with the spirit and with the letter of the Instructions." No such person was to serve "as a regular agent for your office or conduct espionage on behalf of the Military Intelligence Division." Mindful of the need for information, however, Dunn added an important caveat: he would "heartily welcome" someone "having no formal connection to M.I.D." who "merely volunteers information." Intelligence "which comes freely to us," he said, "is still highly desirable."[13]

Seattle had already gotten the message. During the strike, agents of the supposedly defunct Minute Men Division of the American Protective League had furnished information directly to Military Intelligence using reporting forms supplied by the army. Seattle justified the use of these volunteer agents as a reasonable response to the "revolutionary-strike emergency," noting that they gathered only intelligence needed by the army commander. On February 26, Seattle promised Washington that the "investigation of radical movements has been discontinued," adding that "considerable information continues to come in from volunteer informants."[14]

---

12. Morrison's February 14, 1919, wire from Butte is in Glasser Files, box 3. For more information on the Seattle strike, see Robert L. Tyler, *Rebels of the Woods: The IWW in the Pacific Northwest* (Eugene: University of Oregon Press, 1967), pp. 145–46; Robert K. Murray, *Red Scare: A Study in National Hysteria, 1919–1920* (Minneapolis: University of Minnesota Press, 1955), pp. 58–66, 194–95. For a radical's view, see Harvey O'Conner, *Revolution in Seattle: A Memoir* (New York: Monthly Review Press, 1964); more objective is Robert Friedheim, *The Seattle General Strike* (Seattle: University of Washington Press, 1964). For the route of the "Red Special," see William Preston, Jr., *Aliens and Dissenters: Federal Suppression of Radicals, 1903–1933* (Cambridge, Mass.: Harvard University Press, 1963), pp. 199–200.

13. Acting director of MI to F. W. Wilson, February 19, 1919, MI Microfilm, reel 6, p. 659.

14. Office of MI, Seattle, to director of MI, February 26, 1919, ibid., p. 474. For a sample of Minute Men reporting on MI forms, see p. 439.

Thus was a compromise reached before Marlborough Churchill returned to provide more definite leadership. Relying on alumni of the American Protective League and other volunteers, Military Intelligence began to restore its network. Local APL units simply changed their names and continued their spying for the army in a new war to save the country from the resurgent radical threat. New York's Trevor, chafing under the restrictions that would not allow his men to attend radical meetings, relied on reports from former agents willing to continue their work. He also researched his existing files and prepared an elaborate map, of which he was enormously proud, pinpointing the location of traditional radical meeting places in the metropolitan area. On this he overlaid an "ethnic map" showing the distribution of foreigners and "those born in the United States with one or both parents of foreign origin." The resulting color-coded product showed those zones "in which trouble may be expected to arise."[15]

At the Chicago headquarters of the Central Department, intelligence officer Crockett had intensified his work with former APL members, with especially good results in the Windy City and in Cleveland. The reports from volunteer informants attending radical protests of the treatment of "political prisoners" so incensed him that he recommended a program of counterpropaganda. Dunn cut him off quickly with the comment that under the January restrictions, "it is not a function of Military Intelligence to carry on propaganda or counter-propaganda of any description."[16] Crockett's understudy in the Central Department, First Lieutenant Donald C. Van Buren, handled the northern portion of the large district. By early March he had established close ties with former members of the American Protective League in Cleveland who had organized themselves into the Loyal American League. Alarmed by the appearance of radical literature aimed at workers and soldiers, the league, led by Arch C. Klumph, developed a citizens' spy network, published a weekly intelligence bulletin, and lobbied legislators for action against "the present revolutionary doctrines and plans for revolu-

15. See the April 22, 1919, report on a speech by Scott Nearing at the Rand School, ibid., reel 5, pp. 266–67. Trevor's map is described in his February 27, 1919, memorandum to the director of MI, reel 12, pp. 225–26. Trevor's plan to use troops "in the event that the radical agitation which is now being pushed by fiery propaganda [takes] the form of direct action" is in office of MI, New York, to George R. Ryer, April 22, 1919, reel 12, pp. 382. See also Trevor to director of MI, May 2, 1919, reel 12, pp. 414–18.

16. Acting director of MI to intelligence officer, Central Department, March 18, 1919, ibid., reel 10, p. 442. See department intelligence officer, Chicago, to director of MI, March 13, 1919, p. 443, and acting department intelligence officer, Chicago, to director of MI, January 7, 1919, p. 95.

tion being formulated by all the Bolsheviki organizations in this territory."[17]

When Churchill arrived a month later, it took him only a matter of days to size up the situation and realize the mistake Baker had made in issuing the January restrictions after the Stevenson matter. On April 18 he turned down Trevor's request to install a dictagraph in a room adjacent to the offices of a particularly notorious Russian, telling him to obtain whatever information he could without "using detective methods."[18] Ten days later, he made the decision to restore Military Intelligence to a wartime footing. In a circular letter to all intelligence officers, he formally rescinded the January limitations, replacing them with the following:

> Accurate information, so far as it may be obtained in a legitimate manner, is desired regarding radical activities and the persons engaged therein. Accurate information is desired as to societies and other movements radical or otherwise among demobilized soldiers and as to the leaders thereof.
>
> In obtaining information care must be taken not to excite antagonism or apprehension. Officers and agents who attract attention to themselves or their work are worse than useless. It is proper to collect literature and to send representatives into meetings for the purpose of reporting the same and also to converse with well informed persons, but not to interrogate individuals in a summary and inquisitorial manner nor to institute searches and seizures.[19]

There is no evidence that Churchill sought the approval of Secretary of War Baker for the reactivation of the army against the Reds at home. Once again, at another critical moment for Military Intelligence, Baker was out of the country, and he did not return from his long-delayed trip to France until mid-May. Had he been available, or had Churchill chosen to cable him, the renewal of army snooping might not have occurred, for Baker always seemed relatively unperturbed by the specter of Bolshevism. Yet Churchill could hardly have hidden these activities from his civilian chief for long. Subsequent authorizations for additional money and space certainly came to the secretary's attention.[20] Perhaps the two had reached an unspoken agreement, with Baker assuming that Churchill had in mind only a limited effort and the general determined to keep his boss from hearing any more horror

17. Van Buren to Crockett, March 12, 1919, ibid., reel 10, pp. 64–65.

18. Churchill to intelligence officer, New York City, April 18, 1919, ibid., reel 14, p. 72.

19. The April 28, 1919, "circular letter" reactivating MI for domestic espionage can be found in ibid., reel 4, p. 649, and reel 13, p. 327.

20. Churchill to adjutant general, October 3, 1919, Record Group 165, MID, 10560–295/2, National Archives.

stories about illegal methods in Military Intelligence. The intelligence general was clearly driven by a deep sense of emergency, particularly with the approach of May 1, the traditional day for radical labor action since the Haymarket affair of 1886. Signs of increased radical militancy were everywhere after the Seattle strike. In the Northwest, anarchist posters had been found with the ominous warning: "We will dynamite you!"[21] On the very day that Churchill ordered his agents once more into the fray, authorities found the first bomb that spring.

The terrorist's device of April 28, intended for Seattle's Ole Hanson, was so poorly wrapped that it was discovered and disarmed. The following day, however, a similar package arrived at the Georgia home of former U.S. Senator Thomas W. Hardwick. In the resulting explosion, his maid lost both her hands. A total of thirty-six mail bombs were eventually accounted for, and the damage might have been extraordinary had their makers been better at their craft. The terrorists, however, failed to calculate the number of postage stamps required to ensure delivery of their explosive parcels. Several of the packages were found together, spotted by an alert New York postal employee who, upon reading the description of the Georgia bomb, recognized its mates as among the items held for insufficient postage. These, along with the remainder located in other post offices, were disarmed.[22]

The revelation of the plot for multiple and simultaneous assassinations caused a predictable backlash, and May Day parades were the occasion for considerable violence. Radicals, police, and vigilantes clashed in Boston. In New York a Tom Mooney rally and the offices of the Socialist newspaper the *Call* were attacked by soldiers and sailors. Trevor told Churchill that the radicals were to blame for the mob action because they "irritate the average citizen, whether soldier or civilian, to a degree that he is ready to resort to violence to suppress a movement which he regards as being inefficiently dealt with by the authorities." A Red flag parade in Cleveland met rough treatment from veterans and, in the words of a former MI officer, "all right thinking citizens." The interference with the parade was led by men of the Loyal American League, in cooperation with the police. Army officers were reported on the scene

21. Quoted in Murray, *Red Scare*, p. 69.
22. The bombs were identical: seven by three inches, wrapped in plain paper bearing Gimbel Brothers return address, with a large stamp proclaiming "SAMPLE," and containing a wooden tube filled with TNT. Targets included Senator Lee S. Overman, Oliver Wendell Holmes, Jr., John D. Rockefeller, J. P. Morgan, Judge Kenesaw Mountain Landis, Commissioner of Immigration Frederic C. Howe, and Attorney General A. Mitchell Palmer. A picture of the parcel sent to Morgan is in the unpaged photographic section of John Higham, *Strangers in the Land: Patterns of American Nativism, 1860–1925* (New Brunswick: Rutgers University Press, 1955). See also Murray, *Red Scare*, pp. 68–73.

ripping up the offending crimson symbols. The former intelligence man thought the whole affair "splendid work" and "a beautiful job."[23]

Trevor had agents at seven radical meetings in New York on May Day, and he continued to monitor any function that caught his attention, adding names to his growing list of radical speakers. When, later in the month, philosopher Will Durant spoke on the League of Nations at the Labor Temple, Trevor enrolled him as a "Radical Socialist Lecturer." He did so despite the innocuous nature of the agent's report, which noted that "Prof. Will Durant is not a member of the Socialist Party. He considers himself to be a socialist, but the Socialist Party does not agree with him."[24]

No doubt with Baker's encouragement, Churchill hoped to restrain Military Intelligence from resorting to the illegal measures that had characterized its activities the previous fall. Yet its position was precarious, and pressure from the right was mounting in the face of an increasingly obvious threat of violence from the left. Shortly before the news of the mail bombs, Ralph Easley of the now thoroughly right-wing National Civic Federation wrote Churchill to express his pleasure that the chief was "back on the job" and his dismay about current events, especially the number of veterans being won over by the Reds. "I have been amazed," Easley added, "to hear of so many I. W. W.'its [sic] and Bolshevists holding important positions in various governmental Departments and some of them in the Military Intelligence Division." Churchill defended the loyalty of his men and cautioned that "our laws are very clear concerning the action of the Federal authorities in matters of civil disorder." He added, however, that he did not intend "to split hairs when we are threatened with a menace like the present radical movement."[25]

23. Trevor's May 2, 1919, report to Churchill, MI Microfilm, reel 12, pp. 402–7, has attached to it a vivid account of the fighting outside the Mooney protest at Madison Square Garden. For Cleveland, see S. C. Moule to Captain Metzerott, May 2, 1919, reel 10, p. 49. Murray, *Red Scare*, pp. 73–78, describes the unrest in major cities. Violence did not occur everywhere. Socialists in Dayton, for example, managed to keep their headquarters intact as a result of good community relations. See John T. Walker, "The Dayton Socialists and World War I: Surviving the White Terror," in Donald T. Critchlow, ed., *Socialism in the Heartland: The Midwestern Experience, 1900–1925* (Notre Dame: University of Notre Dame Press, 1986), pp. 117–21. For a December 1, 1918, Plant Protection Section report on Bolshevism in Dayton, see Record Group 165, entry 104, Bolsheviki File, General Correspondence, National Archives, Suitland.

24. The summary of Durant's speech is in George J. Starr to W. L. Moffat, Jr., May 28, 1919, MI Microfilm, reel 12, pp. 464–65; the list of speakers, pp. 472–76. See p. 447 for an account of the May Day meetings in New York and p. 433 for the resolution passed at the Mooney mass meeting, which included a call for a general strike.

25. Easley to Churchill, April 25, 1919; Churchill to Easley, April 28, 1919, ibid., reel 34, pp. 121–24. Easley's paranoid charge that there were radicals on the staff on MI was

What Churchill did do, in the spring of 1919, was to split hairs with his men over methodology. When his Pittsburgh office told him that confidential informant number 836 was in a position to engineer the election of "an under-cover man, preferably an overseas enlisted man," as president of the Soldiers, Sailors, and Marines' Union, which they insisted on calling a "soviet," Churchill ordered them to forget the plan. Such "procuring" was not "expedient" or "within the contemplation" of his April 28 order. The people in Pittsburgh had to limit their activities to "sending representatives to the meetings" or to the use of voluntary informants.[26] He responded similarly at the end of May, when he received a report that an army agent in Chicago had picked the pockets of Ludwig C.A.K. Martens, the Russian unofficial trade representative whose New York office Trevor had wanted to bug. Churchill came down hard on such "irregular" techniques. "This office," he fired back, "does not sanction any such methods and asks that the agents be instructed accordingly."[27] These restrictions were consistent with Churchill's concept of a limited espionage system designed to keep the army in the negative intelligence arena but to avoid severe criticism. In preparation for seeking congressional funding for his expanded operations, he had his Negative Branch draw up a concise statement of his philosophy: "While the Military Intelligence Division is not a censor of individual conduct, nor an agency for the administraton of justice, the activities of individual agitators and leaders cannot be overlooked as a source of information relative to the nature of movements which they promote. To this extent[,] records of their past and present activities should be developed."[28]

Attorney General Gregory and his assistant John Lord O'Brian had

probably a result of Stevenson's dismissal and the restrictions on MI—obviously the work of a terrible conspiracy. He might have had Lippmann in mind, or perhaps Carlton J. H. Hayes. See notes 43 and 66 below for other possibilities. Easley soon formed, within the National Civic Federation, a "Department on the Study of Revolutionary Movements" and became especially concerned about the Young Men's Christian Association, the Federal Council of Churches of Christ in America, and the Interchurch World Movement. He monitored these menacing groups with a "Committee on the Study of Socialism in the Churches" (Marguerite Green, *The National Civic Federation and the American Labor Movement, 1900–1925* [Washington, D.C.: Catholic University of America Press, 1956], pp. 398–414). See also the federation material, including copies of its *Review*, in Lusk Committee Papers, L0039, box 1, folder 17, New York State Archives, Albany.

26. Intelligence officer, Pittsburgh, to director of MI, May 6, 1919, and director of MI to Edward Flood, May 10, 1919, MI Microfilm, reel 8, pp. 664–66.

27. Department intelligence office, Chicago, report, May 26, 1919; director of MI to intelligence officer, Central Department, June 2, 1919, ibid., reel 14, pp. 26–30.

28. Memorandum from MI4 to Churchill, May 13, 1919, Record Group 165, MID, 10560–221/10, National Archives.

struggled to maintain some legal sanity during and just after the war. When, for example, Gregory was asked by a Senate resolution to investigate a series of pro-Russian, and thus presumably revolutionary, meetings in Washington in early February, he had responded that no one there had called for the violent overthrow of the United States government and let the issue drop.[29] Gregory, however, was a lame duck looking forward to the naming of his successor. An interim director led the Bureau of Investigation, and O'Brian was closing up Justice's War Emergency Division. Churchill could not have anticipated that the new attorney general and his assistants would be anything but critical of Military Intelligence. A. Mitchell Palmer, whose appointment Wilson handled by transatlantic cable, became the nation's premier Red hunter and gave his name to a notorious episode in American history, the Palmer Raids. No one reacted more energetically to the May Day bombs than did the new chief legal officer, who had already earned a tough reputation as alien property custodian. By the time Palmer learned that he was one of the intended targets, the calm O'Brian was cleaning out his desk. In his place came a young law school graduate who headed a new agency created by Palmer. Though its actual name was the General Intelligence Division, the unit that J. Edgar Hoover led into the Red Scare was usually called by a more descriptive title: "the Anti-Radical Division."[30]

Despite a massive search involving the entire federal investigative establishment, including the military, the May Day bombers were never found. Even more distressing, the blasts continued. In a second wave on June 2, the new attorney general came very close to death. Palmer and his wife had retired when an explosion shattered the front of their house at 11:15 P.M. Their neighbors, Franklin and Eleanor Roosevelt, had just entered their home across the street, and the assistant secretary of the navy rushed over to find the Palmers shaken but unhurt. Apparently the lone bomber had tripped on the walk, destroying himself and sparing the Palmers the full effect of the blast. Seven other bombings that were

29. August R. Ogden, *The Dies Committee: A Study of the Special House Committee for the Investigation of Un-American Activities, 1938–1944* (Washington, D.C.: Catholic University of America Press, 1945), pp. 14–15.

30. William J. Flynn of the Secret Service took over the Bureau of Investigation on July 1, 1919. Hoover had started as a clerk in the Department of Justice in the summer of 1917, working for O'Brian in the War Emergency Division; his appointment with the General Intelligence Division came two years later. See Stanley Coben, *A. Mitchell Palmer: Politician* (New York: Columbia University Press, 1963), p. 207; Joan M. Jensen, *The Price of Vigilance* (Chicago: Rand McNally, 1968), pp. 260–62; Richard G. Powers, *Secrecy and Power: The Life of J. Edgar Hoover* (New York: Free Press, 1987), pp. 43–55.

clearly part of the same conspiracy occurred in eastern cities on June 2. Terrorism had come to America. The pink handbills, entitled "Plain Words," found at several bombing scenes established that beyond a doubt. They were clear enough: "We will kill . . . there will be destruction; we will destroy," and were signed, "The Anarchist Fighters."[31]

Washington police had the circular as evidence, the fragments of the anarchist's body, the initials K.B. on a collar, a derby hat with the label "Lamson & Hubbard, Boston," and a revolver that turned out to have been purchased by Luigi Calisieri from the Iver Johnson Sporting Goods House of the same city. With those clues, the authorities reached the easy conclusion that the assassin was from or near Boston. They also assumed that the bombings were a protest against the treatment of Luigi Galleani, leader of a band of Italian anarchists, who had been arrested by the Department of Justice and was being held for deportation. Churchill was eager to help, and he immediately ordered all his units to cooperate with the Department of Justice. He also sent one of his operatives with a Washington detective to Massachusetts on a tour of Italian communities, searching for information on a radical resident who had recently disappeared.[32]

Not all the branches of Military Intelligence accepted the ethnic identification of the bomber. In Pittsburgh, where attempts had been made against a federal judge and an immigration official, army agents agreed with the local authorities' assessment that the bombings were the work of the Union of Russian Workers. They reasoned that it had to have been Russian immigrants because one of the charges on the pink sheets was "you have deported us." It was easily determined that "the only persons deported here and elsewhere, with a few possible exceptions, have been Russian agitators." The army agents in Pittsburgh were so intense in their investigation that when the police rounded up fifteen suspects, most of them Russians, an MI operative allowed himself to be publicly arrested and placed in jail with them for three days. Although the ruse worked to the extent that the army spy gained the confidence of his targets, all he learned was that they knew nothing about the bombings, which they thought had been "engineered from the outside, and that in their judgment it was an unfortunate move and would act as a

---

31. Good descriptions of the blast at the Palmer home are in Coben, *Palmer,* pp. 205–6, and Murray, *Red Scare,* pp. 78–79. Palmer was so upset, Roosevelt said, that he reverted to the "thees" and "thous" of his Quaker rearing (Jensen, *Price of Vigilance,* p. 273).

32. Churchill's order went out on June 3, 1919, by telegram, MI Microfilm, reel 14, p. 875. The intelligence report, dated June 22, 1919, by the army agent who accompanied the Washington detective to Massachusetts is on pp. 841–43.

bommerang [sic] to the cause."[33] On that last point the unfortunate souls were entirely correct.

In Cleveland, where the mayor's house had been blown up, Military Intelligence identified Karl Blum as a suspect, based on his incriminating initials, his record as an anarchist, the warrant outstanding for his arrest and deportation, and the fact that he had been missing since early June.[34] The investigation also established the existence of a number of bizarre fringe groups. The "Double Trinity" and the "Group of Avengers" never emerged from the shadows and may not even have existed, but two terrorist groups issued printed statements in the summer of 1919. The Knights of the Red Star served notice: "Should the police dogs, brass buttoned or otherwise, as well as some judges . . . dare to mistreat any one who falls into their clutches as a real or SUSPECTED member of those they term 'Red,' we shall wreak vengeance on the guilty in such a bloody manner that will rid the country of these dogs and hangmen before long."[35] A similar "Proclamation to the People" announced the creation of "Liberating and Punitive Detachments of the People's Army," described as "a small but well equipped, disciplined, trained and hardened army" serving as "the people's warriors in the cause of the welfare of the working people." Also protesting against police cruelty, this group promised to "strike fear and terror into the hearts of our enemies."[36]

The radical leadership insisted that the bombs had been planted, as John Reed said, by "some one who was interested in terrifying the ruling class into destroying the radical labor movement in this country." Algernon Lee, directing the Rand School, also suspected provocateurs from "private detective agencies in the pay of unofficial organizations who have wrapped themselves in the flag of the United States." An agent for the Bureau of Investigation concluded, as he told Congress in 1924, that

33. Intelligence officer, Pittsburgh, to director of MI, June 12, 1919, ibid., pp. 860–63.
34. Department intelligence officer, Chicago, to Bliss Norton, June 20, 1919, ibid., p. 765.
35. This untitled and undated three-page statement, typed in Russian, was picked up in Chicago by a Military Intelligence agent who arranged for it, and the one quoted below, to be translated. English versions of both proclamations and the agent's report are attached to department intelligence officer, Chicago, to director of MI, July 3, 1919, ibid., pp. 720–34. It is possible that the Double Trinity was the "central directing body" of the Knights of the Red Star. See the fascinating interrogation of a former intelligence officer from czarist Russia who had followed these radicals to the United States and who became a settlement worker in Gary, Indiana: Van Buren, intelligence report, June 12, 1919, pp. 774–82. See also Spolansky and Janovsky, intelligence report, June 11, 1919, pp. 772–73, and Van Buren, intelligence report, June 13, 1919, p. 771.
36. "Proclamation to the People," ibid., pp. 727–28. See also the file "Bombing Outrages" developed by the Plant Protection Section (just going out of business in the summer of 1919) in Record Group 165, entry 104, National Archives, Suitland Records Center.

there "never was anything to the Palmer explosion. . . . I think that was a stage-set proposition, done for a purpose solely."[37] Recent scholarship, however, suggests that the authorities were correct in their assumption that Italian anarchists were responsible. Luigi Calisieri was never found, but there is substantial evidence that Carlo Valdinocci was involved in the bombings and may have blown himself up on the attorney general's doorstep. Andrea Salsedo admitted that he had printed "Plain Words" before jumping, presumably, from the fourteenth floor of the building in which the Justice Department held him.[38]

The attack on his home propelled an already concerned Palmer fully into paranoid politics. When Baker wrote his cabinet colleague to express his sympathy for the shock to the Palmer family, the attorney general responded that he intended to use his position "as a means of putting an end forever to those lawless attempts to intimidate and injure, if not destroy, organized government in this country."[39] Palmer secured an appropriation of half a million dollars from Congress and brought in William J. Flynn, former head of the Secret Service, to lead a strengthened Bureau of Investigation. He also created the General Intelligence Division under his special assistant, J. Edgar Hoover, who began to build the card index system that became the basis for his famous files.[40]

On June 17, Churchill appeared before Congress to request funds to fight the radicals. He knew he had to be extremely careful to avoid indicating his intention to reinvigorate his Negative Branch and resume a major domestic intelligence effort. He allowed his discretion to slide over into outright deception. "Investigation of disloyal persons by the military authorities," he stated before the Senate Military Affairs Comittee in a prevarication that had certainly been approved by Baker, "has been discontinued since the armistice." He noted that it was important

37. The agent was testifying against Harry M. Daugherty, who had just resigned as attorney general in the aftermath of the Teapot Dome scandal (U.S. Senate, *Hearings before the Select Committee on Investigation of the Attorney General*, 68th Cong., 1st sess., *Investigation of Honorable Harry M. Daugherty, Formerly Attorney General of the United States*, 3 vols. [Washington, D.C.: U.S. Government Printing Office, 1924], 3:2902). Reed and Lee are quoted in Robert W. Dunn, ed., *The Palmer Raids* (New York: International Publishers, 1948), p. 17, a fascinating view of the Red Scare from the far left.

38. The best evidence of the Italian anarchists' involvement in the bombings of the spring of 1919 is in William Young and David E. Kaiser, *Postmortem: New Evidence in the Case of Sacco and Vanzetti* (Amherst: University of Massachusetts Press, 1985), pp. 14–26.

39. Palmer to Baker, June 9, 1919, Papers of Newton D. Baker, microfilm reel 8, p. 212, Manuscript Division, Library of Congress.

40. Murray, *Red Scare*, pp. 193–94, attributes Hoover's index card system to his youthful work in the Library of Congress, but it seems remarkably similar to the procedure already established by Van Deman in Military Intelligence, a collection from which Hoover drew heavily. See also Paul L. Murphy, *The Meaning of Free Speech: First Amendment Freedoms from Wilson to FDR* (Westport, Conn.: Greenwood, 1972), p. 68.

for the army to monitor attempts to persuade "enlisted men and discharged soldiers . . . to form councils of soldiers and sailors similar to those in Russia" but stated that the army's paramount mission was to prepare for the coming Red attempt to overthrow the government. Then he titillated the committee with Trevor's colorful maps showing "the haunts of Bolshevists, anarchists, and other extreme radicals." He was awarded $400,000.[41]

Despite his disclaimer, Churchill's intentions were obvious to the *New York Times*, which ran the story under the headlines "Army Has Charts of Red Activities" and "Says Intelligence Officers Have Anarchists and Bolsheviki under Surveillance." Nor were they lost on a former officer, who wrote Walter Lippmann at the *New Republic* that Churchill's argument was "nothing more than a subterfuge to overcome the perfectly proper objection which could be raised to a permanent system of government espionage." Furthermore, he added, "the army has no jurisdiction or proper concern with *discharged* soldiers." In his opinion, the typical army agent was "totally ignorant as to where liberalism ends and radicalism begins. . . . And in his desire to justify his existence, he develops an abnormal capacity for 'seeing things.'" Allowing Military Intelligence to regain "the same free rein which it exercised months ago," when it showed "an utter disrespect for the clear and undisputed civil rights of full fledged American citizens" and "recognized no limits in its efforts to secure information," was "violently antidemocratic" and "a clean-cut and unmistakable step in the direction of militarism."[42]

Lippmann, still loyal to his old boss Secretary Baker, chose not to address the issue in the *New Republic*, telling Ralph Hayes, again Baker's secretary, that "all the men here believe that no one understands the matters involved better than the Secretary of War himself." Such was not precisely the case, for when Hayes asked Churchill to provide a basis for a response to Lippmann, he received the old order of November 20, 1918, with no mention of the subsequent policy restrictions of January that had been rescinded in April. On June 27, Hayes told Lippman that all was well, quoting at length from the dead November demobilization letter.[43] As far as the *New Republic*, the office of the secretary of war, and

---

41. *New York Times*, June 18, 1919; Jensen, *Price of Vigilance*, p. 276.

42. A copy of the anonymous letter to Lippmann, dated June 18, 1919, is in Record Group 165, MID, 10560–277, National Archives.

43. Lippmann to Hayes, June 19, 1919, ibid., 10560–277/3; Hayes to Lippmann, June 27, 1919, ibid., 10560–277/7. Churchill had the Negative Branch attempt to determine the author of the incriminating letter. Although inconclusive, its best guess was Washington lawyer Alexander S. Lanier, who while an MI captain during the war had written President Wilson that the government's case against the IWW was severely flawed; see W. G. Smiley,

the Congress knew, Military Intelligence had no plans to get into the Red Scare in any significant manner.

Just as he had done during the war, Baker failed to exercise any control over Military Intelligence until matters got completely out of hand. An honest man himself, he trusted Churchill. But he was a naive reformer and missed every warning sign when a stern word or a well-chosen dimissal could have changed the history of Military Intelligence. Baker had remained calm during the panic over the bombings, which he attributed to "poor witless devils." He decried the "chronic suspicion and scandal-mongery" of Palmer, Congress, and the press, and even said, "I do not myself think 'Bolshevist peril' anything to be afraid of."[44] Such was Baker's optimism that as the nation plunged into the terrible summer of 1919, he reported proudly to his radical friend Florence Kelley that though her call for the repeal of the espionage law was not likely given the mood of Congress, executive clemency for political prisoners was "really being exercised steadily."[45] Sometimes, however, he seems to have sensed the failure of Wilsonian idealism. As he neared New York after an almost mystical experience at Versailles, where goodness and wisdom seemed so clearly in the ascendant, the harbor pilot brought on board several newspapers. When he saw the "futilities which made up the head-lines of those papers," Baker "felt as though I had fallen overboard into a cold sea."[46]

His despair was understandable. United States troops were in Siberia, and friends of the Russian Bolsheviks agitated openly at home; black Americans were rising in angry protest; drastic postwar cost-of-living increases were precipitating a season of labor violence; and the Mooney supporters had called a general strike for July 4. The panic and suspicion so dreaded by Baker had seized America, and Military Intelligence was headed directly into the hysteria. Lippmann's *New Republic* was on Churchill's list of journals "sympathizing with Bolshevism." A distant paradise felt so threatened by a visiting professor's lectures on Russia

memorandum for general Churchill, June 26, 1919, 10560–277/5; Churchill to Hayes, June 27, 1919, 10560–277/6; and Melvyn Dubofsky, *We Shall Be All: A History of the Industrial Workers of the World* (Chicago: Quadrangle Books, 1969), p. 429.

44. Baker to D. C. Westenhaver, June 13, 1919, Baker Papers, reel 9, pp. 12–13, and to Norman Thomas, August 9, 1919, reel 8, pp. 328–29.

45. Kelley to Baker, June 19, 1919, and his June 21 response, ibid., reel 7, pp. 584–86. Baker corresponded regularly with Kelley and was president of her National Consumers' League. This association did not go unnoticed. For an attack on Kelley for her role as president of the Intercollegiate Socialist Society, her association with the Rand School, and her status as "one who constantly fulminates against capitalists and capitalism," see Mrs. Frederick Nathan to Baker, June 28, 1919, reel 8, pp. 127–28.

46. Baker to D. C. Westenhaver, June 13, 1919, ibid., reel 9, pp. 12–13.

that the Hawaiian Vigilance Corps resolved that no further speakers "will be brought to Honolulu until their past history, sympathies and ideals have been thoroughly vouched for." [47]

Baker allowed troops to be placed on standby in Chicago and Boston for the anticipated Independence Day eruption. During the week of June 30 to July 6, the intelligence office of the Northeastern Department stayed open around the clock as a "precaution against bomb outrages." Central Department intelligence chief Crockett mobilized a hundred former members of the American Protective League and provided them with "temporary credentials" as agents of Military Intelligence. [48] MI was back. Although the organization Churchill rebuilt in the summer of 1919 was not as large as the one recently dismantled, his cadre of experienced officers was able to expand and renew operations rapidly. In addition to the hundreds of agents under the authority of the several department intelligence officers, Churchill maintained three offices reporting directly to him, in New York, Philadelphia, and St. Louis. When, in October, Secretary Baker sought to eliminate unnecessary rental space outside Washington, Churchill successfully defended the expense for these branches as necessary for the "observation of persons whose activities are suspected of being inimical to the interests" of the nation. [49] The secretary of war's tacit approval merely amplified a capitulation to the hysteria that he had made on September 29, 1919, when he renewed the department commanders' blanket authority to respond directly, without waiting for a presidential proclamation, to local requests for federal troops to suppress domestic disturbances. [50]

Like the army's abuses, Baker's ambivalence toward civil liberties has been overshadowed by the excesses of his colleague A. Mitchell Palmer

47. Other pro-Red journals on the Negative Branch's list included the *Nation* and the *Dial* (MI Microfilm, reel 14, p. 609). See the July 24, 1919, report from the Hawaiian Department's intelligence officer on University of California Professor Alexander Kaun, reel 8, p. 749.

48. Intelligence officer, Northeastern Department, to director of MI, July 3, 1919, ibid., reel 14, p. 838; department intelligence officer, Chicago, to director of MI, July 7, 1919, reel 10, p. 744. See also Murray, *Red Scare*, pp. 114–17.

49. Churchill to adjutant general, October 3, 1919, Record Group 165, MID, 10560–295/6, National Archives. Whatever Baker's distaste for the world of negative intelligence, he never sought to avoid contact with Churchill, who, during this period and especially regarding the Siberian adventure, briefed Baker personally and sent memoranda directly to him. See the July 28 and September 15, 1919, memoranda from Churchill to the secretary of war, Baker Papers, reel 7, pp. 156, 174.

50. Baker's September 29, 1919, message went to all commanders and governors; it is in Glasser Files, box 4.

in the Department of Justice, whose famous Palmer Raids have come to symbolize the crisis. It would be a mistake, however, to make Palmer the single villain in the postwar panic. The attorney general certainly expressed the worst of the Red Scare, but he did not create it, and the Wilson administration allowed his activities to flourish. The question of the president's responsibility for the general repression remains unclear. His well-known obsession with the fight over the ratification of the Versailles Treaty and his physical incapacity in the fall of 1919 are traditionally cited in his defense. Historians who see his fear of the left overwhelming his love of civil liberty cite his call for a peacetime sedition act and his continued application of repressive wartime measures after hostilities had ended.[51]

Baker was a loyal supporter of Wilson, following his line on the treaty to the bitter defeat. Perhaps the president failed to restrain Palmer for the same reasons that the secretary of war could not handle Military Intelligence: there was too much else going on, and the topic was too mean-spirited for progressive moralists. Both Baker and Wilson probably assumed that their respective subordinates shared their dilemma over civil rights for radicals. Churchill occasionally expressed some qualms about the role of the military. Once Palmer had identified Red-baiting as an issue that could lead him to the White House, however, there was no stopping him. The situation in 1919 and early 1920 was, then, somewhat different from that of the war years. During the conflict, it had been the Department of Justice that had restrained an abusive army acting illegally. In the Red Scare, the flagrant repression by Justice brought down on its head the wrath of the liberals, and the military largely escaped the criticism and censure that followed once the passion was spent.

Palmer's strategy was simple: the Alien Law left over from the war would be used to round up radical foreigners and ship them out of the country. On August 12, 1919, the new head of the Bureau of Investigation, William J. Flynn, sent a confidential order to his special agents notifying them of the emphasis on deportation. "The Bureau requires," he said, "a vigorous and comprehensive investigation of Anarchistic and similar classes, Bolshevism, and kindred agitation advocating . . . sedi-

---

51. For evaluations of Wilson in this respect, see Murray, *Red Scare*, pp. 200–295, and Harry N. Scheiber, *The Wilson Administration and Civil Liberties, 1917–1921* (Ithaca: Cornell University Press, 1960), p. 53. Robert H. Ferrell, *Woodrow Wilson and World War I, 1917–1921* (New York: Harper & Row, 1985), has a chapter on the problem of civil liberties.

tion and revolution, bomb throwing, and similar activities."[52] The key evidence came to be merely membership in an organization considered by the attorney general to be subversive.

Large-scale raiding of radical headquarters by bureau agents did not begin until November 7, when the Union of Russian Workers' offices were hit in New York and other cities. The best-known raids, when four thousand radicals were taken in twenty-three states, occurred on January 2, 1920.[53] This effort, supervised by J. Edgar Hoover, has received notoriety because of its size and Palmer's ballyhooing in his early run for the Democratic presidential nomination. In numbers of agents, informants, raids, or arrests, however, Palmer's effort was fairly evenly matched by the combined efforts of Military Intelligence and the state governments of New York and Illinois. It was, moreover, a former Military Intelligence volunteer who led the very first raid of the Red Scare.

When Archibald Stevenson's association with Military Intelligence was cut short by Baker's reaction to his testimony before the Overman Committee in January 1919, the great Red hunter was by no means put out of action. Stevenson's anti-radical mania may have existed independently of his relationship with the army, but his connection with the army demands an examination of his subsequent career. While still with Military Intelligence, Stevenson had hoped to persuade the state of New York to launch an investigation of radicalism. The army rejected this idea, but Stevenson did not let it go and, even while being dumped by Baker, he was using his not insignificant influence to pursue the plan. His vehicle was the Union League Club in New York, and in early 1919 Charles E. Hughes, president, appointed Stevenson chairman of a special committee to study the Reds. That report, printed on March 13, 1919 was entitled *Bolshevism* and contained a call for the state legislature to launch an investigation.[54]

On March 20, 1919, the assembly authorized $30,000 for a Committee to Investigate Seditious Activities in the State of New York. Named after its chairman, Clayton R. Lusk, the Lusk Committee was the country's first Red-hunting legislative body to hire its own agents and to run its

52. Flynn to all special agents and employees, August 12, 1919, MI Microfilm, reel 14, pp. 398–403.

53. Murray, *Red Scare*, remains a good, general account of Palmer and his methods; on the raids, see pp. 196–97, 212–17. Coben, *Palmer*, has a hint of sympathy for an attorney general pushed to extremism by his assistants.

54. The Union League Club report is in Lusk Papers, L0040, box 1, folder 18.

own operations against radicals. There was no confusion over the real purpose of the group; when the Underwood Typewriter Company sent a bill for rented machines, it was addressed to the "Joint Committee to Suppress Seditious Activities."[55] In the course of its work, the committee spent $80,000, not including the services of numerous state policemen and volunteers. Former members of the American Protective League were especially willing to help. Lusk's brother-in-law William McDermit, head of the APL's New Jersey division, was more than obliging, as was his New York counterpart, who continued to use the stationery of the supposedly defunct vigilante group.

Although the effort bore his name, Lusk did not run the operation; nor did the state attorney general, Charles D. Newton, whose appointment as chief counsel was a political gesture to assure support from the state police. The real head of the Lusk Committee was associate counsel Archibald Stevenson, supported by his former Military Intelligence boss John B. Trevor, who had been demobilized in June and added to the Lusk effort as a special deputy attorney general. Leading the investigative unit was Rayme W. Finch, a former Bureau of Investigation agent with whom Stevenson, while with Military Intelligence, had cooperated in a raid on Baldwin's civil liberties office.[56] Because the espionage program of the Lusk Committee was comparatively brief, small, and intense, and especially because it kept very good records, it is possible to bring its work into fairly sharp focus, which is not always the case for the more diffuse efforts of Military Intelligence or the Department of Justice. This little Red Scare, moreover, serves as a fine example of the general practices in use at the time. Setting up headquarters in the Prince George Hotel in New York, the Lusk Committee never had more than two dozen agents and an equal number of support staff on the payroll. Equipped with identification cards, guns, and press credentials

55. Materials on the early organization of the Lusk Committee are in ibid., folders 17 and 18.

56. Ibid., folder 13; Jensen, Price of Vigilance, p. 275; Murray, Red Scare, pp. 99–102; Lawrence H. Chamberlain, Loyalty and Legislative Action: A Survey of the Activity of the New York State Legislature (Ithaca: Cornell University Press, 1951), pp. 11–12. The raid on the National Civil Liberties Bureau occurred on August 31, 1918, with Stevenson leading a group of volunteers from the Union League Club calling themselves the Propaganda League. Finch later arrested Baldwin. See Peggy Lamson, Roger Baldwin, Founder of the American Civil Liberties Union: A Portrait (Boston: Houghton Mifflin, 1976), pp. 82–90. There was a natural rivalry between the Palmer and Lusk efforts that Hoover never forgot. In 1921 he suggested to Military Intelligence that Finch was in the pay of the British secret service. See Theodore Kornweibel, Jr., ed., Federal Surveillance of Afro-Americans (1917–1925): The First World War, the Red Scare, and the Garvey Movement (Frederick, Md.: University Publications of America, 1986), reel 22, pp. 559–73.

supplied by the police, the Lusk agents ran networks of informants, sent stenographers to radical meetings, committed burglaries, stole letters and telegrams, hauled in suspects for secret interrogations, secured witnesses for the open hearings of the committee, testified before executive sessions, and in raids on radical headquarters, confiscated tons of literature and office correspondence.[57]

These last items make the Lusk records, now in the New York State Archives, a treasure trove of information on radical activity in New York and the nation in 1919. The stenographic records of speeches and interrogations are invaluable and include wonderfully ephemeral material such as the rantings of George A. Till, a street orator in Buffalo. Also from Buffalo came a daily *Local Bulletin* produced by the Secret Service Committee of the Niagara Frontier Defense League.[58] Some topics are filed separately, as in the case of "Investigations—Negroes"; others are named after the agent, as in "Investigations—Operator Betty Thompson Reports," which contains her eyewitness accounts of the meetings of the Friends of Freedom for India and the Friends of Irish Freedom.[59] Reports also came in from the "Secret Service" of Brooklyn's Confederation of Christian Men and Women of America, who, the letterhead said, were "Banded together to destroy Socialism, the Enemy of Religion and Country."[60]

Stevenson routinely shared information with the Department of Justice and to a lesser extent with Military Intelligence. Trevor could count on favors from MI's New York branch that he had just left and from the department intelligence officer at Governor's Island, but Stevenson was still persona non grata with the Department of the Army. When Major General Leonard Wood occupied Gary, Indiana, during the great steel strike, Finch volunteered his files on Bolshevism in the steel industry. Officially, however, Military Intelligence could not reciprocate, and when the New York attorney general made a formal request to Churchill for information on an indicted radical group, Secretary Baker overruled both his intelligence commander and the chief of staff in denying access

57. On gun permits, including one for Stevenson, and press credentials, see Lusk Papers, L0039, box 1, folder 19. For files on staffing, L0040, box 1, folder 20.

58. The Buffalo material is in ibid., L0038, box 5, folders 11–13, and L0040, box 1, folder 1, folder 20. The preferred stenographer in New York was William F. Smart, who also worked for the army and Bureau of Investigation. Two volumes of his transcriptions for Justice, nearly fifteen hundred pages, are in folder 17.

59. On black Americans, see ibid., L0038, box 2, folder 1; Thompson's reports are in folder 2. Additional material on Irish nationalism is in L0039, box 1, folder 14.

60. Lusk was a member of the Brooklyn group, headed by John T. Oates (ibid., L0040, box 1, folder 1).

to MI's files. Baker was afraid that the use of stenographic notes taken by army agents at radical meetings would publicize, in Churchill's words, "War Department investigations that might possibly be taken exception to."[61]

From June 1919 to January 1920, the Lusk Committee conducted a very brisk operation. To educate the assemblymen on the Red threat, Trevor gave them each a copy of Tunney's thriller *Throttled,* along with a survey of state laws on "anarchy, sedition, treason, syndicalism and kindred activities." The staff accumulated lists of radical organizations and meetings, along with a wonderful collection of photographs, and informants were wormed into the radical underground. One fascinating undercover operation involved placing the young and unreliable Margaret Scully as a typist for Emma Goldman, who was awaiting deportation. Scully's reports illuminate the life of a remarkably liberated woman playing spy in 1919. The reports of Julia Preston, Agent 100 in Binghamton, are more staid. With Finch's encouragement, she had her sister take over when she left for a two-week vacation.[62]

Formal hearings by the Lusk Committee were held in New York City, Buffalo, Utica, and Rochester, but its most sensational work was its raids on radical headquarters, which began before either Military Intel-

61. Director of MI to intelligence officer, New York City, July 14, 1919, MI Microfilm, reel 12, p. 746. For Lusk's relations with local MI units, see Lusk Papers, L0039, box 1, folder 38, and L0040, box 1, folder 27; with the bureau, L0039, box 1, folder 36. Trevor never forgave Baker for dismissing Stevenson and cracking down on MI. Shortly after leaving the army, he wrote that the secretary's actions were due either to a "misconception of the activities" of the army or "to innate sympathy with the radical intelligensia." This claim is in Trevor's long argument for a centralized intelligence agency to combat radicalism in MI Microfilm, reel 15, pp. 867–87.

62. Scully's reports are in Lusk Papers, L0038, box 1, folder 14, and box 2, folder 7; Preston's reports run from August 5, 1919, to February 21, 1921, and are filed, along with those of other non–New York City informants, in L0038, box 5. Reports on antiradical legislation are in L0039, box 1, folder 16. See L0040, box 1, folder 27, for the use of *Throttled.* Photographs are spread throughout the files, but an especially good collection is in L0039, box 1, folder 26. Fairly high-quality photos are also in the committee's printed report: New York Legislature, Joint Legislative Committee Investigating Seditious Activities, *Revolutionary Radicalism: Its History, Purpose and Tactics with an Exposition and Discussion of the Steps Being Taken and Required to Curb It,* 4 vols. (Albany: J. B. Lyon Company, 1920). Logs of 123 radical meetings attended by Lusk agents are in L0027, box 1, folder 1; that box also contains numerous stenographic records of radical meetings in December 1919, including a "Mass Meeting" of the New York Communist party, two sessions on "The Truth about Mexico," and a "Labor Mass Meeting on India." Other extraordinary materials include a two-inch file on the 1916–17 birth control movement led by Margaret Sanger and Frederick A. Blossom, obtained either through liaison or confiscation, and a British intelligence summary on radicalism in the United Kingdom, L0039, box 1, folders 5 and 35.

ligence or the Department of Justice had remobilized.[63] On June 12, Stevenson and his men raided the Russian Soviet Bureau, headquarters of Ludwig C. A. K. Martens, "the man with 200 million dollars to spend and no customers." Martens was authorized by the Russian Bolshevik government to develop trade relations. The State Department, however, refused to recognize his credentials, and though Martens tried to do what he could unofficially, his presence was anathema to the patriots. The picking of Martens's pocket by an army agent in Chicago had riled Churchill in May, but the intelligence chief continued to keep him under close observation. Shortly after the Russian representative set up his office in the World Tower Building in New York, where his secretary was Santeri Nuorteva, Churchill told the State Department that Martens represented "the largest and most dangerous propaganda undertaking thus far started by Lenine's party in any country outside of Russia."[64] Of especial interest to Churchill were any Americans who might aid or comfort this obvious spy. Among those he reported to the Department of Justice for "giving important information" to Martens were Charles A. Beard, incorrectly listed as a professor at Columbia University, and former South Dakota senator and anti-imperialist Richard F. Pettigrew.[65]

Churchill also believed that one of Martens's missions was to develop a counterespionage system within the radical community to root out government spies. His informant, close to Martens, led him to believe that the Russians had plants in both Naval Intelligence and the Department of Justice, but he decided not to share this information for fear that his man would be uncovered.[66] Martens was certainly concerned about espionage, and a major rift developed among American Bolsheviks when he, along with Nuorteva, accused Louis C. Fraina, international secretary of the Communist party of America and delegate to the 1919 Third International, of being an agent for Palmer. An amazing inquiry by

63. For the open hearings, see L0026, box 1, folders 22–24.

64. Churchill to State Department, April 16, 1919, MI Microfilm, reel 14, pp. 90–91. A detailed report on Martens's background prepared by MI on April 12 is on pp. 102–4; the entire file on Martens runs from reel 13, p. 882, to reel 14, p. 552. See also Stevenson's early report, printed by the Union League Club, *Report and Resolutions in Opposition to the Russian Soviet Mission*, dated April 10, 1919, in Lusk Papers, L0040, box 1, folder 26.

65. Churchill to Frank Burke, September 20, 1919, MI Microfilm, reel 14, pp. 129, 241.

66. Wrisley Brown, memorandum for file, September 20, 1919, ibid., reel 14, p. 240. Marguerite Harrison believed a Moscow agent in Churchill's office was the cause of her exposure as an MI spy. She was imprisoned in Russia, and her information arrived after the suspect had been demobilized. No action was taken (Harrison, *There's Always Tomorrow: The Story of a Checkered Life* [New York: Farrar & Rinehart, 1935], p. 430).

the party resulted, published under the title *Stenographic Report of the "Trial" of L. C. Fraina.*[67]

The Lusk Committee kept a two-man surveillance team on Martens and bugged his office, and in November it forced him to testify under subpoena. When he refused to answer all the committee's questions, it found him in contempt, and Martens fled to Washington to turn himself over to the Senate Foreign Relations Committee. The Lusk group was happy enough with his appearance that it published his testimony and made copies available to public libraries. While Martens testified before Congress, Hoover was busy building a case for his deportation, using Military Intelligence's extensive files. The State Department intervened, however, and struck a deal that allowed the Russian to leave voluntarily. He sailed on January 22, 1921, on the SS *Stockholm*, taking with him his wife and two small children. Along with fifteen hundred others, army agents attended a farewell meeting for him at which Robert Minor was the principal speaker.[68] For the next year, Military Intelligence tracked down rumors that Martens planned to return to the United States, and the Bureau of Immigration was on the alert to prevent his entrance.[69]

The other chief enemy of the Lusk Committee was the Rand School of Social Science. Founded in 1906 with funds from a trust left by Carrie D. Rand, a former abolitionist, the institution had become a labor college, owned by the American Socialist Society, the organization that had been fined for publishing Scott Nearing's *Great Madness*. In 1919 the school

67. The report is in MI Microfilm, reel 33, pp. 261–300. Strangely enough, the charges against Fraina originated with a real government agent, and the testimony of another undercover operative cleared him. Tried again in Moscow in 1920, Fraina eventually absconded with Bolshevik funds. He resurfaced under the name Lewis Corey and became one of the editors of that masterpiece of the 1930s, the *Encyclopedia of the Social Sciences*. He taught at Antioch College and died in 1953, shortly before the government rescinded his deportation order; see Bernard K. Johnpoll and Harvey Klehr, *Biographical Dictionary of the American Left* (New York: Greenwood Press, 1986), pp. 141–43.

68. Martens's testimony before Lusk is in Lusk Papers, L0026, box 1, folders 16 and 17, L0038, box 2, folder 15, and MI Microfilm, reel 14, pp. 439–534. Results of the surveillance are in L0038, box 2, folder 15. See also the Lusk report, *Revolutionary Radicalism*, 1:27–28. Hoover's deportation brief was completed on December 7, 1920 (MI Microfilm, reel 14, pp. 271–323); the note that it was "prepared from the files of the Military Intelligence Division" is on p. 247; see also a December 29, 1919, "Memorandum Brief," by Hoover, pp. 404–38. A handbill announcing Martens's speech in Chicago on May 25, 1919, uses the "200 million dollars" slogan, p. 60. Martens's testimony before the Senate is on pp. 150–56. The farewell speeches are summarized, along with a list of those departing with Martens and their cabin accommodations, in a January 27, 1921, Military Intelligence letter to the Bureau, reel 14, pp. 371–73.

69. Department of Labor to W.H. Cowles, November 23, 1921, MI Microfilm, reel 14, p. 325.

claimed to have six thousand students under the direction of Socialist Algernon Lee. Stevenson and his men swarmed into the school on June 21, the same day they went after the local iww and other radical organizations.[70] After those raids, the Lusk effort settled into its hearings and more traditional spying until November, when, spurred by Hoover's raid on Russian radicals in New York, agents of the committee entered seventy leftist headquarters and arrested five hundred men and women.

Having set the tone and methods for the rest of the intelligence community, the Lusk Committee was the first to quit the Red Scare. After criticism from Charles Evans Hughes and the New York City Bar Association, Stevenson announced in January 1920 that his committee knew enough about "seditious activities" that it could advise the legislature "on the question of repressive measures." Having secured the eviction and imprisonment of Socialists in the state assembly, the committee turned its attention to education and "Americanization" as remedies. Formal investigations ended on December 31, and in early January, Stevenson began laying off his staff and reduced his switchboard to a single line on February 16. In the spring the committee finished and printed its lengthy report, a portion of which was a national survey of successful Americanization programs. The final theme of the committee was the high cost of living, particularly the price of sugar. The offices were shut down for good on July 1, 1920.[71]

70. For a history of the Rand School, see Lusk Committee, *Revolutionary Radicalism*, 2:1450–75; Chamberlain, *Loyalty and Legislative Action*, p. 21; and Murray, *Red Scare*, p. 101. Director Lee protested the raid in a June 21, 1919, letter to Lusk, Lusk Papers, L0040, box 1, folder 22.

71. On Americanization, see Lusk Papers, L0026, box 2, folder 1, and volumes 2 and 3 of the Lusk report, *Revolutionary Radicalism*. Details on the committee's shutdown are in L0040, box 1, folder 17; on the cost of living, see L0026, box 2, folders 8 and 9, and L0038, box 1, folders 11 and 12. For Hughes's complaint about Lusk, see Ferrell, *Woodrow Wilson*, p. 212.

CHAPTER 10

The Red Scare

M ilitary Intelligence entered the Red Scare after the Lusk Committee and was not ready for substantial operations until the late summer of 1919. By that time, Palmer, Hoover, and Flynn were also geared up, allocating fully half of the resources of the Bureau of Investigation to combating radicalism. State governments were also involved, and by 1921 thirty-five of them plus the territories of Alaska and Hawaii had laws against sedition. Some of these predated the 1919 hysteria, such as New York's Criminal Anarchy Statute passed in 1902 in reaction to President William McKinley's assassination, but most such legislation resulted from the Red Scare. Generally called "criminal syndicalist" laws, they were aimed at the Reds, and thirty-two states had acts specifically forbidding the flying of the Red flag. A number of bills of a similar nature were introduced at the national level, and one actually passed the Senate on January 10, 1920, but the House failed to approve it.[1]

By late 1919, American public opinion had caught up with the suspicious minds of Military Intelligence. Politicians such as Robert M. La Follette, George W. Norris, William C. Bullitt, and Frederic C. Howe, long the subject of army concern, were now widely regarded as parlor reds. Colleges and universities, especially Barnard, Wellesley, Radcliffe, Chicago, and Yale, were also viewed with alarm, as were individual faculty members such as James Harvey Robinson of Columbia, E. A. Ross of Wisconsin, and Felix Frankfurter and Zechariah Chafee of Harvard. At the height of the scare, a radical was defined, as one scholar has concluded, as a "pro-German, a Russian or other foreigner, a person who sent bombs through the mails, a believer in free love, a member of

1. For summaries of these state laws, see E. F. Dowell, *A History of Criminal Syndicalism Legislation in the United States* (Baltimore: Johns Hopkins Press, 1939); Paul L. Murphy, *The Meaning of Free Speech: First Amendment Freedoms from Wilson to FDR* (Westport, Conn.: Greenwood, 1972), pp. 38–58; Robert K. Murray, *Red Scare: A Study in National Hysteria, 1919–1920* (Minneapolis: University of Minnesota Press, 1955), pp. 230–34; U.S. Congress, Hearings before a Special Committee of the House of Representatives to Investigate Communist Activities in the United States, 71st Cong., 2d sess., *Investigation of Communist Propaganda*, 6 parts (Washington, D.C.: U.S. Government Printing Office, 1930), pt. 5, vol. 3, pp. 425–58.

the IWW, a Socialist, a Bolshevist, an anarchist, a member of a labor union, a supporter of the closed shop, or anyone who did not particularly agree with you."[2] By November, the Negative Branch was so concerned about the "ominous conditions prevailing" that it recommended to Churchill that the staff be increased to "undertake a comprehensive plan for the study and treatment of all radical movements." A month later an alarming army report, passed on to the navy, which gave it to Franklin D. Roosevelt, predicted a "nation-wide terrorists' campaign . . . by Germans, Russians, and Mexican Terrorists. . . . The Terror will surpass anything that ever happened in this country."[3]

MI eagerly followed the deportations and the raids by the Lusk Committee and J. Edgar Hoover, and in the last six months of 1919 even the weekly intelligence summaries prepared for the secretary of war were unusually hysterical about the Bolsheviks, the IWW, the Rand School, strikers, pacifists, Negro subversion, the Nonpartisan League, and the International Workers' Defense League. The last had been inspired by the defense of Tom Mooney and was linked by the army to "the most dangerous anarchist and disruptive groups in the United States," especially Emma Goldman and Martens. The trials of IWW members still continuing in the West were monitored with great interest by Churchill, as were reports of radical infiltration of the American Federation of Labor. Roger Baldwin and his civil libertarians also remained natural targets, as did Robert Minor, whom the army regarded as "emboldened" after his release from Van Deman's trap in Europe. The study of nationalism generated by Hayes earlier in the year had become a standard feature in the reports, but the emphasis had shifted from the Irish and Hindus to the Zionists and Japanese.[4]

2. Murray, *Red Scare*, p. 167; for the parlor reds, see pp. 170, 176–77.

3. Wrisley Brown, memorandum for Churchill, November 13, 1919, Record Group 165, MID, 10560–221/9, National Archives; ONI memorandum for the secretary of the navy, December 20, 1919, ONI: General Files, Assistant Secretary of the Navy Papers, Franklin D. Roosevelt Library, Hyde Park, N.Y.

4. After Baker's clampdown in January, MI had shielded its continuing interest in domestic intelligence by deleting the "Internal Conditions" section of the *Weekly Intelligence Summary*, which went to him. By summer, however, the army's concern about the Reds was so great that that component was resumed with the August 16, 1919, issue. All of these reports, which represent the most finished of MI's products and had a global scope, are reprinted in Richard D. Challener, ed., *United States Military Intelligence, 1917–1927*, 30 vols. (New York: Garland, 1978); the August 16 summary is in 9:1556–64. The collection of MI's targets is based on this and subsequent reports. For the army's file on the International Workers' Defense League, see Randolph Boehm, ed., *U.S. Military Intelligence Reports: Surveillance of Radicals in the United States, 1917–1941* (Frederick, Md.: University Publications of America, 1984), reel 7, pp. 857–96 (hereafter cited as MI Microfilm).

The demobilization forced on Military Intelligence as part of the overall reduction of the army required a heavy reliance on volunteers. The army had only eighteen positions allocated for the Corps of Intelligence Police.[5] The supply of volunteers, however, continued undiminished. The St. Louis branch office was active, with several informants, especially Agent 66, who provided high-quality information on radicals. In St. Paul, Minnesota, private detectives were once again hired from the Northern Information Bureau. In Boston, the army worked with the state adjutant general's office, the intelligence section of which had begun investigations of the "Bolshevik problem" just as the war ended. Also available in Massachusetts was the old APL division that had renamed itself the Massachusetts Security League and was conducting operations against the Reds.[6]

By far the most active army intelligence center was Crockett's in Chicago. Not only was he one of the few MI officers who remained in place from the war through the Red Scare, but he also had excellent relations with the American Protective League and local and state authorities. In Chicago he worked directly with the state attorney general's office, the Anarchist Squad of the local police, and a revived APL that had appeared as the Patriotic American League. Crockett's influence reached throughout his department, and in Cincinnati he directed the information collection effort of A. Clifford Shinkle, another APL alumnus. Crockett had lined up all the former APL state inspectors, with good results in nearly every case. His man in Indianapolis was William C. Bobbs, of the Bobbs-Merrill Company, who pushed Crockett for money for a "salaried representative." In Cleveland and Gary, he had the help of the Loyal American Leagues. Crockett's approach to former APL leaders had the advantage that they brought with them many of their earlier volunteers, giving him a substantial number of agents to plant in radical meetings.[7]

5. U.S. Army, *The History of the Counter Intelligence Corps in the United States Army, 1917–1950 (with Limited Tabular Data to 1960)*, 30 vols. (Baltimore: U.S. Army Intelligence Center, 1959), 4:17, in Record Group 319, National Archives.

6. The St. Louis material is in MI Microfilm, reel 11, pp. 294–340, and reel 13, pp. 673–869. For Minnesota, see reel 12, pp. 937, 955–57; for New England, reel 11, pp. 813–1023, and Lusk Committee Papers, L0040, box 1, folder 25, New York State Archives, Albany.

7. Department intelligence officer, Chicago, to Bobbs, June 19, 1919, MI Microfilm, reel 13, p. 138. See also department intelligence officer, Chicago, to H. H. Seaman, May 28, 1919, p. 9, with the note "Above letter sent to all former State Inspectors, American Protective League, Central Department." For a sample report from a former APL member, see Frank Schwilk to A. Clifford Shinkle, June 26, 1919, p. 43. See also F. M. Pond to department intelligence officer, Chicago, June 6, 1919, and department intelligence officer, Chicago, to director of MI, June 9, 1919, reel 9, pp. 812–13. Activities in Chicago for the last half of 1919 are in reel 10, pp. 696–1029.

Crockett's success was not replicated in other areas, and the limitations on personnel made it impossible to provide truly national coverage. Before 1919 ended, however, a solution was devised, which, if not perfect, did guarantee reports from every corner of the map: army recruiters were given an intelligence mission. Citing the need to be "more fully informed of the progress of radical activities" and the "insufficient information" coming from the Department of Justice, the army dispatched questionnaires, authorized by the secretary of war, to all recruiting stations on October 20, 1919. The instrument asked for the number and location of radicals and their propaganda organs, along with an estimation of the attitude of the general population and the chief source of antiradical propaganda. Some recruiters answered these fairly complex questions in a general and vague fashion, but others went to considerable effort to contact local and state authorities. A few reports were quite detailed, such as the "Who's Who File" on radicals in Trinidad, Colorado. One recruiter continued to send reports after his retirement. But relying on untrained recruiters could give Washington little more than a feeling for areas that might be experiencing increasing radical action.[8]

In addition to the numerous units of the American Protective League, now reorganized under various names, and the network of recruiters and reserve officers, Military Intelligence had another important ally in its fight against radicalism: the American Legion. Founded in early 1919 by Theodore Roosevelt, Jr., Hamilton Fish, and a handful of other officers, the legion quickly mushroomed into a force of a million veterans dedicated to saving the country from the threat of radical agitators. With interlocking memberships in local vigilante groups, the legionnaires raided so many offices, prevented so many speeches, broke up so many meetings, and mobbed so many radicals that Roger Baldwin's civil libertarians could not keep track of the outrages. The most controversial event occurred in Centralia, Washington, on November 11, 1919, during an Armistice Day parade sponsored jointly by the legion and the local Protective Association. Remembering the sacking of its hall in May 1918, the iww was armed and ready for trouble. The details of that fateful day remain disputed. A recent scholarly study has concluded that though the patriots probably planned to run the radicals out of town, they did not intend to precipitate the firefight that ensued, leaving four legionnaires dead. After the arrest of the iww leaders, a lynch mob seized

---

8. The questionnaire from the adjutant general to all recruiting officers, October 20, 1919, and the responses are in "Letters to Recruiting Officers and Officers Detailed to the R. O. T. C.," Record Group 165, MID, 10560–453/2, National Archives.

Wesley Everest, who, as he was being castrated, hanged, and shot, is reputed to have said, "Tell the boys I died for my class."[9] After Centralia, the legion leadership made a determined effort to have members cease, as the Illinois commander said, "the taking of the law into their own hands and taking summary actions against organizations and individuals whom they believe to be disloyal."[10] Legionnaires continued, however, to act as "individuals" in their vigilante work.

Former servicemen of a more radical persuasion joined the avowedly Marxist World War Veterans, also known as the Private Soldiers and Sailors Legion. Military Intelligence, along with the entire counterrevolutionary effort, public and private, regarded this group, which claimed seven hundred thousand members, with intense hatred. Although it was virtually destroyed during the Red Scare, MI watched its remnants until 1922.[11] Another group that appeared in 1919 and caused the army no end of concern was the Committee of Forty-Eight, whose name clearly indicated that it was a conspiracy. Actually it was a political organization led by former Bull Moose Progressives to support Robert M. La Follette for president, and its unfortunate title stemmed from its desire to create a new liberal party throughout the forty-eight states. The dangerous Americans who signed the initial call for a conference included Herbert Croly, Will Durant, Charlotte P. Gilman, Frederic C. Howe, and Ohio State University historian Arthur M. Schlesinger, Sr. At a meeting in St. Louis in late 1919, attended by Military Intelligence agents, a platform was adopted calling for the nationalization of railroads, grain elevators, public utilities, and natural resources. Other planks called for civil rights for women and blacks. The organization clearly was pro-labor and antitrust.

Crockett's best undercover source, Agent 7, reported that funds for the Committee of Forty-Eight came from two New York groups, the single-taxers and the Socialist Party of America, although the latter had tried to keep its support secret. He also linked the committee to the hated National Civil Liberties Bureau, the radical Nonpartisan League

9. The best study of the American Legion is William Pencak, *For God and Country: The American Legion, 1919–1941* (Boston: Northeastern University Press, 1989). See also Murray, *Red Scare*, pp. 87–90, 181–89. Robert L. Tyler, *Rebels of the Woods: The IWW in the Pacific Northwest* (Eugene: University of Oregon Press, 1967), blames the legion for charging the IWW hall. Particularly useful for studying the details of the Centralia episode are early and conflicting analyses reprinted in *The Centralia Case: Three Views of the Armistice Day Tragedy at Centralia, Washington, November 11, 1919* (New York: Da Capo, 1971).

10. American Legion of Illinois, special bulletin, November 26, 1919, in MI Microfilm, reel 11, p. 260.

11. G–2, Governor's Island, to G–2, War Department, January 25, 1922, ibid., reel 20, p. 406; Pencak, *God and Country*, p. 51.

of the upper Midwest, and various labor organizations. In its *Weekly Intelligence Summary* for February 21, 1920,the army concluded that the effect of the committee's association with these groups, "all of such vivid hue, all of them moving in the extreme circles of disruptive radicalism, was to give the Committee of Forty-Eight a decidedly 'red tinge.'" Military Intelligence sent agents, disguised as reporters, to visit the committee's New York headquarters, and others intercepted its mail. This surveillance continued through the group's Chicago convention in July 1920, when La Follette refused its nomination for president.[12]

Crockett always insisted, even to Churchill, that he did not know the identity of Agent 7, who was handled and salaried by the head of Cleveland's Loyal American League. It is not surprising that Crockett went to enormous lengths to protect this agent, a masterful provocateur who regularly dined with Big Bill Haywood in Chicago. When the several Red groups, particularly the American Communist party and the Communist Labor party, convened in Chicago at the end of August, Agent 7 was there to assist in their self-destruction. With the Communists already separated into left and right wings and native and foreign-language groups and split over policy matters such as relations with labor unions, 7 did not create the intense animosity that existed within the radical ranks, but he hoped to exploit it. "As soon as the Convention delegates arrived in Chicago," he reported, "I started working on splitting the delegates in as many factions as possible." After noting that Haywood was "closely working with the Bolsheviki Agents in America, Canada, and Mexico and that he expects something serious to happen," Agent 7 concluded, "we are sitting on dynamite."[13]

12. The Committee of Forty-Eight held on until the 1924 election, after which it was dissolved. It is described in Walter Nelles, *A Liberal in Wartime: The Education of Albert De Silver* (New York: Norton, 1940), pp. 208–9; and James S. Olson, *Historical Dictionary of the 1920s: From World War I to the New Deal, 1919–1933* (New York: Greenwood Press, 1988), p. 73. The Lusk Files, L0039, box 1, folder 8, have several documents on the group, including the December 1919 platform adopted in St. Louis. Military Intelligence's dossier on this liberal failure is in MI Microfilm, reel 14, p. 976, to reel 15, p. 9, and includes Agent 7's "The Origins of the 'Committee of 48,'" dated January 22, 1920. See also reel 12, pp. 367–75, containing the original call for "A Conference of Americans," and an early MI memorandum on the group dated April 23, 1919. The "red tinge" assessment is in the *Weekly Intelligence Summary* for February 21, 1920, in Challener, ed., *Military Intelligence*, 12:3087–88.
13. Agent 7's report, with the inclusive dates of August 28 to September 5, 1919, in MI Microfilm, reel 11, pp. 6–10. Murray, *Red Scare*, pp. 33–56, has a good account of the splintering of the Bolsheviks, who began calling themselves Communists in 1919, but the detail of 7's report is fascinating. The bureau also had an agent at the meetings; his reports, along with the literature he collected, are in MI Microfilm, reel 11, pp. 11–52. Crockett continued to monitor the Chicago Communist community and to collect its publications

Crockett had also inserted one of his own officers with credentials as a delegate of the Communist Labor party. His specific mission was to obtain a complete roster of those attending and to get their pictures using "flashlight photography." Washington was generally pleased with his products, but there was some embarrassment when the New York office pointed out that Chicago had misidentified the well-known John Reed.[14] Churchill told Crockett, "Your reports on the radical conventions in Chicago have provided us with a more complete set of actual circumstances of those conventions, better arranged and more judicially interpreted than we have received from the public press, the Department of Justice, or any other source. I think the subject has been extraordinarily well covered."[15]

Churchill may have felt that Crockett needed a bit of praise, since he had shortly before been forced to reprimand the Chicago officer for his handling of the press. That occasion did not involve a violation of Churchill's code for domestic spywork, but a nasty little quarrel between Military Intelligence and the Bureau of Investigation, with Chicago's two morning newspapers, the *Tribune* and the *Herald and Examiner*, taking sides. The bitter competition between the papers was complicated by the fact that both intelligence agencies had former reporters working for them, with the result that the *Tribune* was the army's paper and the *Herald and Examiner* supported the bureau. Each agency accused the other of leaking confidential information to its pet, and the *Herald and Examiner* had made some unflattering comments about Crockett in several of its stories. Matters came to a head after the bombing of Palmer's house, when Churchill ordered all his units to cooperate with the Department of Justice. Crockett wired back that such sharing was "inadvisable" because "all information obtained by us and given to the Department of Justice is immediately published in the local press." Churchill showed the wire to the bureau, and a first-rate interagency fight developed.[16]

Churchill ordered a formal investigation, dispatching one of his officers to Chicago. The most important finding was that, though there

and fliers; the entire file runs from reel 10, p. 844, to reel 11, p. 293. Melvyn Dubofsky, *We Shall Be All: A History of the Industrial Workers of the World* (Chicago: Quadrangle Books, 1969), p. 449, says that ONI also had agents at the conventions.

14. Intelligence officer, Central Department, to director of MI, September 16, 1919, MI Microfilm, reel 11, pp. 131–33; director of MI to intelligence officer, Central Department, January 13, 1920, p. 196.

15. Director of MI to Crockett, September 23, 1919, ibid., reel 11, p. 113.

16. Crockett telegram to Milstaff, Washington, June 6, 1919, MI Microfilm, reel 14, p. 802; Churchill to acting chief, Bureau of Investigation, June 12, 1919, p. 783.

was "marked hostility" of a personal nature between Crockett and his people and several of the bureau agents, nobody was intentionally revealing confidential information. The particular leaks cited by Crockett were written off as lucky guesswork by reporters. At least part of the problem was that the press routinely visited the offices of Military Intelligence, and Crockett had established the practice of giving scoops to *Tribune* reporters who brought him information. That favoritism had irked the *Herald and Examiner*, which had responded by linking up with the bureau. The presence of a new bureau superintendent in Chicago promised to ease the personal conflict, and Churchill prohibited Crockett's office "from having any dealings with newspaper representatives in relation to official matters."[17]

In mid-August Churchill visited Chicago to see for himself that proper liaison was back on track, and Crockett presented him with a much greater problem: the Department of Justice, he charged, was determined to uncover Agent 7. Following up with a letter, the Chicago officer recounted the history of his deal with Cleveland's Loyal American League, which had agreed to underwrite 7's expenses and salary "in consideration," Crockett said, "for our making no effort to ascertain informant's name." That arrangement, he reminded Churchill, had resulted in reports that were "the best and most complete that we have yet obtained from the inside of the radical ranks."[18] In July Agent 7 had reported a plot by the IWW to assassinate the United States attorney in Kansas City, and the information was duly passed along to the Department of Justice. When he learned of the alleged threat against him, the official naturally wanted to know the source of the report so he could make his own estimation of its credibility. When bureau agents went to Cleveland, Crockett was furious. Agent 7 became a bit perturbed when he heard Big Bill brag that the Justice Department was about to do his work for him and expose a spy.[19]

When Churchill made an issue of the case with the bureau, it immediately denied putting any pressure on Crockett for the identity of his source. The matter ended by early September, but for months afterward, when Churchill forwarded reports to the bureau, many of them to

17. See two memoranda for Lieutenant Colonel Brown, July 24 and 29, 1919, ibid., 930–42. Churchill's ban on contact with the press is in director of MI to intelligence officer, Central Department, August 1, 1919, p. 929.

18. Crockett to Churchill, August 18, 1919, ibid., reel 15, p. 13.

19. Van Buren, memorandum for Crockett, August 30, 1919, ibid., reel 10, p. 788; Frank Burke to Churchill, September 10, 1919, pp. 789–91, and reel 11, pp. 292–93; intelligence officer, Central Department, to Churchill, December 24, 1919, reel 15, p. 108.

the attention of J. Edgar Hoover, he always added the line: "It is requested that this information be used in such a way as not to uncover the agent."[20] Although the assassination attempt never materialized, Agent 7 remained at work, fighting the radicals of the Midwest. Until his departure from Chicago, Crockett refused to send his most sensitive reports through normal channels.[21] In an age when modern security classification markings were in their infancy, 7's reports were among the few stamped secret and sent for Churchill's eyes only.

The upheaval that Agent 7 had predicted for some time came with the steel strike of 1919. That year was, in addition to being one of race riots, bombings, and Communist agitation, also one of great strikes, and Seattle had set the precedent for violence and repression. By the spring there were more than three hundred strikes every month, and the army once again patrolled the streets of traditionally hot spots such as Bisbee, Arizona, and Butte, Montana. Troops were also dispatched to the West Virginia coal fields during a November strike, where they cooperated with the American Constitutional Association, a superpatriotic organization funded by the coal companies. In mid-July Crockett calculated that there were 150,000 men on strike in Chicago, and he expected more. "Russian, Poles, Lithuanians predominate," he wired Washington. "Russian radicals dominate. Situation critical."[22]

The best-remembered labor action of 1919 was the Boston Police Strike, which catapulted Governor Calvin Coolidge to the vice-presidency. Boston had been relatively quiet since the mob actions of May Day, but the policemen's strike, which began on September 9 over wages and working conditions, saw rioting, looting, and eight deaths. The army's Northeastern Department was not prepared to move into the city because it had only one map. Coolidge, however, handled the strike with his National Guard, using equipment loaned to him by the army, and the federal troops on standby were never used. Until the guard and volunteers restored order it was a frightening time for Military Intel-

20. For a sample of Churchill's warning, see Churchill to Frank Burke, February 14, 1920, ibid., reel 34, p. 1033.

21. Department intelligence officer, Chicago, to director of MI, June 15, 1919, ibid., reel 14, p. 770.

22. Crockett telegram to Milstaff, Washington, July 19, 1919, ibid., reel 10, p. 853. Record Group 60, Glasser Files, box 7, National Archives, has a list of strikes and riots in which troops were committed. See Murray B. Levin, *Political Hysteria in America: The Democratic Capacity for Repression* (New York: Basic Books, 1971), p. 202, for a description of the American Constitutional Association. Murphy, *The Meaning of Free Speech*, p. 65, and Murray, *Red Scare*, p. 111, give identical accounts of the number of strikes per month down to August.

ligence, which worried that the 425 radicals it was holding at Deer Island for deportation might attempt a breakout.[23]

This background of labor violence prepared Crockett for trouble in the steel industry. He had monitored the increasing radicalism in Gary, Indiana, since late 1918. On December 30, he sent a letter to the mayor warning him of the Bolshevist activity.[24] He continued to investigate rumors of strikes until Military Intelligence went into temporary remission after the Stevenson affair in January. In the spring, upon a request for help from the chief of police, and after Churchill had switched MI back on, Crockett was able to insert an undercover agent into Gary. The steelworkers went out on strike in late September, and on October 4 the first rioting occurred. Crockett dispatched Lieutenant Donald C. Van Buren, who arrived in Gary at four in the morning and cruised the wide-awake city in a staff car. "The situation was very tense," he later recalled, "you could feel it in the air and see it on the street," where "great crowds of union pickets paraded up and down." General Leonard Wood, commander of the Central Department, was prepared to move the following day when the governor asked for troops.[25]

General Wood, former commander of the Rough Riders, was already a thorn in the side of the Wilson administration. Earlier in the year, the president had written Baker, "Personally I have no confidence either in General Wood's discretion or in his loyalty to his superiors."[26] Having been denied a combat command during the war, he hoped for a presidential nomination as a Roosevelt progressive and an antiradical. Leonard Wood hit Gary hard, placing it under military control and taking over the city hall as his command post. He issued a proclamation calling for order and had Military Intelligence haul in labor leaders and anyone else suspected of being an agitator. MI interrogated them, but it

23. Box 3 in the Glasser Files has the Boston folder, but there is related material in boxes 5 and 8. Military Intelligence accounts of the police strike are in Challener, ed., *Military Intelligence*, 9:1926–38. See also Murray, *Red Scare*, pp. 122–34, and Francis Russell, *A City in Terror, 1919: The Boston Police Strike* (New York: Viking Press, 1975).

24. Crockett to W. F. Hodges, December 30, 1918, Glasser Files, box 4.

25. Van Buren's account of these events is in U.S. Senate, Hearings before the Committee on Education and Labor, 66th Cong., 1st sess., *Investigation of Strike in Steel Industries*, 2 vols. (Washington, D.C.: U.S. Government Printing Office, 1919). The description above is in 2:909 (hereafter cited as *Investigation of Steel Strike*).

26. Wilson to Baker, January 13, 1917, in Papers of Newton D. Baker, microfilm reel 3, p. 12, Manuscript Division, Library of Congress. For a complaint about Wood's politics from the dean of the John Marshall Law School, see Edward Lee to Homer S. Cummings, March 21, 1919, reel 7, p. 90. Wood's biography is Jack C. Lane, *Armed Progressive: General Leonard Wood* (Novato, Calif.: Presidio Press, 1978).

was the general himself who laid down the law on proper civilian conduct.[27]

On October 6, responding to his energetic department commander and apparently without approval from Washington, Van Buren got tougher. After an intermission of nearly a year, the army sleuths renewed the methods Churchill had specifically forbidden: Van Buren's men arbitrarily detained and interrogated hundreds without benefit of warrant, and they raided not only offices and meeting halls but private homes. The Gary police became an arm of Military Intelligence, and the deputized Loyal American League worked full time for Van Buren. In addition to supplying maps and laying out routes for the movement of troops into Gary, the Chicago Patriotic American League provided the army with its blacklist of suspected Reds and those "who openly talk socialism." So many prisoners were taken that Wood erected a barbed-wire pen as a holding facility across from army headquarters.[28]

The raiding and interrogations generally went on all night, sometimes until five-thirty in the morning. Lieutenant Van Buren, a 1914 graduate of Harvard Law School, preferred to surprise private domiciles after midnight to assure that the residents would be at home. The country house of Paul Glaser, an attorney working for the strikers, was one of the first to be hit by the army agents, who entered by smashing open the door. Glaser was regarded as so serious a threat that his telephone was tapped as well.[29] The radical lawyer was so hated by the military that after the strike the army had denaturalization proceedings instituted against him. As a result of the testimony of Van Buren and other intelligence officers, Glaser was found guilty of harboring sympathies for "revolutionary factions," and his citizenship papers were canceled. This was the first case, MI boasted, of denaturalization "as a result of radical activities."[30]

27. An October 7, 1919, memorandum from the intelligence officer, Central Department, to director of MI, summarizes the taking of Gary, Glasser Files, box 4.

28. The stockade is described by Van Buren, who maintained that it was not heavily used, in *Investigation of Steel Strike*, 2: 950–51. For vigilante assistance, see Glasser Files, box 4.

29. As Roger Baldwin had attempted in New York during the war, Glaser met with Military Intelligence and tried unsuccessfully to negotiate. For the "listening apparatus," see MI report, November 1, 1919, MI Microfilm, reel 13, p. 88; for other material on Glaser, pp. 78–87. The Glaser raid and others are described in *Investigation of Steel Strike*, 2:976. In addition to hoping to find weapons and revolutionary literature, MI had added liquor to its list of contraband for which a conviction might be obtained.

30. Assistant chief of staff, intelligence, Chicago, to director of MI, June 8, 1920, MI Microfilm, reel 13, pp. 184; intelligence report, May 29, 1920, p. 198. Van Buren initiated the action to revoke Glaser's citizenship (*Investigation of Steel Strike*, 2:925). Glasser Files, box 4, has additional material on Glaser. The other major threat the army identified in the

The actions of Military Intelligence in Gary hardly represented the low profile Churchill had envisioned when he reenergized his agency. The operation was entirely too open, too visible, and too heavy-handed. There was no escaping public attention, and on October 16, the *Pittsburgh Post* reported that the army had a list of seven hundred suspects and that "every third man on the streets . . . seems to be a Government official."[31] As with any dragnet, there were also mistakes. John Wehner and his wife, mild-mannered Americans living near Lottaville, Indiana, were sound asleep when army intelligence operatives bashed down their door. Initially the Wehners were shocked, but they accepted the agents' apology for their mistake and returned to bed. When a second army team burst in on them, Mrs. Wehner went into hysterics, and a physician had to be summoned. Mr. Wehner was a bit overwrought himself, as he told his congressman, that two different raiding teams could make the same mistake in one evening. He sent the army a bill for the doctor and the door. After an investigation by the inspector general, who called the affair "an unfortunate and regrettable mistake," the Wehners received an official apology.[32]

As charges mounted in the press, army officials stonewalled. Military Intelligence had made no arrests, Churchill told the chief of staff on October 18, in response to an inquiry from the secretary of war. All that had occurred was the interrogation of "criminal suspects who have been arrested by local police." Wood's inspector general found no basis for the numerous complaints that army agents were working hand-in-glove with the private detectives of U.S. Steel to intimidate the strikers with threats of deportation. "The activities of the Intelligence Department," his November 13 report concluded, "have been confined to interrogating persons reported to be radicals." The arrests, and he used that word, were of those who had violated General Wood's rules against the congregation of three or more strikers.[33]

great 1919 steel strike was William Z. Foster, a Socialist and IWW member before the war, who, in his boring-from-within phase, had become an American Federation of Labor organizer. Material on Foster is in Glasser Files, box 4; his testimony is in *Investigation of Steel Strike*, 1:380–429. See also Murray, *Red Scare*, pp. 135–36, 143–44. After the strike Foster visited Russia and joined the Communist party, in which he served as a senior leader until his death in 1961. See the essay on Foster in Bernard K. Johnpoll and Harvey Klehr, eds., *Biographical Dictionary of the American Left* (New York: Greenwood Press, 1986), pp. 137–41; and Arthur Zipser, *Workingclass Giant: The Life of William Z. Foster* (New York: International Publishers, 1981).

31. The *Post* clipping is in Glasser Files, box 5.

32. Material on the Wehner incident is in ibid., boxes 4 and 5.

33. Churchill's October 18, 1919, report to the chief of staff and A. L. Dade's November 13, 1919, report to the commanding general, Central Department, are in ibid., box 4. See

Though he protected his agents in the field, Churchill must have known that Gary represented a complete breakdown of his system designed to keep Secretary Baker uninformed and therefore reasonably happy about Military Intelligence. On October 24, one of the cardinal rules laid down by Baker was broken: after the trouble with Stevenson, no army agent was ever again to testify before Congress. Yet Lieutenant Donald Van Buren, on October 24, 1919, in the midst of the strike, testified before a Senate committee investigating the affair.[34] Van Buren tried to do right by Churchill. He downplayed the stockade for military prisoners, and he stressed the number of guns and quantity of revolutionary propaganda seized. He specifically denied any interest in the American Federation of Labor strike, which he said had not been investigated in any "way, shape, or manner, except as it came in contact with the activities of radicals." Yet his summaries of hundreds of interrogations, his descriptions of numerous raids, and his claim that Military Intelligence had "directed to a great extent the efforts of the local police" were all too suggestive of the very large presence army spies had assumed in Gary.[35]

Even Attorney General Palmer, just then planning his famous raids, was not prepared to defend the actions of the War Department. When the secretary of labor accused both the army and the Bureau of Investigation of abusive methods and coercion in Gary, Palmer's office maintained that, though its agents had acted "in a perfectly proper manner," the overzealousness had come from Military Intelligence and former members of the American Protective League. A representative of the attorney general gave an accurate summary of the activities of the army and its associated vigilantes when he reported that they were "acting in an extremely high-handed manner, were raiding private homes at unreasonable hours, were seizing literature, documents, holding hearings and confining individuals as military prisoners and on the whole subjecting the Government to a great deal of just criticism."[36] The Department

also Joan M. Jensen, *The Price of Vigilance* (Chicago: Rand McNally, 1968), pp. 279–80.

34. The circumstances that led to Van Buren's appearance remain obscure, but it is difficult to imagine Churchill, much less Baker, having approved. It was a rushed inquiry in perilous times, and somehow Van Buren slipped through.

35. The whole of Van Buren's testimony is in *Investigation of Steel Strike*, 2:906–52. David Brody, in *Labor in Crisis: The Steel Strike of 1919* (Philadelphia: J. B. Lippincott, 1965), p. 136, disputes Van Buren's conclusions: "No evidence ever revealed Bolshevik control of the strike in Gary. Even the charges of local radical activity were ludicrously exaggerated."

36. Of the correspondence between the cabinet members in October 1919 in the Glasser Files, box 4, see especially William B. Wilson to the attorney general, October 11, 1919; Baker to William B. Wilson, October 12, 1919; and John Creighton, memorandum for Scott, October 16, 1919.

of Justice, however, did not press vigorously against the army's methods. With Churchill's assurances to the secretary of war and the Gary situation in hand, Military Intelligence managed to survive the rest of the year without another major crisis.[37]

Churchill's efforts to get his agents out of the limelight were aided immensely by the attention given to raids mounted by the Lusk Committee and the Department of Justice. On November 7, Hoover's men arrested hundreds of members of the Union of Russian Workers around the country, and on the following day Stevenson renewed his raids in New York City. In Chicago, Crockett had opposed Hoover's raid, believing Agent 7's report that the radicals had inside information and were expecting to be visited. Crockett, whose relations with the bureau seem to have improved only slightly, preferred to work with the Illinois state attorney, who wanted to develop a program similar to the Lusk effort. When Crockett left Chicago in late 1919, his successor adopted the same policy and was delighted when the Illinois police swung into action with a raid on the IWW and the two Communist party headquarters on January 1, arresting about two hundred people. The Central Department's intelligence office notified Churchill that the Department of Justice had been deliberately excluded from the state action because there was "considerable animosity" between the Illinois and federal agencies. That there was a startling lack of cooperation was demonstrated the following day, when Justice launched its own raid in Chicago, netting 223 alien radicals.[38]

Hoover's famous January 2 raids were not limited to Chicago but included thirty-three cities in twenty-three states, resulting in the arrest of four thousand radicals. The Department of Justice's methods mirrored those used by Military Intelligence in Gary. Suspects who were American citizens were turned over to the state authorities for prosecution under antisyndicalist laws, while aliens were held for deportation hearings. Sending the Reds back to Russia became the favorite tactic of federal intelligence agencies, using the legislation made available late in the war. There were at least two problems with this new weapon. First, at least some of the Reds wanted to go to Russia, and that, in the natural order of the world of negative intelligence, meant they should be restrained from doing so. The initial attempt by the army to have a Russian alien deported resulted in just that dilemma. "We were collecting evidence looking toward his deportation," the Seattle office reported

37. The troops were removed from Gary in January 1920, and MI monitored the city for some time afterward; see the reports in MI Microfilm, reel 13, pp. 65–286.
38. Assistant chief of staff, intelligence, Chicago, to director of MI, January 7, 1920, ibid., reel 7, pp. 198–202.

on October 14, 1918, "when along comes his application for a passport to return to Russia. What can best be done with him? Manifestly he must not be allowed to return to Russia to make trouble for us there and, on the other hand, he is making lots of trouble for us here."[39]

The second problem experienced by both the military and the Department of Justice in securing deportations was that, though they made the arrests, the Department of Labor's immigration office rendered judgment on the question of exile. By the fall of 1919 it had become clear to both agencies that Labor did not share their sense of urgency. In October, Van Buren used his appearance before Congress to complain of Labor's refusal to deport many aliens submitted to it. He said that it was necessary to "get a man with a lighted bomb in his hand" to prove to the immigration board that he was an anarchist worthy of deportation.[40] The biggest deportation occurred in late December, when the "Soviet Ark," as the press called the troopship *Buford*, left New York with 249 aliens, including Emma Goldman as one of the three women on board.[41] Some

39. Office of MI, Seattle, to intelligence officer, San Francisco, October 14, 1918, ibid., reel 34, p. 463. The individual involved was Leon Green, the mysterious Russian firebrand who nearly shut off electric power in the Seattle strike of early 1919. MI reported his alias as "Butowetsky." The *New York Times*, February 9, 1919, called him "Leon Rikowsky, alias Leon Green." Carlton J. H. Hayes, in a memorandum for Cook, September 21, 1918, MI Microfilm, reel 34, p. 468, noted that preventing Green's return to Russia was "an end devoutly to be sought by us." The deportation case against this "Russian I. W. W.-Bolsheviki" was later dropped. Green became a naturalized citizen and was sought by the army during the 1919 Seattle strike and in Chicago, after which he went to Russia. In late 1920 MI opposed his return to the United States. The file on him is reel 34, pp. 440–98. Some labor leaders thought him an agent provocateur, but Military Intelligence considered him "one of the four or five really important leading Russian advocates of direct action and Bolshevism in the country" (Weekly Intelligence Situation Survey for the Week Ending January 14, 1920, reel 19, p. 935). In late 1920, MI noted his return from Russia as an "active emissary of Lenine" (Mathew C. Smith to W. L. Hurley, December 10, 1920, reel 34, p. 440). See Robert L. Friedheim, *The Seattle General Strike* (Seattle: University of Washington Press, 1964), pp. 45–46, 150–51; and Harvey O'Connor, *Revolution in Seattle: A Memoir* (New York: Monthly Review Press, 1964), pp. 136–37. O'Connor, p. 142, notes that in 1923 Green was expelled from his Chicago union for accepting bribes from management.

40. *Investigation of Steel Strike*, 2:939. The real foot-dragger was Frederic C. Howe, commissioner of immigration in New York, who supervised Ellis Island and was a well-known liberal, having been called as early as 1916 "a half-baked radical with free love ideas" (*New York Times*, July 17, 1916). Rather than bow to the wishes of the intelligence agencies and violate due process, Howe resigned. MI never like Howe; see office of MI, New York, to director of MI, April 29, 1919, MI Microfilm, reel 12, p. 396, for a report on him that questions his membership in the Committee of Forty-Eight and his association with Scott Nearing. Howe's 1925 autobiography, *Confessions of a Reformer*, has been reprinted (Chicago: Quadrangle, 1967).

41. The best description of the deportation scene, which occurred in the early morning hours of December 21, is in Alice Wexler, *Emma Goldman in Exile: From the Russian Revolution to the Spanish Civil War* (Boston: Beacon Press, 1989), pp. 9–20.

3,000 others were still detained on deportation warrants, and the tension with the Department of Labor increased in early 1920, when the immigration board began to dismiss cases at an alarming rate.

In the meantime, as Palmer and Hoover grabbed headlines with their Red hunt, Military Intelligence had quieted down considerably. Though no formal changes in policy were announced immediately following the publicity of MI's role in Gary, it seems obvious that Baker's concern had filtered down through Churchill. The army, however, did not close up shop. Intelligence officers across the country continued to send to Washington weekly summaries of radical activities and labor unrest, and the Negative Branch used these to compile confidential national reports. With the Department of Justice and several states dramatically involved in the suppression of Reds, the reports of Military Intelligence suggest a sense of victory that may also have been responsible for the relative decrease in army activity. Field units, however, continued to monitor radicals. The Chicago office worked with the Illinois state attorney in the prosecution of those arrested in the recent raids. In New York, army agents remained frequent visitors at radical lectures, as did their colleagues in other cities. From Arizona, Military Intelligence ran informants across the border, where it was reported that "several men of Russian or German appearance" had organized a railroad strike.[42]

The case that ended Secretary Baker's long patience with Military Intelligence developed out of its Graft and Fraud Section and involved a civilian volunteer named John C. Hammond. A newspaperman, Hammond had worked with the American Protective League and the Department of Justice during the war. His application for a commission in Military Intelligence had been slowed by a derogatory report that questioned his financial dealings and evaluated him as "bright, but he is a great bluff, toots his own horn incessantly, and refers to Colonel House, Mr. Tumulty and others as though they were his bosom companions." Despite that assessment, Hammond's application was still in process when the Armistice ended his candidacy. Hammond remained an investigative reporter, and a year later he used his contact with Marlen Pew, former press officer for the secretary of war, to relay information to Baker concerning leaks on forthcoming Supreme Court decisions. Baker passed this data on to the Department of Justice, which used it to obtain several indictments.

42. Assistant chief of staff, intelligence, Chicago, to state attorney, January 2, 1920, MI Microfilm, reel 1, p. 364; assistant chief of staff, intelligence, Chicago, to director of MI, January 22, 1920, reel 15, p. 99. On New York, see M. K. Bundo to William L. Moffat, Jr., February 10, 1920, reel 9, pp. 190–92; on Boston, intelligence officer, Northeastern Department, to director of MI, January 3, 1920, reel 3, p. 245.

The Department of War's opinion of Hammond rose sharply. When he again communicated to Pew that former army officers were conspiring to use their connections to obtain confidential information on the sale of army surplus material, Baker suggested to Churchill that he hire Hammond to conduct the investigation. Still uncertain of the reporter, Churchill enrolled him on an expenses only basis and assigned civilian agent Robert Dawson, who had been a New York policeman, a Corps of Intelligence Police inspector, and a commissioned officer in MI, to work with him. The files of the resulting investigation were destroyed, but subsequent summaries make it clear that Hammond's work went "far outside of matters of legitimate concern to the Military Intelligence Division and many of them are palpably made up of mere gossip." After he had done his damage, he was judged "wild and erratic" and "a dangerous man to entrust with the conduct of confidential investigations." Another report indicated that Hammond's "collateral inquiries" related to the "conduct of public men."[43]

These fascinating references aside, Hammond's principal case involved the sale of surplus phenol, commonly known as carbolic acid. Derived from coal tar, phenol was used as a disinfectant and, as an ingredient in picric acid, for explosives. The military had carloads of it when the war ended. As it did with other surplus material, the army released the phenol at well below the market price, contracting with the Monsanto Company to handle the sales for a commission. Hammond never produced any evidence of fraud on the part of Monsanto, but in his attempt to do so he created his own company, Roberts Chemical, as a cover to trace the distribution of the phenol. In the course of his investigation, he managed to buy several carloads for his company and to turn a tidy profit, which he told Military Intelligence he used to defray his considerable expenses.

Despite MI's continuing misgivings about Hammond's methods, all was well until early March, when Hammond submitted a report suggesting "irregularities of a grave character" on the part of a high-ranking naval officer. Against the advice of his deputy director, Alexander B. Coxe, Churchill decided to take the matter to the secretary of war.[44] For the first time, Baker realized how wide-ranging the investigation had become. Baker was so alarmed at the scope he saw in Hammond's report that he finally took decisive action to restrain Military Intelligence. In a

43. Alexander B. Coxe to Frank Burke, May 14, 1920, and Wrisley Brown, memorandum for McCain, May 25, 1920, in Alexander B. Coxe, Sr., Papers, J. Y. Joyner Library, East Carolina University, Greenville, N.C.
44. Coxe, memorandum, April 22, 1920, ibid.

long letter to Churchill, the secretary made his attitude plain enough. No doubt as a courtesy, he expressed confidence that Churchill, "from our conversations," agreed with his policy of a limited role for Military Intelligence. Nevertheless, he restated it fully for the record: "It is of the highest importance that the Military Intelligence Division should not permit itself to become a general investigating body interesting itself in the private relations or business of people, or either duplicating or interfering with the interests and activities of other agencies of the Government."[45]

Baker also provided the specific parameters in which Military Intelligence could act, and they were very limited. Churchill's division had a "field of action" that covered "all allegations of misconduct, involving disloyalty, graft, or fraud, by military officers, or wrong-doing of like character by other persons in conjunction with members of the Army." Baker specifically disallowed following up on any leads that might take the army out of its sphere. Such information was to be turned over to the appropriate federal agency, "as a matter of comity, but no further investigation or inquiry with regard thereto will be undertaken by the Military Intelligence Division." Churchill seemed almost relieved, and the following day he ended all investigations of radicals. A week later in Memorandum 40, he quoted the secretary's policy verbatim, telling his men that for the army the Red Scare was over.[46]

It was almost over for Attorney General Palmer. When the Red terror he had predicted for May failed to materialize, the public began to tire of his panic. The civil libertarians' ranks had increased as moderates reacted against the Lusk-inspired eviction of five Socialists from the New York State Assembly. Liberals found an opportunity to attack Palmer and his methods during a public airing of the feud between Justice and Labor over the deportations.[47] Assistant Secretary of Labor Louis F. Post, who had quashed hundreds of deportation warrants for aliens because they were denied counsel and otherwise injured, had become Palmer's special enemy. When Palmer attempted to have Post impeached, the hearings backfired on the attorney general. Post was cleared, and abundant testimony revealed abuses by the Department of Justice. Although no action was taken against Palmer, he remained on the defensive in subsequent congressional investigations during the rest of his term.

---

45. Baker, memorandum for Churchill, March 11, 1920, in Record Group 165, MID, 10560–367/1–2, National Archives, and in Coxe Papers.
46. Director of MI, Memorandum 40, March 19, 1920, Record Group 165, MID, 10560–630/1, National Archives.
47. Murphy, *Meaning of Free Speech.* pp. 87–88.

When a bomb exploded near the Morgan Building in New York in September, killing thirty-three people, there was no hysteria. Instead, Palmer, Hoover, and Flynn had become subjects of public ridicule.[48]

The months after Baker's March 1920 crackdown were not happy ones for Military Intelligence. In early April, Churchill entered the hospital with an inflammation of a facial nerve, leaving Coxe as acting director. Hammond was furious over the end of his connection with MI. Insisting that the termination of his Monsanto investigation represented an obstruction of justice, he threatened to sue and to call for a court-martial of Coxe and his senior officers.[49] No doubt out of concern that the entire matter might be revealed, Coxe tried to generate a positive image for Military Intelligence by granting an interview to a reporter. The resulting story in the *Washington Herald*, especially the following section, was almost too defensive:

No Spy Hunting Here

The division . . . is anxious for home folks to be clear on one point about which misunderstanding is universal. "M. I." is not engaged in running down Bolshevist intriguers or German secret agents in the United States. It is not spy-hunting among our own people. It is not "shadowing" American citizens or looking for illicit wireless installations on roof-tops.

It is not hounding people with enemy-sounding names. It is not a "protective league," nor is it a "pussy-foot" or "gum-shoe" organization. It is engaged in high-grade, professional military work—work long pursued by other great countries but until the war woefully neglected by the United States. "M. I." is merely trying to put "prepared" in preparedness. Not much money is being spent on its activities.[50]

48. Post did not stop all deportations; more than five hundred people were expelled in small groups in 1920 and 1921, but there were no more arks (Murray, *Red Scare*, pp. 247–59). Sources on the deportations and the practices of the Justice Department include Constantine M. Panunzio, *The Deportation Cases of 1919–1920* (1921; rpt. New York: Da Capo Press, 1970); Louis F. Post, *The Deportation Delirium of Nineteen-Twenty: A Personal Narrative of an Historic Official Experience* (1923; rpt. New York: Da Capo, 1970); R. G. Brown et al., *Illegal Practices of the United States Department of Justice* (1920; rpt. New York: Arno Press, 1969); Robert W. Dunn, ed., *The Palmer Raids* (New York: International Publishers, 1948); U.S. House of Representatives, Committee on Rules, Hearings, 66th Cong., 2d sess., *Attorney-General A. Mitchell Palmer on Charges Made against Department of Justice by Louis F. Post and Others* (Washington, D.C.: U.S. Government Printing Office, 1920); U.S. Senate, Committee on the Judiciary, Hearings, 66th Cong., 3d sess.: *Charges of Illegal Practices of the Department of Justice* (Washington, D.C.: U.S. Government Printing Office, 1921).

49. The Coxe Papers are very helpful on Hammond's charges and Churchill's illness. See especially Agent 298, sealed memorandum to Pratt, April 29, 1920, and Coxe to Van Deman, June 2, 1920.

50. The clipping from the *Washington Herald*, July 20, 1920, is in the Coxe Papers.

Coxe's effort was not entirely successful, and rumors persisted into the summer of 1920 that the army operated a domestic spy system. One pointed inquiry asked whether Military Intelligence "undertakes to scrutinize and report on the aims and activities of political organizations within the United States."[51] Despite its firm denials, the withdrawal of the army from domestic espionage was gradual. Hoover continued to use the military's vast files, requesting information on the Interchurch World Movement and such liberals as Felix Frankfurter, Zechariah Chafee, Louis Post, and Raymond Robins.[52] From time to time, local army units assisted state officials in their prosecutions of radicals, as the Pittsburgh office did in September. Reports on radical meetings dribbled in from released informants who still used their coded numbers or, more often, from local police units.[53]

By this time, however, the principal sources of information for Military Intelligence were the responses by reserve and recruiting officers to another series of questionnaires that had been sent out in April and November 1920. These officers were told not to make "any special investigations or inquiries" but simply to acquire from the local Bureau of Investigation or police department information on "the radical situation now obtaining." They were to estimate the number of Communists, Socialists, anarchists, and members of the IWW in their districts. They were also to establish whether there were "any public officials in your area who are either disloyal to the Government, or sympathetic to the extreme radical doctrines."[54] Most reports reflected the general apathy that had invaded the country by the end of 1920. In December, the San Francisco recruiter reported that the wartime IWW membership of twenty thousand had dwindled to twenty-five hundred. After consulting

51. Paul Hanna, "Query Addressed to Colonel Coxe," August 16, 1920, Record Group 165, MID, 10560–465/1, National Archives.

52. Hoover to Churchill, May 13, 1920, MI Microfilm, reel 11, p. 796; Hoover to C. E. [sic; Dennis E.] Nolan, September 27, 1920, reel 15, p. 551.

53. Arthur M. Scully to Coxe, September 29, 1920, ibid., reel 4, p. 644. The last coded agent report came from Agent 41 on September 22, 1920, and concerned the "connection of the I.W.W. and United Communist Party with Farmer Labor Party" (reel 19, p. 786). MI also obtained, probably through liaison, the minutes of the IWW's May 1920 convention in Chicago (reel 15, p. 227). Most reports on radical meetings in late 1920 omitted any reference to sources; a sample is in reel 12, p. 764, but the reel contains several of that type; or see a similarly unattributed report on Scott Nearing's speech in New York on October 15 in reel 9, p. 166.

54. Director of MI to recruiting officer, Newark, Ohio, November 11, 1920, ibid., reel 19, pp. 289–90. The questionnaire for April 17, 1920, has not been found, but the responses that cite it indicate that it asked for the same information. See the April reports from recruiters in Oklahoma City, Grand Rapids, and New York, reel 19, pp. 299–301, 355, 357–58.

with the Department of Justice and the American Legion, the Grand
Rapids recruiter put the number of ıww members at twenty-five, with
twice that many Communists and a hundred Socialists. The chief recruiter in Spokane, who had a large sector covering parts of Washington
and Idaho and all of Montana, reported that "the I.W.W. are rather
snowed under at present in this part of the Northwest" and that "radical
elements have about stopped trying to control affairs." The report,
he said, was based on information from army recruiters who traveled
throughout the area and "have made it their business to inform themselves on this subject."[55]

One purpose of the questionnaire was to help on a matter that
occupied a good deal of Military Intelligence's time in 1920: developing
an estimate of the strength of the radicals in anticipation of the day when
the army would be called in to suppress a revolution. An earlier attempt
to have J. Edgar Hoover provide this information had proved futile.
When asked for the number of radicals, he replied that "the membership of radical organizations is not a fair test of the amount of radical
activity."[56] On March 20, Washington asked all intelligence officers at
the headquarters of the several geographical commands to calculate "the
strength of violent revolutionary forces." The army planners wanted the
radicals' "combat strength," meaning "those who would actually join a
revolution." Organizations cited as definitely revolutionary were the
ıww, the World War Veterans, the Union of Russian Workers, the two
Communist parties, and "Anarchists." The Socialists and the Nonpartisan League were classified as nonviolent but containing individual
members who might be more radical. Washington also demanded estimates on the number of blacks, Germans, Irish, other alien groups, and
"the unorganized criminal element of the department that would join
any movement of violence."[57]

The Central Department intelligence officer went to enormous and
somewhat tedious lengths to arrive at a figure for radical strength. The
reduction followed from the assumptions that 32 percent of Americans
were wage earners, 12 percent of those workers were organized, and 30
percent of those in unions were "radically inclined." Taking a quarter of

55. See the following recruiting office reports to the director of MI: San Francisco,
December 3, 1920, ibid., reel 19, pp. 517; Grand Rapids, December 9, 1920, p. 348;
Spokane, November 27, 1920, pp. 1022–24.

56. Hoover to Nolan, November 3, 1920, ibid., reel 11, p. 963.

57. A sample of the director of MI's March 20, 1920, form letter to departments is the
one to assistant chief of staff, intelligence, Southern Department, ibid., reel 19, pp. 117–18;
responses start at p. 102.

that last calculation, the office reported 15,435 "real radicals" in Illinois. Ohio had nearly as many, and other states in the large department had decreasing numbers, down to South Dakota with only 2,171.[58] Other MI offices were less sophisticated. The Southern Department sent in an "extremely conservative" estimate of fewer than 4,000. The Southeastern command simply reported that radical strength was "negligible."[59] In November 1920 a General Staff College study took all the reports and applied some secret formula to come up with impressive levels:

Radical organizations [membership]	380,000
Radical individuals belonging to semi-radical or semi-revolutionary organizations	322,000
Individuals who adhere to the above groups but who are not carried on their rolls	200,000
Unorganized aliens	40,000
Unorganized negroes	50,000
Unorganized criminals	50,000
Total	1,142,000 [60]

Hoover refused to comment on such outrageous figures. He apparently preferred to gauge radical strength by analyzing the leftist press. He told the army that he subscribed to 251 "ultra-radical" newspapers, over half of them in foreign languages.[61] The army, however, persisted in its estimation, using the same numbers in a confidential lecture at the General Staff College on December 16. Here senior officers also received a map identifying the "most dangerous localities" as Chicago, Cleveland, New York, Seattle, and San Francisco.[62] This clearly exaggerated view of radical activity surprised the intelligence officer in Boston, who had counted fewer than a thousand "bona fide radicals" but found that Washington had him credited with 10,244. Unfortunately for

58. Assistant chief of staff, intelligence, Chicago, to director of MI, April 30, 1920, ibid., pp. 102–4.

59. G–2, Fort Sam Houston, to director of MI, April 23, 1920, ibid., pp. 105–6; department intelligence office, Southeastern Department, to director of MI, April 10, 1920, p. 109.

60. Memorandum for W. C. Babcock, November 12, 1920, ibid., p. 983.

61. Hoover to W. W. Hicks, November 24, 1920, ibid., pp. 980–82.

62. W. W. Hicks, "Estimate of the Radical or Revolutionary Situation in the United States," December 16, 1920, ibid., reel 34, pp. 961–70.

the historian, the clarification he requested was handled by that hateful device the telephone.[63]

These figures of radical strength were included in the estimates of the situation attached to a series of operation guides for domestic emergencies called War Plans White. When the intelligence analysts gave their projections to the new War Plans Division, the numbers were again inflated. War Plans assumed in 1920 that the "well organized movement for the overthrow of the Government" would put 600,000 militants into the field immediately "and there could be mobilized in thirty days nearly 1,500,000." The first stage of the takeover, the worried planners hypothesized, would be nonviolent, but strikes would paralyze the transportation system. Then revolutionary shock troops would "seize all food depots and make distribution to the starving people thereby getting them as friends and in the same way . . . get control of the local government."[64]

Apart from its estimates for War Plans White, Military Intelligence remained heavily involved in censorship. In late 1920, the army produced a "List of Newspapers and Other Publications Considered Undesirable for Circulation in Posts or Cantonments." This blacklist of over five hundred items included the *Birth Control Review*, the agnostic magazine the *Crucible*, the *Dial*, three publications by the Women's Peace party, Jack London's *A Good Soldier*, Scott Nearing's *Great Madness*, all sorts of Hindu, Irish, and Yiddish publications, an unidentified speech by Senator La Follette, the *Nonpartisan Leader*, and, from Georgia, the agrarian radical and race-baiting *Watson's Magazine* along with an entry entitled "Watson's Editorial on the War."[65]

Equally interesting to the army, as it faced the limitations on its direct role in combating the left, were private organizations that might take up that mission. The most comprehensive list that emerged was "Associations Engaged in Propaganda against Bolshevism." The sixty-five patriotic organizations included many expected names: the American

63. Assistant chief of staff for MI, First Corps Area, to director of MI, February 26, 1921, ibid., reel 20, p. 489; a handwritten note on the bottom indicates that the response was made by telephone.

64. This hysterical projection was developed in early 1920 and is quoted in "Emergency Plan White, War Department (General Policies and Instructions), 1923," Record Group 407, Adjutant General, box 99, National Archives. No field reports ever hinted at any such radical conspiracy; War Plans merely applied the model it perceived as having worked in Russia. For evidence that Military Intelligence feared that it was being supplanted by the new War Plans Division, see a special MI committee's memorandum for the director of MI, July 7, 1919, Coxe Papers.

65. The list is attached to Churchill's telegram to assistant chief of staff for MI, Fort Sam Houston, July 16, 1920, MI Microfilm, reel 19, pp. 835–47. "Under no circumstances," Churchill ordered, "can list be made public."

Legion, the American Bankers Association, Chamber of Commerce, Kiwanis Club, Rotary Club, and Knights of Columbus. Along with the previously established Loyal American Leagues of Gary and Cleveland, the Loyal Legion of Loggers and Lumbermen in the Northwest, the National Civic Federation, and the National Security League, the list contained more recent additions: the Committee of Fifteen ("some place in N.E. Dept."), the All American Alliance of Texas, and the Law and Order League and the National Defenders in east Tennessee. Alaska had its One Hundred Percent Americans, Indianapolis its National Americanism Association, Boston its Order and Liberty Alliance, and Louisiana its Self Preservation and Loyalty League (" against Negroes"). The *Zero Hour* magazine came out of Oklahoma, while Wheeling, West Virginia, had a group with the intriguing title Cooperative Readjustment Society.[66]

Another fascinating document of late 1920 was "Brief Sketch of the Important International Movements or 'Isms' and Certain Combinations of these Movements (Intrigues) with which the Military Intelligence Division is Concerned." In that view, anarchism was made up of "educated propagandists and young students—men and women with half-baked ideas." Bolshevism represented "the efforts of a small group of international demagogues to get control of the governments of the world by fomenting and exploiting the social and economic unrest of the lower orders of society." Emanating from Soviet Russia, "this unspeakable doctrine" was disseminated by the "well established" and "intimate connection of the Jews and Jewry with Bolshevism." Of the three classes of Jews, "the Nationalist, Zionist, and the International," the aims of the first two were "laudable." The International Jew represented the real threat: "generally a brilliant, egoistical radical, some times an idealist dreaming of ultimate world domination by the Jews, but more frequently a thorough-going radical, using his keen wits for purely personal gain." Other frightening signs in America and around the world included labor strikes, Pan-Latinism ("the antithesis of Pan-Americanism"), Pan-Orientalism ("new and unfocused"), and Socialism. The last, the report said, was best typified in the United States by the efforts of the Nonpartisan League to develop farm cooperatives.[67]

66. The unsigned list of "Associations Engaged in Propaganda against Bolshevism," June 19, 1920, is in ibid., pp. 829–30.
67. The "Brief Sketch of Important International Movements or 'Isms'" is unsigned and undated, except for a stamp that it was received in the War Department on November 6, 1920 (ibid., reel 34, pp. 871–77). For an objective view of the "radical Jewish subculture" in East Harlem, see Richard Polenberg, *Fighting Faiths: The Abrams Case, the Supreme Court, and Free Speech* (New York: Viking, 1987), pp. 18–27.

In a similar study for the General Staff College, titled "Bolshevism," Colonel Andrew Moses linked the Russian peril to the Jews, the iww, and the Nonpartisan League. "Dangerous aliens," he concluded, "should be deported without delay." Native radicals were to "be watched and intelligent counter propaganda used to promote Americanism."[68] Department intelligence officers and military attachés around the world were alerted in 1920 to monitor signs of a variety of international conspiracies, including "International-Jewry, Japanese-Siberian, Japanese-Russo-German, Pan-Latinism, and Bolshevist-German-Islamic." Intelligence officers at home and abroad were also to report "any items of information coming to your notice" concerning the following broad topics:

Anarchism	Labor
Bolshevism	League of Nations
Christendom	Latinism
Commerce	Pan-Americanism
Feminism	Pan-Orientalism
Finance	Pan-Turanianism
Heathendom	Socialism
Islam	Tactics[69]
Jewry	

Military Intelligence's role in the Red Scare never received the publicity associated with the Palmer Raids and the deportations, yet the army was at the forefront in the battle against radicalism. Moreover, it seemed virtually impossible to extricate the military from that role. Churchill attempted to do so, apparently genuinely, when the war ended. His own paranoia, no doubt fanned by the shadowy Van Deman and the alarmist reports from intelligence officers in the field, made it impossible for him to remain reasonable when faced with the dramatic events of 1919. Even the secretary of war proved unable to control Military Intelligence. Within little more than a year, Baker twice attempted to end the army's domestic spying. His March 1920 restrictions had more success, but ultimately he was unable to keep army agents out of radical meetings, and he could never change the deeply conservative and suspicious mentality that dominated Military Intelligence and the officer corps.

Nevertheless, the army's spying empire did decline in 1920. Though

68. Andrew Moses, "Bolshevism," October 1, 1920, MI Microfilm, reel 34, pp. 884–911.
69. The June 10, 1920, letter from the acting director of MI to military attachés has a note: "Similar letr to I[ntelligence] O[fficer]s 10110–2048" (ibid., pp. 876–77).

Baker's admonitions no doubt had at least some temporary effect, as did the fear of public exposure, the most effective means of restricting Military Intelligence proved to be drastic cutbacks in personnel and financing. By the second half of 1920, not only was the army's intelligence operation a mere skeleton of its former vigorous self, but Churchill and Van Deman were no longer in charge. In the 1920s and 1930s, the shriveled agency could look for aid only from the private sector, and in those years its activities were mild indeed when compared to its heyday during World War I and the Red Scare. Even so, and with all the restrictions, fears, and reductions, the army's loathing for the American left persisted.

CHAPTER 11

Interlocking Directorates
of the 1920s

The year 1920 saw the exit of Ralph Van Deman and Marlborough Churchill from the Military Intelligence Division. The founding father was never welcome in Washington, and after a brief stint as deputy to Churchill, he left for the Philippines in March 1920. Churchill's future was equally unspectacular. When he stepped down as director of Military Intelligence in August 1920, the reduction in force under way cost him his temporary rank of brigadier general. Since Congress had required that all regular army officers be demoted one grade in their permanent rank, Churchill, who had been a lieutenant colonel, found himself a major. After nonintelligence assignments in Washington, in June 1922 he became the assistant chief of staff for intelligence at the geographical command headquartered in New York. There is no evidence that Churchill's departure represented a reprimand from his military or civilian superiors. His rapid advancement during the war simply seems to have worked against him in this time of extensive retrenchment. After Churchill left, the Washington office remained very sensitive to public disapproval of political spying, but some field units resumed their old habits.[1]

Following passage of the National Defense Act of 1920, the army went through changes in structure and nomenclature. The six departments were regrouped into nine corps areas. Under the new system, the Eastern Department, for example, became the Second Corps Area, and the department intelligence officer became the corps' assistant chief of staff for intelligence. This terminology was applied to the War Depart-

---

1. Van Deman was promoted to brigadier general in 1927 and held several commands in the United States and received a second star shortly before his retirement to San Diego in 1929; see Ralph E. Weber, ed., *The Final Memoranda: Major General Ralph H. Van Deman, USA Ret., 1865–1952, Father of U.S. Military Intelligence* (Wilmington, Del.: Scholarly Resources, 1988), p. xxi. See also the article on Van Deman in G. J. A. O'Toole, *The Encyclopedia of American Intelligence and Espionage* (New York: Facts on File, 1988), pp. 461–63; for Churchill, pp. 114–15. On the demotion of regular officers, see Alexander B. Coxe to Churchill, May 28, 1920, Alexander B. Coxe, Sr., Papers, J. Y. Joyner Library, East Carolina University, Greenville, N.C.

ment when General Pershing became army chief of staff in 1921 and brought his model, which he had developed in France, to the general staff in Washington. After that, there was an assistant chief of staff for intelligence in the War Department, more or less in charge of the several assistant chiefs in the corps areas. The shorthand designation, also created in France, for these positions was G-2. Consequently, the corps area G-2s communicated with the general staff G-2 in Washington, and soon G-2 was the generic term for army intelligence. Though the corps areas G-2s were nominally under the control of their local chiefs of staff, their connection with Washington was resented by commanders and other staff officers. The Military Intelligence Division in Washington was the only general staff component that could deal directly with its corps counterparts; others had to go through the corps commander. Military Intelligence, furthermore, used its own communications code, and only G-2s possessed the key.[2]

Pershing arrayed his general staff into five divisions, each headed by an assistant chief; hence intelligence, G-2, was the second division on the staff. The National Defense Act, however, had allocated slots for only four generals as assistant chiefs. Since one division had to suffer and intelligence lacked seniority, the cut was made there. When Churchill's successor, Brigadier General Dennis E. Nolan, left shortly before the new staff system went into effect on September 1, 1921, he was replaced by Colonel Stuart Heintzelman. In the politics of the general staff, intelligence was, as an army historian has said, "merely a junior partner," a status made obvious because its chief was only a colonel.[3]

In his tenure, General Nolan initiated a series of evaluations of army intelligence that very nearly ended the existence of the Negative Branch. An October 1920 report remarked that "the activities of this branch are being gradually reduced" and suggested that "a more descriptive name for the branch might not be out of place." Shortly thereafter, another evaluation suggested that the branch should be given new missions or abolished.[4] The following year an analysis found "no active work" in negative intelligence being conducted, beyond receiving information

2. For materials on organization and G-2 communication, see Record Group 165, MID, 10560–484/1, National Archives.

3. Bruce W. Bidwell, *History of the Military Intelligence Division, Department of the Army General Staff, 1775–1941* (Frederick, Md.: University Publications of America, 1986), p. 256. This source is excellent for sorting out the complex organizational changes. See the article on Nolan in O'Toole, *Encyclopedia of American Intelligence*, p. 329.

4. James L. Collins, memorandum for the director of MI, October 12, 1920, and Mathew C. Smith, memorandum for the director of MI, October 13, 1920, both in Record Group 165, MID, 10560–1–A, pt. II, National Archives.

from the Department of Justice, local police, and "from the American Legion; and from various individuals," who provided intelligence "voluntarily without being requested to do so."[5] At that time the Negative Branch had only 3 officers and 7 civilian employees, and a subsequent review by experts from the Bureau of Efficiency found their work to be "in duplication with that of the Department of Justice" and recommended a reduction to 1 officer and 1 civilian. The total strength of the Military Intelligence Division on June 30, 1921, was only 45 officers and 100 civilians. By early 1922, this number had been reduced to 24 officers and 66 civilians with a budget of $165,000. As a gauge of the severity of the cutbacks, there were, in 1922, only 104 officers on the entire general staff in the War Department.[6]

After Churchill's departure, the Negative Branch remained so sensitive to criticism that no formal investigations were ordered by the Washington command center. When Lincoln Steffens gave a speech in town on January 7, 1921, the branch stirred briefly into action but was careful to cover itself by having two secretaries volunteer to attend and take notes.[7] Another moment of panic occurred shortly afterward when a former artillery officer reported that his contact with the western IWW convinced him that they were planning a march on Washington, where they would find jobs in hotels and poison the food and generally cause a "reign of terror." Field units were alerted, but no evidence developed to support the claim.[8] In March, the chief of staff rejected a plan to allow Denver agents to receive "radical data" from the Pinkertons. The final memorandum refusing the deal cited possible "injury" to the army, but an earlier draft was more blunt: "Should such an agreement be entered into and knowledge thereof obtained by radical organizations, it would subject the Military Intelligence Division to severe criticism."[9]

5. "Organization and Function of the Negative Branch," August 24, 1921," ibid., 10560–489.

6. Memorandum for the G-2, December 29, 1921, 10560–563/27, ibid.; U.S. Bureau of Efficiency, "Report on the Requirements for Civilian Personnel in the Military Intelligence Division of the General Staff," November 1, 1921, 10560–563/1; Heintzelman, memorandum for the budget officer for the War Department, December 31, 1921, 10560–563/30. For strength figures, see Bidwell, *History of Military Intelligence*, p. 257.

7. Memorandum for Hicks, January 10, 1921, in Randolph Boehm, ed., *U.S. Military Intelligence Reports: Surveillance of Radicals in the United States, 1917–1941* (Frederick, Md.: University Publications of America, 1984), reel 34, pp. 930–31 (hereafter cited as MI Microfilm). The women reported that "the audience consisted mostly of foreigners, many of whom were heard conversing in foreign tongues." They described Steffens as having "small eyes and a nervous expression."

8. H. P. Kayser, memorandum for file, January 27, 1921, and G-2, Fort Sheridan, to director of MI, February 4, 1921, ibid., reel 20, pp. 196–97.

9. G-2, Fort Sam Houston, to director of MI, March 10, 1921, and the response of March 25, 1921, ibid., pp. 666, 668. The unused draft is on p. 667.

Another sign of Washington's concern for limiting its exposure was the closing of its files. By early 1921, access was limited to the Department of Justice, and a form letter was developed for the routine denial of patriotic organizations wishing to see the secrets hidden in the army dossiers.[10] Such restraint did not exist, however, in the field. The rapid turnover of officers associated with the demobilization and reorganization meant that there were in place at the headquarters and subordinate units of the corps areas a new crop of men who had not had their fingers burned by Baker or Churchill. Moreover, the manuals directing the widespread collection effort during the war seem to have had a longer shelf life than the letters restricting the domestic intelligence mission. Many units did not know they had been mothballed.[11]

Military Intelligence's enemies in 1921 were the traditional ones. Reports on the Finnish Socialists led by Santeri Nuorteva continued until late 1921, and the foreign movements of Louis C. Fraina (the "Italian Jew Communist"), Louise Bryant (widow of John Reed, who had died in Moscow on October 17, 1920), Big Bill Haywood, Emma Goldman, and other radicals were carefully followed by the army in cooperation with the State Department.[12] Military Intelligence's best vantage point for monitoring the flow of Americans in and out of Russia was Riga, Latvia, a hotbed of espionage. At home, the Second Corps Area had the most energetic domestic intelligence program, led by Parker Hitt, who before the war had written the first book on cryptology published in the United States. Hitt continued to watch the Rand School, the World War Veterans, the National Defense Committee (fighting for the remaining political prisoners and for deportees "still rotting on Ellis Island"), the Communists, the blacks, and the IWW. Hitt was especially concerned about that last organization, and in the summer of 1921 he had an informant inside it.[13] Third Corps Area headquarters, at Fort Howard,

10. Mathew C. Smith, memorandum for chiefs of MI4 and MI8, March 16, 1921, Record Group 165, MID, 10650–630 FW, National Archives.

11. Bidwell, *History of Military Intelligence*, p. 277.

12. The largest file on the Red Finns is in MI Microfilm, reel 9, pp. 230–808; a similar file on Fraina is in reel 33, pp. 80–385; Haywood's file runs from reel 5, p. 392, to reel 6, p. 114; those for Emma Goldman, Alexander Shapiro, and Alexander Berkman are in reel 3, pp. 692–945. The file on John Reed and Louise Bryant is in reel 33, pp. 579–892. For an interesting and late report on Reed, see J. Edgar Hoover to Alexander B. Cox[e], August 14, 1920, reel 33, pp. 888–89. See Alice Wexler, *Emma Goldman in Exile: From the Russian Revolution to the Spanish Civil War* (Boston: Beacon Press, 1989), pp. 24, 33–34, 58, 123, 256, for a view of MI's success against Goldman.

13. These reports are in MI Microfilm, reel 15, pp. 39–846, except for the file on the World War Veterans, which is reel 20, pp. 210–478, and that on the Communists, which runs from reel 20, p. 903, to reel 21, p. 320. On Hitt and the blacks, see Theodore Kornweibel, Jr., ed., *Federal Surveillance of Afro-Americans (1917–1925): The First World War, the Red Scare, and the Garvey Movement* (Frederick, Md.: University Publications

Maryland, was also active, as were First Corps in Boston and Eighth Corps at Fort Sam Houston. By 1922, however, reports from the field had dwindled sharply. The dying Negative Branch managed to generate only a few products, the most interesting of which was a March 6, 1922, list of "Red and Pink" newspapers and periodicals. It was sent to the State Department to prevent radical reporters from receiving passports and included nearly 150 publications. Among the honored were the *A.F. of L. Weekly News Letter* ("semi-radical"), the *Birth Control Review* ("liberal and semi-radical"), the *Butte Daily Bulletin* ("radical in policy"), the NAACP's *Crisis* (for which a characterization was apparently unnecessary), *La Follette's* ("a liberal and radical paper"), the *Nation* ("organ of the radical intellectuals"), the *New Republic* ("radical"), the *Nonpartisan Leader* ("radical"), the *South Dakota Leader* ("radical"), the *Survey* ("radical"), and *Upton Sinclair's Magazine* ("extremely radical").[14]

All G-2s shared a common requirement. Each had to provide the intelligence estimate for his respective War Plan White, the emergency mobilization scheme for handling a civil disturbance within the United States. Orders went out for the development of such plans in the fall of 1920, but progress had been hampered by the reorganization. One early result was the frantic effort to establish the "strength" of the radical enemy. Another was the use of army recruiters as sources, a practice that was reinforced and approved by the chief of staff on the basis that, as one G-2 said, "the collection of information necessary for the preparation of the plan requires reliable agents throughout the Area."[15]

Of all the G-2s, the one at Third Corps Area probably took his planning task the most seriously and was the first to produce an extensive "intelligence annex" for the corps area's Plan White. The Maryland intelligence office was given to total paranoia. The G-2 saw "in progress a systematic and well directed movement which has for its intermediate object the overthrow of the Constituted Authority in the United States." This terrible prospect was even then being achieved by subverting "the

of America, 1986), reel 21, pp. 904–76 (hereafter cited as Surveillance of Afro-Americans Microfilm). When Churchill took over as Second Corps Area G-2 in the summer of 1922, he apparently ended Hitt's surveillance program. For Hitt's early work in cryptology, see John Patrick Finnegan, *Military Intelligence: A Picture History* (Arlington, Va.: U.S. Army Intelligence and Security Command, 1985), pp. 16–17.

14. The March 6, 1922, "List of Red and Pink Publications in United States" is attached to State Department memorandum, P. A. Adams to U2, March 9, 1922, in the State Department files in Surveillance of Afro-Americans Microfilm, reel 18, pp. 918–33.

15. On the renewed use of recruiters, see acting chief of staff to director, War Plans Division, September 3, 1920, 10560–305/16, and Churchill, memorandum for the adjutant general, October 20, 1919, 10560–305/2, in Record Group 165, MID, National Archives.

home, the press, the school and the Church." There were twenty-five different methods used in this vicious propaganda war, including the radical press; radical speakers; radical "social gatherings"; motion pictures "designed to foment class hatred"; and boring-in of schools, unions, and "the negro masses." Esperanto "and other devices for a universal language" were tools for the "furtherance of internationalism." The most pernicious threat, or at least the one with the longest description, involved "the formation of interlocking directorates by means of which religious, pacifist, social uplift, co-operative, liberal, industrial and racial groups, organizations, elements, federations and societies are linked together as a working whole under the general direction of radical leaders."[16]

By 1923 the War Department had produced a fairly modern and thorough set of instructions for developing what was then called Emergency Plans White, including a fill-in-the-blank presidential proclamation committing troops after state authorities had confessed their inability to handle an insurrection. Such a proclamation was paramount because, shortly before leaving office, Newton Baker had restored the "true relationship" in the federal system and had rescinded his blanket authority for commanders to act on a governor's request.[17] Noting that commanders had their own plans "for the complete military occupation and control of their corps area," the War Plans Division justified this preparedness by referring to the "fall and winter of 1919–20 [when] social unrest was at its height." The intelligence requirement before troops were committed involved maintaining a current estimate of the situation that measured and described "Radical Forces" and projected "Radical action." No other sources of disturbance were considered by Washington, not even a race riot. It was always the radicals.[18]

As the old threat from groups such as the IWW and the Bolsheviki diminished, so did the intensity of the G-2s. By 1922 very little collection and reporting was occurring. In fact, the whole domestic intelligence program was on the verge of withering for lack of a decent-sized enemy. Then, so suddenly that the military seemed surprised, the pacifists were back. The Washington naval disarmament conference,

16. MI Microfilm, reel 20, pp. 857–60. Other items on the early development of War Plans White are in Record Group 60, Glasser Files, box 9, National Archives. All communications on this subject were originally classified secret.

17. Baker, memorandum for chief of staff, December 2, 1920, Glasser Files, box 9.

18. "Emergency Plan White, War Department (General Policies and Instructions), 1923," Record Group 407, Adjutant General, box 99, National Archives. Later versions of Plan White, down to 1946, along with other color-coded plans (Orange was for war with Japan, Green for Mexico), are in boxes 99–102.

which produced the Five Power Treaty of February 6, 1922, breathed life into peace groups that had been formed during the war and spawned new ones. By spring, the Women's International League for Peace and Freedom was so active that the army quartermaster general sent a messenger to its office to collect literature, which he promptly gave to his colleague, the G-2.[19] A few months later, Churchill, as G-2 in New York, requested from Washington "a summary showing the various pacifist and anti-military organizations in the country, their aims, purposes and interlocking directorates."[20] The information he received was not comforting.

There were numerous groups ranging "from a violent red to a light pink" in which the work by women was particularly prominent. In fact, the report to Churchill said, "the activities of all women's societies and many church societies may be regarded with suspicion." Using an especially tortured logic, the study of interlocking directorates produced a trail that led from the Women's Joint Congressional Committee, the National League of Women Voters, and the National Women's party to the Women's International League for Peace and Freedom. Members of that pacifist group were linked to the Joint Amnesty Committee, which led the army analysts to the Labor Defense Council and then straight to the Communists.[21]

The most active of the peace groups was the Women's International League for Peace and Freedom, all the more frightening because its international secretary was New York lawyer Madeline Doty, wife of none other than Roger Baldwin, whose civil liberties bureau had changed its name to the American Civil Liberties Union in 1920. Despite such an obvious conspiracy, the army ran no formal investigations against those groups in the early 1920s, contenting itself with filing away information from the press and volunteers.[22] Nor did it attempt to suppress or disrupt another pacifist threat, the National Student Forum. Considered by the army as an outgrowth of the National Student Committee for

19. J. M. Carson to S. Heintzelman, April 12, 1922, MI Microfilm, reel 19, p. 708.
20. Churchill to Cowles, December 14, 1922, ibid., reel 22, p. 1028.
21. Cowles to Churchill, December 9, 1922, ibid., pp. 1025–27. The chief of the Negative Branch apologized to Churchill for not providing more elaborate information, citing a shortage of "officer and clerical" help. See also reel 19, p. 531, for a May 13, 1922, memorandum for Cowles that connects Carrie Chapman Catt and Jane Addams with "many pink organizations" and Mrs. Raymond Robins with "real red organizations." The interlocking directorate analysis assumed that a moderate group was linked by its most radical board member to the most extreme organization to which that member belonged.
22. The file on the Women's League, containing a good deal of information from the 1930s, is in ibid., reel 19, pp. 529–732.

the Limitation of Armaments and the Intercollegiate Liberal League (formerly the Intercollegiate Socialist Society), the forum was essentially a speaker's bureau. When posters announcing a program called "The Causes of War" appeared on campuses in New York in May, the Washington G-2 decided that they were "socialistic and indirectly contain propaganda against the Army of the United States." A "discreet inquiry" was ordered. The Ninth Corps G-2 in San Francisco reported that support for the "dangerous socialistic organization" came mainly from "the editors of the *Nation*, the *New Republic* and kindred radical publications." [23]

The Department of Justice was also interested in the National Student Forum and told the army that though some of its speakers were "very true Americans," there were others whose "sincerity of Americanism is gravely doubted." Among those who had "socialistic and anarchic tendencies" was the familiar Roger Baldwin. Military Intelligence's analysis of the speakers had Baldwin down as an "Intellectual Anarchist." George Creel, by virtue of his membership in the ACLU, received a similar designation. Oswald Garrison Villard, incorrectly listed as "Arnold," was a double threat because he was editor of the *Nation* and a member of ACLU's executive committee; he was tagged as "an advocate of revolutionary socialism." [24]

Military Intelligence felt hamstrung by its inability to move decisively against the students and their speakers. Although it was certain that "all the work of industrial and physical preparation for defense will have been wasted if the younger generation are going to turn out to be pacifists and internationalists," the army could find no way to fight "this insidious propaganda" without going public. [25] The situation was particularly hard for the faculty of the Reserve Officers' Training Corps, who had to face the threat every day on their campuses. As eager agents of Military Intelligence, these officers, in a program just being established, were so angry at times that they took matters into their own hands. "Someone here on the faculty is a member [of the Forum]," reported the military instructor at Coe College in Cedar Rapids, "and keeps us rather busy tearing down posters denouncing armies, R.O.T.C. and so forth. We go on the theroy [sic] that we have as much right to take

23. M. E. Locke to G-2, Second Corps Area, May 13, 1922, and W. R. Slaughter to G-2, War Department, May 27, 1922, ibid., reel 22, pp. 1022–23.
24. "Speakers National Student Forum, Characteristics and Activities of Some Who Have Socialistic and Anarchic Tendencies," n.d., ibid., pp. 1015–20.
25. Locke to G-2, Second Corps Area, October 30, 1923, ibid., p. 1014.

them down as he has to put them up."[26] Washington told him, in direct terms, why their hands were tied:

> You know how suspicious of M.I.D. activities many people are and that it is attacked on the slightest provocation for "military interference in civilian matters." Now if your college authorities took some "decisive" action relative to N.S.F. activities there, basing that action on "facts" furnished by M.I.D., and the matter became public, as it almost certainly would, the fat would be in the fire, and the War Department and M.I.D. again be targets for attacks. For these reasons, M.I.D. cannot afford to go on record in this matter, so please do not mention it in this regard.[27]

Military Intelligence was especially sensitive about such criticism because in the fall of 1922 another embarrassing episode had occurred involving an energetic intelligence officer in the Northwest. The post intelligence officer at Vancouver Barracks in the state of Washington must have believed that the reporting requirement on radical groups in the Red Scare was still in effect because on October 16 he sent a form letter to the county sheriffs in his area. The complete letter was reprinted in the *Nation*, the *Labor Herald*, and other newspapers. The most inflammatory parts are as follows:

> The Intelligence Service of the Army has for its primary purpose the surveillance of organizations or elements hostile or potentially hostile to the Government of this country, or who seek to over-throw the Government by violence.
>
> Among organizations falling under the above heads are radical groups such as the I.W.W., World War Veterans, Union of Russian Workers, Communist Party, Communist Labor Party, One Big Union, Workers International Industrial Union, Anarchists, Bolsheviki, and such semi-radical organizations as the Socialists, Non-Partisan League, Big Four Brotherhoods, and the American Federation of Labor.[28]

The first paragraph was damaging enough, but the inclusion of the American Federation of Labor as a subject of army interest caused a tremendous uproar. Nearly two years before, in the winter of 1920–21,

26. Niederpruem to P. H. Bagby, February 10, 1923, ibid., p. 1012.
27. Bagby to Niederpruem, February 17, 1923, ibid., pp. 1010–11.
28. These portions of the letter are in Bidwell, *History of Military Intelligence*, p. 279; the entire document is reprinted in Frank J. Donner, *The Age of Surveillance: The Aims and Methods of America's Political Intelligence System* (New York: Knopf, 1980), p. 291. See also U.S. Army, *The History of the Counter Intelligence Corps in the Unitd States Army, 1917–1950 (with Limited Tabular Data to 1960)*, 30 vols. (Baltimore: U.S. Army Intelligence Center, 1959), 4:361 (hereafter cited as CIC History), in Record Group 319, National Archives.

the army had been the object of a bitter complaint from Samuel Gompers to J. Edgar Hoover that military agents were spying on AFL affiliates in Oklahoma.[29] This time, the explosion was so great that mere denials would not suffice. In addition to relieving and reprimanding the offending individual, Secretary of War John W. Weeks eliminated the position of intelligence officer at smaller posts and ordered the army to bring the corps area G-2s into line. Accordingly, the adjutant general, responsible for issuing official army policy, notified all commanders that "the Secretary of War is much concerned at reports from time to time of the activities of intelligence officers in the United States." Warning that "harmless and even readily justifiable inquiries arouse suspicion," the general concluded that "it is obvious that the American people are very sensitive with regard to any military interference in their affairs." Information to satisfy a corps commander's need to know about possible domestic disturbances was to be obtained solely "through the proper civilian authorities and by scrutiny of the public press." Otherwise, intelligence officers were to limit their activities to training for their combat intelligence mission. Only the secretary of war could grant exceptions to this policy.[30]

During the following September, the official policy was highlighted in an article on the duties of intelligence officers in the *Army and Navy Journal*. Warning field units against excessive zeal, the piece cautioned that "the intelligence officer is not a policeman. He is not a diminutive edition of a Burns-Pinkerton detective."[31] Even though the restrictions on Military Intelligence seemed clear, some individual officers continued to create embarrassing incidents for the army. When a reserve

29. Hoover to Nolan, December 28, 1920, and January 29, 1921; Mathew C. Smith to Hoover, February 3, 1921, MI Microfilm, reel 20, pp. 156, 160, 166. The Oklahoma incident resulted from the Eighth Corps Area G-2's "economical and psychological" survey, which asked for, among other things, membership numbers for a variety of organizations, including the American Legion, churches, and groups "affecting in any way the social and industrial life." The Fort Sill intelligence officer asked the local Department of Justice agent for information on the AFL, and so the story of an army "investigation" of labor unions developed. The G-2's broad interest doubtless stemmed from his work on the corps' War Plan White. His attitude was especially militant. If investigations of "recognized labor unions which show no trace of radicals could not be easily justified," he told Fort Sill, such was not the case for "our enemies the Radicals." Later he referred to the "Radicals" as "our avowed enemies." See the file on the incident, reel 20, pp. 156–66. The same G-2 had, on August 27, 1920, queried Washington for information on radicals in his area, along with a request for the number of union members and the names of labor leaders (Glasser Files, box 9).

30. Bidwell, *History of Military Intelligence*, p. 278; CIC History, 4:37.

31. Quoted in Rhodri Jeffreys-Jones, *American Espionage: From Secret Service to CIA* (New York: Free Press, 1977), p. 122.

captain announced his support of Robert M. La Follette for president, the G-2 in Chicago attempted to have him drummed out of the army and created a brief cause célèbre for the liberal press. Shortly afterward, army and navy intelligence officers in New York complained that Maxwell Anderson and Laurence Stallings's play *What Price Glory* was obscene and damaging to the morale of the military, especially the Marine Corps. Mayor John F. Hyland disagreed, and once again the intelligence community was held up to public censure.[32]

Military Intelligence was not responsible for the most famous case of army involvement in civilian affairs, but inevitably it was blamed for the "Spider Web Chart" in the mid-1920s. The chart, which must rank as the masterpiece of all the analyses of interlocking directorates, was completed in early 1923 by Lucia R. Maxwell, who chaired the Patriotic Committee of the League of American Pen Women. Unfortunately for the army, she was also the librarian of the Chemical Warfare Service, headed by Brigadier General Amos A. Fries. As a caption for her chart, Maxwell selected a line from the Lusk report: "The Socialist Pacifist Movement in America is an Absolutely Fundamental and Integral Part of International Socialism." The chart consisted of three columns, one of organizations and two of women who belonged to them. The spider web effect was created when she drew numerous lines connecting the women to the groups of which they were members. The results were amazing and proved to the satisfaction of many patriots that apparently innocuous organizations were under the control of Moscow. Included in the web of subversion were the General Federation of Women's Clubs, the Women's Christian Temperance Union, the National Congress of Mothers and Parent-Teachers Associations, the American Home Economics Association, the national board of the Young Women's Christian Association, the League of Women Voters, and the American Association of University Women.

Maxwell gave the original chart to President Warren G. Harding and sent copies to Attorney General Harry M. Daugherty and his special assistant, J. Edgar Hoover. Daugherty confessed, "I do not know how I should have got along without it." Hoover called it "a magnificent piece of work," noting that "one can gain more in my estimation from an examination of such a chart than he can from reading voluminous reports dealing with the same subject." He urged her to continue the good

32. These two cases are cited in ibid., pp. 122–23.

work.[33] On the bottom of some of the copies were the following lines, generally attributed to Maxwell:

Miss Bolsheviki has come to town,
With a Russian cap and a German gown,
In women's clubs she's sure to be found,
For she's come to disarm AMERICA.

She sits in judgement on Capitol Hill,
And watches the appropriation bill,
And with her O.K., it passes—NIL
For she's there to disarm AMERICA.

She uses the movie and lyceum too,
And alters text-books to suit her view,
She prates propaganda from pulpit to pew,
For she's bound to disarm AMERICA.

The male of the species has a different plan,
He uses the bomb and the fire brand,
And incites class hatred wherever he can,
While she's busy disarming AMERICA.

His special stunt is arousing the mob,
To expropriate and hate and kill and rob,
While she's working on her political job,
AWAKE! AROUSE!! AMERICA!!![34]

The extent to which the chart had been circulated in the army became all too obvious on March 7, 1924, when the commander of Fort Bragg, Brigadier General Albert J. Bowley, addressed the Columbus, Ohio, Chamber of Commerce and called Frederick J. Libby of the National Council for the Prevention of War a Russian agent. When pacifists

33. Hoover to Lucia Maxwell, May 19, 1923, MI Microfilm, reel 19, p. 533. Daugherty is quoted in Norman Hapgood, *Professional Patriots* (New York: Albert & Charles Boni, 1927), p. 106, which contains a good description of the chart. See also Paul L. Murphy, *The Meaning of Free Speech: First Amendment Freedoms from Wilson to FDR* (Westport, Conn.: Greenwood, 1972), p. 192; and William Pencak, *For God and Country: The American Legion, 1919–1941* (Boston: Northeastern University Press, 1989), p. 9.

34. The poem is in Hapgood, *Professional Patriots*, pp. 104–5, and in the *Woman Patriot*, "Dedicated to the Defense of the Family and the State AGAINST Feminism and Socialism," 2 (June 1, 1927): 84. This entire issue of the *Woman Patriot* is in MI Microfilm, reel 19, pp. 578–85. Though the magazine is a hysterical attack on Hapgood, it is nevertheless valuable for information and documents on the fight over the Spider Web Chart.

protested, he cited the Spider Web Chart as his source.[35] Moreover, both Secretary Weeks and General Fries had made speeches attacking peace groups, especially Libby's organization and the Women's International League. There is considerable evidence that Fries knew of Maxwell's work, approved it, and allowed her to send out copies from his office.[36]

The copy of the Spider Web Chart that appeared in Henry Ford's *Dearborn Independent* on March 22, 1924, did not carry the poem, but the version acquired by the Women's Joint Congressional Committee did. More important, the women also knew about Lucia Maxwell's connection with the military. On April 2, the chair of the committee, Maude Wood Park, delivered an indignant letter to Secretary of War Weeks. Quoting all five verses, she told him plainly that the 12 million women voters in the seventeen women's groups represented by her committee could not understand "why an employee of a government bureau should be permitted, with the knowledge of the head of the bureau, to attack the women's organizations of the country." She said the poem was "scurrilous and libelous and insulting to every woman voter" and called the Lusk-inspired heading "scurrilous, libelous and criminal." The chart itself, she said, was "false and inaccurate."[37]

No male chauvinist ever beat a hastier retreat than did Secretary Weeks. He apologized profusely and ordered General Fries to track down and destroy all copies of the chart in the War Department.[38] Despite Fries's protests that the chart was Maxwell's private effort, the fact remained that she had provided copies to the army, one of which had found its way to Military Intelligence. Fries dutifully located every copy he could and asked for its destruction. As the furor with the women's groups raged, MI was monitoring, through press clippings and liaison with Hoover, the convention of the Women's International League for Peace and Freedom and was using Maxwell as a consultant.[39] After

35. Murphy, *Meaning of Free Speech*, pp. 193–94; Bowley's speech is summarized in Hapgood, *Professional Patriots*, pp. 116–18.

36. For the case against Fries, see Joan M. Jensen, "All Pink Sisters: The War Department and the Feminist Movement in the 1920s," in Lois Scharf and Joan M. Jensen, eds., *Decade of Discontent: The Women's Movement, 1920–1940* (Westport, Conn.: Greenwood Press, 1983), pp. 199–222. See also Hapgood, *Professional Patriots*, pp. 113–31, for public comments by Fries and other army officers and civilian officials against the pacifists.

37. Park to the secretary of war, April 2, 1924, reprinted, with editorial comment, in the June 1, 1927, issue of the *Woman Patriot* cited above.

38. Weeks to Park, June 2, 1924, reprinted in Hapgood, *Professional Patriots*, pp. 105–6.

39. Fries to J. H. Bogart, April 23, 1924, MI Microfilm, reel 19, p. 534; Walter O. Boswell, memorandum for chief, MI4, May 23, 1934, p. 548; Madden telegram to Boswell, May 12, 1924, p. 613.

another complaint from the Women's Joint Congressional Committee, Weeks wrote on May 2 to acknowledge that the caption and the poem had "no bearing" on the group and that it was "in no way connected with most of the persons to whose activities the Chemical Warfare Service had found objection." This time he sought to separate Fries from Maxwell, stating that the chart has been "presented erroneously as a poster issued by the Department." Such work, he said, was not the function of the army because it did not "possess the information which would justify an attempt to analyze the correctness or incorrectness of the chart."[40]

Despite the fight over the Spider Web Chart, the army was out of domestic intelligence by 1924, having already issued "War Department Policy Number 27, Subject: Confidential Information on Individuals." Once again, the principle was affirmed that in peacetime the army should not collect information concerning civilians. Release of data from the files of Military Intelligence was also forbidden.[41] Earlier, the Negative Branch had come to recognize that "present radical activities in the United States, from a national aspect, appear to be insignificant and with remote bearing on the military situation." What work was being done, a 1921 study had found, represented "largely wasted effort." Consequently, the Negative Branch was eliminated as a separate unit, and its national situation survey was discontinued. Corps Area G-2s were also told that their overriding concern with "radical activity and labor movements" was misplaced and that they should concentrate on developing maps for troop transportation should an emergency occur. As an example, the report noted that the G-2 of the Fourth Corps Area needed to cease concern with the left and begin to develop "definite information readily available for use in moving troops from Camp Jackson and loading them on boats at Charleston."[42] In 1925, the War Department G-2 asked for permission to have the corps area G-2s forward periodic reports to him on "groups and organizations which might be involved in internal disorders or in aiding an enemy." Although he

40. Weeks to Parks, May 2, 1924, ibid., p. 652, and reprinted in the *Woman Patriot* issue cited above. With the 1927 appearance of Hapgood's exposé of superpatriot organizations, a complaint came from Ida L. Jones, general secretary of the YWCA, who still thought the Spider Web Chart a product of MI. The War Department's G-2, Colonel James H. Reeves, told her that his division "never criticizes adversely either individuals or organizations" (Jones to Reeves, April 26, 1927, MI Microfilm, reel 19, p. 566; Reeves to Jones, April 30, 1927, p. 569; see also Stanley H. Ford to Jones, May 20, 1927, p. 570).

41. Policy No. 27, March 31, 1923, War Department Policies Book No. 1, 10560–630/6w, Record Group 165, MID, National Archives.

42. John B. Barnes, memorandum for the director of MI, August 30, 1921, 10560–1–A pt. II, ibid.

stressed that he wanted the information strictly for planning purposes, the deputy chief of staff turned him down flat, telling him to rely entirely on liaison with the Department of Justice.[43] For the remainder of the decade, the G-2 made no attempt to regain a domestic mission, and each year the office's annual report carried the same statement:

> The collection of information by G-2 regarding the radical situation in the United States is confined to that which appears in the public press. The information collected is studied in connection with the possible effect of the radical situation upon the execution of any existing or proposed war plans. It is also studied in connection with the effect upon the efficiency of the Army of the United States at the present time, especially with reference to the military training in schools, colleges and activities of pacifists or radicals.[44]

The year 1924 also saw the official withdrawal of the Department of Justice from political intelligence. One of the casualties of the Teapot Dome scandal was Attorney General Daugherty, and after his resignation the Senate launched an investigation into the department that focused on the abuses of the Bureau of Investigation, particularly allegations that director William Burns had used his position to funnel business to his private detective company. President Calvin Coolidge's new attorney general, Harlan Fiske Stone, accepted Burns's resignation and issued a new policy that "the Bureau is not concerned with political or other opinions of individuals. It is concerned only with their conduct and then only with such conduct as is forbidden by the laws of the United States."[45] To implement this policy and oversee a reduction in the

43. Bidwell, *History of Military Intelligence*, pp. 280–81. The deputy chief who scotched the plan was Major General Dennis E. Nolan, who back in 1920 had succeeded Churchill as director of Military Intelligence.

44. Quoted in Bidwell, *History of Military Intelligence*, p. 281.

45. Quoted in Paul L. Murphy, "Communities in Conflict," in Alan Reitman, ed., *The Pulse of Freedom: American Liberties, 1920–1970s* (New York: Norton, 1975), p. 40. See also Eleanor Bontecou, *The Federal Loyalty-Security Program* (Ithaca: Cornell University, 1953), p. 91; Donald O. Johnson, *The Challenge to American Freedoms: World War I and the Rise of the American Civil Liberties Union* (Lexington: University of Kentucky Press, 1963), p. 173; Joan M. Jensen, *The Price of Vigilance* (Chicago: Rand McNally, 1968), p. 288. For the charges against Daugherty, which were numerous and fascinating, along with a wonderful look at the Department of Justice from 1919 to 1924, see U.S. Senate, Hearings before the Select Committee on Investigation of the Attorney General, 68th Cong., 1st sess., *Investigation of Hon. Harry M. Daugherty, formerly Attorney General of the United States*, 3 vols. (Washington, D.C.: U.S. Government Printing Office, 1924) (hereafter cited as *Investigation of Daugherty*). The most inquisitive senator was Burton K. Wheeler, from Butte, Montana, who had resigned as federal attorney to protest army methods in late 1918.

number of agents, Stone appointed J. Edgar Hoover temporary director of the bureau, a position that became permanent in January 1925.[46]

Another signal of the collapse of the American intelligence community came in 1929, when Secretary of State Henry L. Stimson shut down State's decoding program, the Black Chamber.[47] Only Naval Intelligence was left as a functioning spy agency, and since World War I the navy had kept fairly closely to matters of direct naval importance, generally steering clear of the surveillance of radicals. Two exceptions to this policy were the burglaries of the pacifist Federal Council of Churches of Christ in America in 1924 and of the New York headquarters of the Communist Party of America in 1929. The latter incident resembled an old-style raid, with considerable vandalism. "We even swiped the check books and bank books," the team leader claimed, "to create even more trouble." Visiting diplomats were always fair game for Naval Intelligence, and during the Washington Naval Conference they intercepted and deciphered the messages of foreign governments. The particular enemy, correctly as it turned out, was Japan, against whom the navy ran numerous covert operations, including a break-in at the Japanese consulate in New York. Japanese visiting the United States were routinely followed by navy agents. Once they ransacked an American professor's luggage, having mistaken it for that of a Japanese.[48]

The Military Intelligence files of the late 1920s contain slim pickings indeed. J. Edgar Hoover stopped sending his reports on the radical press in early 1926, although he did continue to provide reports on

46. Hoover testified before the Senate investigating committee only days after his interim appointment. The chairman, Smith W. Brookhart, told him his job was "to get rid of those professional double-crossing detectives." "Most positively," replied Hoover. "We do not intend to have anybody in the service of that character" (*Investigation of Daugherty*, 3: 2452). It is now clear that Hoover had no intention of ending his surveillance of radicals. For overwhelming evidence of his secret campaign in the late 1920s against the ACLU and leftist groups, see David Williams, "'They Never Stopped Watching Us': FBI Political Surveillance, 1924–1936," *UCLA Historical Journal* 2 (1981): 5–28. Hoover's relatively small espionage program was on such a close-hold basis that even Military Intelligence was unaware of its existence.

47. Jeffreys-Jones, *American Espionage*, p. 134, advances the novel thesis that, having learned that the U.S. code had been compromised, the public announcement of the end of cryptographic espionage was simply a ruse. The cutback was real enough, however, to drive its guiding genius, Herbert O. Yardley, away in disgust. On Yardley, see O'Toole, *Encyclopedia of American Intelligence*, pp. 504–5.

48. These cases are discussed in Jeffrey M. Dorwart, *Conflict of Duty: The U.S. Navy's Intelligence Dilemma, 1919–1945* (Annapolis: Naval Institute Press, 1979), pp. 41, 45–46. See also pp. 3–5 for the fascinating 1930 story of President Herbert Hoover's Watergate-like use of navy agents to break into the Democratic party's New York office, only to find it empty. A good deal of material on the navy's worldwide espionage program in the 1920s is in Record Group 38, ONI, "Suspect" and "CAP" files, National Archives.

alleged Communists in the army.[49] Subversion of the troops, along with fear of the pacifists, was the theme, to the extent there was one, of Military Intelligence's quiescent domestic program. Walter Trumbull and Paul Crouch symbolized the threat, for they composed the first Communist "cell" discovered in the army. They were privates at Schofield Barracks in Hawaii and were court-martialed in 1925 for, as their handbills said, "the crime of thinking, and organizing in behalf of the working class." Their sentences of twenty-six and forty years, respectively, at Alcatraz, were later reduced to one and three years. Trumbull began a speaking tour as soon as he was released, as did Crouch when he got out in June 1927. The few remaining agents in the Corps of Intelligence Police were used to cover their speeches, while at the War Department the effort to counter subversion in the army seems to have been in the hands of a single master sergeant.[50]

Limited resources offered no alternative. Starting the decade with a budget of $400,000 and a total staff of 234, the Washington intelligence headquarters had shrunk by 1930 to 75 people working with slightly more than $57,000. The 1930s saw even further decline, bottoming out in 1934 with a staff of 70 on a budget of $26,650.[51] These practical restraints and a policy produced by public criticism resulted in nearly complete inactivity in negative intelligence during the late 1920s. Only one case when an agent observed a meeting that did not involve Trumbull or Crouch has been found. On July 16, 1926, "a soldier" (probably a clerk) of the New York G-2's office attended and reported on a debate on the resolution "Our present form of Government is in the best interests of the Masses" between Communist Jay Lovestone and George H. Mann of the National Security League, moderated by Scott Nearing.[52]

In the War Department, the G-2 prepared only one staff study of radicalism after 1924. This analysis, done in the summer of 1927, maintained that radicals aimed to destroy the home, religion, patriotism, and national defense, but the information was very general and contained none of the saucy details typical of earlier reports. It was, however, even

49. Reports on the radical press from 1923 to 1926 are in MI Microfilm, reel 23, pp. 2–217.

50. Ibid., reel 21, pp. 1–320, contains general information on the threat of Communist infiltration of the military, along with agents' reports on Crouch and Trumbull and reports from Hoover on the same subject. The handbill, entitled "The Perfect Soldier" and announcing a March 18, 1926, speech by Trumbull is on p. 78. See Bidwell, *History of Military Intelligence*, pp. 281–82, for the countersubversion work of Master Sergeant John J. Maurer.

51. Complete staffing and budget figures from 1920 to 1941 are charted in Bidwell, *History of Military Intelligence*, p. 258.

52. Emer Yeager, memorandum for G-2, War Department, July 22, 1926, MI Microfilm, reel 21, pp. 55–58.

more exaggerated, claiming that there were "at least 5,000,000 who are radically inclined." To reach that number, the report had to count all the people who had voted for Robert M. La Follette in his 1924 race for the presidency on the Progessive party ticket. Including them made perfect sense to the army because La Follette's platform had been "more or less socialistic."[53]

A similar report, untitled, had been completed in the previous spring by a Military Intelligence reserve officer on training duty with the Second Corps Area G-2. A rambling attack on pacifism, communism, and internationalism, the report does not appear to have been circulated at the highest levels of the War Department. Its bibliography, however, is fascinating: a list of private organizations offering information on "subversive activities." Located in New York City were the American Defense Society, the Military Order of the World War, the National Security League, and Key Men of America. Washington, D.C., had the Daughters of the Revolution and the Reserve Officers' Association, while the Sentinels of the Republic and the Public Service League were head-quartered in Boston. The Better America Federation operated out of Los Angeles, and Chicago was home to the Military Intelligence Association of the Sixth Corps Area, Inc.[54]

The formal withdrawal of the Bureau of Investigation and the military from spying on subversives was well known to thousands of Americans, and when they undertook to fill that void, the business of patriotism boomed. The reserve officer who compiled the above list was clearly well connected to that industry, but his inventory was far from complete. He omitted perhaps the most important, the National Civic Federation, which, under Ralph M. Easley, had been active since the war in opposing radicals. In 1924 Easley, who had excellent relations with the Bureau of Investigation while Burns was in charge, hired former MI volunteer and Lusk investigator Archibald Stevenson to head a Free Speech Committee of thirty lawyers to defend the occasional need to trample on civil liberties. One critic who attended a federation meeting saw Easley, the "dean of our prodigious, professional patriots," moderating while Stevenson peeked through the door "like a sinister gargoyle." Stevenson's contribution to great quotations was "We stand with the American people, and the American people are opposed to change."[55]

53. Stanley H. Ford, memorandum for the chief of staff, July 13, 1927, ibid., reel 22, pp. 1030–42.

54. Joseph A. Marion, the Second Corps Area G-2, forwarded the undated report in a memorandum for G-2, War Department, June 6, 1927, ibid., reel 23, pp. 288–302.

55. Marguerite Green, *The National Civic Federation and the American Labor Movement, 1900–1925* (Washington, D.C.: Catholic University of America Press, 1956), pp. 421–45.

Also missing from the reservist's list was the National Patriotic Builders of America, Inc., of New Rochelle, New York, whose president, Daisey A. Story, told Secretary of War Dwight F. Davis in 1928 that the Communists had "235 nuclei in the Army and Navy and 18 soldier clubs, with a membership of 785 soldiers."[56] Another omission was the American Vigilant Intelligence Federation in Chicago. Founded in 1923 by Harry A. Jung, head of the National Clay Products Industries Association, the group was so paranoid about Jews, immigrants, and Communists that even the American Legion was leery of it.[57]

The legion was at least as good a source on the Reds as the Daughters of the American Revolution (DAR). Happy to work with local intelligence officers, the veterans kept blacklists, published a *Bi-Weekly Report on Radicalism,* and kept informants in "various communist organizations."[58] The DAR was especially active in hunting radicals in the late 1920s, when its president-general was Grace H. Brosseau and Elsie W. Walker was first chair of the National Defense Committee.[59] Other groups not on the officer's list included the National Patriotic League, the Associated Industries of Cleveland (which said in 1930 that "one of our problems is to watch this radical movement"), the Constitutional League of America, the American Constitution Association, the American Citizenship Foundation, the United States Flag Association, the National Association for Constitutional Government, the Civil Legion, the Allied Patriotic Societies, the National Patriotic Council, the United States Patriotic Society, the Industrial Defense Association, and the American Coalition of Patriotic Societies (founded in 1929 by John B. Trevor, former head of the Military Intelligence office in New York).[60]

---

56. Dwight F. Davis to Mrs. William C. Story, October 6, 1928, MI Microfilm, reel 21, pp. 176–78. Although the G-2 called the report greatly exaggerated, the secretary ordered copies sent to all corps area commanders (Stanley H. Ford, memorandum for the chief of staff, October 8, 1928, pp. 174–75).

57. N. E. Hewitt to Dwight F. Davis, November 13, 1928, and Stanley H. Ford, memorandum for the adjutant general, ibid., reel 21, pp. 271–73. This report on communism in the military was also dispatched to army commanders. For more on Jung, see Pencak, *For God and Country,* p. 165; Murphy, *Meaning of Free Speech,* p. 174; and James S. Olson, *Historical Dictionary of the 1920s: From World War I to the New Deal, 1919–1933* (New York: Greenwood Press, 1988), p. 13.

58. Pencak, *For God and Country,* pp. 163–64. For information on the legion's subcommittee on "communism and radical activities," see U.S. Congress, Hearings before a Special Committee of the House of Representatives to Investigate Communist Activities in the United States, 71st Cong., 2d sess., *Investigation of Communist Propaganda,* 6 parts (Washington, D.C.: U.S. Government Printing Office, 1930), pt. 1, vol. 4, p. 394 (hereafter cited as Fish Hearings).

59. Murphy, *Meaning of Free Speech,* p. 197.

60. After the war, Trevor had turned to fighting for immigration restriction and, as an

Many of these groups were small and, like the Civil Legion organized in 1926 by Chicago attorney Frank Comerford, short-lived. Others became formidable institutions. Of those formed in the 1920s, perhaps the most aggressive was the Better America Federation. Growing out of the Commercial Federation of California in 1920, this Los Angeles group, like most of the others, was supported by big businesses. In 1921 Better America succeeded in having the *Nation* and the *New Republic* banned from the public schools of Los Angeles, and in 1923 it engineered the arrest of Upton Sinclair for disturbing the peace.[61] Of the several groups that played at the spy game and published "intelligence bulletins" by the late 1920s, the Better America Federation was emerging as one of the most serious. Another spry private group operated out of Minneapolis and kept its identity secret from Military Intelligence, though it provided weekly reports on radical activities. This anti-Communist, anti-black group managed to place an agent at the national convention of the Communist Party of America in Chicago in 1926.[62]

Military Intelligence's irregular contact with most of these groups was supplemented by reports from individuals. Francis R. Welsh was a private citizen whose fear of radicalism had been excited by the Lusk Committee report. From his home in Philadelphia, he conducted his own personal investigation into the Communists and radical groups such as the ACLU.[63] Other informants were officers in the army reserves, who, despite specific regulations issued after the Vancouver Barracks incident

adviser to U.S. Representative Albert Johnson, was one of the major contributors to the concept of quotas by national origin expressed in the immigration restriction law of 1924. John Higham interviewed Trevor in 1949 for his *Strangers in the Land: Patterns of American Nativism, 1860–1925* (New Brunswick: Rutgers University Press, 1955), pp. 314, 319–21, 324, 394. In the Cold War, Trevor's coalition continued to fight communism and call for strengthening the Federal Bureau of Investigation and the Central Intelligence Agency (Olsen, *Historical Dictionary of the 1920s*, p. 10). For additional information on these groups and their leaders, see Hapgood, *Professional Patriots*, and Murphy, *Meaning of Free Speech*.

61. Howard A. DeWitt, *Images of Ethnic and Radical Violence in California Politics, 1917–1930* (Saratoga, Calif.: R&E Research Associates, 1975), pp. 100–101. See also Edwin Layton, "The Better America Federation: A Case Study of Superpatriotism," *Pacific Historical Review* 30 (May 1961): 137–47.

62. The anonymous reports were forwarded to Washington from the Eighty-eighth Division headquarters in Minneapolis. They are attached to R. W. Case to G-2, War Department, MI Microfilm, reel 23, pp. 230–87.

63. See Welsh's untitled report of April 1, 1925, ibid., reel 20, pp. 1000–1002; other undated reports are on pp. 993–95, 998. The army informed Welsh that it had "nothing to do with any such civilian activities" and sent his reports to the Department of Justice (Mark Brooks to director, Bureau of Investigation, April 7, 1925, p. 996; S. C. Sturgis to the adjutant general, April 3, 1925, p. 999). See also Welsh's testimony before the Fish Hearings, pt. 1, vol. 4, pp. 111–58.

of 1922, continued to spy on the Reds. The Cleveland chapter of the Reserve Officers Association, for example, arranged to have a Methodist preacher attend the Communists' 1927 May Day activities.[64] The New York reserve headquarters wrote its members in late 1926 urging opposition to the peace activists. Among the groups on the list to be watched were the American Federation of Teachers and the Women's Christian Temperance Union. Also in 1926, the Indiana Reserve Officers' Association asked its fellows to oppose the American Association of University Women for aiding the National Council for the Prevention of War.[65]

No doubt the most active intelligence officer in the reserves was Captain Harry C. Lear of Detroit. Out of one office, he ran the Michigan Department of the Reserve Officers Association and the American Centre of the International Entente against the Third International and published the *Industrial Intelligence Bulletin*. He was also connected with ROTC and with the National Guard and communicated directly with the War Department's G-2, Colonel Stanley H. Ford, who promoted him and suggested that copies of his reports be sent to J. Edgar Hoover.[66] In Chicago, former army spies created their own private group in 1923, the Military Intelligence Association of the Sixth Corps Area, with no official connection to the army. The group caused a good deal of noise in the area by opposing radical meetings, especially those of Jane Addams, but it remained small and apparently conducted no formal investigations.[67] The Military Order of the World War was made up of former officers, and though it was much smaller than the American Legion, it was just as outspoken against "parlor bolsheviks, agitators, internationalists, communists, Bolsheviks and anarchists." The group publicly attacked historian Charles A. Beard and in 1927 suggested that Columbia University's Carlton J. H. Hayes, a former intelligence officer, be "kicked out of the university bodily."[68]

If the entire membership of these organizations, especially the American Legion, the DAR, and the Ku Klux Klan is counted, there were

64. Herbert Turner to G-2, War Department, April 30, 1927, MI Microfilm, reel 21, p. 2.

65. The New York and Indiana letters are reprinted in Hapgood, *Professional Patriots*, pp. 123–28. The latter caused an uproar because it was mailed postage-free in envelopes supplied by the army.

66. Ford to Lear, February 10, December 14, 1928, MI Microfilm, reel 21, pp. 205, 270; Lear to Ford, February 4, November 13, December 11, 1928, pp. 169, 172, 206.

67. See the association's October 31, 1923, report, "Communism: A World-Wide Program of Conquest and Revolution," by Ralph E. Duncan, ibid., reel 23, pp. 218–29.

68. Hapgood, *Professional Patriots*, pp. 172–74; the Sixth Corps Area association is described on pp. 176–77.

plainly far more anti-Communists than there were Communists in the late 1920s. That roaring and materialistic decade saw no successes for the radicals, and the general public had little time for social issues. Tom Mooney remained in jail, and in 1927 Nicola Sacco and Bartolomeo Vanzetti, the two most famous anarchists of the period, who were arrested during the Red Scare for robbery and murder, went to their deaths.[69] Flush times produced few angry young men, but when the decade ended so did the prosperity. In the Great Depression, the work of private organizations was not sufficient to combat a resurgent radicalism. Once again, Military Intelligence awakened.

69. Military Intelligence seems to have been uninvolved in either the investigation or the hysteria associated with the trial of the two famous anarchists.

CHAPTER 12

The Great Depression

The trauma of the early 1930s—massive unemployment, unprecedented misery, and a Republican administration hamstrung by its laizzez-faire philosophy—brought a renewal of both radical activity and repression. With the great and violent 1929 Gastonia, North Carolina, textile strike as a prelude, 1930 saw street fighting and the highest level of Communist activity since the Red Scare. Organizing the unemployed into councils, the Communists led a march of the hungry on Washington in 1931. The following year a much larger and less radical army of discontented veterans descended on the capital. Not since World War I, as the Better America Federation told Chief of Staff Douglas MacArthur, had "the general revolutionary activity throughout the United States been more intensive and portentious."[1] In early 1933, the chairman of the Anti-Radical Committee of the Detroit Council of National Defense informed Naval Intelligence that conditions were so bad in the automobile city that military reserve units had pulled out their White Plans to face the revolution. Rumors carried in the Detroit press and repeated in intelligence reports had it that "40 to 60 Moscow trained riot organizers" were preparing for a showdown with "350 Secret Service men." In 1934, the army passed to J. Edgar Hoover the report that Leon Trotsky had secretly entered San Francisco to lead the workers in revolution.[2]

Congress was not long in facing the new threat from the left, and in early 1930, after much lobbying by the National Civic Federation, the

1. Margaret A. Kerr to MacArthur, July 30, 1932, in Randolph Boehm, ed., *U.S. Military Intelligence Reports: Surveillance of Radicals in the United States, 1917–1941* (Frederick, Md.: University Publications of America, 1984), reel 22, pp. 72–73 (hereafter cited as MI Microfilm).

2. Commandant, Ninth Naval District, to director of Naval Intelligence, February 17, 1933, MI Microfilm, reel 29, p. 687; Hoover to C. K. Nulsen, September 24, 1934, reel 25, p. 309. There is some disagreement in American historiography as to the level of turbulence in the Depression. Most historians downplay the labor and radical violence, as well as the intensity of vigilante and private antiradical groups, but Bruce Nelson, *Workers on the Waterfront: Seamen, Longshoremen and Unionism in the 1930s* (Urbana: University of Illinois Press, 1988), and Harvey Klehr, *The Heyday of American Communism, the Depression Decade* (New York: Basic Books, 1984), suggest that a slight upward revision in the estimation of the temperature of the times may be in order.

House of Representatives authorized a special committee to investigate communism. Led by Hamilton Fish, Republican from New York and one of the founders of the American Legion, the committee undertook a national survey that lasted nearly a year.[3] Dominated by superpatriot organizations, the Fish Committee provided the most thorough and hysterical study of the American left since the Lusk investigation of 1919. Although the chairman occasionally observed that the committee was limited to a scrutiny of communism and had no authority to investigate "socialism, radicalism, pacifism, and what not," his admonitions were generally futile. The ultra right insisted on describing the conspiracy to undermine America.[4]

More than any other threat, it was the Young Pioneers, the children's branch of the Young Communist League, that dismayed the committee. With the motto "Smash the Boy Scouts" and units in sixty-three cities, the Young Pioneers had taken their fight to the schools, where their un-Americanism was obvious in their refusal to give the pledge of allegiance to the flag.[5] From Fish's perspective, however, the most important function of the committee was to bring to the public's attention the deplorable fact that the federal intelligence community was not authorized "to deal with the communistic activities."[6] In building a case for national intervention, the Fish Committee amassed a wonderful survey of both the right and the left in 1930. All the great players appeared. The director of the speakers bureau of the Better America Federation reported its membership at five hundred and cited its missions as sponsoring an annual collegiate oratorical contest on the Constitution and gathering information on "subversive movements" for dissemination in

3. Ralph Easley of the National Civic Federation described his role in getting the hearings approved in a May 22, 1930, letter to War Department G-2 Colonel Stanley H. Ford, MI Microfilm, reel 23, pp. 322–23.

4. U.S. House of Representatives, 71st Cong., 2d sess., *Hearings before a Special Committee to Investigate Communist Activities in the U.S.*, 6 parts (Washington, D.C.: U.S. Government Printing Office, 1930), pt. 5, vol. 3, p. 327 (hereafter referred to as Fish Hearings). Fish himself was hardly a liberal. In a radio address he once charged that the nation's major universities were "honeycombed with Socialists, near Communists and Communists" (quoted in William Pencak, *For God and Country: The American Legion, 1919–1941* [Boston: Northeastern University Press, 1989], pp. 241–42; see also *New York Times*, November 30, 1930).

5. Fish Hearings, pt. 3, vol. 1, pp. 1–72. Copies of the Young Pioneers' organ, *New Pioneer*, along with over six hundred pages of other Communist publications from the early 1930s, are grouped together in MI Microfilm, reels 26 and 27. The *New Pioneer* featured a fascinating comic strip called "Pioneers"; see reel 26, p. 969, for an episode in which "children of jobless parents" march on city hall and force the mayor to keep their school open in the summer "as a feeding center."

6. Fish Hearings, pt. 5, vol. 2, p. 109.

its bulletin. The real culprit, according to Better America, was Roger Baldwin's American Civil Liberties Union, which had "utilized its dastardly political influence to have our Department of Justice prohibited from investigating radicalism." Calling the motives of the ACLU "all bad," the group cited it as a "typical respectable friend or aid society" to the Communists, a relationship only too apparent, since William Z. Foster was on the ACLU's board. In an update of the Spider Web Chart, the federation gave the committee a copy of "The Tie That Binds," which showed the "interlockage" between "Radical, Pacifist, Defeatist, Socialist and International Societies."[7]

The National Security League agreed that it was "only common sense" to allow the Department of Justice to spy on the Communists. An officer of the Birmingham Ku Klux Klan reported that his concern over the lack of federal action had led his group to create its own surveillance program.[8] Fish also welcomed Father Charles Coughlin of the Shrine of the Little Flower in Royal Oak, Michigan, who railed against the Illuminati, Socialists, Communists, Henry Ford, and J. P. Morgan. The committee even printed his sermons as exhibits.[9] Fish was less kind to A. Philip Randolph, the president of the Brotherhood of Sleeping Car Porters, whose name was introduced into the committee's official record with the parenthetical notation "Colored." A fascinating and tense exchange occurred with Fish when Randolph tried to explain why blacks were discontented. Fish saw an otherwise complacent black population agitated by the insidious propaganda of the Communists.[10] Also testifying was Nelson E. Hewitt, statistician of the American Vigilant Intelligence Federation in Chicago. Along with supplying numerous documents to the committee, he claimed that the private spy group had infiltrated many Communist meetings in Chicago and throughout the nations.[11]

The only official Military Intelligence representative to appear before the Fish Committee, the G-2 of the Ninth Corps Area in San Francisco, limited himself to a discussion of "communist activity in the military service," which he found "wholly ineffective." A number of reservists

7. The testimony of the Better America Federation is in ibid., pt. 5, vol. 3, pp. 1–136, 329–423; the comment on the ACLU and Justice is on p. 335; the chart is inserted between pp. 78 and 79. Baldwin's defense of the ACLU, and his denial that he was a Communist, is in pt. 1, vol. 4, pp. 405–17. See also the testimony of Upton Sinclair, founder of the ACLU branch in southern California and Socialist candidate for governor, pt. 5, vol. 3, pp. 324–29.

8. The National Security League testimony is in ibid., pt. 3, vol. 1, pp. 227–36; the Klan is in pt. 6, vol. 1, pp. 193–200. The Klansman reported that his unit's interest in Communists sprang "mainly from the fact [that] they were teaching social equality between the whites and the blacks."

9. Ibid., pt. 4. vol. 1, pp. 18–70.

10. Ibid., pt. 3, vol. 1, pp. 242–51.

11. Ibid., pt. 4, vol. 2, pp. 331–32.

and former army intelligence officers, however, reported in detail on their operations against the left. Reserve Major Walter L. Furbershaw of Chicago attacked the ACLU for aiding the Reds, described his personal campaign of surveillance, and gave the committee Communist documents. Jacob Spolansky, of Detroit, testified that he had been in Military Intelligence during the war and had worked as a covert agent for Hoover during the Red Scare. "I participated," he claimed, "in every major operation instituted by the Government against the anarchists and communists." He left the Department of Justice in 1924 and wrote on radicals for the *Chicago Daily News* before being hired as an expert on communism by the Detroit Employers Association and the National Metal Trades Association. The Fish Committee, while in Detroit, also heard from Harry C. Lear, now a major in the Military Intelligence reserve. He had been active against Communists for the past five years and noted that he forwarded his reports to the army, navy, and Department of Justice.[12]

Edwin M. Cason, of the Atlanta police department, told the committee that his ability to recognize Communist literature stemmed from his service with Military Intelligence during the war, and he amplified the testimony of officers from other police radical squads around the country that they were receiving no help from the federal government.[13] These local police operated under criminal syndicalist and Red flag laws which had remained on the books, and in some cases had been strengthened, since the Red Scare.[14] Despite the obvious concern of law enforcement authorities and the Fish Committee's recommendation for a harsh crackdown on the Reds by the Justice Department, including deportation, no federal version of the states' syndicalist laws was enacted. J. Edgar Hoover refused to unleash his agents, afraid that liberal criticism would destroy the limited espionage program he had kept hidden from even his supporters. The small peacetime army likewise hesitated to renew its fight against radicalism. The warnings of the Fish Committee seemed unheeded in Washington.[15]

12. The G-2's report is in ibid., pt. 5, vol. 2, pp. 117–34; Furbershaw is in pt. 4, vol. 2, pp. 338–400. Spolansky is in pt. 4, vol. 1, pp. 174–282; Lear is in pp. 116–20.

13. Ibid., pt. 6, vol. 1, pp. 232–35. The longest police report, offering an extensive set of documents on communism in the 1920s, came from Captain William F. Hynes of Los Angeles (pt. 5, vol. 4, pp. 2–1572). Seattle and Portland each had a full-time police investigator infiltrating the Communists (pt. 5, vol. 1, pp. 90–105, 140–45).

14. The Fish Committee had the Library of Congress prepare a summary and analysis of these various state laws (pt. 5, vol. 3, pp. 425–58).

15. For more on the Fish Committee, see August R. Ogden, *The Dies Committee: A Study of the Special House Committee for the Investigation of Un-American Activities, 1938–1944* (Washington, D.C.: Catholic University of America Press, 1945), pp. 20–32. For Hoover's strategy, see David Williams, " 'They Never Stopped Watching Us': FBI Political

Retired Major General Ralph Van Deman was not about to let the forces of evil overwhelm the country, however, and after the Fish report he decided to take action. From his home in San Diego, Van Deman opened his spy shop in early 1932. Working as feverishly as he had during the war, he soon built a semiprivate agency that left the other patriotic groups in the dust. He had the contacts and the ability to sell the same service he had offered in 1917. With no federal agency fighting the radicals, Van Deman once again became the clearinghouse. Ever secret, never appearing before a congressional committee or seeking publicity in any way, he managed to secure the support of private and official agencies, state and national. The arrangements Van Deman made with the army, the navy, and the Federal Bureau of Investigation (which added Federal to its name in 1935) remain obscure, primarily because his files, now housed in the National Archives, are only partially open. It is clear, however, that after 1940 Van Deman had an official relationship with the Federal Bureau of Investigation (FBI) and received funds from the army to underwrite the cost of his work. Van Deman ruled a large and sophisticated spy network until his death at the age of eighty-six in 1952. The bulk of his material then went to Military Intelligence, where it was incorporated into files used by the army, navy, and FBI until the early 1960s.[16] Whether the army had a formal agreement with Van Deman in the 1930s, there was certainly a friendly working arrangement at the local level. Within months after setting up for business, Van Deman began receiving reports from the intelligence officer of the Eleventh Naval District in San Diego and, somewhat later, from the G-2 of the Ninth Corps in San Francisco.

He also established close ties with the Better America Federation and the American Vigilant Intelligence Federation. He received information from Archibald Stevenson, who had become chairman of the Subversive Movements Department of the National Civic Federation, and he stayed in touch with John Trevor, who continued to agitate for stronger deporta-

Surveillance, 1924–1936," UCLA Historical Journal 2 (1981): 18.

16. Records of the army's acquisition of the Van Deman files are in Record Group 319, ACSI Files, box 28–24–4, National Archives, Suitland Records Center. A description of them, based on an army report prepared by this writer, along with an account of their 1971 transferral to the Senate Internal Security Subcommittee, is in New York Times, September 7, 1971. The Van Deman papers themselves are in Record Group 46, Records of the U.S. Senate, Internal Security Subcommittee of the Senate Judiciary Committee, 1951–1975, Van Deman's Investigative Files, National Archives (hereafter referred to as Van Deman Files). The FBI also has a file on Van Deman, available in the agency's Reading Room in Washington, which sheds considerable light on his World War II relationship with the bureau and with the army, as well as on the bureau's decision not to fight the army over custody of Van Deman's files.

tion laws. The radical squads of the San Diego and Los Angeles police departments shared the reports of their informants with him, as did various county sheriffs. He worked with several private detective agencies and had harmonious and productive relationships with the Industrial Association of San Francisco and the Associated Farmers of California, Inc., both of which had their own intelligence networks fighting the radical threat from the wharves of San Francisco to the lush fields of the Imperial Valley.[17] In addition, he received occasional intelligence from the Border Patrol and the Coast Guard, and he directed the work of a number of concerned private citizens who reported to him.[18] An assistant postmaster aided him by providing tracings of the addresses on suspicious envelopes. Eventually Van Deman secured copies, and sometimes the originals, of radical correspondence intercepted by unknown means.[19] Van Deman directed his informants in covert operations against labor, Communist, and fascist organizations, and his files are a marvelous window on the fight against subversion in the 1930s.

The deepening depression and obvious Communist activity eventually forced the military to change its policy of not spying on civilians in peacetime. When a new War Department G-2, Colonel Alfred T. Smith, asked on February 19, 1931, for permission to lift the restrictions, Chief of Staff Douglas MacArthur's initial reaction was to reject the proposal. In June, in response to an inquiry on communism from a National Guard officer in Florida, the army dutifully referred him to the Fish Committee, noting that "the War Department does not make any investigation of individuals or groups outside of the military service, nor engage in any acts which might savor of military espionage of our own people."[20] Shortly thereafter, MacArthur agreed to allow, on a temporary basis, field intelligence units to forward to Washington monthly reports on radicalism. This arrangement was formalized on December 11, 1931, when instructions from the adjutant general required each corps area headquarters to provide secret monthly summaries on "The General

17. California in the 1930s was especially tense. See Nelson, *Workers on the Waterfront;* Charles P. Larrowe, *Harry Bridges: The Rise and Fall of Radical Labor in the U.S.* (New York: Lawrence Hill, 1972); and Cletus E. Daniel, *Bitter Harvest: A History of California Farmworkers, 1870–1940* (Ithaca: Cornell University Press, 1981).

18. In the thirteen boxes of the Van Deman Files presently open to the public, covering the period from January 1932 to late 1939, there are no reports from the Department of Justice.

19. The tracings are in ibid., R-679, R-684a, and R-689a, box 3, and in R-970, box 4. Box 7 has numerous files with intercepted letters.

20. Albert E. Barrs to F. Trubee Davison, June 11, 1931, and Davison to Barrs, June 22, 1931, MI Microfilm, reel 23, pp. 387–88.

Subversive Situation."[21] The initial cause for the renewal of domestic surveillance seems to have been the formation of Unemployed Councils by the Communists and the announced plan by those groups for a National Hunger March on Washington for December 7, 1931.[22] Only about sixteen hundred marchers came to the capital, and there was no difficulty with the police. Communist agitation mounted with the new year, and in March a confrontation in Detroit between the radicals and police armed with machine guns left four dead and sixty wounded.[23]

Because the 1931 directive allowed for the collection of information only through liaison and from the press, Military Intelligence reporting in early 1932 remained fairly general, containing comments on pacifists, bank closings, unemployment, relief efforts, and natural disasters, along with descriptions of local hunger demonstrations. Some units were able to get information from police or private organizations with agents inside Communist groups, but most of the army reports were so inferior that the Washington G-2's office began a systematic evaluation of each summary in order to train units grown unaccustomed to collecting domestic intelligence. Some of these early submissions are, nevertheless, very interesting. A February 15 memorandum from Portland, Maine, for example, revealed the work of a "secret agent" of the Veterans of Foreign Wars who had infiltrated a group who "call themselves Socialists, but are actually Communists."[24] Military Intelligence also became briefly concerned about the New History Society, led by Alice C. Chanler, a prominent New Yorker and convert to the Bahai faith. The reserve officer assigned to investigate found that it was "Utopian, futile, and wholly

---

21. On MacArthur's decisions, see Bruce W. Bidwell, *History of the Military Intelligence Division, Department of the Army General Staff, 1775–1941* (Frederick, Md.: University Publications of America, 1986), pp. 281–82. The New York reserve office issued similar reporting instructions on October 14, 1931, spurring the unit in Rochester to send informers to radical meetings and to give "much secret advice" to the American Legion and other patriotic groups (Robert J. Halpin to commanding general, Ninety-eighth Division, November 3, 1931, MI Microfilm, reel 24, pp. 585–86). The December order activating local reporting has not been located, but subsequent reports all cite it as a reference. The summaries, which began in January 1932, are in reels 24–32, except for those from the Ninth Corps Area, which have been lost. Although the formal monthly requirement was discontinued on March 14, 1934, corps areas were encouraged to make reports as necessary. In 1935, the security classification was reduced to "confidential" and the messages were dubbed "informal reports," a practice which continued until World War II.

22. For the Communist plan of organization for the march and for defense against expected attacks by the American Legion, see "Directives on the Organization and Tasks of Defense Groups during the National Hunger March, December 7, 1931," in MI Microfilm, reel 27, pp. 414–23.

23. Klehr, *Heyday of American Communism*, pp. 56–60.

24. Lucius C. Bennett to commanding general, First Corps Area, February 15, 1932, MI Microfilm, reel 24, pp. 97–98.

innocuous . . . made up largely of emotionally unbalanced women."[25] The G-2 at Fort McPherson in Atlanta expressed no fear in his first report about Red action among the blacks, deciding that the "vast majority of the Negroes are not sufficiently intelligent to grasp the Communistic doctrines."[26]

That Military Intelligence was rusty and slow to respond was evident when it was caught off guard by the famous Bonus March of 1932. Under the Adjusted Compensation Act of 1924, veterans were given certificates for a bonus payable in 1945. With the Depression, demands had risen for immediate payment, and when President Herbert Hoover vetoed the Bonus bill, calls for a march on Washington developed. Elements of the Bonus Expeditionary Force (BEF) were on the move when G-2 Smith met with Chief of Staff MacArthur on May 24 to discuss the possible implementation of Plan White for the nation's capital. A check with the Washington police produced the estimate that a force of up to seven thousand veterans would reach Washington by June 8, and coordination with the Department of Justice revealed the disconcerting news that it had no special plans for supplying timely information to the army. More distressing was the report "from reliable sources" that the march was being used by the Communists "as a forerunner and foundation for a series of national demonstrations planned to agitate the recognition of Russia by the United States." Passing that information to all corps area G-2s, Washington ordered them to provide "an informal daily air mail report" on the progress of Bonus marchers in their districts. Also beginning on May 25, and each day thereafter, the Washington G-2 gave MacArthur a national situation summary. On May 26, Colonel Smith told MacArthur that "neither the Department of Justice nor the local police of Washington appear to have the information which the War Department has as to the real [Communist] purpose behind this demonstration."[27]

25. Andrew Ten Eyck to G-2, Second Corps Area, n.d., probably April 1932, ibid., pp. 654–56.

26. "Military Intelligence: The G-2 Estimate of the Subversive Situation in the Fourth Corps Area," January 1, 1932, ibid., reel 28, pp. 169–73.

27. Alfred T. Smith, memorandum for the chief of staff, May 25 and 26, 1932, ibid., reel 21, pp. 764, 748; William H. Wilson to G-2, Sixth Corps Area, May 25, 1932, p. 765; Paul C. Paschal, memorandum for the G-2, May 25, 1932, pp. 762–63. Army estimates of the role of Communists in the Bonus Army were incorrect; the Bonus leadership was definitely anti-Communist. See Klehr, *Heyday of American Communism*, pp. 60–61; and Benjamin Gitlow, *The Whole of Their Lives: Communism in America—A Personal History and Intimate Portrayal of Its Leaders* (New York: Charles Scribner & Sons, 1948), pp. 229–34. The reporting requirement generated a large file on the Bonus March in MI Microfilm, running from p. 321 of reel 21 to p. 206 of reel 22. Reel 27, pp. 223–64, has copies of the New York *B.E.F. Crusader* and the Washington *B.E.F. News* for the summer of 1932. All military communications about the march were classified secret. Despite MI's claim, Hoover in the Department of Justice was concerned about Communist influence in the

After personally viewing a march of five thousand veterans, Smith intensified the intelligence effort on June 10 when he demanded coded radio reports of the progress of other units to Washington. Special emphasis, the orders said, was to be placed on identifying "communistic elements and names of leaders of known communistic leanings."[28] The G-2 told MacArthur that "the communists have utterly failed in what they started out to do," but he anticipated that "they will undoubtedly continue working and will increase their efforts to spread propaganda and unrest [and] the longer the veterans are congregated here the greater will the danger become." He thought it imperative "that their departure be encouraged in every practical way."[29] As names of veterans were received from the police, Smith had the army's personnel files searched for information on these individuals, until MacArthur ordered the effort terminated on June 20.[30]

Army units collected information throughout the country, primarily by the close liaison Washington had urged with local Justice agents and police. The most active corps area G-2s seem to have been in Chicago, where considerable information was gained from the American Vigilant Intelligence Federation, and at Fort Sam Houston. The latter requested permission to insert an intelligence policeman into a Bonus group in Dallas "and have him hobo it with them to Washington [and become] a persona grata in the group while at the capitol." Such a covert operation required the approval of the secretary of war, and by the time Patrick J. Hurley gave his authorization, the Bonus element had already left Texas. Having missed his opportunity, the Eighth Corps Area G-2, Colonel L. B. Clapham, complained to Smith in Washington that

> Some Government agency should take positive action to obtain first-hand reliable information on the plans and tendencies of this [Bonus] force. . . . We realize fully the War Department's policy in restrictions regarding non-interference . . . and the reasons back of such a policy. Nevertheless, I believe the Army could do a great deal more in gaining information . . . and do so with utmost discretion and secrecy. . . . I believe that we could work without such restriction and close the door "before the horse is stolen."[31]

BEF. See Williams, "They Never Stopped Watching Us," pp. 15–16.

28. Quoted in Roger Daniels, *The Bonus March: An Episode of the Great Depression* (Westport, Conn.: Greenwood Press, 1971), p. 159. Smith's description of the June 7 parade is in his memorandum for the chief of staff, June 8, 1932, MI Microfilm, reel 21, p. 662.

29. Smith, memorandum for the chief of staff, June 8, 1932, MI Microfilm, reel 21, pp. 663–64.

30. Smith's memorandum for the chief of staff, June 21, 1932, has the handwritten note: "This report [from personnel files] not sent. Discontinued on June 20th, 'by order of Chief of Staff'" (ibid., p. 545).

31. L. B. Clapham to Smith, June 8, 1932, ibid., pp. 667–68. For the tardy approval of

When Washington failed to respond, the Texas G-2 gave up and did not propose to penetrate the next group of marchers who came through later in June. Had he done so, his man could have provided the continuity lost when Van Deman's informant, who had joined the group in Los Angeles, left it at Dallas and made his way to Washington alone. At El Paso, however, this particular caravan had been interviewed by army agents from Fort Bliss. These operatives and Van Deman's plant cited dissatisfaction with Royal W. Robertson, who led the contingent of 150 cars and two small airplanes and who was thought to be pocketing much of the money he raised along the way. Van Deman's agent and other army reports did not agree with Fort Bliss's assessment that the Robertson group was "under Communistic Influences." Colonel James Totten certainly did, seeing Communists everywhere. When he learned that Hollywood's Metro-Goldwyn-Mayer motion picture studio intended to provide transportation for another body of marchers from California, he told Washington that the studio was "100 per cent Jewish as to controlling personnel," involved in politics, and possibly funded by the Soviet Union.[32]

Remaining somewhat calmer than his Texas subordinates, the Washington G-2 relied heavily on the district's police department for information. Relations between the agencies were good, and a steady stream of reports came in from the Crime Prevention Bureau, which undertook to maintain an accurate count of the number of veterans in their several encampments. Military Intelligence also augmented its staff with reserve officers, who circulated among the protesters and took notes at speeches. Other army teams ran a series of reconnaisance missions tracking the veterans' locations and numbers. Though estimates varied, and those from the Veterans Administration were usually the lowest, the district police put the number on July 4 at just over twenty thousand. Bonus ranks decreased sharply after Congress agreed to advance a small

the covert operation, see Smith, memorandum for the adjutant general, June 7, 1932, p. 684.

32. Hq., Eighth Corps Area, to the adjutant general, June 27, 1932, ibid., p. 858; also quoted in Daniels, *Bonus March*, p. 160. On Fort Bliss, see William Nalle to G-2, Eighth Corps Area, June 25, 1932, MI Microfilm, reel 21, pp. 859–60. The debriefing of Van Deman's informant is in Van Deman Files, R-1015, box 4. The Van Deman Files have several items on suspected Red influence in Hollywood in the 1930s, including a Better America complaint about James Cagney (R-543, box 2), an undated copy of a letter from Will Rogers to Harry A. Hopkins (R-670c, box 3), literature from the Workers Film and Photo League of Hollywood (R-745, box 3), a Naval Intelligence report on communism at MGM (R-1620, box 7), and a Better America agent's report of a 1936 meeting of the Hollywood Anti-Nazi League in Defense of American Democracy, sponsored by Eddie Cantor, Frederick March, and Dorothy Parker and attended by navy agents (R-1709 and R-1709a, box 7). Similar 1937 navy reports to Van Deman are in R-1813 and R-1948, box 8.

portion of the money, still payable in 1945, to enable the frightening veterans to get out of town.

Although communication between BEF commander Walter E. Waters and Washington Police Superintendent Pelham D. Glassford had generally been open and cordial, conditions began to deteriorate in late July, when an estimated six thousand die-hards remained. Most of the veterans were camped in the flats along the Anacostia River, but some had taken over vacant government buildings scheduled for demolition. When the district commissioners ordered the downtown sites evacuated, Colonel Smith told MacArthur that, though Robertson appeared ready to leave, Waters had "adopted a defiant attitude." The crisis came down to a building at Third Street and Pennsylvania, N.W., which, according to an army report, had been reinforced by recalcitrant veterans armed with clubs. Smith blamed the problem on the district authorities, who had failed to enforce earlier eviction notices. "The psychological effect of so many false starts," he told MacArthur, "is sure to give the bonus marchers the idea that they have the authorities 'bluffed.' This has undoubtedly lessened to a great degree the chance of evicting the bonus marchers without the use of force."[33]

The intelligence chief proved entirely correct, and on the following day, when police attempted to oust the marchers, violence erupted, leaving four dead. When the district government asked President Hoover for military help. General MacArthur, assisted by his aide Major Dwight D. Eisenhower, led the troops in clearing the downtown area and then proceeded to raze the shanty town in the Anacostia flats. There is some argument about whether President Hoover had intended for MacArthur to move against all the veterans, but there is no doubt about the effect of the Bonus March on Military Intelligence.[34] Having been once again turned on, the army ventured further into espionage against subversives. The official line in Washington remained that Military Intelligence did not actively collect information on civilians, but the Bonus March left field

33. Smith, memoranda for the chief of staff, July 22 and 27, 1932, MI Microfilm, reel 22, pp. 106–7, 137–38.

34. Secretary of War Patrick J. Hurley's order to MacArthur was "Surround the affected area and clear it without delay." He did not explain if he meant only the occupied buildings in the government triangle or if he meant to include all the camp sites (Hurley to MacArthur, July 28, 1932, ibid., reel 22, p. 99). Hurley's press release of August 3, 1932, defending the army and accusing the BEF of having come "more and more under the influence of a number of so-called red, radical agitators after many of the genuine veterans had left," is in reel 21, pp. 503–5. MacArthur's after-action report is reprinted in Daniels, Bonus March, pp. 291–307. Donald Lisio, The President and Protest: Hoover, Conspiracy, and the Bonus Riot (Columbia: University of Missouri Press, 1974), should be used in conjunction with Daniel's work in examining Hoover's and MacArthur's roles.

units with well-developed sources: volunteer informants, reserve officers and ROTC instructors, patriotic societies, law enforcement agencies, press reports, and direct observation by army agents.

Uncertain as to what kind of information Washington desired, intelligence officers in the field tended to report whatever came to them. In the late summer of 1933, the War Department told the Chicago G-2 that at the national office "the clerical force here is not sufficient to make use of such detailed information." Washington itself was unsure of what data it required. Though it was obvious, as Chicago was told, that "the fact that a number of communists held a picnic need not be reported," it was equally true that "names of leaders are valuable." In the end, Washington confessed, there was "no rule of thumb."[35] Lacking firm instructions, the G-2s filled their monthly surveys of the general subversive situation with a wide variety of information and made special reports highlighting particular events. The 1931 requirement included general questions about public attitudes, and the very nature of the Depression made subversion and possible subversion very broad topics. The February 7, 1933, submission from the First Corps Area in Boston was typical. "Former loyal and patriotic citizens" were reported to be "particularly bitter against the local banks," and a "confidential meeting" of businessmen led by the Boston Emergency Relief Campaign was reported in detail. A Catholic priest told the group that the church "holds that it is not immoral for a man to steal food if he is hungry and does not have money to buy it" and that "if we ignore the 'distant thunder' caused by discontent, revolution would result."[36]

Of the twenty-seven items included in a May 9, 1933, report from the New York G-2, seventeen came from the press, seven from volunteer informants, and three from handbills (called "dodgers") picked up by agents on the street. Seven of the entries involved pacifist meetings, mostly on university campuses. Six focused on the activities of radical and nationalistic foreigners in the United States and an equal number on Communist meetings and office locations. Farm and labor unrest were mentioned three separate times. Two items discussed student protests at Columbia University: one over the firing of a professor and another against the famous Scottsboro, Alabama, convictions of several black youths for rape. Anti-Nazi activities were mentioned twice. A rally at Union square "in a protest demonstration against Hitler and his government" drew 10,000 people. The other involved "15,000 communists and

35. C. K. Nulsen to T. A. Clark, September 15, 1933, MI Microfilm, reel 29, p. 876.
36. Fox Conner to the adjutant general, February 7, 1933, ibid., reel 24, pp. 226–30.

sympathizers" at Madison Square Garden, organized "by the Communists with the support of some liberals." The election in Buffalo of seventeen representatives from "fifty organizations representing trade unions, fraternal organizations, and political societies" to attend a "Free Tom Mooney Congress" in Chicago was the subject of a single entry.[37]

Prominent names in the summary included Nicholas Murray Butler, president of Columbia University, cited for his connection with the Carnegie Endowment for International Peace, and Roger Baldwin and Malcolm Cowley, who spoke against Hitler at the Madison Square Garden event. Norman Thomas and Heywood C. Broun were reported for playing similar roles at Union Square. Jeannette Rankin and Mary H. Swope were listed for their appearance before a mass meeting of the Women's International League for Peace and Freedom on the steps of the city hall in New York. Reinhold Niebuhr was included as one of the Columbia faculty who had signed an anti-ROTC petition. Of the sixty-three names in the report, twenty-four were educators. In its evaluation, the Washington office asked for further information on "any direct support to pacifist organizations by the Carnegie Endowment for International Peace" and noted that the analysis of widespread pacifism among the students of Columbia University "corresponds with reports from other colleges."

Concern about student pacifism was so great that in late 1933 the Sixth Corps Area G-2 ordered his press relations officer to attend and report on a national meeting of the Student Congress Against War at the University of Chicago. Since Communist party secretary Earl Browder was a speaker, it "was evident from the beginning that the Congress was under Communistic influence, if not control." Scott Nearing and Jane Addams also addressed the delegates, who were "of foreign appearance with the Jewish type predominating."[38] When communist-front organizations led student antiwar strikes each spring from 1934 to 1936, their

37. J. E. Woodward to the adjutant general, May 9, 1933, ibid., pp. 1018–31. The following paragraph is from the same source. Attached to this secret report, selected only as a sample, are statements from volunteer informants; the evaluation by Washington is on pp. 1032–33. In the Van Deman Files, information on the Mooney cause is in boxes 8–13. Almost always, the army reports of this period were marked by an unprofessional hysteria and a distinct rightist orientation, but occasionally a product was more objective and informative. See, for example, the February 7, 1933, report from a reserve officer detailing the problem of hunger in Los Angeles County and the crisis of food cooperatives caught in the struggle between conservatives and radicals (MI Microfilm, reel 23, pp. 501–5). The August 18, 1932, report, "Survey of the Negro Population in New York City," is also by a reserve officer and is less racist than most of its kind for the period. See reel 27, pp. 218–22.

38. Grattan McCafferty to commanding general, Sixth Corps Area, January 4, 1933, MI Microfilm, reel 33, pp. 615–22.

activities on New York and New Jersey campuses were monitored by the Second Corps Area.[39] Van Deman's 1936 list of "Radical Professors and Teachers" included John Dewey, John Dos Passos, Felix Frankfurter, Sidney Hook, Reinhold Niebuhr, Rexford G. Tugwell, and Howard W. Odum.[40]

A movement among blacks was identified by Military Intelligence in the fall of 1933 when reports starting coming in from the Midwest that Japanese agents were organizing, to quote the membership card, a "Pacific movement of the Eastern World aiming to establish a confraternity among the darker races of the World." The proper title seems to have been the Fellowship of God and the Brotherhood of Man, but the general term used by Military Intelligence was "Pacific Movement."[41] The G-2 in Kansas City regarded the program as "simply a racket," but, as he told Washington, "some of my colleagues, apparently, hold different opinions. The 'Pacific Movement' has almost as many investigators as it has members: Immigration Service, Secret Service, Dept. of Justice, and Kansas City Detective Squad, while the Navy is in full cry."[42] His army colleagues were also alarmed, and a few months later the Baltimore G-2 ordered an inquiry that would "of course be held as 'secret' and the investigation must be made with discretion." In Wichita, the Military Order of the World War hired a black "free lance social worker and preacher" to infiltrate the Pacific Movement and send his reports to Military Intelligence. J. Edgar Hoover shared with the army reports from a Pittsburgh "colored" informant handled by the local police. Despite urgings from the Washington G-2, Hoover refused to open his own investigation or to instigate deportation proceedings. By late 1935 the army, in a letter to Harry Jung of the American Vigilant Intelligence Federation, expressed an opinion it could have reached two

39. Joe N. Dalton to Charles K. Nulsen, January 14, 1936, ibid., reel 25, pp. 359–61; Carl H. Strong to G-2, Washington, April 12, 1935, pp. 329–32; Dalton to G-2, Washington, April 30, 1936, pp. 441–44. Military Intelligence noted Joseph P. Lash, future friend and biographer of Eleanor Roosevelt, as one of the leaders of the 1936 strike.

40. "Radical Professors and Teachers," February 3, 1936, Van Deman Files, R-1375, box 6. R-970, box 4, contains the book by Nelson E. Hewitt, statistician of the American Vigilant Intelligence Federation, *How "Red" Is the University of Chicago?* (Chicago: Advisory Associates, 1935). For an account of Communist-sponsored organizations for college students, most notably the National Student League, see Klehr, *Heyday of American Communism*, pp. 309–423.

41. The membership card is in MI Microfilm, reel 32, p. 327.

42. J. M. Moore, "Special Report on 'Pacific Movement' (Jap-Negro)," October 25, 1933, in National Archives, *Correspondence of the Military Intelligence Division Relating to "Negro Subversion" 1917–1941* (Washington, D.C.: National Archives, 1986), microfilm project number M1440, reel 4, p. 306 (hereafter cited as Negro Subversion Microfilm).

years earlier: the Pacific Movement was an insignificant moneymaking scam.[43]

After the summer of 1932, Military Intelligence headquarters kept a watchful eye for other marches on Washington. As early as November, MacArthur's G-2 notified him that based on the *Daily Worker*, to which MI subscribed, three marches were planned; repeats of the hunger and bonus marches and a new one by farmers. Of these, the G-2 accurately concluded that the first two were definitely Communist-controlled, and his erroneous assumption of "a probability that the farmers' march is inspired by communists" was based solely on the *Daily Worker*'s support for it.[44] The agrarian protest never materialized into a major threat, but the second Hunger March in December 1932 was carefully monitored by the army.

Both Military Intelligence and the Better America Federation obtained copies of a map labeled "Columns of the National Hunger March." The marchers were scheduled to reach Washington on December 4. With their calls to "Defeat the Bosses Hunger Program" and "Help the Unemployed Millions in their Fight against Starvation and Misery," the radicals demanded a federal grant of $50 to each unemployed worker, plus $10 for each dependent, for "winter relief." The radicals also wanted "immediate unemployment insurance at the expense of the bosses and government." Corps area G-2s followed the progress of the several columns from around the country and provided sensational reports of their being armed with guns, blackjacks, and tear gas. The Operations

43. C. K. Nulsen to Harry A. Jung, November 21, 1935, Negro Subversion Microfilm, reel 4, p. 435; O. A. Dickinson to G-2, War Department, December 16, 1933, pp. 315–16; Hoover to Nelson, June 12, 1934, p. 341. Other correspondence with Hoover is in the complete file on the Pacific Movement, ibid., pp. 301–439, and Theodore Kornweibel, Jr., ed., *Federal Surveillance of Afro-Americans (1917–1925): The First World War, the Red Scare, and the Garvey Movement* (Frederick, Md.: University Publications of America, 1986), reel 20, pp. 547–630. It includes early alarmist reports from the navy, as well as evidence of a brief 1936 panic that American blacks were being recruited to fight for Ethiopia against Mussolini. In World War II, the leader of the Pacific Movement was jailed for pro-Japanese activities (Morris Schonbach, *Native American Fascism during the 1930s and 1940s: A Study of Its Roots, Its Growth and Its Decline* [New York: Garland, 1985], p. 219). In the 1930s, the navy had a full espionage program against Japanese-Americans on the West Coast run by the I-V(S) group of the Thirteenth Naval District. The craft employed was so sensitive that even in reports classified secret it was "not considered desirable to set forth the methods of obtaining information." See commandant, Thirteenth Naval District, to chief of naval operations, March 27, 1936, Record Group 38, ONI, Oriental Desk, box 1, National Archives.

44. Alfred T. Smith, memorandum for the chief of staff, November 1, 1932, MI Microfilm, reel 22, pp. 239–43. For a February 24, 1933, "Special Report on Farm Movement," including information on the Farmers Holiday Association and the United Farmers League, see reel 32, pp. 295–96.

Branch of the army's national intelligence office, assuming the role of the defunct Negative branch, studied the group in Washington and placed its number at thirty-two hundred. After marching on Capitol Hill and meeting with the vice-president and Speaker of the House, the group was given safe passage to the Maryland line by New York Congressman Fiorello La Guardia.[45]

The G-2's Operations Branch in Washington also monitored two other marches in the spring of 1933. In a report to the chief of staff, the May 8 Scottsboro Protest March was characterized as consisting of "about 1,400 persons in the parade, of which about 90% were a low order of negro and the other 10% were a lower order of white persons."[46] Only about 2,000 veterans showed up for the second Bonus March held later in May, and President Franklin D. Roosevelt, just inaugurated on March 4, defused the protest by offering the veterans jobs in the newly created Civilian Conservation Corps.[47]

The original Bonus March produced one other group that attracted Military Intelligence's interest: the Khaki Shirts, founded in the summer of 1932. Most of the early members had been in the BEF, including Khaki Shirt National Commander Arthur J. Smith. Initial reports regarded the group as "communistically inspired," but before long the analysts of the Operations Branch saw the connection with Mussolini's Black Shirts. The assistant G-2 in Baltimore listened to one of Smith's followers address a crowd of two hundred on August 1 and noted the definite "no Reds or radicals wanted" theme. Reports about Smith's background varied, but it was clearly established that he had served with the British from 1914 to 1918 before enlisting in the American army. Other information had him as an aviator in several revolutions, including

45. Klehr, *Heyday of American Communism*, places the number of hunger marchers at twenty-five hundred. See his description of their Washington activities, pp. 66–68. The army files on the march are scattered in the reports from the corps area G-2s. See especially reel 22, pp. 209–340; reel 24, pp. 214–42, 796–943; reel 29, pp. 455–509. In the Van Deman Files, box 1, see a pamphlet on the hunger campaign put out by the National Committee of Unemployed Councils, *Why We March for Unemployment Insurance* (New York: Workers Library Publishers, 1932). Also in box 1 is a February 2, 1933, San Diego police report on a meeting of the local Unemployed Council attended by agents of Naval Intelligence. In the same location can be found ten issues of the *Hunger Fighter*, the "Organ of the Jobless of Los Angeles County," from October 1932 to December 1934.

46. Nulsen, memorandum for the chief of staff, May 9, 1933, MI Microfilm, reel 21, p. 601. There are several reports on the Scottsboro case spread throughout box 3 of the Van Deman Files.

47. Klehr, *Heyday of American Communism*, p. 281, says the second Bonus March had "a more decided Communist tinge than its predecessor," an assessment substantiated by the army reports in MI Microfilm, reel 21, pp. 585–626, and reel 22, pp. 286–406. A third march in 1934 involved only fourteen hundred veterans.

fighting with Pancho Villa in Mexico and with the French Foreign Legion in Morocco. One informant suggested that he had flown for Cesar Augusto Sandino, whose name was later taken by the Sandinistas, against American marines in Nicaragua and that he had "turned down a job running the Bolivian Army at $1600 a month and expenses." Despite Smith's claims of membership in the millions, Military Intelligence eventually wrote off the Khaki Shirts, as the press had done much earlier, as "a one-man racket for the benefit of Art J. Smith."[48]

With the attention given the Khaki Shirts, it is somewhat surprising that Military Intelligence did not investigate America's most famous fascist group, William Dudley Pelley's Silver Shirts. Then again, it was always the threat from the left that drove the army's information collection effort. The paramilitary Silver Shirts did not, however, escape Van Deman's notice; he had four coded agents who successfully penetrated a secret and heavily guarded training camp.[49] The army did take an interest in the Crusader White Shirts, founded by George W. Christians of Chattanooga, Tennessee, with elements in Georgia, Pennsylvania, and California. MI considered Christians harmless, with "a brilliant mind but of erratic temperament."[50] When informants working for the Illinois National Guard reported the existence of an American Nazi movement in early 1934, Military Intelligence judged the source unreliable.[51] Outside the army, however, anti-Nazi sentiment was mounting, and one of the first resolutions introduced into the House of Representatives in

48. Reports on the Khaki Shirts are scattered, but the summary file is in MI Microfilm, reel 22, pp. 346–56; the official membership card is on p. 204, and Smith's photograph on p. 449. Copies of the newspaper the *Khaki Shirts* are in reel 32, pp. 1012–31.

49. Van Deman Files, R-364, R-368, box 2; R-783, box 3; R-1581bc, box 7. The camp's location was also coded, but box 1 has an undated (probably 1933) Silver Shirt "Official Dispatch," from Asheville, North Carolina. See also R-351, box 2, for a file on "The American White Guardsmen," which proclaimed itself "secret, military and patriotic, confining its membership to White Americans." For the Silver Shirts and other fascist groups, see Schonbach, *Native American Fascism*.

50. R. M. Howell, memorandum to G-2, War Department, March 12, 1934, MI Microfilm, reel 22, p. 438. See reel 28, pp. 777–81, for Christians's "General Orders," which closed with "Strike hard, straight and swiftly. Get what you start out to get." Reel 28, pp. 269–70, has the 1933 issue of a far-right publication out of Chicago called the *Vigilante*, but the best collection of ephemeral products of the extreme right in the 1930s is in the Van Deman Files. Among these are "Secret Nature and Significance of Communism" and "Secret Nature of the Currency Shortage." These two "Confidential" bulletins put out by the "Foundation for Christian Economics, Private Information Service for Members Only" in the winter of 1932–33 are in box 1. A report from the Civic Council of Defense of California, Inc., in Long Beach found even *Scholastic Magazine* too far to the left (R-940 and R-948, box 4).

51. Joseph C. Hatie to G-2, Sixth Corps Area, February 9, 1934, MI Microfilm, reel 29, pp. 1047–97.

1934 called for a "Special Committtee on Un-American Activities" to investigate Nazi and "certain other propaganda activities." Although the inquiry was largely the effort of Congressman Samuel Dickstein of New York, and it was frequently called the Dickstein Committee, the chairman was John W. McCormack of Massachusetts.

This first un-American activities committee did investigate Nazism and fascism and included in its list of subversive and racist organizations the Silver Shirts and, no doubt to the chagrin of the Chicago G-2, the American Vigilant Intelligence Federation, but it was the "other" in its charge that caught the attention of the military and patriotic organizations, which were once again happy to reveal the Red menace.[52] The testimony of the head of the National Civic Federation and Archibald Stevenson, now the federation's general counsel, was much the same as it had been in 1930: when the ACLU forced the Department of Justice out of the business of spying on the Reds, that work was taken over by private societies. Now money and congressional authority were required to put J. Edgar Hoover back on the job. Margaret Kerr, executive secretary and office manager of the Better America Federation, provided detailed data on Communist activities in California. She herself had infiltrated a Communist cell in Los Angeles, and, among Communist "co-operating organizations," she cited the ACLU and the Women's International League for Peace and Freedom. Representatives from the American Legion, the national Chamber of Commerce, and the Benevolent and Protective Order of the Elks also testified. Particularly interesting was the statement from retired Major General S. D. Butler, winner of two medals of honor, that the fascists had asked him to lead a political army of veterans. Local police amazed the committee with alarming figures on Communist membership; New York City was said to have seventy-five thousand hard-core Reds.[53]

When the War Department's G-2, Alfred T. Smith, appeared before the committee in late 1934, he wore the stars of a brigadier general,

52. See Ogden, *Dies Committee*, pp. 32–37; Schonbach, *Native American Fascism*, pp. 139–51, 233–35; and Walter Goodman, *The Committee: The Extraordinary Career of the House Committee on Un-American Activities* (New York: Farrar, Straus and Giroux, 1968), p. 10, for an account of the McCormack hearings. For an example of the racism of Harry A. Jung of the American Vigilant Intelligence Federation, see his 1935 pamphlet, *Communism and the Negro*, in Negro Subversion Microfilm, reel 4, pp. 427–34.

53. U.S. House of Representatives, Public Hearings before the Special Committee on Un-American Activities, 73d Cong., 2d sess., *Investigation of Nazi Propaganda Activities and Investigation of Certain Other Propaganda Activities* (Washington, D.C.: U.S. Government Printing Office, 1935), pp. 46–60 (hereafter referred to as Nazi Propaganda Hearings). Kerr's testimony is on pp. 112–22; Butler's, pp. 8–20; on New York Reds, p. 184.

reflecting Military Intelligence's final acceptance as a full member of the general staff. He chose his words very carefully, opening with the disclaimer that during peacetime the army "does not investigate individuals or groups in civil life, nor does it engage in any activities which might savor in the slightest degree of military espionage of our own people." Nevertheless, he said, Military Intelligence undertook "to keep itself informed" concerning "what appear to be subversive activities," especially those relating to "national defense." This collection effort, he insisted, was limited to "liaison with Federal, State, county, and municipal authorities, and a scrutiny of the press. Information is received when voluntarily submitted by patriotic organizations and individuals, but is never requested." Active investigations were conducted only against "un-American activity within the Army."[54]

Smith cited the 1925 military convictions of Crouch and Trumbull, two dishonorable discharges handed out in 1933 and 1934, and a 1932 on-post Communist cell that had been "placed under surveillance [and] soon disintegrated." He and his navy counterpart thrilled the committee with examples of Communist literature aimed at soldiers and sailors. Most titillating of all was navy Commander V. L. Kirkman's testimony that the Communists regularly used young women "chosen for their good looks" to incite "mutiny, rebellion, sabotage and assassination."[55] Smith, who was completing four years as intelligence chief and was soon to receive his own brigade, did not provide the details of several cases at variance with the policy he had outlined to Congress. The dilemma for intelligence officers was how to handle civilian Communists who were recruiting soldiers without becoming involved in the collection of information on those civilians. At Fort Sam Houston, for example, the G-2 sent one of his clerks undercover to befriend a known Communist soldier. The resulting contact turned into a substantial case lasting two years and leading to the surveillance of "certain civilians who are directly interested in fomenting discord among enlisted men." There was a good deal of uncertainty about the legality of the operation, but ultimately the army satisfied itself that the agent was interested in the civilians "only to the extent that the Army is affected."[56] Outside the continental United States, the army had fewer qualms. A 1934 investigation of the Hawaiian Freethinkers' Club clearly intruded into the civilian

54. Ibid., pp. 106–7.
55. Quoted in *New York Times*, December 19, 1934.
56. G-2, Eighth Corps Area, to G-2, War Department, May 2, 1934, and February 5, 1936, MI Microfilm, reel 22, pp. 551, 701. The entire file is on pp. 694–701.

arena, and in Puerto Rico the army ran full-fledged operations against the nationalists.[57]

Only six weeks before Smith's appearance in the McCormack hearings, the commanding general at the Presidio in San Francisco had reported the existence of a "very small, but highly organized, group of Communist soldiers" and had requested approval of "a plan to introduce a few thoroughly reliable enlisted men into the Communist Party" in an effort to identify the "soldier defectives." Clearly designed to go off post, the plan received Smith's blessing but failed for lack of concurrence by the other assistant chiefs of staff. Instead, Smith allocated $200 for the Presidio to buy informants "so long as the policies of the War Department . . . are not violated."[58] The California G-2 reported to Washington an expenditure of only $55, and it seems likely that he assumed his superiors preferred not to know what he was doing and forwarded no more reports. He did, however, develop close ties with Van Deman, and the latter's files disclose an active Military Intelligence on the West Coast. It seems reasonable to expect that other G-2s conducted operations similarly hidden from Washington.

The San Francisco Military Intelligence office corresponded so frequently with the retired Van Deman that a rubber stamp ("VanD") was developed in 1936 to facilitate routing to him. Much of the information the army obtained in California came from informants, apparently hired by the Industrial Association of San Francisco, which voluntarily gave the results to the G-2, who passed them on to Van Deman. Accordingly, labor problems, especially in the maritime industry, dominated the reports.[59] The largest other topic concerned the agitation of Communists in the military and especially in the New Deal's famous Civilian Conservation Corps (CCC). The army ran the CCC camps, and its concern for ideological purity was considerable.[60] Here the corps area G-2s had

57. For Hawaii, see ibid., pp. 568–77. A copy of a Freethinker's membership card is in the Van Deman Files, R-1215, box 5. A great deal of information on Puerto Rico in the 1930s is in MI Microfilm, reels 25 and 26.

58. The Presidio commander's October 1, 1934, letter to the War Department is in ibid., reel 22, p. 495. The case is reviewed in a September 30, 1935, "Summary of anti-Subversive Measures," pp. 716–18.

59. The earliest report from the Ninth Corps Area G-2 to Van Deman is dated September 3, 1935, and concerns communist infiltration of the American Federation of Labor (Van Deman Files, R-1063, box 4). Other confidential army reports appear in boxes 4 and 5. Overall, the material from the Eleventh Naval District in San Diego, Van Deman's best source, exceeds that of the army.

60. Box 1 of the Van Deman Files has several issues of the communist newspaper *Forester's Voice* for the CCC camps, along with *Soldier's Voice* and *Shipmate's Voice*. See

no fear of violating policy because, so far as Washington was concerned, the CCC camps came under the same protection from sedition enjoyed by military posts.

As the camps were first being set up in the spring of 1933, the War Department began to receive reports of, as the Baltimore G-2 put it, "the interest taken by some of our pacifists and pink (or worse) friends in the C.C.C."[61] On May 10, a secret letter went to all corps area commanders requiring the addition of a section on agitation in the CCC to the monthly subversive situation report. The G-2s naturally levied a reporting requirement on CCC district commanders, who passed it down the chain of command. These secret orders became public in early 1936, when the *Daily Worker* published those from the Nebraska CCC district headquarters. After a polite but embarrassing inquiry from the Office of Emergency Construction Work, the secretary of war approved the following justification: "The well known and often publicized efforts of subversive elements to cause trouble and dissatisfaction among members of the CCC necessitate the taking of these measures in order that the War Department may be aware of the situation."[62]

Another leak in early 1936 caused even more problems for the military. After McCormack's hearings, both the army and the navy had worked closely with him and other conservative congressmen in drafting a bill to make it illegal to disseminate radical propaganda to servicemen. When Texas's U.S. Representative Maury Maverick, whose name was truly descriptive, obtained a navy document entitled "Communist-Affiliated and Communist-Aiding Organizations in the United States," he made it public. Both the ACLU and the Federal Council of Churches were included, and they complained bitterly. Citing "continuing evidence that the Naval and Military Intelligence Departments are still collecting and disseminating, at least in Army and Navy circles, information of a character to which we call attention," the ACLU urged President

R-363, box 2, for a list of "9th Corps Area CCC Enrollees Discharged for Radical Activities," covering the period from June 1933 to February 1934. See R-1293, box 5, for a G-2 report on Jehovah's Witnesses in the CCC who refused to salute the flag.

61. J. C. Pecham to G-2, War Department, May 29, 1933, MI Microfilm, reel 19, p. 718. See also the August 25, 1933, memorandum for the chief of staff, subject: "Subversive Activities in the Civilian Conservation Corps," reel 22, pp. 461–62.

62. The inquiry from the assistant to the director of Emergency Construction Work is Guy D. McKinney to the adjutant general, January 22, 1936, ibid., reel 32, p. 378. The justification approved by the secretary of war also contains a summary of the several orders for spying in the CCC. See F. H. Lincoln, memorandum for the adjutant general, February 14, 1936, p. 383. Material on the CCC is contained in the several reels holding reports from the corps areas, but the Second Corps Area was perhaps the best in collecting and forwarding examples of literature aimed at the CCC. See reel 25, pp. 206–95.

Roosevelt to order that "no agency of the Military and Naval forces should engage in any propaganda whatever intended to create prejudice on political issues."[63]

Roosevelt was certainly not afraid of the Communist threat, either domestic or foreign, and it was under him that diplomatic relations were restored with the Soviet Union. He was, by the same token, no blind civil libertarian, and he loved the game of intelligence. Accordingly, he gave the ACLU only a vague response at the very time that he was moving to strengthen his administration's ability to investigate subversives on the right and the left.[64] After the 1936 fuss over the McCormack bill, however, the army resumed its cautious approach, at least on the national level. Only occasional informal reports came in from the field, and reserve Lieutenant Colonel Walter Furbershaw of Chicago seems to have been running the only army-controlled penetration of the Communists.[65] In the summer of 1937, when Ralph Easley of the National Civic Federation complained that "the Government at Washington is helpless with respect to defending our nation against the subversive forces seeking its destruction," Secretary of War Harry H. Woodring reminded him of "the continuing policy of the War Department to conduct no investigations of subversive activities among the civilian population."[66] With Congress about to enter another, shriller investigation of the Reds, and with war clouds gathering over Europe, that situation was about to change.

63. The navy document was dated April 1, 1935, but the release did not occur until nearly a year later. The navy's report to the president and the ACLU's letter of March 17, 1936, are in Official Files, 18x and 2111, Franklin D. Roosevelt Library, Hyde Park, N.Y. For the army's favorable opinion of the McCormack bill, including the response to an inquiry from Representative Maverick to Brigadier General Harry E. Knight, who had succeeded Smith as G-2, see MI Microfilm, reel 22, pp. 611–31. The bill never passed, but versions were introduced until 1939 (p. 768).

64. For Roosevelt's "low key approach" to the far left, see "Communism," in Otis L. Graham, Jr., and Meghan R. Wander, eds., *Franklin D. Roosevelt, His Life and Times: An Encyclopedic View* (Boston: G. K. Hall, 1985), pp. 71–72. Jeffrey M. Dorwart, *Conflict of Duty: The U.S. Navy's Intelligence Dilemma, 1919–1945* (Annapolis: Naval Institute Press, 1979), p. 84, describes Roosevelt's defense of the navy from the ACLU and his verbal instructions to Hoover to enter the fight against subversives. For Roosevelt's "fascination with spies and spying" and his connection with ROOM, a secret intelligence group supporting the navy and including Kermit and Theodore Roosevelt, Jr., and William Vincent Astor, see pp. 114, 162–71.

65. For a typical report from Furbershaw, see A. L. Hamblen to G-2, War Department, October 15, 1938, MI Microfilm, reel 30, pp. 659–61.

66. Easley to Woodring, June 25, 1937, and Woodring to Easley, July 7, 1937, ibid., reel 23, pp. 303–5.

CHAPTER 13

Delimiting Military
Intelligence

The late 1930s saw the appearance of a new generation of professional Red haters. The largest group was Gerald L. K. Smith's rabid Committee of One Million, whose members were given badges to investigate Communists and who numbered nearly a million by 1942. The favorite book of the far right was Elizabeth Dilling's *The Red Network: A "Who's Who" and Handbook of Radicalism for Patriots*. She gloried in the term *professional patriot*, and among her cohorts to whom she dedicated her book were "the men of the Chicago Military Intelligence." So strange were these times that even former secretary of war Newton D. Baker, who had become a conservative corporate lawyer, was listed by Dilling as a "Communist-Recommended Author." Eleanor Roosevelt was included as "Socialist sympathizer and associate; pacifist."[1]

The era's new and longer-lasting House Un-American Activities Committee was led by Martin Dies, Jr., of Texas. Established on May 26, 1938, the Dies Committee eventually included even nudism in its definition of subversion. Dies was the first to point a finger at the federal government, not only for failing to repress radicals but also for having them on the payroll. In early 1939, he was responsible for an unsuccessful attempt to impeach Secretary of Labor Frances Perkins for her laxity in not deporting the radical West Coast labor leader Harry Bridges. The following year, Dies announced that he had a list of a dozen Communists on the staff of the Tennessee Valley Authority. He sent Roosevelt the names of over a thousand suspected subversives who were federal employees.[2]

1. Dilling's *Red Network*, published privately in Chicago in 1934, has been reprinted (New York: Arno Press, 1977). On the Committee of One Million, see Glen Jeansonne, *Gerald L. K. Smith: Minister of Hate* (New Haven: Yale University Press, 1988), pp. 64–79. For the army's uncertainty over what to make of Smith, see G-2, Third Corps Area, to G-2, War Department, July 29, 1937, in Randolph Boehm, ed., *U.S. Military Intelligence Reports: Surveillance of Radicals in the United States, 1917–1941* (Frederick, Md.: University Publications of America, 1984), reel 27, pp. 882–84 (hereafter cited as MI Microfilm).
2. Eleanor Bontecou, *The Federal Loyalty-Security Program* (Ithaca: Cornell Univer-

In the late 1930s Roosevelt directed the creation of the modern federal internal security system. He was clearly reacting to pressure from Dies, and much of the information available on that early system comes from the administration's defensive responses to the congressman. It is also true that Roosevelt had a genuine dislike for fascists such as the Silver Shirts. Though he may have desired to focus on the far right, he was willing to accommodate Dies and his own intelligence community by including the Communists as targets in his surveillance system. In answering Dies's complaints, the FBI claimed that it had begun "building up a system of internal security" as early as 1935. That effort moved quickly enough that in the spring of 1938 liberals in the Congress, led by Senators Robert M. La Follette, Jr., and the venerable George W. Norris, were worried about an American Gestapo.[3]

The federal intelligence community seems to have been eager to respond to the new domestic threat, but as in World War I, there was uncertainty and disagreement within that community over which agency would rule. Unlike 1917, however, the argument was resolved. J. Edgar Hoover's Federal Bureau of Investigation emerged as the supreme authority on domestic intelligence. Hoover's first approval from Roosevelt came in an August 24, 1936, meeting at which the president authorized Hoover to investigate fascists and Communists. As Hoover's biographers have suggested, the FBI director took a limited mandate from Roosevelt and "initiated a broad, intensive investigation of domestic radical activities that extended to spying on the nation's college campuses."[4] Whatever Roosevelt's inclinations, Hoover had the advantage over the army and navy, and he never relinquished it. In late 1938,

sity Press, 1953), pp. 8–10; August R. Ogden, *The Dies Committee: A Study of the Special House Committee for the Investigation of Un-American Activities, 1938–1944* (Washington, D.C.: Catholic University of America Press, 1945).

3. Materials on the La Follette investigation are in the Official Files, 1581, Franklin D. Roosevelt Library, Hyde Park, N.Y. The best source on Dies and late 1930s internal security measures is Official Files, 10-b, a large collection including the "FBI Numbered Reports," number 109 of which describes the system set up in 1935. Also in 10-b is a 1939 order from Roosevelt, responding to FBI reports of a Silver Shirts arms cache in southern California, that "the whole area around Long Beach and San Diego should be examined with a microscope inside and out." In President's Secretary's Files, 77, see Roosevelt to Hoover, January 21, 1942, wherein Roosevelt asks about William Dudley Pelley, founder of the Silver Shirts and publisher of the *Galilean*, and notes, "Now that we are in the war it looks like a good chance to clean up a number of these vile publications."

4. Athan G. Theoharis and John S. Cox, *The Boss: J. Edgar Hoover and the Great American Inquisition* (Philadelphia: Temple University Press, 1988), p. 176. Hoover's August 24, 1936, meeting with Roosevelt, and subsequent sessions involving the president, Hoover, the attorney general, and the secretary of state, are described in detail on pp. 173–76.

Roosevelt authorized $150,000 for Hoover's use in investigating "counter-espionage activities."[5]

This level of presidential approval, based on a detail in the FBI's appropriation that allowed it to handle investigations requested by the Department of State, was insufficient for Hoover. He wanted this limitation removed and a clear statement that the FBI had primary authority for domestic intelligence. To achieve these goals, he had to forestall an effort in early 1939 by State to establish itself as the coordinator for such work, and he had to control the army's and navy's reentry into domestic investigations. At this time Roosevelt's internal security program involved a large "interdepartmental committee," including representatives from the Departments of State, Treasury, War, Navy, Justice, and the Post Office. The committee was supposed to act as a "clearing house for data," but most of the cases were being conducted by the FBI, army, and navy. To perform its part of this mission, the army, on April 17, 1939, formally reintroduced negative intelligence, housed this time in the more appropriately labeled Counter Intelligence Branch.[6]

Hoover's approach was to attack the interdepartmental committee as unworkable and likely to repeat the violations of civil liberties that had occurred in World War I. He convinced Attorney General Frank Murphy to advise the president that the large committee was "neither effective nor desirable." The best way to handle espionage, counterespionage, and sabotage, the attorney general said, was to limit this work to the three agencies, the FBI, the army, and the navy, that "have perfected methods of investigation and have developed channels for the exchange of information, which are both efficient and so mobile and elastic as to permit prompt expansion in the event of an emergency."[7]

Roosevelt agreed, and on June 26, 1939, in a confidential memorandum to the cabinet members, he reduced the membership on the interdepartmental intelligence committee to the FBI, army, and navy. The intelligence directors of these three were to coordinate their activities, and all matters "involving actually or potentially any espionage,

5. Ibid., p. 177. See the footnote on this page that supports the conclusion that "Roosevelt knew that the FBI was already investigating dissident activities." FBI reports to Roosevelt, beginning in April 1938, are in the President's Secretary's Files, 76 and 77, Roosevelt Library.

6. Bruce W. Bidwell, *History of the Military Intelligence Division, Department of the Army General Staff, 1775–1941* (Frederick, Md.: University Publications of America, 1986), pp. 2841–85. During this period it was always spelled Counter Intelligence, two words.

7. Attorney general to Roosevelt, June 17, 1939, Official Files, box 10-b, Roosevelt Library.

counter-espionage, or sabotage" were to be "controlled and handled" by them. Hoover had reduced the field.[8] In September, when he learned that New York City planned to revive the old Bomb Squad as a "special sabotage squad," he again raised the specter of vigilante action to generate a presidential statement that the FBI had "charge of investigative work in matters relating to espionage, sabotage, and violations of neutrality regulations" and called for local authorities "promptly to turn over to the nearest representative" of the FBI any information on those subjects.[9] Now only Military Intelligence and the Office of Naval Intelligence were competing with Hoover.

In making his move, Hoover could count on the support of the navy, which, a naval scholar has concluded, had been "under the spell of the FBI" since the June 1939 agreement.[10] In dealing with the army, there were two other pressures on Hoover in the spring of 1940. The American Legion was eager to become World War II's version of the American Protective League, and like the APL, it was prepared to work for the army if the FBI was not interested. Hoover's solution was to establish the FBI's American Legion Contact Program, which eventually involved thousands of volunteer informants and lasted until 1966.[11] Hoover also had to head off Martin Dies, who was urging the president to create a home defense council, a superagency to coordinate the FBI, MI, and ONI. The FBI director was able to have Roosevelt inform Dies that he had "perfected arrangements for the coordination of all investigative activity relating to matters of this kind under the FBI."[12]

As it turned out, Hoover had very little difficulty in dealing with

8. The June 26, 1939, letter from Roosevelt to the attorney general, the postmaster general, and the heads of State, Treasury, War, Navy, and Commerce is in ibid. and Record Group 165, MID, entry 203, National Archives. It is discussed in Bidwell, *History of Military Intelligence,* p. 396; Jeffrey M. Dorwart, *Conflict of Duty: The U.S. Navy's Intelligence Dilemma, 1919–1945* (Annapolis: Naval Institute Press, 1979), p. 105; and Theoharis and Cox, *Boss,* p. 178. In typical Roosevelt fashion, he told the State department that he did not mean to exclude it. Though, he said, "the principal work in this country should be done under the leadership of the F.B.I., G-2 Section of the War Department and O.N.I. of the Navy Department [,] this does not mean that the intelligence work of the State Department should cease in any way" (Roosevelt to secretary of state, June 26, 1939, Official Files, 10-b, Roosevelt Library).
9. Quoted in Theoharis and Cox, *Boss,* p. 208.
10. Dorwart, *Conflict of Duty,* p. 118.
11. Athan Theoharis, "The FBI and the American Legion Contact Program, 1940–1966," *Political Science Quarterly* 100 (Summer 1985): 271–86; William Pencak, *For God and Country: The American Legion, 1919–1941* (Boston: Northeastern University Press, 1989), pp. 312–15.
12. Roosevelt to Dies, June 10, 1940, Official Files, 1661a, Roosevelt Library; Hoover to Edwin Watson, June 3, 1940, ibid. See also Theoharis and Cox, *Boss,* p. 213.

Military Intelligence. The War Department's new G-2, Brigadier General Sherman Miles, was no match for Hoover, who by then was famous for his crime fighting in the 1930s. Miles, taking command as acting G-2 only a month before Hoover proposed that the FBI control all domestic investigations, admitted that he knew "nothing about negative intelligence, except that it is a huge subject and which will require a very large system." Noting that he lacked experienced officers, he contacted Ralph Van Deman and Alexander B. Coxe and asked them to come to Washington to help.[13] Furthermore, Van Deman had become a Hoover enthusiast. As early as March 1937 the retired general had offered to give his subversion files to the FBI.[14] The following year, when Hoover was vacationing in San Diego, Van Deman tried unsuccessfully to see Hoover regarding a "plan to organize some sort of a group for the purpose of counter-espionage work."[15] Although Hoover denied any knowledge of such a plan, he asked Van Deman to stay in touch with the FBI's Los Angeles office and promised that "if the occasion arises I shall be happy to call upon you."[16] In 1939, Van Deman again failed to see Hoover when the latter visited California, but the basis for a close relationship was laid by Hoover's agents, who kept in contact with the general. Through those channels, Van Deman sent advice to Hoover on the need to avoid "some of the mistakes" committed during World War I involving the "relationship between the Bureau and the Army and Navy Intelligence."[17]

According to his former deputy Alexander Coxe, Van Deman was ready to accept Hoover's hegemony over internal matters. "Now that the F.I.B [sic] has been enlarged, given funds, and otherwise put on its feet," Coxe told G-2 Miles, "there should be little trouble in getting them to take over all counter espionage work in the civil population." He and Van Deman believed, he said, that "the Army should confine its efforts at counter espionage to the military establishment." Coxe also urged against the military having any relationship with "civilian spy hunting organizations such as 'The American Protective League' during World War I." Such groups, he said, were "very dangerous, in that they are

13. Miles to Coxe, May 17, 1940, Alexander B. Coxe, Sr., Papers, J. Y. Joyner Library, East Carolina University, Greenville, N.C. For Hoover's prestige by 1937, see Theoharis and Cox, *Boss*, pp. 154–55.
14. R. R. Roach, memorandum for D. M. Ladd, July 18, 1945, in the FBI file on Ralph H. Van Deman, available in the Reading Room of the FBI's headquarters in Washington, D.C. (hereafter cited as FBI Van Deman file).
15. Van Deman to Hoover, October 24, 1938, FBI Van Deman file.
16. Hoover to Van Deman, November 1, 1938, ibid.
17. H. B. Wood to Hoover, October 6, 1939, ibid.

hard to handle and may get out of hand." Better to let the bureau worry about them.[18] Perhaps the founding fathers of Military Intelligence remembered the criticisms their agency had undergone back in the Red Scare and in the 1920s. Perhaps, over the years, their philosophy about the role of the military in American society had changed. Perhaps they were simply being practical and accepting that with its increasing need for foreign intelligence, the likelihood of a combat role, and the perceived necessity of fighting subversion within its own ranks, the army had neither the need nor the ability to duplicate services the FBI could render adequately. Moreover, cooperating with the FBI could provide the authorization and financial basis for augmenting the army's own investigative arm for combat and foreign intelligence and for internal security within the military. Miles may very well have regarded Hoover's proposal as a godsend.

At any rate, Miles had very little time to decide. Hoover had called a National Intelligence Conference in his headquarters for May 31, 1940. Miles asked Van Deman and Coxe to accompany him to this "highly confidential conference" where the question of the coordination of domestic intelligence was to be decided. Also attending were Assistant Secretary of State Adolf A. Berle, Director of Naval Intelligence admiral Walter S. Anderson, and Hoover and his staff.[19] The group met to consider a plan Hoover had sent to them in a May 29 memorandum. Hoover had proposed that during peacetime his agency would be responsible for all investigations of nonmilitary personnel involved in "allegations of espionage, sabotage and such related matters," for protecting critical industries, and for monitoring "Un-American" groups. He promised to share this information with the army and the navy through weekly conferences and designated liaison officers. In time of war, Hoover proposed that "in so far as it is possible," the military would not involve itself in "the investigation or prosecution of civilians."[20]

With the military ready to be convinced, Hoover had little difficulty gaining approval of his plan. In his words, Coxe and Van Deman "expressed themselves as being literally astounded at the thoroughness,

18. Coxe to Miles, May 20, 1940, Coxe Papers.

19. Hoover describes the conference in an untitled memorandum, dated June 2, attached to a June 3, 1940, letter from him to Brigadier General Edwin M. Watson, FDR's secretary who handled intelligence matters (Official Files, 10-b, FBI Numbered Files, 109, Roosevelt Library). See also Hoover to Van Deman, August 14, 1940, FBI Van Deman file. The absence of Marlborough Churchill from these proceedings is striking. He was either out of favor or in ill health; he died on July 9, 1942.

20. Quoted in Theoharis and Cox, *Boss,* pp. 211–12.

magnitude, and soundess of the coordinated program."[21] Van Deman was thrilled. As he told Hoover:

> I want to say, again, how delighted I am with the spirit of understanding and cooperation which was evident in all of the agencies. . . . With such an attitude it should be a comparatively easy task to work out the organizations and procedure necessary to accomplish the very onerous task which lies before this country. I mean it should be comparatively easy in comparison with the job we had in 1917. At that time we were confronted by the same task but then not only was there no suitable organization in existence but we encountered opposition on every hand.[22]

Van Deman and Miles also attended a second meeting in Hoover's office on June 3 and reached "a complete agreement on the delineation of responsibility." Miles wrote to Coxe, who had returned to his home in El Paso, Texas, that the arrangement that had been signed and forwarded to the president for his approval would "definitely establish our authority to act." Rather than seeing the agreement as a capitulation, Miles regarded it as a positive mission statement for Military Intelligence. This success, he told Coxe, was attributable "very largely to the fact that you and General Van Deman were here and that I was able to cash in on your experience and reputation."[23]

The document, signed by President Roosevelt on June 5, 1940, was known as the Delimitation Agreement. In it, Hoover received complete responsibility for all counterintelligence investigations involving civilians within the United States and its territories, except for the Panama Canal Zone, Guam, Samoa, and the Philippines. In those locations, the army controlled spying in the Canal Zone and the Philippines, and the Navy handled Guam and American Samoa. At home, however, the investigations of the army and the navy were to be limited to their own establishments, including civilian employees. The FBI also obtained specific authority to work with "civilian groups designed to combat 'Fifth Column' activities."[24]

Despite Van Deman's assessment, the vagueness of the Delimitation

21. Hoover's June 2, 1940, untitled memorandum cited in note 19.
22. Van Deman to Hoover, July 3, 1940, FBI Van Deman file.
23. Miles to Coxe, June 4, 1940, Coxe Papers.
24. The Delimitation Agreement is in Record Group 165, MID, entry 66, National Archives, and quoted extensively in Bidwell, *History of Military Intelligence*, pp. 397–98, and Theoharis and Cox, *Boss*, pp. 212–13. A subsequent decision by Roosevelt gave Hoover responsibility for the Western Hemisphere, which he maintained until he lost all overseas control to William Donovan's Office of Strategic Services. See Bidwell, *History of MI*, pp. 397–98, and Theoharis and Cox, *Boss*, p. 216.

Agreement and the natural impulse of investigative agencies to investigate meant that Military Intelligence did not withdraw completely from internal affairs. Both the army and the navy considered it necessary only to "coordinate" their domestic intelligence activities with the FBI, and both continued to justify additional investigative agents by claiming that the FBI could not respond to their needs. Sometimes, as in the case of Furbershaw in Chicago, the army simply hid its investigations from the FBI and the navy.[25] The army felt that Hoover was not moving quickly enough in developing a plant protection system or in countering the fifth column, each an FBI responsibility under the Delimitation Agreement. Eventually, Hoover placed nearly twelve thousand informants inside plants designated by the War Department, but on the matter of countersubversion, the army moved ahead on its own.[26] Moreover, the new director of Naval Intelligence, Captain Alan G. Kirk, did not get along with Hoover, and the navy could no longer be counted on to support the FBI against the army. Kirk was especially concerned that Hoover's agents were operating in Guam and Samoa, areas awarded to the navy under the agreement. It is clear that neither the army nor the navy was entirely out of Roosevelt's intelligence program because the respective intelligence chiefs took turns providing daily briefings for the president.[27]

Hoover felt that General Miles failed to understand his subordinate role, and the FBI director expressed particular displeasure over the G-2's independent calling of meetings of intelligence chiefs. Insisting that "there should be no overlapping or duplication," Hoover asked for a revised Delimitation Agreement in early 1941. Although it took a year for Hoover to gain Roosevelt's approval, when it came on February 9, 1942, the FBI was granted control over all inquiries "involving civilians in the

25. The army's claim that the deception was "to safeguard the operative against possible identification" is certainly plausible, but the caution also kept the FBI from exercising its option to take over the case. Furbershaw's information was sent to the FBI in "piecemeal" and "redrafted form" (G-2, Sixth Corps Area, to G-2, War Department, February 8, 1941, and C. H. Bonestead to William Bryden, April 5, 1941, MI Microfilm, reel 31, pp. 454, 654).

26. For conflicts between the army and the FBI over plant protection and countersubversion, see Bidwell, *History of Military Intelligence*, p. 398, and Rhodri Jeffreys-Jones, *American Espionage: From Secret Service to CIA* (New York: Free Press, 1977), p. 166. For a classic ONI defense of its need for more agents, undated but probably 1940, see confidential memorandum, Op-16-A-1, Record Group 38, ONI, Oriental Desk, box 1, National Archives. Dorwart, in *Conflict of Duty*, p. 123, describes the ingenious measures the navy used to continue its own investigations. Beginning in March 1939, Hoover sent volumes of information to MI. The army's file "FBI Correspondence" in Record Group 165, MID, entry 66, National Archives, shows him working hard to keep his promise of support.

27. Dorwart, *Conflict of Duty*, p. 153.

United States."[28] The army was to rely entirely on the FBI for information on subversion. The role of Military Intelligence in American life had finally been fully delimited, if in fact it was possible to curtail an investigative agency growing rapidly from the pressure of another world war.

When World War II started in Europe in September 1939, the U.S. Army had fewer than 200,000 troops, and the G-2's staff in the War Department totaled only 69 people on a budget of slightly over $89,000. At that time, the Counter Intelligence Branch had 3 officers, but within a year its Counter Subversion Section alone had a staff of 14 with 62 subordinates serving in the nine corps areas. By 1941, with the United States still not in the war, there were 848 people, three-fourths of them civilians, in the Washington G-2's headquarters, and the budget had nearly quadrupled. In July 1940 a branch of the Washington office was opened in New York City, followed by others in Miami and San Francisco.[29] The army's countersubversion effort, called the CS system, was aimed at rooting out Communist, fascist, and Japanese sympathizers in its own ranks. Orders for reporting on such individuals has been issued as early as 1937, and in 1940 a major campaign began to crush them in the army. Later that year, all headquarters and installations, down to the smallest camp, were required to have an intelligence officer who was to oversee the work of informers. Plans called for "at least one operative in each fifty men."[30]

Beginning in November 1940, each corps area G-2 had to provide Washington a "Special Report on the Subversive Situation" showing its implementation and staffing of the CS program.[31] One of the earliest and most thorough of the reports came from the G-2 in New York. Analyzing the effect of Stalin's purges and his pact with Hitler, he reported that "it is becoming less intellectually fashionable to be avowedly a fellow-traveler." This happy change was regarded as part of "a natural curve" producing "a swing back from cynicism and contempt for things termed bourgeois, and toward a renewed patriotism, to the refutation of pacifism, involved in the breakdown of all disarmament and an avalanche of events demonstrating its absurdity." Although these

28. Quoted in Theoharis and Cox, Boss, p. 215.
29. Bidwell, History of Military Intelligence, pp. 258, 399. The main concern of the branch offices was foreign intelligence; for their records, see Record Group 165, MID, entry 203, National Archives.
30. The CS system, with a fairly objective report on the major Communist and fascist organizations and leaders, is described in a November 25, 1940, document entitled "Subversive Elements in the United States" (MI Microfilm, reel 23, pp. 817–88).
31. These reports are arranged by corps area in MI Microfilm, reels 24–32.

"Pink losses" were encouraging, the analysis saw the "practical Communists" becoming stronger as "drifters, malcontents, radicals and agitators by natural inclination are constantly joining the ranks." Particularly disconcerting was the Congress of Industrial Organizations (CIO), in which there was "much Communist feeling" since "Radical Unionism has tasted blood in recent years." Blacks were reported to be "rapidly growing race-conscious and aware of the possibilities for benefit through racial solidarity. Many of them have embraced Communism." Listed as a "'fellow-traveler' organization" was the American Civil Liberties Union, "a 'high-brow' counterpart of the International Labor Defense—which is avowedly Communistic."[32]

This report contained a particularly fascinating section entitled "Subversive Elements in the New York City School System." The "serious proportion of the 'left wing' tendencies" in education was subscribed to the influence of the teacher-training programs at Hunter and City colleges, both of which stressed "sociology with a 'left wing' approach," were "attended predominantly by Jewish students," and were "decidedly more to the left than is healthy." Cited for special mention were the Faculty Club of Hunter College and the High School Principals Association ("Sixty percent of all New York City High School principals are Jewish"). As if the point had not already been made, the report concluded that "the Jewish population in New York City appears to be particularly susceptible to the influences of the Communist Party."[33]

Paranoia also reigned in Chicago, where new intelligence officers were discovering old enemies. As early as the spring of 1940, the unit there launched an investigation of the local chapter of the ACLU. Sources cited by the alarmed G-2 included the Fish report, now a decade old, and Elizabeth Dilling's thriller *The Red Network,* which was "surely correct, as otherwise suits against the author would have caused its withdrawal." Also mentioned as valuable were interviews with naval colleagues, former officers, and the redoubtable Harry A. Jung, whose reputation had survived, at least in Chicago. The army report concluded that the ACLU was "definitely communistic" and "composed of people

32. G-2, Second Corps Area, "Special Report on the Subversive Situation," dated November 20, 1940, is in ibid., reel 26, pp. 671–725. When Hitler attacked the Soviet Union, the FBI and MI were aware that the "Communist Party has issued instructions to speed up production for National Defense [in the United States] rather than to hinder it," but their attitude toward the Communists did not change (G-2, Sixth Corps Area, to G-2, War Department, June 26, 1941, reel 31, p. 1049).

33. G-2 Second Corps Area, "Special Report on the Subversive Situation," dated November 20, 1940, ibid., reel 26, pp. 671–725.

who are Communist sympathizers and who furnish the 'respectable front' for the Communist Party."[34]

By 1940 the traditional counterintelligence obsession with names was also evident. No doubt the army would have rediscovered this tool itself, but this particular exercise may have been prompted by J. Edgar Hoover's Custodial Detention Program, a listing of subversives to be arrested when the emergency came, which he had started in June. The army's concern grew tremendously with the passage of the Selective Service Act in September 1940; from a counterintelligence aspect the draft meant the wholesale induction of subversives. At first, Military Intelligence thought it could simply reject such draftees. When the G-1, the personnel chief, pointed out that "public opinion will force the Army to state the reasons for rejection," the decision was made to "procure the names of the suspected men" and, once inducted, "maintain a close surveillance over the suspected individuals through company commanders and selected enlisted men." The problem was to get the names. Hoover promised in late December to give Military Intelligence a list of "persons suspected of being members of subversive organizations," but impatient G-2s took matters into their own hands.[35]

On at least one campus (Columbia University, certainly the most feared educational institution in the East), an agent from the Corps of Intelligence Police was stationed in the fall of 1940 "to uncover possible subversive personnel." At the University of Iowa, agents working for the Seventh Corps Area G-2 were busy collecting the names of "German-born professors . . . who are outspoken Nazi sympathizers."[36] In September 1940, the Baltimore G-2 began compiling a "Red Book," listing "the names of any officers, enlisted men or civilians who any competent

---

34. G-2, Sixth Corps Area, to G-2, War Department, May 9, 1940, ibid., reel 31, pp. 123–24. In World War II, Dilling was indicted for sedition (as was William D. Pelley of the Silver Shirts), but the case was dropped after the judge's death caused a mistrial (Jeansonne, *Smith*, pp. 75–84).

35. G-1 to G-2, October 22, 1940; Hoover to Miles, December 10, 1940, MI Microfilm, reel 22, pp. 921, 926–27. One army promise to have the Counter Intelligence Branch cooperate is in Sherman Miles to directors of FBI and ONI, November 4, 1940, reel 23, pp. 815–16. For Hoover's continuing difficulty in getting army and navy assistance in "consolidating the inventories of Intelligence activities," see his letter to G-2 Miles, December 2, 1940, reel 23, p. 810. The navy had a leg up in the race for names: in 1940 it hired the counsel for the Dies Committee and gained access to those files (Dorwart, *Conflict of Duty*, p. 122). In Seattle, the navy's intelligence office produced a two-inch-thick "Black Book" on Japanese-Americans. Names, descriptions, surveillance information, and maps detailing centers of Japanese populations stretching into British Columbia made this a thorough job (Record Group 38, ONI, Oriental Desk, box 11, National Archives).

36. C. M. Busbee to G-2, Second Crops Area, November 26, 1940, MI Microfilm, reel 22, p. 922; G-2, Seventh Corps Area, to G-2, War Department, November 1, 1940, reel 32, p. 513.

officer, in his review of cases and handling of correspondence, has believed suitable for custodial detention." The office hoped to examine the Pennsylvania state police's file of fifteen thousand suspected subversives for additional names.[37] By 1941 all corps areas were flooding Washington with material under such titles as "Monthly Intelligence Report," "Monthly Report on Labor Conditions," and "Lists of Disloyal or Subversive Persons." Vito Marcantonio, U.S. representative from New York, made that last roster. The Second Corps Area G-2 told his superiors in Washington that information from "a highly confidential source" had revealed Marcantonio to be "actively sympathetic to the Communist movements." The report also noted, without analysis, that the congressman "spends at least a large part of two days of each week in conference with Mayor Fiorello H. La Guardia."[38] Other reports reflected the activity of agents who were once again attending radical and labor meetings. The navy too was hard at work on its own suspect lists of the right, the left, and the miscellaneous, but the special target of Naval Intelligence continued to be the Japanese on the West Coast.[39]

Agents from the intelligence office at the Quartermaster Depot in Philadelphia were especially active, with operatives using such code names as Sail Dog 3 penetrating local CIO unions. At a May 13 labor meeting, three of the seven persons attending were army informants. In June, at a larger meeting, the army agent was shocked when "out of the clear sky the Chairman said: 'If there are any F.B.I. men or Naval Intelligence Officers present I wish they would please pay their dues as we can use the money.'" The Philadelphia office also followed blacks, Communists, and other suspects. In April, an agent covered a meeting of "an alleged liberal group" which had assembled for a program called "Our Stake in Civil Liberties," a protest against a bill in the legislature to "set up a little Dies Committee in this State." Of the seventy-five people in attendance, most were reported to be "of non-Aryan extraction."[40]

The Chicago G-2 went so far as to open "an undercover investigative

37. G-2, Third Corps Area, to G-2, War Department, April 30, 1941, ibid., reel 27, p. 982.

38. Acting G-2, Second Corps Area, to G-2, War Department, June 13, 1941, ibid., reel 23, p. 949.

39. Dorwart, *Conflict of Duty*, p. 121, has a general description of the navy's work in this period; the elaborate information collection effort against the Japanese is reflected in the files of the Oriental Desk, cited in note 35.

40. The Philadelphia Quartermaster Depot's "summaries of information" for the spring of 1941 are in MI Microfilm, reel 27, pp. 982–1040, and reel 28, pp. 1–11. The file on labor leader Walter Reuther is in reel 23, pp. 889–940. That on CIO founder John L. Lewis was incorporated into a postwar dossier, two inches thick, and shows that he was the subject of army interest from 1936 to 1954 (Record Group 319, Investigative Records Repository Case Files, X8516607, National Archives).

office" in the city, concealing any connection with the army. There, too, an effort was made to find the "link between the Communist Party and the CIO." In Boston, the G-2 totaled up the number of his investigations for Washington, and his report can probably be used as a gauge of the activity in the other eight corps areas. In the month of July his office dealt with "356 incidents pertaining to suspicious individuals and all manner of subversive events," resulting in seventy-three reports to Washington. Almost half the incidents involved suspected "Pro-Communist" or "Pro-Nazi" machinations, and the miscellaneous category took up nearly a third, but that still left room for twenty-seven labor incidents, forty-seven "Suspicious Activities," and two "Jehovah's Witnesses Activities."[41]

The G-2 for the Fifth Corps Area, working at Fort Hayes in Columbus, Ohio, used the "Special Report" format to forward the handiwork of his agents, who were watching two particularly radical schools a few miles to the south. At Wilberforce University in April, agents attended the Southern Ohio Youth Conference, the purpose of which, they reported, was to gain student "support of the CIO labor movement and conduct an aggressive campaign to prevent American intervention in the present war." Resolutions endorsed at the meeting supported civil liberties and the collegiate peace strike scheduled for April 23 and condemned various conservative state bills. Two months later the Ohio agents were at Antioch College in Yellow Springs to "determine the sympathies of the speakers" at a Conference on Progressive Action and Post-War Reconstruction. Neither the army spies nor their superiors in Washington realized that Lewis Corey, author and lecturer on economics, was in reality the notorious and elusive Louis Fraina, former Bolshevist. Another speaker was Max Lerner, professor at Williams College and guilty of a contributing editorship with the *New Republic* and of using the word *democracy* in a way the agents knew meant "some form of socialism." Lerner even favored "a new world order" and spoke of the "need for an appeal to the masses."[42]

Military Intelligence also worried, as it always had, about the possible subversion of the country's black population. In early 1941, Washington ordered all G-2s to watch for "disaffection or subversive activities of

41. For Chicago, see the April 22, 1941, "Study of Causes for Strikes and Work Stoppages within the Sixth Corps Area," and the May 3, 1941, Monthly Intelligence Summary, MI Microfilm, reel 31, pp. 667–704. For Boston, see the First Corps Area's Monthly Intelligence Summary, August 2, 1941, reel 24, pp. 574–78.

42. G-2, Fifth Corps Area, to G-2, War Department, April 14 and July 2, 1941, ibid., reel 29, pp. 215–20, 310–15.

colored troops." The "directing groups" were thought to be the National Association for the Advancement of Colored People and the Communists.[43] Washington was particularly alarmed at the news that A. Philip Randolph of the Brotherhood of Sleeping Car Porters planned to march one hundred thousand blacks on Washington to protest discrimination in defense industry hiring. It was time once again to review the White Plan, and units at Fort Meyer and the Arlington Cantonment were put on alert, while routes were laid to bring in additional troops from Fort Meade. The Fort Meyer commander ordered practice in the "loading and unloading drill," whether of guns or trucks is unclear. In fact, Washington was so frightened that Roosevelt made a deal with Randolph, who called off the march in exchange for a presidential order forbidding racial discrimination in defense factories and ordering the creation of the Committee on Fair Employment Practices.[44]

And so it went. Military Intelligence was reinvigorated, closely allied with the navy and the FBI and swelling with agents as the total army strength went well over a million. Although technically removed from the civilian arena by presidential order, the army was in fact a junior partner in the fight against domestic subversion by the summer of 1941. As a matter of official policy, however, the army was to rely on the FBI for information on subversion among civilians not affiliated with the military. Hoover had clearly gained the upper hand in making his agency the official investigative body for political intelligence. Military Intelligence had entered that agreement willingly, and though it also clearly assumed that when the bureau failed to meet its needs it had the right to perform its own espionage on the home front, the arrangement remained in force and served as an ultimate cap on such operations. There was certainly a natural tendency for local units to go well beyond the official limits, and with its combat intelligence units and the requirement to conduct investigations of its own personnel, the army maintained a strong agent force. The continued enforcement and strengthening of the Delimitation Agreement, however, created a major and unprecedented deterrent to any thoroughgoing domestic intelligence program by Military Intelligence. What Newton Baker had attempted to do in 1918 and 1920 was now White House policy.

The year 1941 thus stands as a suitable conclusion for this study. With the Delimitation Agreement, the army operated under a new set of

43. The unit reports, originally classified secret, are in ibid., reel 22, pp. 877–959.

44. See the file on the Randolph march in National Archives, *Correspondence of the Military Intelligence Division Relating to "Negro Subversion," 1917–1941* (Washington, D.C.: National Archives, 1986), microfilm project M1440, reel 6, p. 714–18.

rules which guaranteed that its excesses of earlier years would not be repeated. The bureaucratic empire involved in the surveillance of the American left now belonged to J. Edgar Hoover, and if he abused his enormous power, he could be counted on to keep Military Intelligence in check. The army might study and analyze, might even conduct limited investigations, but it would take a major social crisis for the G-2 to risk violating the confining executive order in any systematic fashion. That crisis was not to come for another quarter of a century.

Epilogue

Comparatively little is known about the domestic operations of Military Intelligence from 1942 to 1967. The unhappy truth is that the historic record diminishes drastically in late 1941 and remains extremely hazy during the next twenty-five years. Part of the reason for this obscurity is that, beginning in late 1941, the army went through major organizational changes, with the corps areas disappearing to be replaced by service commands and regional defense commands. The Military Intelligence Division also endured reconfigurations, the most important of which was the appearance of the Military Intelligence Service and the Counter Intelligence Corps (CIC). The foreign exploits of the CIC are fairly well known. CIC agents went ashore with the first American troops in the North African landings of November 1942 and during the war conducted missions around the world. Two of their most famous catches were Tokyo Rose and Ezra Pound.[1] The CIC's domestic role sprang from an order approved by the secretary of war in the spring of 1942 that all G-2s submit a monthly intelligence summary, a "brief résumé of the subversive cases," and special reports as needed. The essential question was, "What subversive activity is in progress within the boundaries of the United States or in adjacent countries?"[2]

Subsequent instructions demanded specific information on foreign nationalities, labor, and blacks, in what came to be called Periodic Reports. The Washington G-2 took these submissions from the several commands and condensed them into a national monthly intelligence report. The national digest for March 6, 1944, contained information on labor, juvenile delinquency, Japanese activities in the internment cen-

1. Stanley I. Kutler, *American Inquisition: Justice and Injustice in the Cold War* (New York: Hill and Wang, 1982), pp. 3–32, 63. Pound's army dossier is XE004765, in Record Group 319, Investigative Records Repository Case Files, National Archives. On the foreign adventures of the CIC, see Ian Sayer and Douglas Botting, *America's Secret Army: The Untold Story of the Counter Intelligence Corps* (New York: Franklin Watts, 1989).

2. Adjutant general to all G-2s, June 19, 1942, Record Group 165, entry 189, North American Branch, National Archives.

ters, the black press, "Negro Unrest," "Negro Tension," Communists, and Mexican-Americans in Texas protesting discrimination.[3] It seems apparent that this reporting mission sometimes resulted in covert operations being conducted by local groups. MI agents in San Antonio, for example, attended a meeting of the Jehovah's Witnesses in August 1943. Other agents in Jackson, Mississippi, monitored the Bahai reading room on the basis that "this religious sect, which advocates social equality as one of its precepts, is regarded as one of the causes of negro unrest in this area."[4] The extent of such undercover work remains unknown because the reports seldom discussed sensitive sources and methods and local CIC records have not been found. Clearly there was concern about the propriety of some methods because in early 1944 Washington reminded the field that "it is not intended that the foregoing instructions should involve the use of your intelligence agents to a greater extent than is indicated by your regularly established counterintelligence investigative jurisdiction."[5] In other words, agents were to adhere to the Delimitation Agreement.

In the middle of November 1943, the G-2s held a conference in New Orleans, and the transcriptions of these sessions provide the best view of Military Intelligence operations. The G-2 of the Third Service Command reported on the structure of his activity, apparently selected as a model. With headquarters in Baltimore, he was linked by teletype to his branches in Philadelphia, Pittsburgh, Richmond, and Norfolk. His staff included 185 intelligence officers, and he claimed to have 8,711 informants in the army and a staggering 3,544 civilian informants. Though his chief mission was to investigate military and civilian personnel for security clearances, the G-2 was equally certain that "our duty is to foresee, report, and if possible prevent disaffection, espionage, sedition, sabotage, racial clashes, riot or other catastrophes which may affect the war effort."[6]

3. Subsequent requirements and the resulting reports are included in the papers of the North American Branch, ibid. Judging from these, the Boston headquarters of the First Service Command had intensive coverage of radicals, including an informant on the executive committee of the Boston chapter of the National Association for the Advancement of Colored People. The length of Boston's reports is surpassed only by those from the Second Service Command, headquartered at Governor's Island in New York, which concentrated on Communists, pacifists, blacks, and labor. A little information on the domestic work of the CIC is in U.S. Army, *The History of the Counter Intelligence Corps in the United States Army, 1917–1950 (with Limited Tabular Data to 1960)*, 30 vols. (Baltimore: U.S. Army Intelligence Center, 1959), in Record Group 319, National Archives.

4. G-2, Southern Defense Command, Periodic Report, August 21, 1943, Record Group 165, entry 189, North American Branch, National Archives.

5. Adjutant general to all G-2s, March 18, 1944, ibid.

6. The revealing transcriptions of the addresses at the secret intelligence officers' conference in New Orleans, November 11–19, 1943, are in ibid.

The terrible race riot in Detroit in June 1943 caused the army to become especially concerned about racial unrest. The G-2 of the Sixth Service Command told the conference that after a disturbance in the Sojourner Truth housing project in April 1942, he had inserted a black CIC agent into the Detroit ghetto, adding a second in January 1943. "The work of these colored agents," he reported, "was of an exceptionally high quality. They made themselves a part of the Negro communities of Detroit and worked in an entirely undercover capacity." He also claimed that they were the first to report the beginning of the riot that started on June 20, 1943. During the riot, teams of two white CIC agents were assigned to each police precinct for liaison, while the black agents stayed in the riot area, conducting "spot interviews." One of them was ordered off the street by a policeman who refused to recognize his CIC badge and credentials. Noting that black leaders had been "very inflammatory," the G-2 could find only "slight evidence of direct subversive activity" behind the riot.[7]

Another intelligence officer at the conference addressed the matter of communist subversion. He understood the "tendency among the unwary to classify anyone as a 'Red' who is not a died-in-the-wool conservative," and he believed that "the Communist situation in this country is dangerous enough without seeing 'Red' in anyone who expresses views which might not find favor with some local chamber of commerce." His fear of the communist threat resulted from their alleged control of many unions affiliated with the Congress of Industrial Organizations, and he felt that there were many Reds in the government and civil defense, with five thousand Communist party members in the army alone.[8]

The CIC's most famous domestic escapade in World War II involved its surveillance of Eleanor Roosevelt. Military Intelligence had spotted Joseph Lash as a student radical years before, and his association with Mrs. Roosevelt brought her under the army's scrutiny. In early 1943, the CIC began intercepting Lash's mail, tapping his phone, and bugging his hotel rooms. On at least one occasion CIC agents surreptitiously entered his room. Learning that Lash was to meet Mrs. Roosevelt in Chicago, the CIC bugged her room in the Blackstone Hotel. Since Lash was in the army, the CIC was technically within the Delimitation Agreement in checking on his loyalty, but that it let the case spill over into direct espionage against the first lady is remarkable. Though the story that President Roosevelt, when he heard of the surveillance on his wife, became so incensed that he ordered the army agents sent to their deaths

7. Ibid.
8. Ibid.

in the Pacific and the CIC disbanded is unfounded, it does appear that Roosevelt did learn of the case. It may be that in reaction to this exposure, the army destroyed many of its domestic files.[9]

The most flagrant violation of civil liberties during World War II was the well-known internment of Japanese-Americans. The army's role in calling for the removal of these citizens from the West Coast and in operating the relocation centers is fairly clear, but the actions of the Military Intelligence Service within the centers remains mysterious, except that the service conducted security checks for internees requesting leave. It is fascinating that it was a Military Intelligence agent who reported the brutality of the relocation internal security agents, a report later denied by Secretary of War Henry L. Stimson.[10]

If the CIC files for 1942 and 1943 were destroyed, the best view of those years, and of the entire war period and just after, may well come from the portion of the Van Deman Files that remains unopened, governed by the fifty-year rule in the National Archives. After his involvement in the meetings that produced the Delimitation Agreement, Van Deman became a confidential source in the FBI's Special Service Contact program. He continued his private spy work and in 1943 began to receive financial aid directly from Military Intelligence's confidential funds.[11] It is known that there are Military Intelligence documents in the unreleased Van Deman Files. Two items from the Sixth Army include a February 18, 1947, *Weekly Intelligence Summary* that referred to Will Rogers, Jr., as a

9. The story of Roosevelt's reaction against the CIC is in Joseph Lash, *Love Eleanor: Eleanor Roosevelt and Her Friends* (Garden City, N.Y.: Doubleday, 1982), p. 461. This account is questioned by Richard G. Powers, *Secrecy and Power: The Life of J. Edgar Hoover* (New York: Free Press, 1987), pp. 265–66. The best treatment of the episode is in Athan G. Theoharis and John S. Cox, *The Boss: J. Edgar Hoover and the Great American Inquisition* (Philadelphia: Temple University Press, 1988), pp. 223–24.

10. For the methods "in variation from the normal procedure," which included choking, beating, and kicking, see Richard Drinnon, *Keeper of Concentration Camps: Dillon S. Myer and American Racism* (Berkeley: University of California Press, 1987), pp. 52, 126, 137–38, 261. See also Roger Daniels, *Concentration Camps USA: Japanese-Americans and World War II* (New York: Holt, Rinehart, and Winston, 1971); and U.S. Commission on Wartime Relocation and Internment of Civilians, *Personal Justice Denied* (Washington, D.C.: U.S. Government Printing Office, 1983). For the navy's interest in Japanese-Americans before and after Pearl Harbor, see the papers of the Oriental Desk, Office of Naval Intelligence, Chief of Naval Operations, in Record Group 38, National Archives. Peter Irons, in *Justice at War* (New York: Oxford University Press, 1983), surveys actions of the intelligence community against suspected Japanese saboteurs on the West Coast, and his description of General John L. DeWitt, chief of the Western Defense Command, as a leader in the call for harsh action against all people of Japanese descent is excellent. See pp. 6, 19–79.

11. The financial relationship of Military Intelligence to Van Deman, which allowed him to hire two clerks, is discussed in documents in the FBI's file on Van Deman, available in the FBI's Reading Room in Washington (hereafter cited as FBI Van Deman File). See esp. J. F. Santoiana to Hoover, October 5, 1951.

"Communist sympathizer" and another summary that reported on activities of the NAACP.[12] After the war, the discussion about who should receive Van Deman's files became a matter of some importance. Because of its financial support, the army felt it owned the collection, and with Van Deman in failing health, the CIC drew up a plan to seize them upon the general's death. The FBI understood that it had the rights to the material under the Delimitation Agreement, yet Hoover's initial reaction in the summer of 1945 was to let the army have the files. "I think it is something we should now stay out of," he noted. "We apparently have all pertinent material anyway. What the Army does should be *immaterial* to us."[13]

Despite continuing physical setbacks, Van Deman stayed at work, and the FBI reassessed its position on the files in 1951. Two aspects of Van Deman's system worried the bureau. First, it suspected that Van Deman had been less than careful in evaluating the reliability of his sources. Second, the eighty-five thousand index cards he had accumulated were of a different size than those used by the FBI, making a merger difficult. Hoover's opinion that his agency already had most of the useful information in the files was again confirmed.[14] When Van Deman died on January 22, 1952, the army acquired the files. Eventually they went to the army's Investigative Records Repository at Fort Holabird, Maryland, then to the U.S. Senate's Internal Security Subcommittee, and finally to the National Archives.

One of the especially interesting questions of the early 1950s is the extent to which the army cooperated with Senator Joseph R. McCarthy in his infamous hearings. Given the army's traditional sympathy for congressional investigations of the left, the allegation that some local units were involved in McCarthy's witch-hunt demands further investigation. There are also indications that the CIC engaged in at least some spying beyond that allowed by the Delimitation Agreement. In the 1950s, one former agent has said, the army maintained records on a Unitarian church in Houston.[15] It is known that CIC agents were operat-

---

12. U.S. Senate, Committee on the Judiciary, 93d Cong., 1st sess., *Military Surveillance of Civilian Politics: A Report of the Subcommittee on Constitutional Rights* (Washington, D.C.: U.S. Government Printing Office, 1973), p. 16.

13. The emphasis on *immaterial* is in Hoover's note in longhand on J. K. Mumford to D. M. Ladd, July 19, 1945, FBI Van Deman File.

14. Of the many memoranda on the fate of Van Deman's collection, the best summary is in A. H. Belmont to D. M. Ladd, October 11, 1951, FBI Van Deman File.

15. U.S. Senate, *Military Surveillance of Civilian Politics*, p. 16. The charge that some local MI units cooperated with McCarthy is in Frank J. Donner, *The Age of Surveillance: The Aims and Methods of America's Political System* (New York: Knopf, 1980), p. 292. See also Earl Latham, *The Communist Controversy in Washington: From the New Deal to McCarthy* (Cambridge, Mass.: Harvard University Press, 1966), p. 403. McCarthy was

ing in the field when federal troops were sent in 1957 to integrate Central High School in Little Rock, Arkansas. Specifics about these activities, however, have never been revealed.[16] It may be that during those years the army did relatively little on the home front and generally abided by the Delimitation Agreement. After the violence at the University of Mississippi in 1962, however, local units seem to have increased their information collection effort, and the army began to consider developing a major domestic intelligence program to support its civil rights work.[17]

It was not until the terrible riots of the summer of 1967 that negative intelligence reappeared on a scale comparable to that of the World War I era. Like Van Deman's creation, this enormously large and sophisticated effort swept up all aspects of the left in its net, but its particular enemies were militant blacks and the anti–Vietnam War movement. For the effort of the late 1960s, a good deal is available thanks to the congressional investigation by Senator Sam Ervin beginning in 1971 and continuing into the Watergate era. Ervin's hearings forced the declassification of a substantial body of material that assists in charting the role of the army in the turmoil of the 1960s. By that time, the CIC had been replaced by the United States Army Intelligence Command, which had about a thousand agents spread around the country for the official purpose of conducting background investigations of persons seeking military security clearances. These agents and those of units called Military Intelligence Detachments at major army commands ran sophisticated counterintelligence operations against the American left in absolute violation of the Delimitation Agreement. Methods included observation of radical meetings and the penetration of radical groups by agents in disguise. Local agents might be dispatched to cover small events, yet the most elaborately coordinated program involved inserting spies into groups coming to Washington for the several antiwar demonstrations. Another major target was the Poor People's Campaign of 1968, when

very hard on MI, calling G-2 Major General Richard C. Partridge "incompetent" (Robert Griffith, *The Politics of Fear: Joseph R. McCarthy and the Senate* [Amherst: University of Massachusetts Press, 1987], p. 217).

16. See Robert W. Coakley, *Operation Arkansas*, OCMH Monograph 158M (Washington, D.C.: Office of the Chief of Military History, 1967).

17. For the early 1960s, see U.S. Senate, *Military Surveillance of Civilian Politics*, pp. 16–17. See also Paul J. Scheips, *The Role of the Army in the Oxford, Mississippi, Incident, 1962–1963*, OCMH Monograph 73M (Washington, D.C.: Office of the Chief of Military History, 1965); and Paul J. Scheips and Karl E. Cocke, *Army Operational and Intelligence Activities in Civil Disturbances since 1957*, rev. ed., OCMH Study 73 (Washington, D.C.: Office of the Chief of Military History, 1971).

black agents infiltrated the caravans to Washington and went into deep cover to penetrate Resurrection City and associated black organizations. Ervin's staff concluded that the military's "surveillance of civilians engaging in political activities in the 1960's was both massive and unrestrained."[18]

Data from these investigations, and from liaison with the FBI, the navy, the air force, and local authorities went into the production of two blacklists: a six-volume set, classified confidential, entitled "Individuals Active in Civil Disturbances" and generally called the "identification list"; and the "Compendium," two secret volumes under the title "Civil Disturbance and Dissidence."[19] Electronic surveillance was also used to monitor radio transmissions of suspected radicals, and a special photographic team under the cover name Midwest Video Associates provided the Pentagon with interviews of radicals. The videotape effort and other special techniques were employed most successfully during the Democratic national convention in Chicago in 1968.[20] The computer, a tool not available to Van Deman, was used extensively by the Pentagon, the Intelligence Command at Fort Holabird, Maryland, and other army units to store enormous amounts of data from the thousands of intelligence reports submitted by agents.[21]

Unfortunately for the historian, the pressure from Ervin's investigation and from lawsuits by civil libertarians resulted in the destruction of far more documents than were released. I was in the Pentagon as a counterintelligence officer during this period, and I served on a special task force created by Chief of Staff William C. Westmoreland to respond

18. U.S. Senate, *Military Surveillance of Civilian Politics*, p. 4.
19. The "Identification List" and the "Compendium" are described in U.S. Senate, Committee on the Judiciary, 92d Cong., 2d sess., *Army Surveillance of Civilians: A Documentary Analysis by the Staff of the Subcommitee on Constitutional Rights* (Washington, D.C.: U.S. Government Printing Office, 1972), pp. 4–20.
20. These techniques and other methods are described throughout the Ervin hearings, in U.S. Senate, Hearings before the Subcommittee on Constitutional Rights of the Committee on the Judiciary, 92d Cong., 1st sess., *Federal Data Banks, Computers and the Bill of Rights*, 2 parts (Washington, D.C.: U.S. Government Printing Office, 1971). See also U.S. Senate, Hearings before the Subcommittee on Constitutional Rights of the Committee on the Judiciary, United States Senate, 93d Cong., 2d sess., *Military Surveillance* (Washington, D.C.: U.S. Government Printing Office, 1974). The 1974 doctoral dissertation by the army officer who broke the story on MI spying has been published: Christopher H. Pyle, *Military Surveillance of Civilian Politics, 1967–1970* (New York: Garland, 1986). See also Richard H. Blum, *Surveillance and Espionage in a Free Society* (New York: Praeger, 1972); Jerry J. Berman and Morton H. Halperin, *The Abuses of the Intelligence Agencies* (Washington, D.C.: Center for National Security Studies, 1975); and Morton H. Halperin et al., *The Lawless State: The Crimes of the U.S. Intelligence Agencies* (New York: Penguin Books, 1976).
21. U.S. Senate, *Army Surveillance of Civilians*, pp. 21–97.

to the Ervin investigation. My job was to reconstruct the documentary trail of the army's surveillance of civilians in the 1960s. I gathered quite a collection, and when my work was completed I shipped a set of the documents to the army's Military History Center. I always assumed that one day I would return to them and write a proper history of those fascinating days. To date, however, I have been unable to locate this material, much less begin the lengthy process for its declassification. The documents were, the army says, turned over to the National Archives some years ago, but, despite the good-hearted efforts of numerous archivists, they remain lost. There is, then, much to be done before the rest of the story can be told, a story that ends with the crackdown on the intelligence community caused by the Watergate crisis. That great event, it will be remembered, began as a simple operation in negative intelligence.

The question of whether Military Intelligence has been removed completely from civilian affairs I leave to the reader. There is much in this account that suggests that no matter how many times the army is told to stay clear of the political arena, moments of great domestic upheaval inevitably attract its involvement. Regardless of national policy, moreover, local commanders and intelligence officers have historically been hard to keep in line. Preparing a scenario of domestic disorder that would rekindle the military's interest is not the function of the historian, but I find it irresistible. Urban disorders or other civil disturbances requiring federal troops have always been occasioned by intelligence work. A sharp increase in sustained terrorist bombings and assassinations at home, especially if military installations and leaders were targeted, would certainly bring in Military Intelligence. Assigning a new mission to the army, fighting drugs, for example, might cause commanders to employ their intelligence capabilities. Since Vietnam, however, the domestic scene has been comparatively quiet. Post-Watergate restrictions, not to mention careful intelligence oversight by Congress, the Department of Defense, and civilian organizations, have effectively curtailed the military.[22] Even the FBI is sharply criticized whenever it appears to have resumed political spying. Perhaps it is a new day.

---

22. For restrictions on the intelligence community, see Brian Michael Jenkins et al., *Intelligence Constraints of the 1970s and Domestic Terrorism* (Santa Monica: Rand, 1982); and Stephen J. Cimbala, ed., *Intelligence and Intelligence Policy in a Democratic Society* (Dobbs Ferry, N.Y.: Transnational Publishers, 1987).

Bibliographical Essay

The archival resources regarding Military Intelligence's interest in American radicals before World War II are rich and relatively unmined. The most vital to my work is Record Group 165 in the National Archives, the surviving documents from the Military Intelligence Division (MID) of the Army General Staff. These are crucial for an understanding of the federal surveillance of radicals in the World War I and Red Scare periods, but their coverage of the 1920s and 1930s is sparse. Serious scholars must examine the entire collection in the main building of the National Archives in Washington, D.C., and in the repository in Suitland, Maryland, though a significant portion of Record Group 165 is available on 34 reels of microfilm: Randolph Boehm, ed., U.S. *Military Intelligence Reports: Surveillance of Radicals in the United States, 1917–1941* (Frederick, Md.: University Publications of America, 1984). Because many of these reports cover numerous topics, the index in the printed guide should be used with care. Similar caution is required when examining the 262 reels of microfilm entitled *Name Index of Correspondence of the Military Intelligence Division of the War Department General Staff, 1917–1941*, microfilm project M1194, produced by the National Archives in 1984. This tool can be valuable, but MID's indexing procedure did not include the often fascinating references to individuals and organizations in the division's more general documents.

One of the especially interesting publications by MID is the *Weekly Intelligence Summary.* These are global in scope and include domestic material only during the peaks of discontent and fear. Students of international politics should find them an excellent source. Fortunately, they have been published: Richard D. Challener, ed., *United States Military Intelligence, 1919–1927*, 30 vols. (New York: Garland, 1978). This edition is based on the holdings in Record Group 165, but copies for the years 1917 to early 1921 can also be found in collection 917 at the Western Reserve Historical Society in Cleveland, Ohio, under the heading "U.S. War Department, Intelligence Reports." These summaries came to Western Reserve from the estate of Newton D. Baker, secretary of war during World War I and the Red Scare. Western Reserve also holds other Baker papers not relating to these years. A great supply of War Department material is available in the Baker Papers in the Library of Congress, Manuscript Division. Most of these are on microfilm and can be obtained through interlibrary loan. I found them very useful in examining Baker's relationships with the leaders of Military Intelligence, with Woodrow Wilson and his cabinet members, and with other reformers.

Another part of Record Group 165 has the revealing title "Negro Subversion." These six microfilm reels are not included in *Surveillance of Radicals in the United States* but can be purchased cheaply. See *Correspondence of the Military Intelligence Division Relating to "Negro Subversion," 1917–1941* (Washington, D.C.: National Archives, 1986), microfilm project number M1440. There is some material to 1941, but the focus is on the years 1917 to 1920. A much larger and far more expensive microfilm collection contains, in addition to "Negro Subversion," other documents from the War Department along with a considerable amount of investigative material from other federal agencies: Theodore Kornweibel, Jr., ed., *Federal Surveillance of Afro-Americans (1917–1925): The First World War, the Red Scare, and the Garvey Movement*, 25 reels (Frederick, Md.: University Publications of America, 1986).

Other important collections in the National Archives include Record Group 38, which contains the documents of the Office of Naval Intelligence. Although they are much smaller than the Military Intelligence files, I found them especially helpful for comparative purposes. Files from the Bureau of Investigation for the years 1908 to 1922 are in Record Group 65 and are available on 955 rolls of microfilm, Archives project number M1085. The poor technical quality makes these difficult to read. In Record Group 60, the Abraham Glasser files are well worth examining by students of the military's involvement with labor and blacks. Working on a special assignment in the Department of Justice, Glasser collected these documents in the late 1930s, and until the opening of Record Group 165 they were the best source on MID. Though most of the material consists of typed copies, I found the collection valuable because of its juxtaposition of documents from the Departments of War, Justice, and Labor.

One collection, not in the National Archives, has too long been overlooked by many students of radicalism in the early twentieth century. I refer to the papers of the Lusk Committee, the 1919 New York State legislature's Joint Legislative Committee to Investigate Seditious

Activities, which I found illuminating in several respects. Located in the New York State Archives in Albany, these papers are fascinating because they contain the "Seized Files" from such groups as the Finnish Information Bureau, the Russian Soviet Bureau, the Rand School, the Industrial Workers of the World, and the National Civil Liberties Bureau. Another part, "Documentary Material," contains radical literature. The collection's administrative files afford a clear view of the methods of this intense investigative effort. The Lusk Committee's report is *Revolutionary Radicalism: Its History, Purpose and Tactics, with an Exposition and Discussion of the Steps Being Taken and Required to Curb It,* 4 vols. (Albany: J. B. Lyon Company, 1920).

Although the relatively few official investigative files in the National Archives for the 1920s and 1930s reflect the limited scope of formal intelligence agencies at the time, the archives do contain the records of the private intelligence machine created by Ralph H. Van Deman, the then retired creator of MID. Located in Record Group 46, Records of the U.S. Senate, Internal Security Subcommittee of the Senate Judiciary Committee, 1951–75, these critical investigative files on radicals are not subject to the provisions of the Freedom of Information Act and are released only after fifty years. At this writing, those up to late 1939 are open. I found them by far the best source on the antiradical movement in the 1930s. The Federal Bureau of Investigation has also made public, as a "pre-processed file," a small collection of papers dealing with Van Deman's relations with that agency. Under the subject "Van Deman," these items can be purchased by calling the FBI's Reading Room and paying a nominal photocopying fee. These papers are most helpful on the relationship of Van Deman to the army and the FBI and on the disposition of Van Deman's files upon his death. Other materials on that matter can be found in Record Group 319, ACSI Files, box 28–24–4, National Archives, Suitland Records Center. The attempt at coordination between the intelligence agencies in the 1930s can also be followed by examining relevant papers, especially Official Files 10-b, in the Franklin D. Roosevelt Library at Hyde Park, New York. There are also some intelligence-related documents in Roosevelt's Assistant Secretary of the Navy, 1913–20, papers at Hyde Park. Although they are limited, I found in these papers many indications of Roosevelt's romance with espionage.

When MID was established, Van Deman's executive officer was Alexander B. Coxe, Sr., who was in Paris during the peace conference and later headed the Negative Branch and served as deputy director and acting director of MID during a critical period. I found his papers at East Carolina University in Greenville, North Carolina, helpful, providing crucial documents unavailable elsewhere. The Coxe Papers also contain numerous letters and photographs from his combat in the Philippines that may prove useful to historians of that campaign. Van Deman himself never spoke or wrote openly about the domestic operations of the agency he created. His memoirs are revealing primarily for understanding the organizational development of MID. They are available in manuscript form at the U.S. Army Intelligence Center and School Library, Fort Huachuca, Arizona, and have recently been printed. See Ralph E. Weber, ed., *The Final Memoranda: Major General Ralph H. Van Deman, USA Ret., 1865–1952, Father of U.S. Military Intelligence* (Wilmington, Del.: Scholarly Resources, 1988). This volume contains a biographical sketch of Van Deman by Marc B. Powe, along with an appendix of documents.

Official histories of Military Intelligence are also limited on negative intelligence but useful on structure. The most available of these works, completed for the army in the 1950s, is Bruce W. Bidwell, *History of the Military Intelligence Division, Department of the Army General Staff, 1775–1941* (Frederick, Md.: University Publications of America, 1986). Another work, U.S. Army, *The History of the Counter Intelligence Corps in the United States Army, 1917–1950 (with Limited Tabular Data to 1960)*, 30 vols. (Baltimore: U.S. Army Intelligence Center, 1959), has been declassified and can be obtained in Record Group 319, National Archives. A portion of that study, all on foreign intelligence and printed in photographic facsimile, has been published as volume 11, under the title *The History of the Counter Intelligence Corps (CIC)*, in John Mendelsohn, ed., *Covert Warfare: Intelligence, Counterintelligence, and Military Deception during the World War II Era*, 18 vols. (New York: Garland, 1989). A simplistic official treatment can be found in *The Evolution of American Military Intelligence*, prepared by the U.S. Army Intelligence Center and School in 1973 and available at the Fort Huachuca library. *The Functions of the Military Intelligence Division*, published by MID in 1918, is obtainable through interlibrary loan. Marlborough Churchill's article "The Military Intelligence Division," *Journal of the United States Artillery* 52 (April 1920): 293–315, can be found in the Coxe Papers. A recent work, Ian Sayer and Douglas Botting, *America's Secret Army: The Untold Story of the Counter Intelligence Corps* (New York: Franklin Watts, 1989), is uninformed in its defense of negative intelligence. G. J. A. O'Toole, *The Encyclopedia of American Intelligence and Espionage* (New York: Facts on File, 1988), has several entries relating to Military Intelligence, but his discussion of the Negative Branch is limited. His uncritical reliance on secondary sources regarding sabotage during World War I is another limitation. John Patrick Finnegan, *Military Intelligence: A Picture History* (Arlington, Va.: U.S. Army Intelligence and Security Command, 1985), is objective about the impact of negative intelligence on MI, but the work's primary concern is combat intelligence and cryptography.

There are a number of government documents, available in most large libraries, that I found indispensable. U.S. Senate, Committee on Military Affairs, 65th Cong., 2d sess., *Hearings, Extending Jurisdiction of Military Tribunals* (Washington, D.C.: U.S. Government Printing Office, 1918), contains Van Deman's only public statement on the domestic role of MID. Considerable organization information on an important private antiradical group is in U.S. House of Representatives, Special Committee, 65th Cong., 3d sess., *Hearings, National Security League* (Washington, D.C.: U.S. Government Printing Office, 1919). The end of volume 2 and the entire third volume of U.S. Senate, Committee on the Judiciary, 66th Cong., 1st sess., *Report and Hearings, Brewing and Liquor Interests and German and Bolshevik Propaganda*, 3 vols. (Washington, D.C.: U.S. Government Printing Office, 1919), are most revealing about the army's and Congress's reactions to the Bolshevik revolution. The army's role in the Gary, Indiana, steel strike is depicted in detail in U.S. Senate, Committee on Education and Labor, 66th Cong., 1st sess., *Investigation of Strike in Steel Industries*, 2 parts (Washington, D.C.: U.S. Government Printing Office, 1919). The intriguing story of L. C. A. K. Martens, the "unofficial" Soviet representative to the United States, is in U.S. Senate, Committee on Foreign Relations, 66th Cong., 2d sess., *Russian Propaganda* (Washington, D.C.: U.S. Government Printing Office, 1920).

The abuses of the intelligence agencies in the Red Scare can be examined in U.S. House of Representatives, Committee on Rules, 66th Cong., 2d sess., *Attorney-General A. Mitchell Palmer on Charges Made against Department of Justice by Louis F. Post and Others* (Washington, D.C.: U.S. Government Printing Office, 1920), and in U.S. Senate, Committee on the Judiciary, 66th Cong., 3d sess., *Charges of Illegal Practices of the Department of Justice* (Washington, D.C.: U.S. Government Printing Office, 1921). The Teapot Dome scandal brought a renewed examination of the practices of the Department of Justice, revealed in U.S. Senate, Select Committee, 68th Cong., 1st sess., *Investigation of Hon. Harry M. Daugherty*, 3 vols. (Washington, D.C.: U.S. Government Printing Office, 1924). Congress's attention returned to radicalism in 1930. See U.S. Congress, Special Committee to Investigate Communist Activities in the United States, 71st Cong., 2d sess.,

Investigation of Communist Propaganda, 6 parts (Washington, D.C.: U.S. Government Printing Office, 1930). See also U.S. House of Representatives, Special Committee on Un-American Activities, 73d Cong., 2d sess., *Investigation of Nazi Propaganda Activities and Investigation of Certain Other Propaganda Activities* (Washington, D.C.: U.S. Government Printing Office, 1935).

Three period pieces helped me appreciate the hysteria of the World War I era. Of interest because of his connections with the New York police department and with MID is Thomas J. Tunney, *Throttled! The Detection of the German and Anarchist Bomb Plotters as Told to Paul Merrick Hollister* (Boston: Small, Maynard, 1919). John P. Jones and Paul M. Hollister, *The German Secret Service in America, 1914–1918* (Boston: Small, Maynard, 1918), is another thriller. Emerson Hough's *The Web* (Chicago: Reilly and Lee, 1919) is the official history of the American Protective League and contains reports, apparently unedited, from many state and local units of this semiofficial domestic surveillance organization. Also of interest are the memoirs of Military Intelligence spy Marguerite Harrison, who was caught and imprisoned in Russia: *There's Always Tomorrow: The Story of a Checkered Life* (New York: Farrar & Rinehart, 1935). Although it is not annotated and is rather journalistic, Henry Landau's *The Enemy Within: The Inside Story of German Sabotage in America* (New York: G. P. Putnam's Sons, 1937), helped me sort out the details of German intrigue in the United States. Sidney Howard's *The Labor Spy* (New York: Republic, 1924) contains nothing on MID but is very interesting in its treatment of private detectives. Even better, however, is a more recent study: Frank Morn, *"The Eye That Never Sleeps": A History of the Pinkerton National Detective Agency* (Bloomington: Indiana University Press, 1982).

General histories of the American intelligence community all suffer from attempting to cover too much. Rhodri Jeffreys-Jones, *American Espionage: From Secret Service to CIA* (New York: Free Press, 1977), is one of the best, but it contains errors on MID and is poor on the early period; to be fair, however, the work is on positive, not negative, intelligence. The best survey is Frank J. Donner's *The Age of Surveillance: The Aims and Methods of America's Political Intelligence System* (New York: Knopf, 1980), but its focus is on the more recent era, offering only an overview of the 1917 to 1968 period. See also Phillip Knightley, *The Second Oldest Profession: Spies and Spying in the 20th Century* (New York: Norton, 1987), and William R. Corson, *The Armies of Ignorance: The Rise of the American Intelligence Empire* (New York: Dial Press, 1977). The recent effort by Nathan Miller, *Spying for Amer-*

ica: The Hidden History of U.S. Intelligence (New York: Paragon House, 1989), is an example of the difficulty in covering the entire history of American espionage.

Of more specialized works, a very good and still useful study is Joan M. Jensen's *The Price of Vigilance* (Chicago: Rand McNally, 1968). Jensen's *Military Surveillance of Civilians in America* (Morristown, N.J.: General Learning Press, 1975), through brief, ranks as the first scholarly treatment of the history of MID. I relied heavily on both. I also made considerable use of the story of the navy's positive and negative intelligence efforts in two admirable works by Jeffrey M. Dorwart: *The Office of Naval Intelligence: The Birth of America's First Intelligence Agency, 1865–1918* (Annapolis: Naval Institute Press, 1979), and, by the same press, *Conflict of Duty: The U.S. Navy's Intelligence Dilemma, 1919–1945* (1983).

Before the records of the several federal intelligence agencies were opened, studies on the abuse of civil liberties during World War I and its aftermath were necessarily limited. Nevertheless, several excellent and still useful works were produced, beginning with Zechariah Chafee, Jr.'s *Free Speech in the United States* (Cambridge, Mass.: Harvard University Press, 1941) and James R. Mock's *Censorship, 1917* (Princeton: Princeton University Press, 1941). Chafee, himself a civil libertarian fighter, was well aware of the role of the army's Counter Intelligence Police in the *Abrams* case, and Mock had a clear view of how Naval and Military Intelligence related to the Wilson administration's censorship program. Lawrence H. Chamberlain, in *Loyalty and Legislative Action: A Survey of Activity by the New York State Legislature* (Ithaca: Cornell University Press, 1951), provides a general analysis of the raids by the Lusk Committee. Robert K. Murray's *Red Scare: A Study in National Hysteria, 1919–1920* (Minneapolis: University of Minnesota Press, 1955) is a landmark in illuminating the abuse of civil liberties, and it was followed by an equally important work: H. C. Peterson and Gilbert C. Fite, *Opponents of War, 1917–1918* (Seattle: University of Washington Press, 1957). Taken together, *Red Scare* and *Opponents of War* provide an excellent survey of the groups and individuals suppressed, but since both had to rely primarily on newspapers, they could not fully examine the government agencies responsible for the suppression.

Harold M. Hyman began this process in his *To Try Men's Souls: Loyalty Tests in American History* (Berkeley: University of California Press, 1959). Although his work contains errors, his use of the papers of the American Protective League allowed him to catch a glimpse of Military Intelligence in action on the home front. By the time Harry N.

Scheiber wrote *The Wilson Administration and Civil Liberties, 1917–1921* (Ithaca: Cornell University Press, 1960), he had sufficient sources to reach the warranted conclusion that Woodrow Wilson should bear some responsibility for the abuses of the intelligence agencies.

The first real examination of the role of Military Intelligence in these activities came in William J. Preston's *Aliens and Dissenters: Federal Suppression of Radicals, 1903–1933* (Cambridge, Mass.: Harvard University Press, 1963). Preston's success with MID was based on his use of army documents in the Glasser files in the National Archives. Joan M. Jensen's research in the America Protective League's papers and the Glasser files allowed her, in 1968, to offer an even more complete portrayal of the army's intelligence system in *The Price of Vigilance*, cited above. So uncertain were these early works regarding Military Intelligence that only two mentioned the critically important creator of negative intelligence, Ralph H. Van Deman. When they did refer to him, Hyman and Jensen misspelled his name. Van Deman, ever in the shadows, would no doubt have delighted in this anonymity. The most recent misspelling of his name occurs in Samuel Walker's *In Defense of American Liberties: A History of the ACLU* (New York: Oxford University Press, 1990).

Despite the work in the 1960s, the role of Military Intelligence remained relatively unknown. Murray B. Levin, in *Political Hysteria in America: The Democratic Capacity for Repression* (New York: Basic Books, 1971), ignored too many existing secondary sources and made the gross error of claiming that "Military Intelligence apparently acted merely as a passive medium of exchange rather than an active collector of information" (p. 191). Paul L. Murphy's work is far superior. See especially his *The Meaning of Free Speech: First Amendment Freedoms from Wilson to FDR* (Westport, Conn.: Greenwood, 1972) and his contribution to the New American Nation Series, *The Constitution in Crisis Times, 1918–1969* (New York: Harper & Row, 1972). I remain perplexed that in his *World War I and the Origins of Civil Liberties in the United States* (New York: Norton, 1979) he was able to write an entire chapter on "Beginnings of the Surveillance State" without once mentioning Military Intelligence. Robert Justin Goldstein, in *Political Repression in Modern America, from 1870 to the Present* (Boston: G. K. Hall, 1978), used the work of Preston, Hyman, and Jensen to piece together a decent summary of the extent of MID's work in World War I. The best demonstration of how well the records of MID in the National Archives can be used to flesh out particular aspects of the story of the federal government and the radicals came with Richard Polenberg's

Fighting Faiths: The Abrams Case, the Supreme Court, and Free Speech (New York: Viking, 1987), which I found invaluable. Another work that used the MID archives, but less successfully, is Linda B. Hall and Don M. Coerver, *Revolution on the Border: The United States and Mexico, 1910–1920* (Albuquerque: University of New Mexico Press, 1988).

The Federal Bureau of Investigation is clearly the major agency in the arena of domestic intelligence for the twentieth century. For an early work, see R. G. Brown et al., *Illegal Practices of the United States Department of Justice* (1920; rpt. New York: Arno Press, 1969). For the same period, see the anonymous *The Police and the Radicals: What 88 Police Chiefs Think and Do about Radical Meetings* (New York: American Civil Liberties Union, 1921). Another fairly early criticism is Robert W. Dunn, ed., *The Palmer Raids* (New York: International Publishers, 1948).

Several scholars are presently doing important work on gaining access to the FBI's files. See especially the following: Kenneth O'Reilly, *Hoover and the Un-Americans: The FBI, HUAC, and the Red Menace* (Philadelphia: Temple University Press, 1983); Richard G. Powers, *Secrecy and Power: The Life of J. Edgar Hoover* (New York: Free Press, 1987); Athan G. Theoharis and John S. Cox, *The Boss: J. Edgar Hoover and the Great American Inquisition* (Philadelphia: Temple University Press, 1988); and William W. Keller, *The Liberals and J. Edgar Hoover: Rise and Fall of a Domestic Intelligence State* (Princeton: Princeton University Press, 1989). Of these, I found Theoharis and Cox, *The Boss*, to be most helpful. David Williams has published two worthy articles: "The Bureau of Investigation and Its Critics, 1919–1921: The Origins of Federal Political Surveillance," *Journal of American History* 68 (December 1981): 560–79, and "'They Never Stopped Watching Us': FBI Political Surveillance, 1924–1936," *UCLA Historical Journal* 2 (1981): 5–28. Another important article is by Athan Theoharis, "The FBI and the American Legion Contact Program," *Political Science Quarterly* 100 (Summer 1985): 271–86. Theoharis and O'Reilly have recently edited a microfilm project of forty-two reels, *Federal Bureau of Investigation Confidential Files* (Bethesda, Md.: University Publications of America, 1990), which should be of enormous value to researchers.

For the Wilson administration, Robert H. Ferrell devotes an entire chapter to civil liberties in his *Woodrow Wilson and World War I, 1917–1921* (New York: Harper & Row, 1985). See also David M. Kennedy, *Over Here: The First World War and American Society* (New York: Oxford University Press, 1980). An older but useful work is Chester R. Milham, "A History of National Espionage Legislation and Its Operation in the U.S. during the World War" (Ph.D. diss., University of Southern California, 1938). Loyd C. Gardner, in *Wilson and Revolutions, 1912–1921* (1976; rpt. Boston: University Press of America, 1982), has a long essay introducing a series of documents, with good information on Americans such as Raymond Robins and William Bullitt, who had contact with Bolshevik Russia. Also useful in looking at the World War I period is William J. Breen's *Uncle Sam at Home: Civilian Mobilization, Wartime Federalism, and the Council of National Defense* (Westport, Conn.: Greenwood Press, 1984). The most recent and comprehensive look at the draft during the war is John W. Chambers II's *To Raise an Army: The Draft Comes to Modern America* (New York: Free Press, 1987).

For particular individuals during the Wilsonian era, see Walton E. Bean, "George Creel and His Critics: A Study of the Attacks on the Committee on Public Information, 1917–1919" (Ph.D. diss., University of California at Berkeley, 1941). More recent information is in Stephen L. Vaughn's *Holding Fast the Inner Lines: Democracy, Nationalism, and the Committee on Public Information* (Chapel Hill: University of North Carolina Press, 1980). Newton D. Baker deserves a better biography. Presently available are Clarence H. Cramer, *Newton D. Baker: A Biography* (Cleveland: World, 1961), and Daniel R. Beaver, *Newton D. Baker and the American War Effort, 1917–1919* (Lincoln: University of Nebraska Press, 1966). For a view of A. Mitchell Palmer being pushed to extremes by his assistants, see Stanley Coben, *A. Mitchell Palmer: Politician* (New York: Columbia University Press, 1963). See also Jack C. Lane, *Armed Progressive: General Leonard Wood* (Novato, Calif.: Presidio Press, 1978).

For the radicals of this period, Benjamin Gitlow's *The Whole of Their Lives: Communism in America—a Personal History and Intimate Portrayal of Its Leaders* (New York: Charles Scribner and Sons, 1948) remains worth examination. Paul Avrich has useful biographical sketches in *Anarchist Portraits* (Princeton: Princeton University Press, 1988). Especially helpful is Bernard K. Johnpoll and Harvey Klehr, eds., *Biographical Dictionary of the American Left* (New York: Greenwood Press, 1986). See also Mari Jo Buhle, Paul Buhle, and Dan Georgakas, eds., *Encyclopedia of the American Left* (New York: Garland, 1990). For the Industrial Workers of the World, see Robert L. Tyler, *Rebels of the Woods: The IWW in the Pacific Northwest* (Eugene: University of Oregon Press, 1967); Patrick Renshaw, *The Wobblies: The Story of Syndicalism in the U.S.* (Garden City, N.Y.: Doubleday, 1967); Melvyn Dubofsky, *We Shall Be All: A History of the Industrial Workers of the*

World (Chicago: Quadrangle Books, 1969); Salvatore Salerno, *Red November, Black November: Culture and Community in the Industrial Workers of the World* (Albany: State University of New York Press, 1989). Dubofsky's work was especially helpful in my study. William Young and David E. Kaiser, *Postmortem: New Evidence in the Case of Sacco and Vanzetti* (Amherst: University of Massachusetts Press, 1985), enlightened me on the details of the Italian anarchist community in the United States.

On the IWW leader William D. ("Big Bill") Haywood, see his autobiography as edited by the Soviets: *Bill Haywood's Book* (New York: International Publishers, 1929). See also Lloyd Wendt and Herman Kogan, *Big Bill of Chicago* (Indianapolis: Bobbs-Merrill, 1953), and Joseph R. Conlin, *Big Bill Haywood and the Radical Union Movement* (Syracuse: Syracuse University Press, 1969). Emma Goldman has rightly received considerable attention. See Richard Drinnon, *Rebel in Paradise: A Biography of Emma Goldman* (Chicago: University of Chicago Press, 1961), and Candace Falk, *Love, Anarchy, and Emma Goldman* (New York: Holt, 1984). Alice Wexler, in *Emma Goldman in Exile: From the Russian Revolution to the Spanish Civil War* (Boston: Beacon Press, 1989), shows excellent work in the State Department archives, where she found some Department of Justice and Military Intelligence reports, but her study could have been strengthened by using the army's large file on the anarchist. The Emma Goldman Papers are available on sixty reels of microfilm from Chadwyck-Healey, Inc., Alexandria, Virginia.

No published biography of Elizabeth Gurley Flynn exists; see Helen C. Camp, "Gurley: A Biography of Elizabeth Gurley Flynn, 1890–1964" (Ph.D. diss., Columbia University, 1980). Ralph Chaplin told his own story in *Wobbly: The Rough-and-Tumble Story of an American Radical* (Chicago: University of Chicago Press, 1948). For individual radicals, see Charles Larrowe, *Harry Bridges: The Rise and Fall of Radical Labor in the United States* (New York: Lawrence Hill, 1972); Robert A. Rosenstone, *Romantic Revolutionary: A Biography of John Reed* (New York: Knopf, 1975); Nick Salvatore, *Eugene V. Debs: Citizen and Socialist* (Urbana: University of Illinois Press, 1982); and Arthur Zipser, *Workingclass Giant: The Life of William Z. Foster* (New York: International Publishers, 1981). On Tom Mooney, see Richard H. Frost, *The Mooney Case* (Stanford: Stanford University Press, 1968), and Estolv E. Ward, *The Gentle Dynamiter: A Biography of Tom Mooney* (Palo Alto: Ramparts Press, 1983). As a biography, Joseph North's *Robert Minor: Artist and Crusader, An Informal Biography* (New York: International Publishers, 1956), is unsatisfactory. See the chapter on Minor in Richard

Fitzgerald, *Art and Politics: Cartoonists of the Masses and Liberator* (Westport, Conn.: Greenwood Press, 1973).

On the great struggle in Seattle, see Harvey O'Connor, *Revolution in Seattle: A Memoir* (New York: Monthly Review Press, 1964), and Robert Friedheim, *The Seattle General Strike* (Seattle: University of Washington Press, 1964). On Boston, see Francis Russell, *A City in Terror, 1919: The Boston Police Strike* (New York: Viking, 1975). *The Centralia Case: Three Views of the Armistice Day Tragedy at Centralia, Washington, November 11, 1919* (New York: Da Capo, 1971) is a collection of older works by Wobbly Ralph Chaplin, American Legionnaire Ben Hur Lampmen, and the Federal Council of Churches of Christ in America. For the great steel strike, see David Brody's *Labor in Crisis: The Steel Strike of 1919* (Philadelphia: J. B. Lippincott, 1965).

An important aspect of the Butte situation is admirably treated in David M. Emmons, *The Butte Irish: Class and Ethnicity in an American Mining Town, 1875–1925* (Urbana: University of Illinois Press, 1989). Also interesting is Cletus E. Daniel's *Bitter Harvest: A History of California Farmworkers, 1870–1940* (Ithaca: Cornell University Press, 1981). Bruce Nelson's *Workers on the Waterfront: Seamen, Longshoremen, and Unionism in the 1930s* (Urbana: University of Illinois Press, 1988) is very well done and quite helpful regarding police Red squads, owners' associations, and vigilantes. I also found Steve Golin's *The Fragile Bridge: Paterson Silk Strike, 1913* (Philadelphia: Temple University Press, 1988) very instructive on the O'Brien Detective Agency as a strikebreaking force. David J. Goldberg in *A Tale of Three Cities: Labor Organization and Protest in Paterson, Passaic, and Lawrence, 1916–1921* (New Brunswick: Rutgers University Press, 1989) made excellent use of FBI and MI archival materials. See also Anne Huber Tripp, *The I.W.W. and the Paterson Silk Strike of 1913* (Urbana: University of Illinois Press, 1987). James R. Green's *Grass-Roots Socialism: Radical Movements in the Southwest, 1895–1943* (Baton Rouge: Louisiana State University Press, 1978) remains a good source on the Green Corn Rebellion of the summer of 1917.

On Scott Nearing, consult his *The Making of a Radical: A Political Autobiography* (New York: Harper & Row, 1972), and Stephen J. Whitfield, *Scott Nearing: Apostle of American Radicalism* (New York: Columbia University Press, 1974). For Lincoln Steffens, see *The Autobiography of Lincoln Steffens* (New York: Harcourt, Brace, 1933). See also Ella Winter and Granville Hicks, eds., *The Letters of Lincoln Steffens*, 2 vols. (New York: Harcourt, Brace, 1938). For accounts of Charles A. Beard's contact with the left and the difficulty it caused him, see Mary R. Beard, *The Making of Charles Beard: An Interpretation* (New York: Exposition Press, 1955); Richard Hofstadter, *The Progressive Historians: Turner, Beard, Parrington* (New York: Knopf, 1968); and Ellen Nore, *Charles A. Beard: An Intellectual Biography* (Carbondale: Southern Illinois University Press, 1983). Carl Sandburg also got into trouble with Military Intelligence. See Herbert Mitgang, ed., *The Letters of Carl Sandburg* (New York: Harcourt, Brace and World, 1968); North Callahan, *Carl Sandburg: His Life and Works* (University Park: Pennsylvania State University Press, 1986); and Herbert Mitgang, *Dangerous Dossiers: Exposing the Secret War against America's Greatest Authors* (New York: Donald I. Fine, 1988).

For Military Intelligence's longtime enemy the American Civil Liberties Union, there are a number of sources, although I feel that the topic still needs study. Walter Nelles, *A Liberal in Wartime: The Education of Albert DeSilver* (New York: Norton, 1940), is by one of the founders of the ACLU and still worth consulting, although it lacks any annotation. Donald O. Johnson, *The Challenge to American Freedoms: World War I and the Rise of the American Civil Liberties Union* (Lexington: University of Kentucky Press, 1963), is helpful. Charles L. Markmann, *The Noblest Cry: A History of the American Civil Liberties Union* (New York: St. Martin's Press, 1965), is based largely on secondary sources and interviews. Peggy Lamson's *Roger Baldwin: Founder of the American Civil Liberties Union* (Boston: Houghton Mifflin, 1976) is useful, despite its lack of footnotes. Although Samuel Walker, *In Defense of American Liberties: A History of the ACLU* (New York: Oxford University Press, 1990), is thoroughly grounded in the ACLU papers, it is weak, as I noted above, regarding Military Intelligence.

A full treatment of the federal intelligence community's relationship with African-Americans must await the forthcoming work by Theodore Kornweibel, Jr. Besides Bernard C. Nalty's *Strength for the Fight: A History of Black Americans in the Military* (New York: Free Press, 1986), which has nothing on intelligence but is informative in other respects, the rest of the related material focuses on race riots. Robert V. Haynes's *A Night of Violence: The Houston Race Riot of 1917* (Baton Rouge: Louisiana State University Press, 1976) is valuable, but the best-covered riot is the one in East St. Louis in 1917. Elliott M. Rudwick, author of *Race Riot at East St. Louis, July 2, 1917* (Carbondale: Southern Illinois University Press, 1964), is also the editor of *The East St. Louis Race Riot of 1917* (Frederick, Md.: University Publications of America, 1985), the microfilmed transcripts of the congressional investigation into the riot, which includes reports from the National Guard troops deployed.

William M. Tuttle's *Race Riot: Chicago in the Red Summer of 1919* (New York: Atheneum, 1970) is also important, as is William Cohen's "Riots, Racism, and Hysteria: The Response of Federal Investigators to the Race Riots of 1919," *Massachusetts Review* 13 (Summer 1972): 373–400.

The classic work on the fear of foreigners remains John Higham's *Strangers in the Land: Patterns of American Nativism, 1860–1925* (New Brunswick: Rutgers University Press, 1955). Higham cites former MI officer John B. Trevor's role in immigration restriction, as does Robert A. Divine, *American Immigration Policy, 1924–1952* (New Haven: Yale University Press, 1957). David H. Bennett in *The Party of Fear: From Nativist Movements to the New Right in American History* (Chapel Hill: University of North Carolina Press, 1988) used the microfilmed Military Intelligence papers but focused mostly on organizations and key individuals, and his view of the 1930s is traditional. Da Capo Press of New York made available in 1970 two much older sources: Constantine Panunzio, *The Deportation Cases of 1919–1920* (the factual and devastating account originally published in 1921 by the Federal Council of the Churches of Christ in America), and Louis F. Post, *The Deportations Delirium of Nineteen-Twenty: A Personal Narrative of an Historic Official Experience* (originally published by Kerr of Chicago in 1923). Another older but useful work is the survey of states in E. F. Dowell's *A History of Criminal Syndicalism Legislation in the United States* (Baltimore: Johns Hopkins Press, 1939).

A bibliographic aid on the left and the right is John Earl Haynes's *Communism and Anti-Communism in the United States: An Annotated Guide to Historical Writings* (New York: Garland, 1987). Although journalistic and dated, Norman Hapgood's *Professional Patriots* (New York: Albert and Charles Boni, 1927) is filled with useful leads. Students of the right should also consult Marguerite Green's published dissertation, *The National Civic Federation and the American Labor Movement, 1900–1925* (Washington, D.C.: Catholic University of America Press, 1956). Though poorly written, Howard A. DeWitt's *Images of Ethnic and Radical Violence in California Politics, 1917–1930* (Saratoga, Calif.: R & E Research Associates, 1975) is informative on the Better America Federation. Researchers should supplement it with Edwin Layton's "The Better America Federation: A Case Study of Super Patriotism," *Pacific Historical Review* 30 (May 1961): 137–47. See also Robert D. Ward, "The Origin and Activities of the National Security League, 1914–1919," *Mississippi Valley Historical Review* 47 (June 1960): 51–65. An excellent and most useful contribution to our view of the right can be found in William Pencak's *For God and Country: The American Legion, 1919–1941* (Boston: Northeastern University Press, 1989).

A classic of rightist paranoia is Elizabeth Dilling's *The Red Network: A "Who's Who and Handbook of Radicalism for Patriots* (1934; rpt. New York: Arno Press, 1977). For the late 1930s and the 1940s, readers should consult August Raymond Ogden's *The Dies Committee: A Study of the Special House Committee for the Investigation of Un-American Activities, 1938–1944* (Washington, D.C.: Catholic University of America Press, 1945) and Walter Goodman's *The Committee: The Extraordinary Career of the House Committee on Un-American Activities* (New York: Farrar, Straus and Giroux, 1968). An excellent study of the rabid anti-Communists of the late 1930s, and a model for obtaining information from the Federal Bureau of Investigation, is Glen Jeansonne's *Gerald L. K. Smith: Minister of Hate* (New Haven: Yale University Press, 1988). Also useful in studying Smith and other mystical rabble-rousers is Leo P. Ribuffo's *The Old Christian Right: The Protestant Far Right from the Great Depression to the Cold War* (Philadelphia: Temple University Press, 1983).

Military Intelligence's concern about radical women in the 1920s is indicated in Joan M. Jensen's "All Pink Sisters: The War Department and the Feminist Movement in the 1920s," in Lois Scharf and Joan M. Jensen, eds., *Decades of Discontent: The Women's Movement, 1920–1940* (Westport, Conn.: Greenwood Press, 1983). See also Gertrude Bussey and Margaret Tims, *Women's International League for Peace and Freedom, 1915–1965* (London: George Allen and Unwin, 1965), and Lawrence A. Wittner, *Rebels against War: The American Peace Movement, 1933–1983*, rev. ed. (Philadelphia: Temple University Press, 1984).

On the 1930s, see Harvey Klehr's excellent *The Heyday of American Communism: The Depression Decade* (New York: Basic Books, 1984). John W. Killigrew's *The Impact of the Great Depression on the Army* (New York: Garland, 1979) has a chapter on the Bonus March, but like most military historians, he neglects intelligence. Instead, see Roger Daniels, *The Bonus March: An Episode of the Great Depression* (Westport, Conn.: Greenwood, 1971), and Donald J. Lisio, *The President and Protest: Hoover, Conspiracy, and the Bonus Riot* (Columbia: University of Missouri Press, 1974). Nothing is available on Military Intelligence's connection with the Civilian Conservation Corps, but see John Salmond, *The Civilian Conservation Corps* (Durham: Duke University Press, 1967). On Franklin D. Roosevelt, see Jeffrey M. Dorwart, "The Roosevelt-Astor Espionage Ring," *New York History* 57 (July 1981): 307–22.

For the period after 1941, there is some World War II material in the files of the North American Branch of the Military Intelligence Service, Record Group 165, entry 189, National Archives. I am still searching for the domestic records of the Counter Intelligence Corps, but its foreign intelligence files are in the Archives' Suitland Records Center. For the internment of Japanese-Americans, see Roger Daniels, *Concentration Camps USA: Japanese-Americans and World War II* (New York: Holt, Rinehart, and Winston, 1971); U.S. Commission on Wartime Relocation and Internment of Civilians, *Personal Justice Denied* (Washington, D.C.: U.S. Government Printing Office, 1983); Peter Irons, *Justice at War* (New York: Oxford University Press, 1983); and Richard Drinnon, *Keeper of Concentration Camps: Dillon S. Myer and American Racism* (Berkeley: University of California Press, 1987). On the McCarthy era, see Earl Latham, *The Communist Controversy in Washington: From the New Deal to McCarthy* (Cambridge, Mass.: Harvard University Press, 1966), and Robert Griffith, *The Politics of Fear: Joseph R. McCarthy and the Senate* (Amherst: University of Massachusetts Press, 1987).

As a result of Senator Sam Ervin's investigation of the 1970s, the army destroyed much of its post–World War II material. A few surviving dossiers are in Record Group 319, Investigative Records Repository Case Files, National Archives. Each file, however, must undergo a security review, and the results are frequently disappointing. Similar restrictions are on another set of files at Suitland. These are in Record Group 319 and have been cataloged as "ACSI Records re Army's Involvement in Civil Affairs." They appear to me, however, to be from the historical section of the U.S. Army Intelligence Command, but at any rate, much of this material remains classified and unavailable. I have yet to find the large collection of documents which I compiled at the Pentagon in the early 1970s and which I believe to be the best source for the military's domestic spying for the period after 1957.

Military historians have also had difficulty using classified material, but the best official study is Paul J. Scheips and Karl E. Cocke, *Army Operational and Intelligence Activities in Civil Disturbances since 1957*, rev. ed., OCMH Study 73 (Washington, D.C.: Office of the Chief of Military History, 1971). See also Robert W. Coakley, *Operation Arkansas*, OCMH Monograph 158M (Washington, D.C.: Office of the Chief of Military History, 1967), and Paul J. Scheips, *The Role of the Army in the Oxford, Mississippi, Incident, 1962–1963*, OCMH Monograph 73M (Washington, D.C.: Office of the Chief of Military History, 1965).

Currently, the best material on the late 1960s can be found in the products of the Ervin investigation. See U.S. Senate, Hearings before the Subcommittee on Constitutional Rights of the Committee on the Judiciary, 92d Cong., 1st sess., *Federal Data Banks, Computers and the Bill of Rights*, 2 parts (Washington, D.C.: U.S. Government Printing

Office, 1971); U.S. Senate, Committee on the Judiciary, 92d Cong., 2d sess., *Army Surveillance of Civilians: A Documentary Analysis by the Staff of the Subcommittee on Constitutional Rights* (Washington, D.C.: U.S. Government Printing Office, 1972); U.S. Senate, Committee on the Judiciary, 93d Cong., 1st sess., *Military Surveillance of Civilian Politics: A Report of the Subcommittee on Constitutional Rights* (Washington, D.C.: U.S. Government Printing Office, 1973); and U.S. Senate, Hearings before the Subcommittee on Constitutional Rights of the Committee on the Judiciary, 93d Cong., 2d sess., *Military Surveillance* (Washington, D.C.: U.S. Government Printing Office, 1974).

Ervin's attention to military spying came after the public disclosure by a former officer on the staff of the Military Intelligence school at Fort Holabird. This officer, Christopher H. Pyle, later did his 1974 political science dissertation at Columbia University on the subject, and it has been published: *Military Surveillance of Civilian Politics, 1967–1970* (New York: Garland, 1986). See also Richard Blum, *Surveillance and Espionage in a Free Society* (New York: Praeger, 1972); Jerry J. Berman and Morton H. Halperin, *The Abuses of the Intelligence Agencies* (Washington, D.C.: Center for National Security Studies, 1975); Morton H. Halperin et al., *The Lawless State: The Crimes of the U.S. Intelligence Agencies* (New York: Penguin Books, 1976); and Stanley I. Kutler, *American Inquisition: Justice and Injustice in the Cold War* (New York: Hill and Wang, 1982). For post-Watergate restrictions on the intelligence community, see Brian Michael Jenkins et al., *Intelligence Constraints of the 1970s and Domestic Terrorism* (Santa Monica: Rand, 1982), and Stephen J. Cimbala, ed., *Intelligence and Intelligence Policy in a Democratic Society* (Dobbs Ferry, N.Y.: Transnational Publishers, 1987).

Index